Television with Stanley Cavell in Mind

TV-Philosophy

Series Editors:
Sandra Laugier, Martin Shuster, Robert Sinnerbrink

Television with Stanley Cavell in Mind
edited by David LaRocca and Sandra Laugier (2023)

TV-Philosophy: How TV Series Change our Thinking
Sandra Laugier (2023)

TV-Philosophy in Action: The Ethics and Politics of TV Series
Sandra Laugier (2023)

Television with Stanley Cavell in Mind

edited by
DAVID LaROCCA
AND SANDRA LAUGIER

UNIVERSITY
of
EXETER
PRESS

First published in 2023 by
University of Exeter Press
Reed Hall, Streatham Drive
Exeter EX4 4QR, UK

www.exeterpress.co.uk

© 2023 David LaRocca, Sandra Laugier, and the individual contributors

The right of David LaRocca, Sandra Laugier, and the individual contributors to be identified as authors of this work has been asserted by them in accordance with the Copyright, Designs and Patents Act 1988.

Television with Stanley Cavell in Mind

A CIP catalogue record for this book is available from the British Library.

This book is published under a Creative Commons Attribution Non-Commercial No Derivatives 4.0 International licence (CC BY-NC-ND 4.0). This license requires that reusers give credit to the creator. It allows reusers to copy and distribute the material in any medium or format, for non-commercial purposes only. If others remix, adapt, or build upon the material, they may not distribute the modified material.

https://doi.org/10.47788/BMYM9359

Further details about Creative Commons licences are available at http://creativecommons.org/licenses/

Any third-party material in this book is published under the book's Creative Commons licence unless indicated otherwise in the credit line to the material.
If you would like to reuse any third-party material not covered by the book's Creative Commons licence, you will need to obtain permission directly from the copyright holder.

Every effort has been made to trace copyright holders and obtain permission to reproduce the material included in this book. Please get in touch with any enquiries or information relating to an image or the rights holder.

This Open Access publication was made possible by funding from the European Research Council (ERC) under the European Union's Horizon 2020 research and innovation programme (grant agreement No 834759).

ISBN 978-1-80413-018-6 Hardback
ISBN 978-1-80413-019-3 ePub
ISBN 978-1-80413-020-9 PDF

Cover image: Stanley Cavell © 2023 David LaRocca

Typeset in Adobe Caslon Pro by S4Carlisle Publishing Services

Contents

Acknowledgements	vii
Contributors	ix
Introduction: The Fact and Fiction of Television: Stanley Cavell and the Terms of Television Philosophy DAVID LaROCCA AND SANDRA LAUGIER	1

PART I: NEW TELEVISION — 29

1. Justifying *Justified* — 31
   WILLIAM ROTHMAN

2. 'You Get Paid for Pain': *Kingdom* and New Television — 50
   MARTIN SHUSTER

3. To See and to Stop: The Problem of Abdication in *Succession* — 67
   ELISABETH BRONFEN

4. When TV is on TV: Metatelevision and the Art of Watching TV with the Royal Family in *The Crown* — 85
   DAVID LaROCCA

PART II: BIG PERFECTIONISM ON THE SMALL SCREEN — 99

5. It's My Party and I'll Die Even If I Don't Want To: Repetition, Acknowledgement, and Cavellian Perfectionism in *Russian Doll* — 101
   MICHELLE DEVEREAUX

6. 'Nobody's Perfect': Moral Imperfectionism in *Ozark* — 121
   HENT DE VRIES

7. A Zigzag of a Hundred Tacks: Narrative Complexity in *The Good Place* — 135
   CATHERINE WHEATLEY

8. Im/Moral Perfectionism: On TV's Two Worlds — 152
   JEROEN GERRITS

PART III: EVERYDAY EDUCATION — 171

9 The Sublime and the American Dream in *Fargo* — 173
   HUGO CLÉMOT

10 TV Time, Recurrence, and the Situation of the Spectator:
   An Approach via Stanley Cavell, Raúl Ruiz, and Ruiz's Late
   Chilean Series *Litoral* — 191
   BYRON DAVIES

11 *Homeland*: An Education in Trust — 222
   THIBAUT DE SAINT MAURICE

12 Small Acts — 236
   PAUL STANDISH

PART IV: POPULAR TV AND ITS GENRES — 263

13 The Event of Television: Sitcoms, Superheroes,
   and *WandaVision* — 265
   STEPHEN MULHALL

14 Love, Remarriage, and *The Americans* — 288
   SANDRA LAUGIER

15 *True Detective*: Existential Scepticism and Television
   Crime Drama — 305
   ROBERT SINNERBRINK

Index — 325

Acknowledgements

OUR FIRST AND DEEPEST THANKS are extended to the roster of contributors without whom this ample and artful book would be but a faint sketch. Their wide and penetrating experience writing on and teaching television, film, and media studies—in a philosophical cast of mind—provides this volume with special purchase on the pertinence of Stanley Cavell for the study of TV. More than providing a much-needed, never-before-attempted retrospective assessment of Cavell's contribution to television studies, this gifted band also managed to supply a sense of Cavell's prospective relevance to ongoing and future considerations of TV as streaming, as broadcast, as viewing and re-viewing, and as an essential feature of our private and public lives.

Not far behind, we continue with ready thanks to Anna Henderson, our capable and clever editor, who helped guide this volume from first conception through final realization. We're very grateful for her sense of the book's ambitions and also of its role in a new series on TV-Philosophy at the University of Exeter Press. Two anonymous referees for the press provided much guidance for refining and clarifying the expression of the project, and we remain appreciative for the time and attention demanded of their labors. During production, we have David Hawkins to thank for capable assistance with project management and Sara Magness for informed and impressive copyediting.

The incubation of the volume goes back years, but first took initial and deliberate shape during a pre-pandemic conference hosted by Sandra at the Université Paris 1 Panthéon-Sorbonne, in June 2019, a year after Cavell's death, entitled *La pensée du cinema: En hommage à Stanley Cavell*. Just a few months later, the world was sent into lockdown—and while the coronavirus disaster unfolded, TV queues were loaded and a global binge was underway. The phase illustrated something fundamental about the contemporary role of television in our lives. Given a palpable shift to the digital stream, we felt it time to take stock of Cavell's once and ongoing insights into this groundbreaking subfield of his multiple, expansive interests. Bonding over our shared love of TV (and film), and of course, our long-standing dedication to the life's work and legacy of Stanley Cavell, we hit upon several overlapping magisteria suited to our shared attention.

Benjamin Cavell's ambitious and accomplished work in television, covering a diversity of genres in popular TV, has been taken by us—from first thoughts about this book and throughout its development—as a propitious sign of the creative power and intellectual value of the topic, and of its promising future life.

David would like to acknowledge the gratifying influence of conversations and correspondence with Garrett Stewart, Robert Pippin, Hent de Vries, Emily Apter, Paul Cronin, Haaris Naqvi, Oscar Jansson, Ricardo Miguel-Alfonso, John Opera, Rita Mullaney, and Alessandro Subrizi. For spells of memorable intensity in Montréal and precious duration in Cortona, *mille grazie* Diana Allan and Curtis Brown. In addition to the elastic and motley pleasures of diurnal life together, I'm lucky also to find company for discovering the salutary effects of TV with my insightful wife, K.L. Evans, and our savvy daughters, Ruby and Star.

Sandra wishes also to thank her children, Marie, Simon, and Ulysse, for having introduced her to great shows, including *Buffy the Vampire Slayer* and *Game of Thrones*, and Jocelyn Benoist for all the time discovering and watching TV series together. She owes thanks to all those on both sides of the Atlantic who have shared with her the long-term project of acknowledging the philosophical importance of TV series in the tradition of Cavell's work on cinema: Martin Shuster, Paola Marrati, William Rothman, Jeroen Gerrits, Arnaud Desplechin, Sylvie Allouche, Hugo Clémot, and Thibaut de Saint Maurice. Many thanks to Tatsiana Zhurauliova for her wonderful editing work and advice, and to Anastasia Krutikova for her support and friendship.

Lastly, we wish to express our gratitude to Stanley Cavell, including but also beyond his work on film and television. His writings—an infinite resource for thinking seriously about almost anything that draws one's interest, coupled with his boldness in opening and defending new topics for exploration—have encouraged and inspired us in pursuing a series philosophy.

This publication has received funding from the European Research Council (ERC) under the European Union's Horizon 2020 research and innovation program (grant agreement N° 834759).

Contributors

David LaRocca is the author or contributing editor of more than a dozen books, including *Emerson's English Traits and the Natural History of Metaphor* (2013). Recipient of a teaching commendation from Harvard Extension School, he served as Harvard University's Sinclair Kennedy Traveling Fellow in the United Kingdom and has held visiting research or teaching positions in the United States at Binghamton, Cornell, Cortland, Harvard, Ithaca College, the School of Visual Arts, and Vanderbilt. Advised by Stanley Cavell during doctoral research, he later edited Cavell's *Emerson's Transcendental Etudes* (2003, published under his bachelor name, David Justin Hodge, as was *On Emerson*, also 2003) and worked as Cavell's research assistant during the time he was completing *Cities of Words: Pedagogical Letters on a Register of the Moral Life* (2004) and *Philosophy the Day after Tomorrow* (2005), and beginning *Little Did I Know: Excerpts from Memory* (2010). A recipient of the Ralph Waldo Emerson Society Distinguished Achievement Award, LaRocca has edited additional books featuring Cavell's work, including *Estimating Emerson: An Anthology of Criticism from Carlyle to Cavell* (2013) and *The Bloomsbury Anthology of Transcendental Thought: From Antiquity to the Anthropocene* (2017), and contributed chapters to *Stanley Cavell, Literature, and Film: The Idea of America* (2013), *Stanley Cavell and Aesthetic Understanding* (2018), and *Understanding Cavell, Understanding Modernism* (2023). LaRocca served as guest editor of a commemorative issue of *Conversations: The Journal of Cavellian Studies*, no. 7 (2019): *Acknowledging Stanley Cavell*, and edited *The Thought of Stanley Cavell and Cinema: Turning Anew to the Ontology of Film a Half-Century after* The World Viewed (2020), *Inheriting Stanley Cavell: Memories, Dreams, Reflections* (2020), and *Movies with Stanley Cavell in Mind* (2021). www.DavidLaRocca.org

Sandra Laugier is Professor of Philosophy at Université Paris 1 Panthéon-Sorbonne, Senior Fellow of Institut universitaire de France, and Deputy Director of the Institut des sciences juridique et philosophique de la Sorbonne (UMR 8103, CNRS, Université Paris 1 Panthéon-Sorbonne). She is also Principal Investigator of the European Research Council (ERC) Advanced Grant project DEMOSERIES (www.demoseries.eu). A former student of the École normale supérieure and of Harvard University, she has extensively published on ordinary language philosophy (Wittgenstein,

Austin, Cavell); moral philosophy (moral perfectionism, ethics of care); classic American philosophy (Cavell, Thoreau, Emerson); and democracy and civil disobedience. Her most recent work focuses on gender studies and popular culture, film, and TV series. She is the translator of most of Cavell's work in French and is an advisor for the publication of Cavell's *Nachlass*. She has been Visiting Professor at the University of Toronto (2022), Boston University (2019, 2021), La Sapienza Roma (2019), Pontifical University Lima (2017), and Johns Hopkins University (2008, 2009); Visiting Researcher at the Max Planck Institute Berlin (2014, 2015); Distinguished Visiting Professor at the Johns Hopkins University (2011); Chaire invitée Facultés Saint-Louis, Bruxelles (2009). Awards include: Senior Fellow of Institut universitaire de France (2012–23), Grand prix de philosophie, Académie française (2022), Chevalier de la Légion d'honneur (2014). Among her publications are: *Why We Need Ordinary Language Philosophy* (University of Chicago Press, 2013), *Recommencer la philosophie, la philosophie américaine aujourd'hui* (Vrin, 2014), *Etica e politica dell'ordinario* (LED, Milano, 2015), *Formes de vie* (ed. with E. Ferrarese, CNRS Editions, 2018), *Nos vies en séries, Ethique et philosophie d'une culture populaire* (Flammarion Climats, 2019), *Politics of the Ordinary: Care, Ethics, Forms of Life* (Peeters, 2020), *Wittgenstein, Politique de l'ordinaire* (Vrin, 2021). *Cavell's Must We Mean What We Say? at Fifty* (ed. with G. Chase and J. Floyd, Cambridge University Press, 2022). She is a columnist at the French journal *Libération*: www.liberation.fr/auteur/6377-sandra-laugier.

Elisabeth Bronfen is Professor of English and American Studies at the University of Zurich and Global Distinguished Professor at New York University. She has published an introduction to Stanley Cavell in German (Junius Verlag), *Mad Men: Death and the American Dream* (Diaphanes, 2016), and *Serial Shakespeare: An Infinite Variety of Appropriations in American TV Drama* (Manchester University Press, 2020).

Hugo Clémot is Lecturer in Aesthetics and Philosophy of Art at Gustave Eiffel University, member of LISAA (EA 4120). After completing a PhD thesis on Stanley Cavell and cinema under the supervision of Sandra Laugier, he wrote several books about film, television, and philosophy—such as *Les jeux philosophiques de la trilogie Matrix* (Vrin, 2011), *La philosophie d'après le cinéma: Une lecture de La projection du monde de Stanley Cavell* (PUR, 2014), *Cinéthique* (Vrin, 2018), and *Serial philosophie: Le paradoxe des séries télévisées* (PUFR, 2022)—and has edited *Enseigner la philosophie avec le cinema* (Les Contemporains favoris, 2015). On the topic of TV series, he has published five articles and eight chapters in journals and edited collections. He has also spoken eighteen times in colloquiums and seminars, and has given fifteen public lectures. Always with Stanley Cavell in mind, he has written about numerous TV series such as *Dexter, Lost, Dollhouse, The Sopranos, The Walking Dead, Sherlock, Game of Thrones,* and *Twin Peaks*.

Byron Davies has taught philosophy at the Universidad del Claustro de Sor Juana in Mexico City and been a Visiting Researcher at the International Institute for Advanced Political Studies 'Ignacio Manuel Altamirano', Universidad Autónoma de Guerrero. He previously held a post-doc at the Institute for Philosophical Research, National Autonomous University of Mexico (UNAM), and before that he received his PhD from the Department of Philosophy at Harvard University. In 2024, he will be on a María Zambrano and a Marie Skłodowska-Curie fellowship in Spain, affiliated with the Aresmur research group in aesthetics and art theory at the University of Murcia. Among his recent publications are 'Found Footage at the Receding of the World' (*Screen*, 2022), 'Cavell on Color' (*Conversations*, 2022), 'The Specter of the Electronic Screen: Bruno Varela's Reception of Stanley Cavell' (*Movies with Stanley Cavell in Mind*, ed. David LaRocca, Bloomsbury, 2021), and 'Accidents Made Permanent: Theater and Automatism in Stanley Cavell, Michael Fried, and Matías Piñeiro' (*MLN*, 2020).

Thibaut de Saint Maurice is a PhD student and researcher in DEMOSERIES, a European Research Council project hosted at Université Paris 1 Panthéon-Sorbonne and funded under the European Union's Horizon 2020 research and innovation programme. His work focuses on the uses of seriality as well as on the moral and political issues of TV series. Between 2010 and 2013, he directed the 'Culture Pop' collection published by Ellipses. He is the author of *Philosophie en séries* (2009), *Philosophie en séries-saison 2* (2010), and *Des philosophes et des héros* (2019). He has also published numerous articles, including 'D'un canapé à l'autre, la série En thérapie, comme spectacle de l'expressivité', *Imaginaire et Inconscient*, vol. 48, no. 2 (2021); 'Hippocrate, critique de la faculté de soigner', *Multitudes*, vol. 84 (Fall 2021); and 'Élargir la vie: les eries contemporaines', *Le Débat*, vol. 194 with Hervé Glévarec. Since 2011, he has been questioning fiction and everyday life in various columns on the French public radio channel France Inter. In 2018, his founded the Paris Podcast Festival, the first French festival entirely dedicated to native podcasts.

Michelle Devereaux is a Leverhulme Trust Early Career Fellow in film and television at the University of Warwick. Her work has recently appeared in *Screen*, *MAI: Feminism and Visual Culture*, and *The Bloomsbury Handbook to Sofia Coppola*. Her monograph, *The Stillness of Solitude: Romanticism and Contemporary American Independent Film*, was published in 2019 by Edinburgh University Press. Her current research relates Stanley Cavell's writing on film, genre, scepticism, and perfectionism to explorations of gender and trauma in contemporary film and television. Research interests more broadly include the influence of post-romantic philosophy on contemporary screen culture, gender and feminist theory, film and television aesthetics, performance and stardom studies, adaptation, genre studies, and the study of affect and emotion both on screen and in spectatorship practices.

Hent de Vries is Paulette Goddard Professor of the Humanities at New York University, where he is a Professor of German, Religious Studies, Comparative Literature, and an Affiliated Professor of Philosophy. From 2014 through 2014, he served as Director of the summer School of Criticism and Theory at Cornell University (SCT), Ithaca. De Vries studied Judaica and Hellenistic Thought (Theology), Public Finance and Political Economy (Law), at Leiden University, The Netherlands, where he obtained his PhD in Philosophy of Religion. Before joining NYU, de Vries directed The Humanities Center at Johns Hopkins University (2009-2017), holding the Russ Family Chair in the Humanities with a joint appointment in Philosophy, and also taught in the Philosophy departments of Loyola University Chicago and the University of Amsterdam, where he held the Chair of Metaphysics and its History (1993-2004). He co-founded and directed the interdisciplinary Amsterdam School for Cultural Analysis (ASCA, 1998-2004). De Vries received visiting positions and fellowships at Harvard, Chicago, Princeton, Brown, Columbia, the Université Saint Louis in Brussels, the University of Amsterdam, the Hebrew University of Jerusalem, and the Université de Paris, Panthéon Sorbonne. Having served from 2007 through 2013 as Directeur de Programme at the Collège International de Philosophie, in Paris, de Vries was the Titulaire of the Chaire de Métaphysique Étienne Gilson at the Institut Catholique de Paris, in 2018. In 2020, de Vries was a recipient of the *Prix du Rayonnement de la langue et de la littérature françaises*, one of the *Grands Prix* awarded yearly by the *Académie Française*. De Vries is the author of seven monographs, notably the trilogy *Minimal Theologies, Philosophy and the Turn to Religion*, and *Religion and Violence* (Johns Hopkins University Press, 1999, 2002, and 2005), and, most recently, *Miracles et métaphysique* (Presses Universitaires de France, 2019) and *Le miracle au coeur de l'ordinaire* (Les Belles Lettres, 2019). Moreover, he is the editor and co-editor of ten multi-author volumes. In 2023, a *Festschrift*, edited by Tarek Dika and Martin Shuster, with an extensive informative introduction and some fourteen critical responses to his work was published under the title *Religion in Reason: Metaphysics, Ethics, and Politics in Hent de Vries*. To this volume, de Vries added a lengthy rejoinder, summarizing his scholarly projects thus far while charting some new directions.

Jeroen Gerrits is Associate Professor of Comparative Literature at Binghamton University, State University of New York, where he teaches courses at the intersection of film, literature, and philosophy. He has published a monograph titled *Cinematic Skepticism: Across Digital and Global Turns* with State University of New York Press (2019), as well as numerous articles and book chapters on Cavell's philosophy in the context of film and TV. Among additional publications are articles on specific television shows, including *Buffy the Vampire Slayer*, *24*, and *The Handmaid's Tale*.

Stephen Mulhall is Professor of Philosophy, and the Russell H. Carpenter Fellow and Tutor in Philosophy, at New College, Oxford. His books include

Stanley Cavell: Philosophy's Recounting of the Ordinary (Oxford University Press, 1994), *The Cavell Reader* (as editor, Blackwell, 1996), *On Film* (which has gone through three editions with Routledge, the most recent being 2016), and *The Self and Its Shadows: A Book of Essays on Individuality as Negation in Philosophy and the Arts* (Oxford University Press, 2013). His most recent book is *In Other Words: Transpositions of Philosophy in J. M. Coetzee's Jesus Trilogy* (Oxford University Press, 2022).

William Rothman is Professor of Cinematic Arts at the University of Miami School of Communication. He graduated from Harvard College in 1965, where Stanley Cavell was his honors thesis advisor, and received his PhD from Harvard in 1974, with Cavell the chair of his dissertation committee. After teaching for three years in the NYU Cinema Studies Department, an NEH grant—Cavell was the project director—brought him back to Harvard, where he taught for many years (including a course in film comedy he co-taught with Cavell). He was for three years the Director of the International Honors Program on Film, Television and Social Change in Asia, which led to his writing and co-producing (with the National Film Development Corporation of India) *Unni*, a feature film directed by the distinguished Indian filmmaker G. Aravindan. He was the Founding Editor of Harvard University Press's 'Harvard Film Studies' series before becoming Series Editor for Cambridge University Press's 'Studies in Film' series. He has published essays on diverse aspects of film and television history, criticism, and theory, and on the writings of Cavell. His many books include *Hitchcock: The Murderous Gaze*; *The 'I' of the Camera: Essays in Film History*; *Reading Cavell's* The World Viewed: *A Philosophical Perspective on Film*; *Cavell on Film*; *Jean Rouch: A Celebration of Life and Film*; *Three Documentary Filmmakers*; and *The Holiday in His Eye: Stanley Cavell's Vision of Film and Philosophy*.

Martin Shuster is Professor of Philosophy and the Isaac Swift Distinguished Professor of Jewish Studies at University of North Carolina at Charlotte. In addition to many articles and book chapters, he is the author of *Autonomy after Auschwitz: Adorno, German Idealism, and Modernity* (University of Chicago Press, 2014), *New Television: The Aesthetics and Politics of a Genre* (University of Chicago Press, 2017), and *How to Measure a World? A Philosophy of Judaism* (Indiana University Press, 2021). With Anne O'Byrne, he is the editor of *Logics of Genocide: The Structures of Violence and the Contemporary World* (Routledge, 2020), and with Henry Pickford, he is currently editing *The Oxford Handbook of Theodor W. Adorno*. His work on television frequently engages with Cavell's work on film and in philosophy, and he is currently working on a collection of essays intended as a follow-up to *New Television*.

Robert Sinnerbrink is Associate Professor of Philosophy at Macquarie University, Sydney. He is the author of *New Philosophies of Film: An Introduction to Cinema as a Way of Thinking* (Second Edition, Bloomsbury,

2021), *Terrence Malick: Filmmaker and Philosopher* (Bloomsbury, 2019), *Cinematic Ethics: Exploring Ethical Experience through Film* (Routledge, 2016), *New Philosophies of Film: Thinking Images* (Continuum/Bloomsbury, 2011), and *Understanding Hegelianism* (Acumen, 2007/Routledge, 2014). He has edited two books—*Emotion, Ethics, and Cinematic Experience* (Berghahn Books, 2021) and *Critique Today* (Brill, 2006)—and is a member of the editorial boards of *Film-Philosophy*, *Film and Philosophy*, and *Projections: The Journal of Movies and Mind*.

Paul Standish is Professor and Head of the Centre for Philosophy of Education at UCL IOE. He has extensive experience as a teacher in schools, colleges, and universities, and his research reflects that range. His *Beyond the Self: Wittgenstein, Heidegger, and the Limits of Language* (Ashgate, 1992) indicates an interest in Wittgenstein and education that spans four decades. He is the author or editor of some twenty books, including *Stanley Cavell and the Education of Grownups* (Fordham, 2012), *Education and the Kyoto School of Philosophy: Pedagogy for Human Transformation* (Springer, 2012), and *Stanley Cavell and Philosophy as Translation: 'The Truth is Translated'* (Rowman and Littlefield, 2017), all in collaboration with Naoko Saito; and *Wittgenstein and Education: On Not Sparing Others the Trouble of Thinking* (Wiley, 2023), co-edited with Adrian Skilbeck. He is life president of the Philosophy of Education Society of Great Britain and co-editor of the *Journal of Philosophy of Education*.

Catherine Wheatley is Reader in Film and Visual Culture at King's College London. She has published widely on questions pertaining to film, ethics, and aesthetics, and the work of Stanley Cavell. Catherine is the author of four monographs—including *Michael Haneke's Cinema: The Ethic of the Image* (Berghahn, 2009), the BFI Classics book on *Caché* (BFI Publishing, 2013), and *Stanley Cavell and Film: Scepticism and Self-Reliance at the Cinema* (Bloomsbury, 2018)—and the editor of a number of essay collections and special issues, including, with Kate Rennebohm, a dossier for the journal *Screen* entitled 'Projecting Cavell'. Catherine also writes regularly for *Sight & Sound* magazine, and is a convenor of the BFI's Philosophical Screens series. She is currently working on articles about the concept of wonder and the everyday in film, and on the question of love, friendship, and the Cavellian couple.

Introduction

The Fact and Fiction of Television: Stanley Cavell and the Terms of Television Philosophy

David LaRocca and Sandra Laugier

Television meets its critics on their own terms, and in their own times. For Stanley Cavell, this meant having a life with cinema—'memories of movies are strand over strand with memories of my life'—long before he had a relationship with television.[1] When *I Love Lucy* premiered, Cavell was twenty-five years old and commencing graduate studies in philosophy at Harvard University, having taken a formal and formidable step away from the life in musical composition and performance that he trained for in previous years at Berkeley and Juilliard.[2] While going to the movies was a regular part of his everyday routine, television viewing was still a novelty in 1951, something more akin to a relationship with a domestic appliance than a mode of art—much less a mode of art one could have philosophical reflections about. The medium would have to mature, as would culture's sensibilities for treating it as an intimate part of daily experience and, in time, serious academic study, including, more broadly and provocatively, the formation of one's character and one's attunement to the lives of others.

Contemporaries of Cavell, older and younger, would find their way to the analytical tools and frameworks for discussing television. As with many things, the timing of one's encounters matters. Though we live in an era praised for the artfulness, abundance, and cultural relevance of TV, earlier ages contended with different circumstances: network dominance, technical limits of broadcast, commercial interruptions, a prominent antagonism between art and commerce. Like photography in the nineteenth century and film in the twentieth, television was another vector of controversy over the purposes and meanings of technological innovations. Thus, questions of ontology (what was or is TV?) and aesthetics (when does TV become art?) are joined with the ethical and epistemological (what is TV good for? what does TV help us know?). What you think of television, then, involves an assessment of when you make contact with the medium, including what sorts of conceptions and preconceptions you bring with you. As with the study of art and media more generally, the interaction between concept and artifact is generally fecund, especially when approached generously.

Yet we cannot foreclose the extent to which some thinkers and theorists, especially looking back over the long arc of TV reception, have raised concerns about the medium's deleterious potential: its apparent agency in human dissipation and degeneracy. While Raymond Williams offered a critical materialist approach equipped with a searing interest in how serious criticism of TV-as-form was possible (having already co-written *Preface to Film* in 1954);[3] Paul Goodman placed TV in the context of social change and worried about its detrimental effects; Norbert Weiner charted a course for the tele-visual via cybernetics; Newton Minow admonished viewers of the 'vast wasteland' of television with its 'procession of sadism';[4] Marshall McLuhan spoke of television as a 'cool medium' that instigates active viewership;[5] Mihaly Csikszentmihalyi posited the notion of 'flow' and TV as its antagonist (in the form of 'mindless entertainment'[6]); Leslie Fiedler regarded television as providing a 'relief from art';[7] and Neil Postman generated a culture critique insisting the shallow offerings of TV underwrite a shallow society,[8] it is Cavell's *philosophical* uptake of moving images—at first, movies, and in time, television—that calls and keeps our attention on the present occasion.

What if spending a lot of time with TV shows—and their characters—is positively transformative for one's character or moral sense (even when those characters are morally depraved), leading not to degeneracy but efflorescence and a tilting towards perfectionism? In this alternate take, television would be a condition for sharing company and receiving instruction, for finding a friend and welcoming a teacher. Instead of adopting Larry David's resolute credo for *Seinfeld*—'no hugging, no learning'—we find reasons for contemplating television's impact on the articulation and exercise of moral perfectionism, an outlook that displaces the prospect of achieving perfection for the more vital aim of incremental improvements, progressive if minor insights. The form and content of television, especially since the new millennium, provides portraits of human behavior and sustains them—thus what we watch and how we behave (and think) are interactive. We have more characters and we have more time with them in their 'worlds'. Could it be that television in the present age has become, perhaps without us noticing or articulating it in so many words, the audiovisual equivalent of the novel—or depending on a character's age or arc, perhaps the *Bildungsroman*? In this analogy, the brevity of films (as we have known them) can suddenly seem like short stories, or poems even. In this comparison, television has become the long-form mode in which viewers have a chance to inhabit their own lives—and over a longer term than film allows—while also productively entering the fictional realms presented to them. Whether the analogy proves productive or divisive, it nevertheless gestures towards the evolving function, and undeniably prominent force, of TV shows in our ordinary experience. Against the polemical gesture of writing off television as a danger to democracy or the proper functioning of the human mind, we claim that TV—understood as an appellation involving form *and* content—is an aesthetic rendering of the philosophical life: providing profound sights and sounds worthy of our enduring critical appraisal.

The Fact and Art of Television

Indeed, the authors commissioned to write entirely new chapters for this volume—all acknowledged analysts of varied media environments—have their own histories of encounter with television to call upon and address, including familiarity with the aforementioned media theorists and critics, among many others. Each new decade confronts the evolution of form (from black-and-white to color, from cathode ray tube to retina monitor, from broadcast with commercial sponsors to cable conglomerates to on-demand streaming by way of subscription, from living room screen to mobile phone display) and content (from situation comedy to soap opera, newscast to prestige drama, talk show to game show, live sports event to multi-season nature documentaries, and so on), and so each new decade demands criticism that takes stock and offers pronouncements that give us pause, perspective and, in alternation, provocation and peace. Yet, whenever someone arrives at the study of television, one must brace for an encounter with the undeniable magic of the medium; or, as Cavell put it, more eloquently and evocatively, with 'something like the sheer fact that television exists, and that this existence is at once among the most obvious and the most mysterious facts of contemporary life'.[9]

Given the range of Cavell's philosophical concerns—especially among the arts of literature, music, painting, theatre, opera, and film—one could substitute them for 'television' in the just-cited sentence and walk away similarly dumbfounded (and thus also eager to sign up for further tuitions of this sort). Yet the mysteriousness of television is, perhaps until recently only challenged by film, compounded by its ubiquity, its intimate presence in our lives—endlessly looked to, seldom looked at.[10] 'Television', as Thomas Streeter suggested, 'is something people do.'[11] We take this fact of television as one of the abiding mysteries of the medium and our contemporary lives spent in its company.

With Cavell, we see a decided turn to the serious watching of, and listening to, television, thereby acknowledging yet bracketing the curmudgeonly chatter about the detriments of 'the boob tube' alluded to above. As befits a philosopher who would write his second book about film (*The World Viewed*, 1971) and his third one on Henry David Thoreau's *Walden* (*The Senses of Walden*, 1972), who would co-found the Harvard Film Archive and the African-American Studies Department at Harvard, Cavell discovered a way to approach the study of television productively—that is, in ways that were attuned to the medium's effects on him, on his thoughts, and the environments he inhabited and helped create. In his case, we may discern how his regard for 'reading' (and listening to) TV extends—and adapts—certain habits familiar to his brand of philosophical film criticism, including the virtuosity of its dispensations in ordinary language.

In the 1970s, for example, TV was TV and film was film. 'It was a time when movies were magical', said celebrated auteur director P.T. Anderson, 'and TV was just something you had in a box at home. Those days are long gone, you know?'[12] In the pandemicine, when theatre-going is interrupted or unsettled—along with film festivals and marquee premieres—and technologies disrupt models and ideas for distribution, the very notion of 'movies' is in flux. As cineplexes began reopening after a long pandemic hiatus, A.O. Scott declared—and asked: 'The movies are back. But what are movies now?'[13] And so, part of the motive in what follows is to track such up-to-the-minute contemporary queries by placing them in intimate conversation with Cavell's more established sense of the form and content of what television was, what cinema was. For instance, Garrett Stewart distinguishes phenomena and our language to describe them when he writes, 'What motion pictures are now is post-*filmic*, not postcinematic.'[14] On one register, then, television natively absorbs the cinematic as an indication of its temporal circumstance. Hence the question that inaugurates (and we think sustains) these opening remarks—when is television?—since the interrogative naturally pushes TV-watchers and cinephiles into dialogue about the parameters of what are clearly evolving, interrelated, transmedial phenomena. Television was historically never filmic (not that stylists such as Alfred Hitchcock and David Lynch didn't make it seem so), but it can and it should now be recognized in many of its current modalities as ably cinematic. No wonder Cavell took an interest in parsing the nature of what were, in his time, different technologies with sometimes overlapping and sometimes distinguishable characteristics. But times change and so must our conceptual frameworks and terms of engagement.

Though one can find scattered remarks on TV in Cavell's writings, the *locus classicus* is his 1982 article 'The Fact of Television', which is engaged with and explicated by our contributing authors throughout the present volume, and situated in the context of related scholarly research on television. In this essay, Cavell writes from the scene in which moviegoers were faced with multiple and contemporaneous fronts: the familiar movie theatre (then just catching wind of the blockbuster and IP-drive content inaugurated in the mid-1970s), broadcast television, cable television, and the uncanny accomplice to the audio cassette, the video cassette (with its capacity to present 'film', to record live television, and in the case of camcorders, to function as the medium of the home movie and for aspiring filmmakers, the means for creating homemade movies).

One of the most enduring observations of Cavell's text on television is his sense that cinematic representations and televisual presentations do different things, stand in different relationships to viewers: a movie screen is something we watch, whereas broadcast signals intimate that the content of a television screen is, in fact, something we witness or surveil. In Cavell's recasting of ordinary language, television offers a 'current of simultaneous event reception' whereas film remains a 'succession of automatic world projections'.¹⁵ Use Jean-Luc Godard's *Numéro Deux* (1975) as a quick clinic on the difference: here Godard's film incorporates an actual TV set, and so the film projects Godard as a succession of automatic world projections while, simultaneously, we see him monitored by the TV within the film frame; obviously, the closed-circuit TV screen in *Numéro Deux* is not the same as the broadcast version that displays live sports or talk shows or breaking news, but it provides a picture of the way we might distinguish the ontology of film from the ontology of television as they would have appeared to Cavell some decades ago. 'The distinction between filming the world and monitoring an event is a decisive one for "The Fact of Television"', Cavell tells us in 'The Advent of Videos'.¹⁶ The temporality of broadcast TV, for instance, collapses the here and the there so that we peer through a monitor—as if through a looking glass, such as a telescope—to see what is happening on the other side (indeed, to monitor it); as television has become increasingly scripted, produced in the same manner as film (though presented according to a different logic), the quality of TV as a site for monitoring has shifted—hence the need for a return and reconsideration of Cavell's early 1980s insights.

The publication time stamp of 'The Fact of Television' is worth dwelling on: Cavell wrote the piece in the wake of Norman Lear's revolution of TV content and cable's emergence as a form of distribution. *My Dinner with Andre*, directed by Louis Malle and released in near proximity to Cavell's article, in 1981, captures something of the frenzied sentiment Cavell responds to in his remarks for *Daedalus*: the eponymous Andre says that people are nowadays 'lobotomized by TV', 'lulled into a dangerous tranquility'. Cognizant of such perturbations, Cavell acknowledges the widespread worry that TV is a threat not just to high culture but to higher thoughts, yet finds such 'disapprovals' about, for example, its addictiveness wanting. That is, he sees reason to turn off the alarm and, instead, turn our attention to the varieties and virtues of the televisual (perhaps especially as they are made manifest in contradistinction with cinema). That TV and cinema have seemingly collapsed into one another in this third decade of the new millennium should be a cause for further inquiries, not a reason to shut them down.

> [Is] there some surmise about the *nature* of the pleasure television provides that sets off disapproval of it, perhaps like surmises that once caused the disapproval of novel-reading or, later, of movie-viewing? If this were the case, one might expect the disapproval to vanish when television comes of age, when its programs achieve an artistic maturity to match that of the great novels and movies. Is this a reasonable faith?¹⁷

Since we approach television more than forty years after Cavell asked these questions, we are in a position to assess outcomes—whether his faith was warranted, whether maturity has been achieved. In his time, he wrote: 'the absence of interest in the medium seems to me more complete, or studied, than can be accounted for by the accidents of taste'.[18] Offense at content—the subject of aesthetic judgment, including disapproval—can distract from attention to the 'aesthetic possibilities of the medium', a refrain, a hope, evident also in his study of film.[19] Possibilities, moreover, that are not given or foreclosed. Pointing out such a distinction does not preclude the ongoing commentary and occasional crisis about the intoxicating, addictive, or otherwise perverse charms of TV. Cavell recalls:

> William Rothman has suggested to me that since television can equally adopt a movie mode or a video mode, we might recognize one dimension of television's 'company' in the understanding of the act of switching from one mode to another as the thing that is always live, that is, effected simultaneously with our watching. This points to the feature of the current (suggesting the contemporary as well as indicating the continuous) in my articulation of this aesthetic medium's physical basis.[20]

A few years after Cavell wrote, the moral and intellectual panic remained febrile, embodied for instance in Allan Bloom's trenchant critique of how television, like radio before it, 'assaulted and overturned the privacy of the home'.[21] Cavell spoke directly to Bloom's concerns in 'Who Disappoints Whom?'. After first underscoring numerous points of agreement between them—that is, of a shared concern with the state of culture, including the academy and the education of the young—Cavell dwelled at more length on a couple of differences, in particular, 'our experience of the modern and the popular in the arts'.[22] Responding to such veritable observations (ones hyper-charged when, in our age, the screen delivers social media[23]), and citing indications of Cavell's faith fulfilled, may require saying that television has, in time, in its ever-evolving medial and aesthetic maturity, become a force for pedagogical and perfectionist possibility.

We may recognize a familiar pattern, one harkening back to the network era and still very present. As Horace Newcomb notes: 'From the late 1940s through the mid-1970s, almost all serious attention to television was filtered through a model of American social science designed to explore and determine the "effects" of the medium. Serious attention was focused on the effects of television on children, on political processes, and on general problems related to the representation of violence on television.'[24] The moral panic about the effects of television on human behavior, thus, has given way to the moral panic about the effects of social media on human behavior (and for an even longer term, the purported detriments of video games, especially hyper-violent ones[25]). If we are prone to dismiss the alarm still audible from the mid-twentieth century, we may wonder about the extent of the analogy to the present time. Several studies suggest that the impact of social media, especially on adolescents, is graver than any perceived among earlier generations of youth who watched television.[26]

Drawing a line of continuity with the study of effects—wherever they may fall on the spectrum of influence, and making a link between concerns about television and social media—we should also cultivate proximity to the many fascinating findings of cognitive studies, especially of film and literature. Scholars such as Lisa Zunshine and Blakey Vermeule favor us with the intelligence necessary for parsing the way our minds interact with the characters we find on the page and the screen, and as importantly, how we can think productively and satisfyingly about how emotional relationships develop between readers and texts—even when we figure them as viewers of television.[27]

By the time Cavell had published his first book on film, *The World Viewed* (1971), 'humanistic approaches to television were fugitive in nature, often appearing in general readership magazines such as the *Nation* or *Saturday Review*'.[28] Cavell began reading film criticism by the likes of James Agee in *The Nation* and Robert Warshow in the *Partisan Review*.[29] Early forays of television criticism in book form were similarly made by journalists such as Gilbert Seldes (*The Public Arts*, 1956), Patrick Hazard (*TV as Art: Some Essays in Criticism*, 1966), and Robert Lewis Shayon (*The Eighth Art*, 1962 and *Open to Criticism*, 1971). Television genre study was enriched by Horace Newcomb's *TV: The Most Popular Art* (1974) and his many editions of *Television: The Critical View* (1976).[30] Meanwhile, during this same period, film as a legitimate field of academic inquiry was just making its first forays into journals and monograph publications as well as achieving residence in departments, programs, and archives; Cavell's contributions to the evolution of film as a bona fide medium for academic study—including within philosophy—are now legendary. As his thoughts on television have been less widely circulated, we hope the present initiative will provide some compensation, thereby inaugurating a new and refreshed series of consideration of Cavell's enduring relevance to the study of television.

During these transformations in the nature of television criticism, TV has made contact with the internet—to a large extent, been absorbed by it—and thus turned back upon us as condition of a life spent with screens of all sizes in nearly all places and times. In our pandemic milieu, we are 'distributed' and have willingly pointed self-surveillance apparatuses at our faces. 'Remote work' is the latest iteration of the televisual, a variation on reality TV. Linked together this way means television-as-life all day long; with Zoom, Teams, WhatsApp, and FaceTime, we are connected by TV feeds; we monitor ourselves and monitor each other. Using TV to understand our predicament, appeals to the logic of the *Brady Brunch* taxonomic grid are tired, yet perpetually relevant. And then, of course, after a long workday of video conferencing, we turn, with relief, from the unscripted televisual space of the monitor to the scripted content of cinematic television.

The restless mobility of the televisual image—incarnating variously in our laptop web browsers or phones, then picked up where we left off on our home screens or digital projectors—has displaced the familiar, seemingly-until-now-fixed location of 'the set' or 'the box'. Here, TV's absorption by the internet coalesces into something like the constantly streaming, descending data of *The Matrix*, not to mention the habituated quality of 'plugging in' as a form of 'tuning out' the rest of the world. As the postmodern parable goes, virtual life becomes life altogether. Soon enough, we are told, the green light—not Fitzgerald's but the Wachowskis'—will be drawn into service in the metaverse and its variants: our avatars will watch TV in virtual communities, while our bodies rest in place, motionless yet filled with emotions. At such intervals as these, we are, once again, left wondering how TV (as we have known it) will evolve. Taking stock of where we are, and have been, is a viable response to charting a course into novel and as yet unarticulated frontiers.

Education in and on TV

The contributors assembled here take it as evident that in Cavell's writing on television—and, indeed, in the topics it touches, such as moral perfectionism—there is much to enchant and much to agitate in one's onward reflections about the role TV has in our lives. Watching television with Cavell is a deeply rewarding venture—and the chapters collected here exemplify just how profitable the enterprise can be.

Readers arriving on this occasion of critical study likely have a sense for television and for Cavell too, but perhaps not the two *already* in conversation. How well known, in fact, is Cavell's 'The Fact of Television', which has been described as 'surprisingly unheralded'?[31] We can point out how the *critical* study of television emerged first from technology studies, communication departments, and realms largely beyond the humanities. Scholars and scientists from many disparate fields—in mechanical engineering, physics, sound technology, the history of science, science and technology studies—found themselves coming to terms with the medium as medium, and alongside them (first as a trickle, then as a deluge), in the discursive arts of media studies, film theory, sound studies, philosophy, and of course, most conspicuously, the precipitate of them all: television studies—to varying degrees, a blend of all the aforementioned disciplines. The bibliographies and frames of reference in what follows chart debts and affordances made possible by these varied and interrelated histories of inquiry and their auspicious offerings. Cavell's thought of television is our collective common ground, but each contributing author takes up the invitation with a different show (or shows) in mind and a varying sense of what Cavell's work portends for the past, present, and future of television studies.

In recent decades, as television has become more cinematic and no doubt with franchises, film has become more like television, Cavell's work calls to us, and so we find ourselves watching and listening to television with Stanley Cavell in mind. As we take stock of the expanse of television history, we are especially intrigued by the changes that have taken place since the turn of the millennium when, it would seem, 'prestige TV' or 'serious TV' or 'complex TV' troubled long-standing binaries such as film and television, the (flatness of the) screen and the ('convexity'[32] of the) tube, the image and the monitor, the stand-alone and the serial, art and commerce, celluloid strip and pixel array, theatrical release and streaming on demand, what is projected and what is broadcast, and so on. Thus, when we read Cavell's 'The Fact of Television', we can appreciate his take from that vantage in time and space, but also wonder what to make of his observations decades later. In our day, in our time, what is distinctive, if anything, about TV as a form or format, a genre or a medium? How do we think with Cavell about what some have called 'cinematic television'?[33] What is the purpose or difference or significance of what TV has become, in relation to the medium that remains cinematic but has become 'postfilmic'?[34] Such lines of investigation preoccupy us in the pages that follow.

In the decades since the coincident burgeoning of screened content and scholarly interest in it, the critical literature on television has tracked the evolution of the medium—from HBO (a name that promises how cinema comes home) to Netflix (a portmanteau that draws together the internet and the onomatopoeia of the mechanical film projector's flicker) to AppleTV+ (which combines three elements: a legacy, luxury computer manufacturer with global impact, an abbreviation, and a glyph inviting open-endedness). These medial exemplars, running roughly from the early 1980s to the present, not only coincide with the appearance of Cavell's remarks on television (*c*.1981), but also provide a generous temporal span in which varied and consequential deliberations over television's meaning—as technological phenomenon, as mass art, as agent of influence in our lives—are found.

Recent books have been devoted to articulating and assessing Cavell's understanding of the ontology of film and the nature of 'reading' films—in the latter case, especially as they are expressive of the genres he proposed (viz., comedies of remarriage on the one hand, and melodramas of the unknown woman on the other).[35] We should like to add to these dynamic libraries of dispatches, this time on the subject of television—yet another salvo in the onward development and expansion of Cavell studies. That said, we proceed with an appreciation for the intellectual landscape of several interrelated subfields, among them cinema studies, television studies, media studies, cultural studies, American studies, as well as philosophy, political theory, and cultural anthropology. Indeed, we see ourselves as joining a vibrant conversation already underway. There are interventions in appreciation: lessons on studying television as cultural artifact (such as *Tele-Visions*) and as repository of philosophical insight (such as *Appreciating the Art of Television*).[36] Attempts are made at addressing the radically and rapidly evolving modes of the medium—from animation to reality TV, from documentary to soap opera, from game show to talk show, and more—as found in *Thinking Outside the Box* and *The Tube Has Spoken*.[37] In the new millennium, as premium television was transforming credentials and criteria, Jan Olsson and Lynn Spigel collected their remarks on a 'medium in transition' under the title *Television after TV*.[38] Soon after, *Television Studies after TV* continued the elegy and the inquiry.[39] Even as we are said to live in the wake of TV, television appears a fecund and ongoing forum for intellectual investigation, as seen in *Television Aesthetics and Style* and *Why Theory?: Cultural Critique in Film and Television*.[40] After Jason Mittell's *Complex TV: The Poetics of Contemporary Television Storytelling*, we find license to explore the moral complexity of television (as in Jeroen Gerrits' chapter) and narrative complexity (as in Catherine Wheatley's chapter), including the ways these two dimensions of contemporary storytelling interact.

And yet, despite the richness and variety of these mostly still-relevant studies, only a rare few directly make contact with Cavell's own enduring observations of television (and film), or mark their debts and points of inspiration. Among the notable exceptions we find Lorenz Engell's *The Switch Image*, and our own Martin Shuster's *New Television* along with William Rothman's serial commentary, such as 'Cavell on Film, Television, and Opera'; Alex Clayton draws from Cavell in productive ways in 'Why Comedy is at Home on Television', as does contributor Byron Davies in 'The Specter of the Electronic Screen', along with Luca Bandirali and Enrico Terrone in their *Concept TV*.[41] Cavell's remarks on TV also figure crucially in Alberto N. García and Ted Nannicelli's 'Television's Temporality: Seriality and Temporal Prolongation'.[42] To up the ante, then, our collective effort, in these pages, sets an agenda where Cavell is essential company to each and every dispatch gathered here, regardless of disciplinary locale or privileged television program. If the invitation to contributors afforded incubation for making connections and developing new pathways, the ambition for the final volume is to present a coordinated forum for systematically improving the clarity of Cavell's sense of television (albeit now in a certain historical register), while also discerning what lessons he offers for the present and future study of this ever-evolving medium and its varied content.

TV series teach us about paying attention to forms of life. A bit like parents, families, and societies, they initiate us into what Wittgenstein defines as *Lebensformen*: vital forms or configurations of human coexistence whose texture is the result of the practices and actions that produce or modify them. They are also ideal sites for perceiving *ways of being*: of people, relationships, and family resemblances. The moral vision of characters is publicly revealed or intimately developed through their use of language—their choice of words, their style of conversation. Television series thus pursue the quest for the ordinary and the 'pedagogical' task defined by Cavell and taken up by popular cinema: that of providing a subjective education through shared experience and expression. Here we are invoking the tradition of ordinary language philosophy that we have inherited from Wittgenstein and Austin and Cavell, all of whom defined language as predicated on voice, conversation, and the practice of both. The creation of sound films constituted a historical step in giving voice to humans (on film), and, within certain genres, to women in particular, as Cavell demonstrated in *Pursuits of Happiness* and later, *Contesting Tears*. TV series are a further technical and narrative development that continue this progression in a more diverse way and by giving a place and voice to a wider variety of people—across time, tradition, race, ethnicity, gender, and linguistic context.

Keep in mind that for Cavell, the importance of cinema is defined by its place in an ordinary form of life. Series shape our everyday experience, including our sense of politics and ethics. Here we may think of the importance, within adolescent culture (and also among many working academics), of the series *Buffy the Vampire Slayer*, whose creator, Joss Whedon, imagined it as a feminist work intended to morally transform a coed audience by showing an apparently ordinary girl who was capable of fighting. Buffy's strength lies in her being at once an ordinary girl and a fearsome killer, and in the powerful and paradoxical way she embodies care (care for her friends, her mother, her sister—as well as for the world, which she saves on a regular basis). This allows her to be a role model for girls as well as for boys; care, in this television portrait, is defined as a capacity shared by both sexes.

After what we may call a 'first wave' in which women advanced towards equal presence in popular series, with sexual rights at stake (invoking the classics, *Sex and the City* [HBO] and *The L Word* [Showtime]), now we are in the heart of a 'second wave' that offers the public tools for cultural analysis of the situation of women, confirming Cavell's point in *Pursuits of Happiness*— that the right to vote does not equal political equality. The series *Unbelievable* (Netflix, 2019), from showrunner Susannah Grant, and based on an investigation by the media outlet Propublica, introduces us to two women detectives in an investigation that leads them to confront a serial rapist ... and a police force that is negligent, grossly incompetent, and brutal towards the victims, who are immediately considered 'not believable'. *Unbelievable*'s originality lies in its focus not on the rapist but on the victims, and (as indicative of its role in the second wave) it also 'takes care' of its viewing subjects by avoiding the graphic display of rape. *Unbelievable* holds its own with its actresses. Looking at them, one wonders if the feminine and feminist power of new TV series is perhaps due to the arrival in force of a whole generation of actresses ready to take this women's genre to the next level, like the comedies and melodramas of Hollywood cinema in the 1930s and 1940s: to name a few, Toni Collette and Merritt Wever in *Unbelievable*; Reese Witherspoon, Nicole Kidman, and Shailene Woodley in *Big Little Lies* (HBO, 2017–19); Regina King in *Seven Seconds* (Netflix, 2018) and *Watchmen* (HBO, 2019); Sandra Oh and Jodie Comer in *Killing Eve* (BBC, 2018–22); Elisabeth Moss in *Top of the Lake* (BBC and Sundance, 2013–17) and *The Handmaid's Tale* (Hulu, 2017–). These are actors who, like the Katharine Hepburns, Irene Dunnes, and Barbara Stanwycks of the last century, do not aim to undergo any kind of male gaze—but resolutely embody self-reliance and female solidarity by building on the work of previous generations.

The presence of strong female characters, when women have long been rendered invisible in cinema, is certainly one of the most striking elements in the transformations brought about by, and in, popular culture and TV series. Similarly, two major HBO works, *Watchmen* and *Lovecraft Country* (Misha Green, D. Lindelof, J.J. Abrams, 2019), revisit a repressed episode of American history (the Tulsa massacre) and, as the film *Black Panther* has already done, radically broaden the audience for Black characters, who have themselves become emblematic, morally discerning, and saviors of a nation or the world. By drawing from a range of popular culture resources—comic books, H.P. Lovecraft fantasy fiction, horror stories, and superheroes—and by featuring women, as well as Black actors, the struggles for equality are given a novel depiction (such as embodied by the late Michael K. Williams, hero of *The Wire*, revisited in *The Night Of*, *When They See Us*, and *Lovecraft Country*); in turn, these series invent a new, exuberant, and instructive violence, articulating gender and race, film and TV (as exemplified by Paul Standish's chapter on Steve McQueen's *Small Axe* [Amazon, 2020] below).

Our Lives in Series

As a further scene of instruction, let's consider when Cavell discusses the way TV time involves 'an order of time incommensurate with film time' with reference to the eleven, weekly hour-length episodes of *Brideshead Revisited*:[43]

> [*Brideshead Revisited*] is equivalent in its effect neither to something on film that would last eleven hours, nor to something that would last eleven weeks (whatever such things would be), nor, I think, to eleven films of an hour each. Not only does an hour signify something in television time that has no bearing on film time, but it is internal to the establishment of its formats that television obeys the rhythm, perhaps even celebrates the articulations, the recurrences, of the order of the week, as does Genesis.[44]

A description of familiar features of everyday life takes on new shape in the light of his diction, and syntax and frames of reference (linking television and Genesis). Film time? Of course, we have for years absorbed (mostly passively) the way movies deploy a three-act structure, continuity editing, voice-over, blocking, etc. that amount to an object we recognize *as a movie*. Even and especially in this case, we have a sense of the (acceptable, practiced, even normative) durational range of a film—as opposed to a music video, commercial, or short film. When a film, for its length, breaks into two parts, we wonder if it is still one movie. We have a customary awareness of a film's temporal limits (nowadays roughly ranging from ninety minutes to two-and-a-half hours) as providing a certain criterion for what can be accomplished in such a span. In the shift to television—with its seasons/series and episodes—all limits are lifted; seasons may have episodes of varying length, and indeed, of varying number; and one is never sure when a TV program is finished (see, for example, *Curb Your Enthusiasm* [2000–], which began at the turn of the millennium and has appeared periodically ever since[45]). And then, of course, there are shows that become movies and movies that become shows; Cavell's own example, the TV show *Brideshead Revisited* (1981) appeared as a feature film in 2008. Michael Mann's celebrated *Heat* (1995) was, in fact, a remake of his own earlier television work, *L.A. Takedown* (1989); a comparison of the two, side by side, offers a unique, single-author lesson on the differences between the creation of television and film in the late twentieth century—along with hints about how historical differences can be elided, for example, the way TV production can adopt cinematic style (as Mann does with *Miami Vice*, 1984–89, and recently with *Tokyo Vice*, 2022; s1:e1), and how films can trade on the prodigality of the serial (as with Mann's own cinematic remake of his cult TV series in *Miami Vice*, 2006). Ingmar Bergman's *Scenes from a Marriage* (1973) began as a television miniseries (with six hour-long episodes), but was soon thereafter condensed into a feature film of 167 minutes. *Saraband*, a sequel featuring the same actors, appeared thirty years later in 2003. In 2021, Hagai Levi wrote and produced a five-part series with the same title for HBO, which begins in a moment of meta-awareness of its production, with the actors preparing to begin the scene. These switchbacks, reconceptions, revisions, and repetitions provide concrete instances with which to test our sense of—and confidence in—the criteria that (have historically) defined and divided film and television, and are increasingly deployed to insist on (and exemplify) their common ground.

Moreover, now that films, such as those linked together by the Marvel Cinematic Universe, have adopted seriality, we see a hybridity that makes each independent film behave much more like an episode in a series; indeed, we may descry this trait as far back as 1977 with the first installment of *Star Wars* (i.e., Episode IV). Cinephiles are often left wondering about the coherency of a film-as-episode: does it hold up on its own terms—or does it need the previous or next installment? Alongside these narrative conundrums, the nature of parasocial relationships remains salient, with viewers invited to bond with, or in today's parlance, 'follow' the exploits and emotional journeys of any number of characters. The exemplarity of such characters can be outsized: Steven Spielberg once quipped that TV was his third parent.[46] We spend days and nights with the characters, and return to them season after season, in a parasocial intimacy from which we draw morals and insights. TV allows for the pleasure of 'keeping something in mind'—and it is a term that informs the very title of this collection.

Not to be missed, then, it is not just the quantity, but the very nature of brief episodic encounters that appears to encourage a habit, indeed, a mode of iterative and perpetual relation; we can allocate the time, perhaps very nearly on a daily basis, to watch an episode of a television show, in a way that we cannot justify watching a standard film with such regularity. And perhaps we would even find ourselves less inclined to watch a short film (lasting a mere thirty minutes) than a TV show lasting 'the same' thirty minutes; why is this a felt difference in our modes of reception? Such emergent dichotomies, doubtless tied to aspects of behavioral psychology, received a talented treatment at the Golden Globes when Tina Fey and Amy Poehler had this exchange:

> FEY: So you may be confused which nominees count as movies and which are considered TV.
> POEHLER: Now TV is the one that I watch five hours straight, but a movie is the one that I don't turn on because it's two hours. I don't want to be in front of my TV for two hours, I want to be in front of the TV for one hour five times.[47]

Cavell was sensible to the quality and pitch of humor—indeed, outright jokes—in the course of philosophical investigation,[48] and this perceptive repartee deserves our attention and our self-reflection. Why is what they say the case? And how does it affect the present and future not so much of television (which appears to have bested its cinematic counterpart) but of film? Cavell's own autobiographical reflections on his moviegoing life—e.g., attending a movie almost daily for a stretch of his life in New York and Los Angeles—remind us how material conditions for viewership doubtless inform possibilities (is there a repertory movie theatre in your neighborhood playing masterworks of cinema day after day, night after night, as there is in Paris' Quartier Latin?).

All the more striking, we learn that, according to surveys, it is the moviegoers themselves who have unlearned going to the movies during the pandemic—and it is those who *used to go* regularly who appear to return the least (who may be permanently lost to the public habit), now preferring the setting of their own home to screen films that are so easily available and in such abundance. People have lost the habit—and we might say the talent and taste—for watching films in movie theatres. Film seems to have joined the domestic, private space, previously associated more closely with TV series, which have in turn acquired a new role as comforter (and company against social isolation) to compensate for the increased withdrawal into the home, and especially as a consequence of lockdown and quarantine. This is just an(other) example of the 'privatization' of cultural life, which may well be a radical change in the 'movie-going lives' Cavell described. What so many moviegoers give up is not film per se, but a form of life (a quite French, and in France a still persistent, *Lebensform*): passing in front of a cinema on the way home from work, or on the way out of the metro or the café, and deciding impulsively to see a film, or making a trip to the cinema as part of a friendship, or a family gathering—all of this now feels part of a distant life, where the cinema was an integral part of daily experience, a portion of a constant mixing of public and private spaces.

One can be forgiven for seeing moviegoing, on these terms, as an allegory of democracy: the (lost?) *agora* in which individuals assemble peaceably to test the terms of common (i.e., shared) civilization, and to walk away with new understanding (of oneself and others), ready to speak new things out in public, in the light of day—maybe today or the day after tomorrow.

Moreover, Cavell notes in *The World Viewed* that you have a different memory of a film depending on who you were with when viewing it. Companionship in the film *experience* is thus central to Cavell's analysis; so also is 'care':

> Rich and poor, those who care about no (other) art and those who live on the promise of art, those whose pride is education and those whose pride is power or practicality—all care about movies, await them, respond to them, remember them, talk about them, hate some of them, are grateful for some of them.[49]

Now, what Cavell says about movies is also true of TV. Everyone cares. And to our gratification, the series has provided a semblance of continuity in the face of the pandemic's destruction of cherished public spaces. Series—and their producers, i.e., the streaming behemoths—have taken care of us during the containment. The series used to accompany ordinary lives, and now they prove to be a resource or a refuge in extraordinary situations. They present 'comfort worlds' which, in turn, have the power to become live and ongoing 'relationships', essential to personal memories and the formation of self-understanding, all the while displacing in-person alternatives: going to coffee shops, traveling, meeting and touching each other. When the world couldn't visit Paris, *Emily in Paris* provided vicarious travel and 'friends' to be among. And series allow their viewers, like the characters in a dystopian series, to perceive the price and the charm of an everyday life that we took for granted—we remember June in *The Handmaid's Tale*, nostalgically watching old videos of *Friends* episodes in the devastated premises of the *Boston Globe*. With *Station Eleven* (HBO, 2021), likewise, we began to feel a demarcation separating Before Times from the present.

The characters of television fiction are so well anchored and clear in their moral expressions—idiosyncratic rather than archetypal—that they can be 'released' and opened to the imagination and use of all viewers, 'entrusted' to us—as if it were up to each of us also to take care of *them*. Indeed, for a fan who has followed a serious series from the beginning, living with the characters for three, four, seven years, and sometimes many more (including repeated viewing, 'restarting' a series), these characters become an *object of care*, even as the series care for us. Hence the great importance of the conclusions to series, which must teach their viewers to go on without them. The final moments of *Lost* (ABC, 2004–10) and *Mad Men* (AMC, 2007–15) are illustrations of the labor that series enact to guide us in separating from their characters, if not leaving their worlds (cherished as a mode of personal memory). As Sandra Laugier discusses in her contribution to this volume, *The Americans* (FX, 2013–18) teaches us how to leave Elizabeth and Philip Jennings, a couple of KGB spies infiltrated in the United States in the 1980s, or perhaps more aptly, to let them leave us. *Banshee* (Cinemax, 2013–16) devotes with admirable concentration its entire last episode to the hero's melancholic farewell to each of the characters, a way for him to free himself from these people in his life, and to find autonomy apart from them.

Part of the hold characters have on us must be attributed to the movie or television actor's mysterious capacity for what Cavell defined as 'photogenesis': making themselves perceptible to spectators and thereby, somehow, constituting the spectator's experience of a character. Thus, the modes of expression of TV series actors (their moral texture, distinctive style of speech and gesture) are a veritable ethical resource offered by popular culture. Episode by episode, season after season, the question of morality is shifted towards the development of a common sensibility, which is both presupposed and educated (or transformed) by the sharing of values. We live with these characters and in time, even when the show ends, they live in us. Such 'serial care' is essential to collective moral survival. And during the present time, the series that we thought had been relocated, progressively detached from our television screens (because they were once broadcast) have reinstalled themselves in the home (thanks to on-demand streaming to our laptops, tablets, and phones). We now consume series and films alike—on the same screen real estate.

It is not accidental that series are (almost) never available in cinemas. At the cinema, film educates, transforms, consoles, but film does not 'take care' of us the way TV series do. Rather, film offers the disturbing experience of a world and of characters bigger than oneself, on a screen which, while presenting this to us, cuts us off from the world, makes the world strange anew. Perhaps this is one answer to the question why it is 'easier' to watch hours and hours of television but harder to devote oneself to a single film, especially a much-vaunted classic. The invention of cinema caused the subversion of what John Dewey called 'the abyss between ordinary and aesthetic experience'.[50] It is now necessary to take into account this redistribution of public and private spaces, the privatization of the public by the mutation of the forms of everyday life where the cinema is secularly embedded.

Popular Art?

As Cavell noted decades ago, playing a movie on TV doesn't make the movie *into* TV; indeed, it may highlight (as it did for Cavell) the way that television-as-a-medium remains in development as a form of art:

> I have begun by citing grounds on which to deny that the evanescence of the instance, of the individual work, in itself shows that television

has not yet come of age aesthetically. (Even were it to prove true that certain television works yet to be made may become treasured instances, as *instances*, such as the annual running of *The Wizard of Oz*—which serves to prove my case, since this is not an object made by and for television—my topic here remains television as it stands in our lives now).[51]

We are on much less certain ground when we capture another phrase, one addressed to *The Wizard of Oz*—as 'not an object made by and for television'—since we are currently inundated with objects that *are* made by and for television and yet claim themselves to be movies (see again how the crop of streaming platforms—Amazon, AppleTV+, Netflix, HBO, etc.—appear comfortable declaring a work 'film' without blushing, as they should, given the long, vaunted history of moviemaking). Cavell continues:

> But movies also, at least some movies, maybe most, used to exist in something that resembles this condition of evanescence, viewable only in certain places at certain times, discussable solely as occasions for sociable exchange, almost never seen more than once, and then more or less forgotten.[52]

Cavell has spoken of how he wrote much of *Pursuits of Happiness* (published the year before 'The Fact of Television') from memories of the seven comedies he wrote about in stunning detail and to pronounced philosophical effect. He did not write from digital databases, nor elaborate notebooks of film quotations nor careful step outlines—just personal memories of the movies. Our present condition requires no such exhaustive memories of movies (and television) comparable to what Cavell was compelled to maintain and retrieve as he composed his masterwork in the 1970s.[53]

Reflection on popular culture and its 'ordinary' objects leads to a transformation of theory and of criticism, as Cavell was one of the first to realize and enact. Cavell was less concerned with inverting artistic hierarchies, or the relationship between theory and practice, than with the transformation necessitated by our encounters with new experiences. The framework that he proposed for cinema—that of cultural democracy—is also a potent one for TV series. To use it, we must also prove the need for TV criticism, and define its form—a challenge raised by Robert Warshow, who, in *The Immediate Experience*, maintained:

> We are all 'self-made men' culturally, establishing ourselves in terms of the particular choices we make from among the confusing multitude of stimuli that present themselves to us. Something more than the pleasures of personal cultivation is at stake when one chooses to respond to Proust rather than to Mickey Spillane, to Laurence Olivier in *Oedipus Rex* rather than Sterling Hayden in *The Asphalt Jungle*.

And when one has made the 'right' choice, Mickey Spillane and Sterling Hayden do not disappear; perhaps no one gets quite out of sight of them. There is great need, I think, for a criticism of 'popular culture' which can acknowledge its pervasive and disturbing power without ceasing to be aware of the superior claims of the higher arts, and yet without a bad conscience.[54]

Cavell shows that a film (taken as a whole, including its actors and production) brings its own intelligence into its making, and that this intelligence itself educates us, leads us to recognize and appreciate our own tastes as movie fans, and thus for coming to know ourselves. This reading is even more valuable for TV series. An ordinary aesthetics of television must defend not the specificity of the individuals who create shows, nor the works as such, but rather the conditions for a common and shareable aesthetic experience. One of Cavell's greatest achievements is to have shown the 'intelligence that a film has *already* brought to bear in its making', which amounts to letting a work of art *have its own voice* in what philosophy will say about it.[55] Or learning what it means to 'check one's experience', to use the expression from *Pursuits of Happiness*[56]—that is, what it means to examine one's own experience and 'let the object or the work of your interest teach you how to consider it'.[57] This means that one must educate one's experience so that one can be educated by it. There is an inevitable, but not regrettable or embarrassing, circularity at work here: *having* an experience requires trusting one's experience. This role of trust in education is what makes TV an essential resource for the aforementioned moral education.

And as Cavell mindfully cautions, the philosophical catch is that the education cannot be achieved before the trusting.[58] For Cavell, there is a parallel between the relationship of cinema to high art and the relationship of ordinary language philosophy to 'high' philosophy. Philosophy, then, is connected to the self-education that television provides, and which can be defined as each person's *cinematographic autobiography*, to use Cavell's concept: the way in which our lives include fragments of movies and series; the way in which we orient ourselves in relation to these key moments, which are just as much a part of our experience as the dreams or real moments that we experienced—and which now haunt us. Our self-image, in a word, is formed and informed by fragments from film and increasingly also from TV; a strange donning of characters or drawing from their experience becomes essential to our own sense of identity and action. Call this cosplay of the imagination. Great television, just as film, presents us with important moments, moments of transformation—moments that in real life are fleeting and indeterminate, or that require years or an entire lifetime to understand (and even then, as so much else, may remain enigmatic and unresolved).

Popular culture does not refer to a primitive or inferior version of culture, but rather to a shared democratic culture that creates common values and serves as a resource for a form of self-education—or more specifically, a form of culture of the self, a subjective perfecting or subjectivation that occurs through sharing and commenting on ordinary and public material that is integrated into ordinary life. It is in this sense that, to cite Warshow again, 'we are all self-made men'. Cinema for Warshow is at the heart of popular culture: 'movies ... are the most highly developed and most engrossing of the popular arts, and ... seem to have an almost unlimited power to absorb and transform the discordant elements of our fragmented culture'.[59] In reading this passage, one cannot help but transfer the remark to television series, which are certainly (even more so than movies) a repository of all of culture, and absorb and recycle elements from music, video games, classical television—and of course, movies. That which Cavell claimed for Hollywood popular movies—their capacity to create a culture shared by millions—has been transferred onto other corpora and practices, in particular onto television series, which have taken up, if not taken over, the task of educating the public. Cavell's argument in *Cities of Words* was both ethical and perfectionist, if we redefine morality in new terms: that is, no longer in terms of 'the good' or definitive judgment, but rather the ongoing exploration of our forms of life. The importance and benefit of extending this aesthetic and ethical method to include television series is equally ethical, for these works are as shared and public as movies were in the twentieth century; they reach a significant audience and play an educational role, and perhaps even more emphatically than cinema, they make it possible to anchor the value of a work in the experience one has of it.

Even as television allows (and may encourage or insist upon) a retreat into the home, it may also provide conditions for a renewed sense of potentiality for democratic conversation—admittedly, as yet to manifest itself. If human civility—both in the conditions for physical 'in-person' congregation and the modes in which we address ourselves, one to the other—has been negatively impacted by this pandemic and this iteration of social media (with its capacity to spread misinformation and hate around the world in an instant), perhaps a future time, not far off, will surprise us with an opportunity to share our hard-won findings, some of them the precipitate of years' or decades' worth of time spent with television shows (either watching them alone or with a small band of trusted others). Like the solitary scholar emerging from the library after an independent sojourn with the classics to find her community—including moral and political agency—so too may we reserve the hope that in years to come television shows will be at once a lingua franca that crosses borders and languages, and also provide the terms and conditions for instantiating a richer, more nuanced understanding of what it means to be—and become—human.

As such, we need to rethink what we mean today by popular culture (which is no longer exactly 'popular' in the social or political sense in which certain arts—songs, folklore—once were, even if popular culture sometimes draws on the resources of these arts) by connecting it more clearly to the Deweyan notion of the public. Television series are sites of the education of individuals, an education that amounts to a form of personal 'perfecting' through sharing and discussing public and ordinary material, which is integrated into individuals' lives and provides a resource for their conversation with others. Thus the democratic experiment returns to us anew under the auspices of television. Cavell's ordinary aesthetics deliberately goes against the traditional critical approach, which is obsessed by art as *a separate domain* and the mystique of the individual creator, as well as with 'representation' and image, to the detriment of the ordinary experience of seeing a movie, which is the subjective—but always shared—experience of public material. For Cavell, cinema is a matter less of aesthetics than of *practice*—an ordinary practice that connects and reconciles the private and the public, the subject's expectation and the shared common experience.

The forms of work that interest the contributors in this book are those that are capable of transforming our existences by educating and cultivating our ordinary experience, not only in the classical sense of training our aesthetic taste, but in the sense of a moral training that is constitutive of both our singularity and representativeness. Cavell, radically combining Emerson's analyses (in the latter's essay 'Experience') and Dewey's (in *Art as Experience*), emphasizes that it is important to be able to educate one's experience in such a way that one can have confidence in it and, in this way, to live it. If cinephilia is a form of education of the self, 'seriesphilia' is even more so. This education does not occur through exposure to a set of universal masterpieces (even if such television classics do now exist), but through the constitution of one's personal list of favorite movies or series, and of scenes and lines of dialogue that are appropriate to various circumstances or occasions in one's life, at which points they are remobilized to pronounced and profound effect.

Cinematographic art, whether in the form of movies or TV series, is 'popular' art because the experience of it underlies ordinary experience. Dewey maintained that aesthetic experience is emblematic of experience in general, and Wittgenstein told us 'ethics and aesthetics are one'; so too this experience of television art is *moral*—both mysterious and ordinary, personal and public. It is ordinary because nothing is more shareable and self-evident than going to see movies or watching shows and talking about them, and these are often moments in which we reaffirm common ground in language. It is a mysterious form of knowledge, this coming to know what counts for oneself, and there is nothing easy or immediate about it. The only source for verifying one's description of what counts is *oneself*—whence comes the role of confidence, of trust in one's own experience,[60] which is the source of moral perfectionism and the only basis for public education and public moral expression.

The redefinition and relocation of the important is the hallmark of Cavell's approach to popular culture. In 'More of the World Viewed', Cavell contests the possibility of determining the importance of a film from a solely theoretical or historical point of view.[61] In art, as in politics, though I exist in a community of inquirers, I alone can say what counts (for me), I alone can determine the importance and significance of the movies or series I see. This personal (or in an Emersonian sense, 'original') relation is, paradoxically, the *democratic* aspect of the experience of cinema, which stands in contrast to the condescension that marks some approaches to the aesthetics and criticism of TV series. In short, moral perfectionism takes individual experience seriously, encourages the individual to articulate what elements of culture are important, and then invites the individual to give expression—not so much in a mood of defense or combat as in an agreeable pitch—to their orientation of the work, to what counts and why.

It is a requirement of individual exemplars of a particular genre that they conform to the identifying features of that genre. For example, given how seductive the character played by James Stewart is to the heroine of *The Philadelphia Story* (1940, dir. George Cukor), the movie could easily have ended with their marriage, a possibility to which the film briefly alludes. But, as Cavell notes, it is the *genre* that decides—just as we know, without needing any confirmation, that *War of the Worlds* (2005, dir. Steven Spielberg) will end with a remarriage (as most catastrophe movies do), and just as genre allows us to understand the perplexing conclusion of *The Affair* (2014–19), which depicts the reconciliation of protagonists who start out as a couple at the beginning of the series. Thus, cinema is full of explicit references to archetypal works within a given genre. TV series are also preoccupied by genre features, and are themselves a compendium of such references: the invocation of films or classical series through the 'citation' of scenes or actors, the repetition of plot points or allusion to character types, and so on.[62] It is, however, the *openness* of genre, and its creative and intertextual potential that enables its productive capacity, including the invention of new genres and subgenres.

TV series inherit the conversational capacities of couples from film's remarriage comedy genre, which bestows on them a particular grammar of expressions, interactions, and emotions. And early twenty-first-century series have supplied an even more diverse and variegated set of forms for narrative and moral reflection, thereby enriching an ever-expanding range of genres and subgenres, among them: mafia/cartel shows such as *Narcos* and *Mafiosa* drawing from *The Sopranos*; political shows such as the French *Baron Noir*, reworking *The West Wing*; metaphysical shows such as *The Leftovers* paying homage to *Lost*; and feminist examples such as *Girls* and *I May Destroy You* reinventing and updating elements from *Sex and the City*. In this way, television genres offer resources for empowering the generations of characters that emerge from their creative potency, not least because they provide an adaptable grammar that can be mobilized to provide both moments of continuity and overlap, and the permission to deviate—and invent. Such genre fluidity also offers the viewer a wealth of resources for exploring and better understanding their own thoughts and feelings, from the perspective of the particular context of the subject's personal reception (e.g., watching a given show at a certain time in one's life, during, after, or before a crucial phase of development). Cavell, citing again Warshow, writes that:

> [Warshow] expresses his sense of the necessarily personal in various ways ... namely, a sense of the writer's having to invent his own audience, of the writer's having to invent all the meanings of experience, of the modern intellectual's 'facing the necessity of describing and clarifying an experience which has itself deprived him of the vocabulary he requires to deal with it.'[63]

Towards TV-Philosophy

As an aid to defining the scope of our consolidated investigations in *Television with Stanley Cavell in Mind*, all of the chapters gathered here are dedicated to television shows produced in the twenty-first century, or, selecting a near-synonymous temporal marker, post-9/11 TV. The delineation may sound arbitrary, but it is fruitful, since it is around this time that the term 'prestige TV' was invented, with customary invocations of *The Sopranos* (1999–2007) as another emblematic point of reference. Suddenly television seemed weighty enough to bear serious philosophical discussion. A scene in the movie *Juliet, Naked* (2018, dir. Jesse Peretz) dramatizes this shift with satirical finesse: in the wake of screening a clip from *The Wire* during a university class, an auditor asks the professor whether students need to have read Euripides' *Medea* in order to understand the TV show—to which he replies humorlessly, 'It wouldn't hurt.' Another indication of a subtle change in the critical stance of some philosophers towards television, and popular culture more generally, can be seen in the bracketed appearance of *Seinfeld and Philosophy* (2000) and *The Simpsons and Philosophy* (2001). These books have authorized the pursuit of such forms of study and added legitimacy to the sophisticated treatment of everyday objects of art. We could trace these instincts back much further to Duchamp or Warhol, but it is sufficient to notice that the coincidence of serious television and serious criticism of television share a time horizon. What accounts for the shift, however, is more mercurial, though it might resolve itself in the Emersonian notion that 'what attracts my attention shall have it'.[64] When philosophers began to watch television in the new millennium, they may have recognized that the aspirations of their craft were coordinate with those seen and heard on screen. Moreover, the expanding study of television—not only by philosophers but by other serious humanist critics—may mark one of those moments when a person's avocations (nighttime binge-watching, say) found purpose and purchase in a person's daylight vocation.

The contributors to this volume, some of whose discerning criticism in this collection has already been mentioned, propel our collective conversation about the meanings of television into new realms—at times drawing from preexisting thinking and transforming it, while at other points, Theseus-like, inventing new ground as they proceed into auspicious territory. Indeed, both inclinations may amount to the same effect: as when Elisabeth Bronfen draws out the Shakespearean core of HBO's celebrated *Succession* (2018–), Paul Standish workshops the nuances of race in Steve McQueen's *Small Axe* (BBC, 2020), and Byron Davies explores lines of affiliation between Cavell's thought and Francophone Chilean filmmaker Raúl Ruiz's late-in-life TV series, *Litoral* (2008). Interventions into the moral landscape of TV as found in celebrated marquee shows such as *Homeland* (2011–20), *Ozark* (2017–22), *Justified* (2010–15), *True Detective* (2014–2019) and *The Good Place* (2016–20) cascade respectively from Thibaut de Saint Maurice, Hent de Vries, William Rothman, Robert Sinnerbrink, and Catherine Wheatley. Stephen Mulhall helps us navigate layers of metareference in Marvel's *WandaVision* (2021–), full as it is with genre engagement through *mise en abyme*, while David LaRocca articulates expressions and achievements of metareflexivity in Netflix's *The Crown* (2016–), and Michelle Devereaux takes further steps with *Russian Doll* (2019–), another series devoted to the representation of repetition and reflexiveness.

As these esteemed shows exemplify, serious television criticism often involves recognizing the presence—and effect—of a creator who is sometimes the same and sometimes different from the showrunner, which, in turn, we have learned is not the same as the director (of a film). These differences have presented challenges for those critics with 'auteurist sensibilities'. Robert Pippin articulates the problem: 'A room full of writers, often rotating in and out, series that are only planned out a few episodes when they begin, lots of interference from HBO or AMC types, many different directors over the course of a series. Even with the notion of an implied, collective author, tracking form and themes can be a mess.'[65] In this context one may judge that a show is not good enough season over season, or even episode over episode in the same season, to warrant sustained close reading. Some worry that no single stretch of a series is on par with the quality of good film—perhaps especially when a television show derives from a film, such as *Fargo* (2014–; see Hugo Clémot's contribution), which began life as a lauded and is now a canonical Coen brothers feature (1996). As Pippin put it in some comments on Martin Shuster's *New Television*: 'the governing intelligence that shapes long form series is collective and perhaps only something like a general sensibility or tonality can be attributed to the showrunner. But this distribution of sensibilities has to have an effect on the kind of artwork that can be made.'[66] As Shuster's chapter in this volume demonstrates, exploring such effects—and articulating what kind of work of art we have when we invoke the name, the location, and the medium of television—will remain a central preoccupation. And all chapters here demonstrate the *understanding* brought by a great number of TV shows to their own making, to paraphrase Cavell on Hollywood film.

In the third full decade of the twenty-first century, television studies has become a robust subfield of media studies. On a parallel trajectory, a subfield of philosophical and literary inquiry called Cavell studies / Cavellian studies has existed for several decades. A further sub-subfield explores philosophy and television, or more specifically *popular* philosophy and *popular* television, in a way that is approachable to a general readership (the various *Philosophy of* and *Philosophy and* titles alluded to above demonstrate this avenue of approach). Our guiding principle throughout the following pages is to find ways of drawing these three realms—television studies, Cavell studies, and the philosophy of popular culture—into intimate, rewarding conversation.

Our unique line of pursuit thus finds us applying serious philosophical attention—and indeed critical analysis—to television by focusing on how Stanley Cavell's work productively informs our understanding and experience of popular television series—now, as we take stock of present circumstances; looking back; and also peering, so far as we can, into the near and further future. We collectively aim to think and rethink what has been seen and heard so that we may prepare for the new instances we encounter, even as we appreciate the many accomplished shows we have lived with, admired, and benefited from. The bounty of television in our age can feel overwhelming: How exactly should I be thinking about such-and-such a show? What is a good show? What is 'the good of TV series'? And how, in fact, does one go about television criticism in a Cavellian spirit? *Television with Stanley Cavell in Mind* offers generative replies to these and related questions.

Notes

1. Stanley Cavell, *The World Viewed: Reflections on the Ontology of Film, Enlarged Edition* (Cambridge, MA: Harvard University Press, 1979 [1971]), xix.
2. Stanley Cavell, *Little Did I Know: Excerpts from Memory* (Stanford: Stanford University Press, 2010), 95.
3. Lola Seaton, 'How Raymond Williams Redefined Culture', *New Statesman*, August 25, 2021.
4. Newton N. Minow, 'Television and the Public Interest', delivered May 9, 1961 at the National Association of Broadcasters, Washington, DC.
5. Marshall McLuhan, *Understanding Media: The Extensions of Man* (Berkeley: Gingko Press, 2003; originally published by McGraw-Hill, 1964), 39.
6. Mihaly Csikszentmihalyi, 'Relax? Relax and Do What?' *New York Times*, August 12, 1993.
7. See Stanley Cavell, 'The Fact of Television', *Daedalus*, vol. 111, no. 4 (Fall 1982), 241. Our page citations come from the article as reprinted in *Themes Out of School: Effects and Causes* (San Francisco: North Point Press, 1984), 235-68; 235-36.
8. Neil Postman, *Amusing Ourselves to Death: Public Discourse in the Age of Show Business* (New York: Penguin, 1985).
9. Cavell, 'The Fact of Television', 235-36.
10. Kevin Townsend, Sophie Gilbert, Megan Garber, and Spencer Kornhaber, 'The "Meta-Emptiness" of *Emily in Paris*', *The Atlantic*, January 7, 2022.
11. Thomas Streeter, *Selling the Air: A Critique of the Policy of Commercial Broadcasting in the United States* (Chicago: University of Chicago Press, 1996), 3.

12 Kyle Buchanan, 'Paul Thomas Anderson Goes Back to the Valley with *Licorice Pizza*', *New York Times*, November 22, 2021.
13 A.O. Scott, 'The Movies Are Back. But What are Movies Now?', *New York Times*, July 15, 2021.
14 Garrett Stewart, *Cinemachines: An Essay on Media and Method* (Chicago: University of Chicago Press, 2021).
15 Cavell, 'The Fact of Television', 252; Cavell, *The World Viewed*, 72.
16 Cavell, 'The Advent of Videos', *Artspace*, May–June (1988), 173. Reprinted in *Cavell on Film*, ed. William Rothman (Albany: State University of New York Press, 2005), 167–73.
17 Cavell, 'The Fact of Television', 237.
18 Cavell, 'The Fact of Television', 236.
19 Cavell, *The World Viewed*, 31. See also *The Thought of Stanley Cavell and Cinema: Turning Anew to the Ontology of Film a Half-Century after* The World Viewed, ed. David LaRocca (New York: Bloomsbury, 2020).
20 Cavell, 'The Fact of Television', 253.
21 Allan Bloom, *The Closing of the American Mind: How Higher Education Has Failed Democracy and Impoverished the Souls of Today's Students* (New York: Simon and Schuster, 1987), 58–59.
22 Stanley Cavell, 'Who Disappoints Whom?', *Critical Inquiry*, vol. 15, no. 3 (Spring 1989), 606.
23 See Nicholas Carr, *The Shallows: What the Internet is Doing to Our Brains* (New York: W.W. Norton & Company, 2010; updated edition, 2020); and Jaron Lanier, *The Arguments for Deleting Your Social Media Accounts Right Now* (New York: Picador, 2018).
24 Horace Newcomb, 'Television', in *Encyclopedia of Aesthetics*, second edition, ed. Michael Kelly (New York: Oxford University Press, 2014), online version, n.p.; rb.gy/4dyq0h. For a digest of representative work from this era, see George Comstock and Marilyn Fisher, *Television and Human Behavior: A Guide to Pertinent Scientific Literature* (Santa Monica: RAND Corporation, 1975).
25 See Patrick M. Markey and Christopher J. Ferguson, *Moral Combat: Why the War on Violent Video Games is Wrong* (Dallas: BenBella Books, 2017).
26 See Jonathan Haidt, www.thecoddling.com/better-social-media and his co-authored research 'Underestimating Digital Media Harm', *Nature Human Behavior*, vol. 4 (April 2020), 346–48. See also Haidt, 'The Dangerous Experiment on Teen Girls', *The Atlantic*, November 21, 2021.
27 Lisa Zunshine, *Getting Inside Your Head: What Cognitive Science Can Tell Us about Popular Culture* (Baltimore: Johns Hopkins University Press, 2012) and Blakey Vermeule, *Why Do We Care about Literary Characters?* (Baltimore: Johns Hopkins University Press, 2011). See also *Introduction to Cognitive Cultural Studies*, ed. Lisa Zunshine (Baltimore: Johns Hopkins University Press, 2010); Amanda Anderson, Rita Felski, and Toril Moi, *Character: Three Inquiries in Literary Studies* (Chicago: University of Chicago Press, 2019).
28 Newcomb, 'Television', *Encyclopedia of Aesthetics*, online version, n.p.
29 Stanley Cavell, *Little Did I Know*, 227–28, 231.
30 Newcomb, 'Television', *Encyclopedia of Aesthetics*, online version, n.p.

31 See *Cognition, Emotion, and Aesthetics in Contemporary Serial Television*, ed. Ted Nannicelli and Héctor J. Pérez (New York: Routledge, 2022), 33.
32 Cavell, 'The Advent of Videos', 172.
33 See Angelo Restivo, *Breaking Bad and Cinematic Television* (Durham: Duke University Press, 2019).
34 See again Stewart, *Cinemachines*, 1, 7, 9–11, 15, 36.
35 Among other recent critical forays in these Cavellian genres, see Catherine Wheatley, *Stanley Cavell and Film: Scepticism and Self-Reliance at the Cinema* (New York: Bloomsbury, 2019); Rex Butler, *Stanley Cavell and the Arts: Philosophy and Popular Culture* (New York: Bloomsbury, 2021); and *Movies with Stanley Cavell in Mind*, ed. David LaRocca (New York: Bloomsbury, 2021).
36 *Tele-Visions: An Introduction to Studying Television*, ed. Glen Creeber (London: BFI Palgrave, 2015 [2006]); *Appreciating the Art of Television: A Philosophical Perspective*, ed. Ted Nannicelli (New York: Routledge, 2017).
37 *Thinking Outside the Box: A Contemporary Television Genre Reader*, ed. Gary R. Edgerton and Brian G. Rose (Lexington: University Press of Kentucky, 2005); *The Tube Has Spoken: Reality TV and History*, ed. Julie Anne Taddeo and Ken Dvorak (Lexington: University Press of Kentucky, 2010).
38 *Television after TV: Essays on a Medium in Transition*, ed. Jan Olsson and Lynn Spigel (Durham: Duke University Press, 2004). And Spigel, of course, has a suite of other books to consider, among them the co-edited volume with Charlotte Brunsdon, *Feminist Television Criticism: A Reader*, second edition (Berkshire: Open University Press, 2008).
39 *Television Studies after TV: Understanding Television in the Post-Broadcast Era*, ed. Graeme Turner and Jinna Tay (New York: Routledge, 2009).
40 *Television Aesthetics and Style*, ed. Jason Jacobs and Steven Peacock (New York: Bloomsbury, 2013); Jason Mittell, *Complex TV: The Poetics of Contemporary Television Storytelling* (New York: New York University Press, 2015); Edward Tomarken, *Why Theory?: Cultural Critique in Film and Television* (Manchester: Manchester University Press, 2017).
41 Lorenz Engell, *The Switch Image: Television Philosophy* (New York: Bloomsbury, 2021); Martin Shuster, *New Television: The Aesthetics and Politics of a Genre* (Chicago: University of Chicago Press, 2017); William Rothman, 'Cavell on Film, Television, and Opera', in *Stanley Cavell*, ed. Richard Eldridge (Cambridge, MA: Cambridge University Press, 2003); Alex Clayton, 'Why Comedy is at Home on Television', in *Television Aesthetics and Style*; Byron Davies, 'The Specter of the Electronic Screen: Bruno Varela's Reception of Stanley Cavell', in *Movies with Stanley Cavell in Mind*; Luca Bandirali and Enrico Terrone, *Concept TV: An Aesthetics of Television Series* (Lanham: Lexington Books, 2021). See also Sandra Laugier, *Nos vies en séries* (Paris: Climats Flammarion, 2019); 'The Conception of Film for the Subject of Television: Moral Education of the Public and a Return to an Aesthetics of the Ordinary', in *The Thought of Stanley Cavell and Cinema*; and *TV-Philosophy* (Exeter: University of Exeter Press, 2023).
42 Alberto N. García and Ted Nannicelli, 'Television's Temporality: Seriality and Temporal Prolongation', in *Cognition, Emotion, and Aesthetics in Contemporary Serial Television*, 29, 33–38.
43 Cavell, 'The Fact of Television', 263.

44. Ibid.
45. *Curb Your Enthusiasm* (2000–) aired for eight mostly consecutive seasons until 2011, then resumed with a ninth season in 2017; the eleventh season began in October 2021.
46. Clélia Cohen, *Masters of Cinema: Steven Spielberg* (Paris: Cahiers du Cinéma, 2010), 8.
47. Maya Salam, 'Amy Poehler and Tina Fey Skewer the H.F.P.A.'s Lack of Diversity', *New York Times*, February 28, 2021.
48. See Thomas Elsaesser, 'Stanley Cavell and Cinema', in *The Thought of Stanley Cavell and Cinema*, which starts with the telling of a joke. See also Stanley Cavell, *Cities of Words: Pedagogical Letters on a Register of the Moral Life* (Cambridge, MA: Belknap Press of Harvard University Press, 2004), 378.
49. Cavell, *The World Viewed*, 4–5.
50. John Dewey, *Art as Experience* (New York: Minton, Balch & Company, 1934).
51. Cavell, 'The Fact of Television', 240.
52. Ibid.
53. Ralph Waldo Emerson, 'Self-Reliance', in *The Complete Works of Ralph Waldo Emerson*, vol. 2 (Boston: Houghton Mifflin and Company, 1904), 88.
54. Robert Warshow, *The Immediate Experience* (Cambridge, MA: Harvard University Press, 2001), xxvii.
55. Stanley Cavell, *Pursuits of Happiness: The Hollywood Comedy of Remarriage* (Cambridge, MA: Harvard University Press, 1981), 10.
56. Ibid.
57. Ibid.
58. Ibid., 12.
59. Warshow, *The Immediate Experience*, xxxviii.
60. Cavell, *Pursuits of Happiness*, 10.
61. Stanley Cavell, "More of the World Viewed," *The Georgia Review*, vol. 28, no. 4 (Winter 1974), 571–631.
62. For more on the nature of cinematic reference and reflexivity, see *Metacinema: The Form and Content of Filmic Reference and Reflexivity*, ed. David LaRocca (Oxford: Oxford University Press, 2021).
63. Cavell, in Warshow, *The Immediate Experience*, 292.
64. Ralph Waldo Emerson, 'Spiritual Laws', in *The Complete Works of Ralph Waldo Emerson*, vol. 2 (Boston: Houghton Mifflin and Company, 1904), 144.
65. Robert B. Pippin correspondence with David LaRocca, February 17, 2021.
66. Robert B. Pippin, comment on Martin Shuster's *New Television: The Aesthetics and Politics of a Genre* (2017), presented at the Modern Language Association meeting, January 6, 2019.

PART I
NEW TELEVISION

1

Justifying *Justified*
William Rothman

In 2010, on a lecture tour of Australia and New Zealand, I met Jason Jacobs, who was writing a book on *Deadwood*, a Western series created by David Milch, also the creator of *NYPD Blue*. The latter was a series I watched regularly, as I had its predecessor, *Hill Street Blues*, for which Milch had been a regular writer. In conversations with Jason about his project, I maintained an attitude of skepticism as to whether any television series could reward the kind of criticism Stanley Cavell had devoted to Hollywood romantic comedies of the 1930s and 1940s. And I had reason to believe that Cavell had my back. In his 1982 essay 'The Fact of Television', he writes, 'To say that masterpieces among movies reveal the medium of film is to say that this revelation is the business of individual works, and that these works have a status analogous to traditional works of art.'[1] Cavell's essay goes on to argue that unlike film, television had produced no individual works with the status of art. It's not that he believed that television had no aesthetic interest. But what that aesthetic interest *is* was the question he investigated by pondering what *television* is. Employing the terminology of *The World Viewed*, he posed the question, what is the medium's material basis? And how are we to account for the pervasive *fear* among intellectuals that television is doing us harm? (Among intellectuals, fear of television in general has since been superseded by fear of Fox News specifically, and of social media in general.)

When I returned home and watched *Deadwood*, my skepticism evaporated. The more of the acclaimed series I watched, the more I agreed with those who argued, like the contributors to this volume, that twenty-first-century television to date had produced numerous great works. The mission of the present volume is to watch great works of television fiction with Cavell's writings in mind, in furtherance of serious television criticism. And yet, in 'The Fact of Television' Cavell had denied that there could be great works of television. Thus, my main business in the first part of this chapter, before

I turn to the great—and quite Cavellian—series *Justified*, is to reconcile this volume's intellectual project with the ideas Cavell expressed in his essay on television.

Masterpieces among movies are individual works that most fully reveal and acknowledge the conditions of the film medium, *The World Viewed* argues. If there are no artistic masterpieces among television's individual works, as 'The Fact of Television' suggests, 'what is memorable, treasurable, criticizable'— what reveals or acknowledges the television medium—must reside not in a program's individual episodes, but in the program 'as such', what Cavell calls its *format*.² Later in the essay, Cavell will refer to a program's format as the 'thing' of aesthetic interest. But this doesn't mean that a program's format is an individual work comparable to a movie, which would in turn imply that among television programs 'as such' there may be masterpieces. How could we find *I Love Lucy* 'as such' to be 'memorable, treasurable',³ except by remembering, treasuring, any episode? And how could we find *I Love Lucy* 'criticizable' if individual episodes are not?

At the time Cavell wrote 'The Fact of Television', soap operas were primarily relegated to daytime, as they had all been before *Peyton Place*, which premiered in 1964. By 1969, *Peyton Place's* once sky-high ratings had so declined that it was cancelled in mid-season, and there were no prime-time American soap operas until *Dallas* (1978), *Dynasty* (1981), and their spin-offs. When Cavell wrote 'The Fact of Television', television's dominant fictional mode was what he calls a *series* (sitcoms like *I Love Lucy*, cop shows like *Dragnet*, Westerns like *Gunsmoke*, and so on). In a series, in Cavell's sense, every episode tells a complete story that begins when a baseline of normality, the realm of the everyday, the ordinary—a crucial concept for Cavell, of course—is disrupted by a crisis and ends with the crisis resolved and a return to normality. Soap operas depart from this pattern, but, Cavell argues, for all their similarities to movie serials, television soap operas are so replete with recurrences and repetition—not least that they are broadcast the same day and time every week—that their continuing stories are best seen as part of the program's format, of the features every episode perfectly instantiates. In effect, the format is a formula for generating a program's individual instances. By contrast, in a movie genre like the comedy of remarriage, what we might think of as the formula—what *Pursuits of Happiness* calls the genre's *myth*—is reinterpreted, revised, by each member of the genre. The formula doesn't generate the instances; the instances generate the formula.

In preparation for offering his definition of the material basis of the medium of television, Cavell cites his one reference to television in *The World Viewed*. That passage invokes André Bazin's assertion that film puts us in the presence of the actor by relaying his presence to us as if by mirrors. Cavell's response was to note that Bazin's idea 'really fits the fact of live television, in which what we are presented with is happening simultaneously with its presentation'. He qualifies this, however. 'In live television what is present to us while it is happening is not the world, but an event standing out from the world. Its point is not to reveal, but to cover (as with a gun), to keep something on view.'[4]

'The Fact of Television' takes up this intuition by defining the material basis of the medium of television—what it is, apart from which there would be nothing we could call television—as 'a current of simultaneous event reception'. Each of these words registers a significant difference between film and television, for *The World Viewed* defined the material basis of the medium of film as 'a succession of automatic world projections'.[5] 'The mode of perception that I claim is called upon by film's material basis is what I call viewing. The mode of perception I wish to think about in connection with television's material basis is that of monitoring'.[6]

'A current of simultaneous event reception' is the material basis for all television formats, and also for all the formats, the individual programs 'as such', those formats support. Beyond this, television is itself a format, at once one *kind* of 'current of simultaneous event reception'—radio is another—and an *instance* of such a 'current'. (We can say 'Television is a current of simultaneous event reception'; we cannot say 'Film is a succession of automatic world projections'.)

Cavell goes on to reflect, in a prescient passage, on ways in which our sense of what television *is* might be affected by future technological developments: 'If the distribution of video cassette recorders and cable television increases, as appears to be happening, to the size of the distribution of television itself, or to a size capable of challenging it, this will make problematic whether television will continue to exist primarily as a medium of broadcasting.'[7] The change this passage anticipates had largely come to pass by 1988, when Cavell published 'The Advent of Videos', in which he returned to a thought he had expressed in another prescient passage of 'The Fact of Television':

> If the increasing distribution of video cassettes and disks goes so far as to make the history of film as much a part of the present experience of film as the history of the other arts is part of their present—hence brings film into the condition of art—it will make less respectable the assumption of the evanescence of the individual movie, its exhaustion under one viewing, or always casual viewings.[8]

In 'The Advent of Videos', Cavell considers some implications of the fact that since he published 'The Fact of Television', this, too, had come to pass. The assumption of 'the evanescence of the individual movie', as Cavell put it, was a repression of film as an art, a repression as old as the art of film itself. By 1988, the proliferation of video cassette recorders and video stores like Blockbuster had for the first time made readily available the lion's share of the great works that have shaped film's history as an art. When Cavell wrote *The World Viewed*, he had to rely on his memories of movies that had become 'strand over strand' with memories of his life. When he wrote *Pursuits of Happiness*, he could check his memories and intuitions with the films themselves. The unprecedented availability of movies in forms that facilitated study made it possible for criticism to begin to undo the repression of the art of film. Our sense of what film *is* was changing. The same can be said of television.

Whether I'm watching a program on a broadcast or a cable channel, regardless of how many channels are available, I can be said to be watching television—the medium whose material basis is as 'a current of simultaneous event reception'. That's why in 'The Fact of Television' Cavell could say that he was not regarding broadcasting—a particular mode of transmission; cable is another—'as essential to the work of television'.[9] But if I was watching an episode I'd recorded on my VCR, I couldn't be said to be watching television. Simultaneity *is* essential to television's material basis, in Cavell's view. But VCRs and DVD players—the same holds for streaming video—eliminate simultaneity. What we're watching isn't a current of simultaneous event reception; it's not a 'current', much less a 'simultaneous' one, and there is no 'event' being 'received'. What we're watching isn't to be called television, by Cavell's criterion. Or if we choose to refer to it as television (as when we call a Netflix series a 'television series'), it registers that our sense of what television is has altered since Cavell wrote 'The Fact of Television'.

When a movie is run on television, Cavell argues, it is no longer experienced *as* a movie; the film's succession of automatic world projections, subjected to the conditions of monitoring, has become a current of simultaneous event reception. No doubt, the experience of watching a movie streamed or played on a VCR or DVD player differs in small and large ways from viewing a film projected on a movie screen with an audience in a theatre. But our mode of perception is still viewing, not monitoring. We experience the movie as a succession of automatic world projections, not as a current of simultaneous event reception.

In defining masterpieces of art as works that most meaningfully reveal or acknowledge that art's material basis, 'The Fact of Television' relies on concepts that figure centrally in *Must We Mean What We Say?* and *The World Viewed*, concepts linked in those books to Cavell's reflections on modernism and the modern. *Pursuits of Happiness* shifted the emphasis from *The World Viewed*'s focus on what it means for something to be a film to what it means for a film to be a remarriage comedy, one artistic medium that film's material basis supports. In 'The Fact of Television', by contrast, Cavell's claims about television formats all derive from his intuition that television's material basis is a current of simultaneous event reception, and the linked intuition that monitoring, not viewing, is the mode of our perception of television. Although 'The Fact of Television' was written after *Pursuits of Happiness*, its focus shifted back to the material basis of the medium as such—as it had to, given the essay's claim that unlike the comedy of remarriage, a television format is not an artistic medium.

Between the 1980s, when Cavell wrote 'The Fact of Television' and 'The Advent of Videos', and 2004, when *Deadwood* premiered, television changed, as I've said. Insofar as the experience of television no longer had to be tethered to monitoring, the arguments in 'The Fact of Television' for denying that television programs can be works of art were rendered moot. So were Cavell's reasons for insisting that we don't experience movies on television *as* movies.

The untethering of television fiction from monitoring was a development whose possibility 'The Fact of Television' in no way denies. It was a development I have no doubt Cavell welcomed, as he surely welcomed the news that his son Benjamin had signed on as a screenwriter for the great—and quite Cavellian—series *Justified*, which premiered in 2010 and ran for six seasons. (He is credited as writer or co-writer of seventeen episodes, among them 'The Promise' [the series finale], and as story editor for the magnificent second season.)

The advent of digital video recorders (TiVo was introduced in 1999), which made 'time shifting' an everyday practice, in tandem with streaming video, was as consequential for television as the advent of videos was for film. It did not undo a repression of television as an art, as videos had for film. Unlike film, television had no prior history as a great art. Hence there was no repression, no failure of acknowledgement, to undo. What made DVRs and streaming video so consequential is that they made it possible for television as a medium of art—television as it had become, that is, or what replaced television as it had been—to be born. What is that art? I don't think of this as a question about the art's material basis. For once untethered from monitoring, a series in Cavell's sense, a soap opera, a miniseries, and a feature-length movie run on television or in a theatre, for all their differences, are all successions of automatic world projections.

In *Must We Mean What We Say?* and *The World Viewed*, the terms 'modernism' and 'medium' are ubiquitous. In Cavell's later writings, they all but drop out. *Pursuits of Happiness* itself is a transitional work within Cavell's authorship, a stage in his ever-deepening recognition of the intimacy of his affinity with the writings of Ralph Waldo Emerson. In writing about movies in his late book *Cities of Words*, his focus, which in *Pursuits of Happiness* had shifted from the material basis of film to the conditions of a particular medium—genre—film's material basis supports, shifted further. It moved to ways in which certain individual movies can also be thought of as Emersonian works, works that earn their place within a tradition of moral perfectionism that *Cities of Words* traces back to the origins of philosophy in ancient Greece, and forward to *Cities of Words* itself.

In 'The Fact of Television', Cavell couldn't write about television the way he wrote about film in *Pursuits of Happiness*, given the essay's contention that unlike a genre like the comedy of remarriage, a television format is not an artistic medium. Nor could he write about television the way he was to write about movies in *Cities of Words*. A television program 'as such' can hardly exemplify an Emersonian perfectionist outlook, cannot in that way be Cavellian, if television's works are, as Cavell puts it, 'to be understood as revelations (acknowledgements) of the conditions of monitoring by means of an aesthetic procedure in which the basis of a medium is acknowledged primarily by the format rather than by its instantiations'.[10]

As I've said, though, in watching a movie on a streaming video site or playing it on a DVR or DVD player, our mode of perception is viewing, not monitoring. We experience the movie as a movie. Thus, it's not even an interesting question whether it's possible for a movie we watch on Netflix, say, to be an Emersonian perfectionist work. Obviously, it can. *The Philadelphia Story*, streamed on Netflix, is still a comedy of remarriage, and everything said about it in *Pursuits of Happiness* and *Cities of Words* still applies.

It's almost as obvious that it's possible for a miniseries, when untethered from monitoring, to be an Emersonian perfectionist work. A miniseries isn't fundamentally different from a very long movie. Dickens novels were published in installments, but those installments have simply become chapters to us, and most novels have chapters. A miniseries has a narrative trajectory known to each episode's writers. In principle, there's no problem in making the protagonist, and ideally other major characters as well, undergo the kind of metamorphosis screenwriters call a 'character arc'—the kind of metamorphosis, so traumatic as to be tantamount to death and rebirth, that the women in remarriage comedies undergo.

In my experience, screenwriting students are apt to suppose that a 'character arc' means that the character starts with a goal and in the course of the film either achieves or fails to achieve it. But in *It Happened One Night*, say, Ellie *thinks* her goal is to get to New York to be reunited with her legal husband, King Westley. The events of the film open her eyes to the fact that what she thought she wanted isn't what she really wants; she discovers, and achieves, her true goal. If a 'character arc' is understood in this way, as requiring the achievement of a new perspective, an onset of self-knowledge, it's clear that the feature film as an artistic medium, which makes 'character arcs' obligatory, has what we might think of as a natural affinity with Emersonian perfectionism.

In what Cavell calls a series, every episode resolves the crisis precipitated by an inciting incident and ends with a return to normality, the realm of the ordinary. Only characters whose role is limited to the episode in which they appear are candidates for the kind of metamorphosis Emersonian perfectionism envisions. In soap operas, too, recurring characters can't have true 'arcs', but for the opposite reason. For every crisis resolved, a new one must take its place, in order that their stories can be continued ad infinitum (or until declining ratings lead the show to be cancelled). Recurring soap opera characters can change, but they can't undergo the kind of metamorphosis that is de rigueur for feature films.

In 'The Fact of Television', Cavell observes that *Hill Street Blues* 'seems to be questioning the feature of a series [in his sense] that demands a classical ending for each instance, hence questioning the distinction between soap opera and series'.[11] *Hill Street Blues* pioneered this hybrid format, as I think of it, when it premiered in 1978, combining elements of a so-called procedural like *Dragnet* and a soap opera. It interwove stories about the professional lives of police officers with continuing stories revolving around their personal lives. *St. Elsewhere*, another early hybrid series, followed the professional and private lives of doctors and nurses at a hospital; *L.A. Law*, employees at a law firm. The 'procedural' side of such a series harks back to the movies Cavell cites in *The World Viewed* about, as he put it, 'men in uniform, which is to say, men doing the work of the world, in consort'[12]—except that in a typical hybrid television series, women as well as men are shown 'doing the work of the world, in consort'. And in some series—*Justified*, for example—there is within the 'consort' one clear protagonist. Others focus on the ensemble of characters who make up the 'consort'. And there are series—*The Sopranos*, *Boardwalk Empire*, *The Americans*—in which it would be more apt to characterize the 'consort' as *undoing* the 'work of the world'.

Writing in 1982, Cavell couldn't know that the hybrid series (along with the miniseries, which can be thought of as a truncated hybrid series no less than as an extended movie) would soon dominate television fiction.

In 2012, Jason Jacobs invited me to contribute an essay for a volume he was co-editing with Steven Peacock. The series I chose to write about was *Justified* because I loved it; because, as I've said, Benjamin Cavell, whom I'd known since he was a little boy, was one of its writers; and because one of his episodes, 'Blowback', the eighth of the first season, impressed me as particularly Cavellian—not because the series protagonist, US Marshal Raylan Givens (Timothy Olyphant), undergoes a 'character arc' in the episode. He doesn't. But a man named Wallace does.

In 'Blowback', Raylan tries to defuse a hostage situation in the marshals' office without any casualties. Wallace, a prisoner with a long history of violence, has corralled two guards and is holding a knife to the throat of one. Knowing he only has fifteen minutes before the TAC team arrives to kill the prisoner, Raylan asks, 'Is there any way we can get some fried chicken in here—spicy?' Just as the TAC team enters and gives Raylan two minutes before they shoot to kill, the food arrives. Raylan takes a bite and promises Wallace that if he lets the guards go, he'll order chicken dinners for him, 'extra spicy', and engage him in conversation, every night for the next three nights. A shot of bourbon seals the deal. Wallace gives up the knife and surrenders, saying he only wanted to be treated like a human being.

It's not that when Wallace first took the guards as hostages he was aware that this is what he wanted. With Raylan's help, he achieves a new perspective, opens his eyes to what he truly desires, which is something all human beings desire, whether or not they know this about themselves. What I found most Cavellian about 'Blowback' is the way Raylan's understanding of the role played by conversation in making us human, and by the realm of the ordinary in general, empowers him to help Wallace awaken to his own humanity, and to the humanity of the guards he had been ready to kill. In this episode, Raylan doesn't achieve a 'character arc' in the same way Wallace does. But the episode made me wonder whether it's *possible* for the protagonist of a hybrid series to undergo the kind of metamorphosis Emersonian perfectionism envisions.

I knew that I couldn't write about *Justified* the way I had written about Hitchcock thrillers in *Hitchcock: The Murderous Gaze*. In that book, I went through five Hitchcock films from first moment to last, endeavoring to articulate, aided by over 600 frame enlargements, the ideas motivating, and expressed by, every line of dialogue, every gesture of the characters, and everything the camera does. Even halfway through its second season, *Justified* already had too many episodes to attend so closely to each one. And in *The Murderous Gaze* I looked at the films through the prism of authorship, taking Hitchcock, as director, to be their author. But *Justified* had numerous directors. In any given episode, the director's role—hence the camera's—is not what it is in films of an 'auteur' like Hitchcock.

At almost every moment, Hitchcock has the camera perform some gesture that expresses a thought—Hitchcock's thought—about what is happening within the film's world. Every such gesture is also a declaration that this film has an author—in Hitchcock's case, an author with a name and a familiar face. For Hitchcock, the camera was an instrument of self-expression. For the director of an episode of *Justified*, the camera is not—must not be—personal in such a way. Nor is the camera an instrument of self-expression for the person credited as the series 'creator', responsible for establishing its format (David Milch for *Deadwood*; Graham Yost for *Justified*). That's why, I now realize, in writing about *Justified* I was never moved to describe a shot, a framing, a cut, or a camera movement, although in writing about films—not just Hitchcock films—it has always been my practice to attend to the camera at every significant moment.

As I've said, when I began writing about *Justified*, the series was in its second season. I had no way of knowing the direction the narrative would take. The writers of the individual episodes didn't have the 'big picture' any more than I did. That's because *Justified*, like virtually all hybrid series as well as soap operas, followed procedures introduced by Paul Monash, the creator of *Peyton Place*, half a century earlier. Daytime soap operas had traditionally been written on a freelance basis. Monash assembled a team of regular writers and two story editors. After conferences with the writers and input from Monash, the story editors gave the two writers assigned to a particular episode a plot outline that kept a few weeks ahead of the shooting schedule. The writers had no 'Bible' outlining the trajectory of the entire series.

Lacking the 'big picture', I chose to focus on *Justified*'s first episode, 'Fire in the Hole', the so-called pilot, and its relationship to the Elmore Leonard story on which it was based.[13] The pilot, written by Yost, takes from Leonard's story almost everything the characters say and do. In the story, however, the crisis precipitated by the inciting incident is fully resolved; the story is self-contained in a way the pilot of a hybrid series cannot be if it is to fulfill its function *as* a pilot. 'Fire in the Hole' isn't the only Leonard story whose protagonist is Raylan Givens. But Leonard's Raylan stories are like the episodes of a series in Cavell's sense, not a hybrid series.

A reviewer for the *San Jose Mercury News* wrote of the collection of Leonard's stories that included 'Fire in the Hole' that the voice telling the story conveys 'a hint of what lordly amusement would sound like if God had worked at a Detroit ad agency'. Never standing on grammatical ceremony, the narrator's voice melds seamlessly with the voices of the characters, continually segueing, within single paragraphs and even single sentences, between paraphrasing characters, quoting them, saying what they're feeling, thinking, imagining or remembering, and expressing his own thoughts. The narrator's 'lordly amusement' conveys that he takes himself to be a bit superior to these characters whose thoughts are transparent to him and whose voices he mimics so deftly. Then again, these characters—especially the men—are wont to look down on each other. The 'lordly amusement' with which he tells this story about characters who are (he wants us to know) open books to him reveals, despite himself, his affinity with them. Like the Sydney Greenstreet character in *The Maltese Falcon*, Elmore Leonard likes a man who likes to talk, whether he be a criminal mastermind like Boyd Crowder (Walton Goggins), the clueless lowlife types who follow him, the murderous underworld figures who vie with him for control of Harlan's drug trade, an officer of the law who goes by the book like Art Mullen (Nick Searcy), Raylan's boss, or a hero like Raylan himself, who struggles to reconcile the dark, fatalistic streak in his nature with the authority vested in his badge and with his personal moral code, symbolized by his cowboy hat.

That Boyd is Raylan's match as a sardonic wordsmith is evident from their exchange before the shoot-out in which—in the story, but not in the pilot—he mortally wounds Boyd:

> 'Your forty-five's on the table but I have to pull,' Raylan said. 'Is that how we do it?'
> 'Well, shit yeah, it's my call. What're you packing?'
> 'You'll pay to find that out,' Raylan said.
> 'Ice water in your veins, huh? You want a shot of Jim Beam to go with it?'[14]

The narrator is too intent on impressing on the reader that he, too, has ice water in his veins to plumb their depths—or his own. This isn't a failure of Leonard's writing; it's internal to the story's way of achieving closure. The pilot episode of a hybrid series must not be complete unto itself; viewers must sense that beneath the narrative ground it stakes out lie rich veins waiting to be mined in future episodes. But how is that possible in this case, given that the pilot leaves its characters' actions and words almost unchanged from a story that is complete in itself?

Part of the answer resides in the alterations Yost did make to the original story. More crucially, perhaps, a television series, like a movie, *shows* rather than *tells*. And the Raylan the pilot shows is not the Raylan the story's narrator tells us about. Like the 'human somethings' projected on the screen in the movies Cavell invokes in *The World Viewed*, the Raylan who appears on the screen is incarnated by a flesh-and-blood human being, the real subject of a camera that filmed him. Viewers don't have to *imagine* Raylan. Then again, viewers lack the *freedom* to imagine Raylan. But readers cannot imagine *this* Raylan. The Timothy Olyphant who incarnates Raylan is a human being. And because human faces, bodies and voices possess 'remarkable expressiveness', as Emerson puts it, *Justified* can grant us access to a kind of poetry, out of reach of the story on which it is based—what Cavell calls the 'poetry of the ordinary', the perception that 'every motion and station, in particular every human posture and gesture, however glancing, has its poetry, or its lucidity'.[15]

Leonard's story cannot empower readers even to imagine what *Justified*'s viewers see with their own eyes when just these 'human somethings', in just these settings, in just these situations, perform just these gestures and speak just these words in just these voices. Timothy Olyphant's Raylan—like Walton Goggins' Boyd, Nick Searcy's Art, Joelle Carter's Ava and Natalie Zea's Winona (and, in the second season, Margo Martindale's monstrous yet all too human matriarch Mags Bennett)—manifests the mystery of human identity, the fact that we are mysteries to each other and to ourselves; that our identities are not fixed. Timothy Olyphant's Raylan possesses an unknownness beyond what any writer can invent.

The ending of 'Fire in the Hole' is the exception that proves the rule that the story's Raylan lacks the depth of *Justified*'s Raylan.

> Raylan stood by, relating the scene step by step as Art rolled Boyd over to look at the exit wound …
>
> 'He have any last words?'
>
> 'He said I'd killed him.' Raylan paused. 'I told him I was sorry, but he had called it.'
>
> Art was frowning now. 'You're sorry you killed him?'
>
> 'I thought I explained it to you,' Raylan said in his quiet voice. 'Boyd and I dug coal together.'[16]

The phrase 'in his quiet voice' conveys that Raylan speaks the last line in a voice typical for him, not in an emotional one. Nor does the narrator's voice betray emotion, whether Raylan's or his own. That Raylan *is* moved is conveyed only by the author's device—no story can use it more than once—of letting Raylan have the last word, as if his 'quiet voice' silences the narrator. There's nothing this narrator *can* say in *his* typical voice.

Walton Goggins is so charismatic that if in the pilot Raylan *had* aimed for Boyd's heart, the series would have taken the bullet. Because in the pilot

Boyd survives the shooting, Yost had to alter the story's last scene. It's not to Art but to Ava, who isn't sorry—nor are we—that she killed her abusive husband, that Raylan confesses that he was sorry he had to shoot Boyd because they had 'dug coal together'. (A line that will be echoed in the series finale.)

From watching Joelle Carter's reaction to Raylan's words, we know, without needing a narrator to tell us, that Raylan's explanation resonates with Ava. In the pilot, Ava, too, is deeper than her counterpart in the story. Having grown up in Harlan County, she knows the immutable bond forged between men who stared down the angel of death when they were miners together. And she has had a crush on Raylan, and he has wanted to kiss her, since they were minors together. Now that she and Raylan, too, have—not for the last time in the series—stared down the angel of death together, Ava has reason to hope that an immutable bond has now been forged between them—a bond that in ensuing episodes will repeatedly be tested.

In both story and pilot, sparks fly when Raylan and Ava first find themselves face to face after so many years. 'Ava was forty now', Leonard's masterful passage begins, 'but he knew those eyes staring at him and she knew him, saying, "Oh my God—Raylan", in kind of a prayerful tone.' Giving Ava the words 'Oh my God—Raylan' slyly intimates that Raylan *is* her God. The slyness is Leonard's, not Ava's or the narrator's. But the narrator's gratuitous 'kind of' adds his typical 'lordly amusement' to the implication that Raylan's arrival at her door is, for Ava, a kind of miracle. The passage goes on:

> 'You remember me, huh?' Ava pushed the door closed. She said, 'I never forgot you,' and went into his arms as he offered them, a girl he used to like now a woman who'd shot and killed her husband and wanted to be held ... He kissed her on the cheek. She kept staring at him with those eyes and he kissed her on the mouth ... He didn't know why he kissed her other than he wanted to. He could remember wanting to even when she was a teen.[17]

When the woman with 'those eyes' is Joelle Carter, who plays this scene with such sincerity, we no more look down on Ava than on Raylan. After their kiss becomes 'serious', we are told that Raylan, like the narrator at story's end, doesn't know what to say. Presumably, he *would* know what to say if he knew he had a reason for kissing Ava other than that he wanted to. Whether he has such a reason is something the story's Raylan doesn't know about himself; nor does this trouble him. Or if it does trouble Raylan that he doesn't know this about himself, that's something the narrator doesn't know about him or doesn't find worth mentioning.

In the pilot, Art is troubled that Raylan had failed to aim for Boyd's heart, that he had let his emotions override his commitment to correct law enforcement practices. In the story, there's no suggestion that Raylan finds it troubling that Art is troubled by this. In the pilot, we know, without needing a narrator to tell us, that Raylan *is* troubled that Art is troubled by him. More generally, Raylan is troubled by what he knows, and by what he does not know, about himself. This is clear from the little scene—it's not in the story—that ends the pilot.

Beer bottle in hand, Raylan shows up in the middle of the night at estranged wife Winona's home, sneaking in through the garden door and almost giving her lover Gary (William Ragsdale) a heart attack. Winona is the only person to whom Raylan feels he can, and must, confess at least part of what is troubling him. In the opening scene, we saw Raylan kill a man in Miami under circumstances so questionable he was transferred to the Lexington, Kentucky office, uncomfortably close to Harlan, where he was born and raised and where his wily criminal father Arlo (Raymond Barry) lives. The troubling thought Raylan confesses to Winona is that he would have killed that man, in his eyes a murderer who deserved to die, even if the man hadn't drawn his gun first—Raylan's fear is that he may have had no reason to kill this man other than that he wanted to, like the singer in Johnny Cash's 'Folsom Prison Blues' who 'shot a man in Reno just to watch him die'.

'When is killing justified?' is a question the pilot raises and addresses, as does every episode of *Justified*. Throughout the series, this question is linked to the question, 'What kind of person is Raylan?' That question, in turn, is inseparable from the question, 'What kind of person does Raylan wish to be?' These are questions *about* Raylan, but also questions *for* Raylan. If he is committed to the Emersonian perfectionist aspiration of 'walking in the direction of the unattained but attainable self', they are questions Raylan must strive to answer.

In Leonard's story, Raylan and Winona have two sons who live in Georgia with their mother and stepfather. Given *Justified*'s interest in father–son relationships, these sons could have been a rich vein for the series to mine. They would have been an obstacle, though, to mining an even richer vein: Raylan's romantic relationships with Winona and Ava, which bring *Justified* into proximity with the Hollywood genres Cavell wrote books about.

That Raylan's ever-changing relationship with Winona would be a thread running through *Justified* is anticipated by the exchange that ends the pilot. 'I've never thought of myself as an angry man', Raylan says thoughtfully. Winona replies, firmly yet gently, as if to a child, but with a hint of amusement less 'lordly' than seductive, 'You're good at hiding it and most people may not see it, but you're the angriest man I have ever known'—another line that will be echoed in the series finale.

Raylan's silence acknowledges that the depth of his anger is something Winona had known about him that he hadn't known about himself. How could he not wish for his relationship with this woman, who knows him better than he knows himself, to have a future? He can't have such a conversation with Ava. But Ava, too, knows something about her hero that Raylan doesn't know about himself: that he *is* a hero. Ava is a part of what is troubling Raylan, a part he is unwilling to confess to Winona. The pilot invites us to expect that Raylan will eventually have to choose between them. But he doesn't know which woman he wants.

In the pilot, real-estate agent Gary, the man then in Winona's life, strikes Raylan—and us—as unworthy of her. Later episodes will bear this out, but not before we and Raylan learn that Gary possesses a trait Winona isn't foolish for valuing: unlike Raylan, Gary knows what he wants. And to get what he wants, he will move heaven and earth—and hell as well. If Raylan decides he does want to win Winona back, he will have to *claim* her, as the Cary Grant character must do, Cavell observes in *Pursuits of Happiness*, if he is to win back his ex-wife in *The Awful Truth*, *His Girl Friday*, and *The Philadelphia Story*. To claim Winona, though, Raylan would have to forgo the heroic quest that, as the series progresses, he—and we—increasingly take to be his mission: saving the world of Harlan, *his* world, from the powers of darkness personified by Boyd Crowder. Boyd is Raylan's soulmate, but also his nemesis. They are on opposite sides of a struggle for the soul of Harlan—and for the affections of Ava, who, unlike Winona, is a daughter of Harlan. If he were to forgo his mission to win Winona, that would mean leaving Ava in Boyd's clutches. Raylan knows that Boyd genuinely loves Ava in his fashion. Raylan also knows that Boyd can't be trusted not to kill her.

In *His Girl Friday*, Walter (Cary Grant), too, has a heroic mission: to help save Chicago, the way Mayor LaGuardia saved New York City, if not from the powers of darkness the film personifies as Hitler, at least from corruption and incompetence. Walter sees Hildy (Rosalind Russell), his once and future wife, as a comrade in his quest, for Walter's world is Hildy's world. But Raylan's world isn't Winona's world. If Raylan were to abandon his quest for the sake of winning Winona, it would be as if Hildy were to marry Bruce Baldwin (Ralph Bellamy), rather than Walter. *His Girl Friday* suggests, in its comically ironic way, that no one like Walter or Hildy whose true home is the newspaper world—or, in *Twentieth Century*, Oscar Jaffe's theatre world (or Howard Hawks' world of filmmaking)—can ever be at home anywhere else.

Justified leads us to think of Raylan's dark, fatalistic streak as the Harlan in his nature. It is expressed in the song, 'You'll Never Leave Harlan Alive', written by Darrell Scott in 1996, and performed by several singers over the closing credits of several episodes, most hauntingly by Brad Paisley at the end of the series finale: 'In the deep dark hills of eastern Kentucky, that's the place where I trace my bloodline. And it's there I read on a hillside gravestone, "You will never leave Harlan alive".' Whether any son of Harlan can ever leave Harlan alive is another question—ultimately answered, surprisingly, in the affirmative—that the pilot invites us to expect the series to answer.

Harlan is a real place not far from modern Lexington, Kentucky, which might as well be—and in the series *is*—Los Angeles. But in *Justified*, Harlan is also a mythical place, as it was in Barbara Kopple's 1976 Oscar-winning documentary *Harlan County, USA*. Harlan pulls the series closer to the world of Flannery O'Connor than to the world of Elmore Leonard's crime fiction. As the series progresses, Raylan will find himself less engaged in his professional life as a US Marshal and increasingly devoted to his mission—at once a moral obligation and a spiritual quest—of saving this Chinatown of family feuds, corruption, corporate greed, and drugs from being engulfed by chaos.

In *Must We Kill the Thing We Love? Emersonian Perfectionism and the Films of Alfred Hitchcock*, I argue that Hitchcock was drawn to the worldview encapsulated in the Oscar Wilde line he never tired of quoting: 'Each man kills the thing he loves', a line that resonates with the Harlan in Raylan's nature. But Hitchcock, like Raylan, was equally drawn to the Emersonian— and Cavellian—outlook exemplified by comedies of remarriage. In *Must We Kill the Thing We Love?* my guiding intuition was that striving to overcome the conflict between these worldviews became the driving force of Hitchcock's art. And in tracing the trajectory of his career, I discerned a dialectical progression that culminated in *Marnie* (1964), in which, as I had come to see it, the Emersonian side of Hitchcock's artistic identity prevailed.

When I began writing about *Justified*, I had no way of knowing whether the Emersonian side of Raylan's nature would ultimately prevail—the deepest of the questions the pilot invites us to expect the series would ultimately have to answer. It prevailed in Hitchcock's case. But Hitchcock didn't trace his bloodline to the deep dark hills of eastern Kentucky. What was at stake for me in this question wasn't whether *Justified* was a work of art worthy of serious criticism. Even halfway through *Justified*'s second season, I had seen enough to have no doubt that the series was, indeed, such a work. What was at stake for me was whether *Justified* would prove to be an Emersonian perfectionist work. Not every truly great series is—*Breaking Bad*, for example, whose protagonist is in a relentless downhill spiral and never achieves the kind of metamorphosis Emersonian perfectionism envisions. In the final episode, his perspective does change. But as in *Citizen Kane*, the onset of self-knowledge is too little and too late to save him.

Winona's 'You're the angriest man I've ever known', the pilot's memorable last line, is tellingly invoked in 'The Promise', *Justified*'s intricately plotted, action-packed finale. In this episode, co-written by Benjamin Cavell, Raylan has an opportunity to kill Boyd, who has just tried to kill him. Ava pleads with him to do it—Boyd has promised to kill her when he gets out of prison, and she and Raylan both know that no prison can hold him if he's dead set on revenge. And Raylan *wants* to kill Boyd, the way he wanted to kill that man in Miami at the beginning of the series. This time, he resists the temptation, making it possible for Art to say to Raylan, approvingly, 'You got Boyd Crowder, and you got him right'. In pursuing Boyd, Raylan had acted so unlawfully, though, that Art, who always goes by the book, knows that he should fire Raylan or even have him arrested. Not wishing to be the kind of person who would do that to someone he loves, Art chooses instead to have Raylan transferred back to the Miami office—a gesture I chalk up as a win for Emersonian perfectionism.

Fast-forward four years. Raylan, symbolically hatless, is at the beach with his and Winona's young daughter, who has been living with her mother and her new husband. When Winona chides Raylan for giving their little girl ice cream, rather than a healthier snack, he defends his decision, provoking her to call him the most stubborn man she has ever known. Raylan replies, knowingly invoking a line in the pilot, 'Better than angry', an assertion Winona doesn't contest—a brilliant way for the series to answer one of the questions hanging over the series from the beginning. Winona knows that Raylan is no longer the angry man he was in the opening episode. That he, too, knows this implies that she no longer knows him better than he knows himself. Raylan has had his 'character arc'. He has overcome or transcended the violent, darkly fatalistic streak in his nature. Evidently, taking the boy out of Harlan has taken Harlan out of the boy. Chalk this up as another win for Emersonian perfectionism.

In the Miami Marshal's office, Raylan looks at an article a colleague in Kentucky sent him that includes a photo of Ava. So Raylan, who is indeed stubborn, makes his way to Lebec, California, and knocks on Ava's door. The last time he had seen her, she was in his custody and in handcuffs, but she escaped and absconded with the $9 million that had been at the centre of all the convoluted plot twists in *Justified*'s sixth and final season.

When Ava opens the door, she explains to Raylan how she had managed to get away from Harlan, who had helped her and then run off with the money. He asks how she's getting by. She says she helps the owner of the ranch work with special needs children, and she looks after the big house, works at the school in town, and does other volunteer work. She, too, has had a true 'character arc'. Of course, the question on Ava's mind—and ours—is whether Raylan will turn her in. She says that there's something she wants to show him that he can't tell Boyd about. To quote from the synopsis on the *Justified* Wiki (yes, there is such a thing!): 'Ava calls and a young boy comes out, the child that she had with Boyd. When Raylan asks his name, she says "Zachariah, [the name of her uncle, who was killed earlier in the episode] the only man in my life who never wanted anything from me".' She tells Raylan that if he's going to take her in, she'll have to make arrangements for her son. He says he's not going to take her in. 'Tearfully she thanks him. He says he hopes she'll be able to sleep better. "You're not the only one I've been afraid to see at my front door", she says.'[18]

After all the tumultuous twists and turns in their relationship, Ava is still the woman with 'those eyes'. Does Raylan want to kiss her? No doubt. But he doesn't wish to be, again, a man who wants something from her. In any case, their relationship can't have a future unless he joins her in hiding. That would mean forsaking his responsibilities towards his own child—and towards Ava. Raylan knows that Boyd is the person she's afraid to see at her front door—and he knows why. So he does what he must do and pays Boyd a visit at his Kentucky penitentiary, where he's in the chapel, preaching to a captive audience of prisoners. Quoting again from the *Justified* Wiki:

> Raylan who's there to tell Boyd, with supporting (forged) documents—Oklahoma driver's license, death certificate—that Ava had died three years earlier in a car crash late one night in West Texas. At first Boyd is saddened, but then gets suspicious as to why Raylan would come all that way to bring him this news. 'Now, you could have called the warden, sent word through my lawyer.' 'You asking why I came', Raylan asks, and when Boyd nods yes, 'Thought it was news that should be delivered in person.' 'That the only reason?' Boyd probes. There's no response other than a smile. 'After all these long years, Raylan Givens, that's the only reason?' They look each other in the eyes for several moments before Raylan says, 'I suppose if I allow myself to be sentimental, despite all that has occurred, there is one thing I wander back to …'
>
> Finishing Raylan's sentence for him, Boyd says, 'We dug coal together', echoing their conversation in the pilot and closing another circle. 'That's right', Raylan says, keeping mum on the fact that he's there to save Ava and her son from Boyd, and to save Boyd from himself, save him from killing Ava, the only thing in the world he ever loved.[19]

Many a hybrid series is simply terminated when the channel or network pulls the plug. But *Justified* arrives at an ending with a sense of necessity to it. The pilot's unanswered questions are answered, and its protagonist's metamorphosis is complete. But what a tortuous, circuitous route it took—seventy-eight episodes with innumerable storylines and plot twists—for the series to get there! This underscores how different the hybrid series is, as a narrative form, from the feature-length movie. For screenwriting students are taught not only that a movie must end with its protagonist achieving a 'character arc', but also that it must arrive at such an ending by as direct a path as possible. No scene is to be superfluous; every scene must move the film forward on the path to its destination.

It has always seemed to me that 'arc' is an apt word for the kind of metamorphosis that the feature film requires in that it connotes a long, curved trajectory, like a rainbow with a pot of gold at the end. Then again, an old movie theatre projector lamp, too, has an arc, in this case a spark that jumps instantaneously from conductor to conductor. In a movie, the protagonist's 'character arc' takes the duration of the film to happen, but when it does, it happens in a flash, like the dawning of an intuition. *What* happens in that flash is the kind of metamorphosis, tantamount to death and rebirth, that is defining for Emersonian perfectionism. But this doesn't seem to me the best way to think about the trajectory of a hybrid series like *Justified*.

Raylan's metamorphosis doesn't happen instantaneously, but incrementally. Is it, then, that in every season, every episode, perhaps in every incident, Raylan has, as it were, a 'mini-arc', with the 'mini-arcs' cumulatively adding up to a metamorphosis tantamount to death and rebirth? This, too, doesn't seem quite right. It strikes me that Cavell's last book, his philosophical memoir *Little Did I Know*, offers an illuminating parallel. In *Little Did I Know*, Cavell tells the story of his life up to the completion of *The Claim of Reason*. In this story, as *Little Did I Know* tells it—this, for Cavell, is its philosophical *point*—the private and the public (in Cavell's own case, life and philosophy) are inextricably intertwined, as they are—this is the guiding intuition in *Cities of Words*—in the movies he understands to be Emersonian perfectionist works. The intertwining of the private and the public, the personal and the professional, is also a defining feature of the hybrid television series.

In *Little Did I Know*, Cavell observes that he has no interest in telling his story in a way that begins with his birth on the south side of Atlanta, Georgia, and continues from there. For such a narrative strikes him 'as leading fairly directly to death, without clearly enough implying the singularity of this life, in distinction from the singularity of all others, all headed in that direction'. Rather, his interest is to see how 'what Freud calls the detours on the human path to death—accidents avoided or embraced, strangers taken to heart or neglected, talents imposed or transfigured, malice insufficiently rebuked, love inadequately acknowledged—mark out for me recognizable efforts to achieve my own death'—with no guarantee, of course, that he will find such 'markers' on the paths his life has taken. His hope was to discover that, and how, the 'excerpts'—the days, the moments—his prose evokes enable him to discern, however partially, the myth his life illustrates, a story that has until then escaped him—'the story of how his life should have come to this, to just these words, to telling just this story'.[20] And he hoped to show that this story wasn't his alone, hoped that readers would see their lives as 'incorporated' in his.

The story of *Justified* is the story of Raylan Givens' professional and personal life from his transfer to Kentucky to four years after he is transferred back to Miami—the period in which Raylan overcomes or transcends what I've called the Harlan in his nature and, like Hitchcock, embraces an Emersonian perfectionist outlook.

As I've said, a television series, like a movie, doesn't *tell*; it *shows*. In a Hitchcock film, it's the director, Hitchcock, who is doing the showing; in a sense, his relationship with the characters, and with us, is part of the film's story. In *Justified*, there is no director whose relationship with Raylan, or with us, is part of the story. Raylan's story is his. But it's not his alone. In *Justified*, Raylan's story, like the story Cavell tells in *Little Did I Know*, includes the lives of all the characters 'incorporated' in his.

Little Did I Know ends its story with the completion of *The Claim of Reason*, the book, adapted from his doctoral dissertation, that enabled Cavell to put his dissertation behind him and declare his existence as a philosopher—the only kind of philosopher who could have written such a book or could have wanted to. But the *writing* of the book that tells this story is inseparable from the story it tells. Writing *Little Did I Know* brought to an end the period of Cavell's life that began where the story it tells ends, the period in which he fully yielded to his yearning for philosophy. *Little Did I Know* is not only under its own question, as Cavell takes all philosophy to be, it also finds the answer it is seeking. For Cavell, philosophy had achieved its end. When he finished telling the story that ends with his rebirth, his creation as a philosopher, he leaves behind this life whose story he has told. Both as the protagonist of *Little Did I Know* and as the teller of the tale, Cavell achieves a true 'character arc'.

In *Justified*, there is no teller of Raylan's tale, hence nothing equivalent to the double role Cavell plays in *Little Did I Know*. Apart from that crucial difference, however, *Little Did I Know* and *Justified* have affinities that illuminate the relationship in a hybrid television series between the individual episodes and the series as a whole. The narrative trajectory of a feature film, which follows as direct a path as possible to the protagonist's 'character arc', is like the kind of autobiography Cavell had no interest in writing that leads 'fairly directly to death, without clearly enough implying the singularity of this life, in distinction from the singularity of all others, all headed in that direction'. *Justified*, by contrast, is akin to the autobiography Cavell did write, which strives to discern how 'what Freud calls the detours on the human path to death—accidents avoided or embraced, strangers taken to heart or neglected, talents imposed or transfigured, malice insufficiently rebuked, love inadequately acknowledged', mark out recognizable efforts to achieve his own death hence to make possible his rebirth.[21]

Looking back on the entirety of *Justified* from the perspective achieved by its ending, all the episodes, with their innumerable characters and plot twists, can be seen as such 'markers' on the paths Raylan had to take for his life to come to this—the paths *Justified* had to take to achieve a satisfying ending to just this story; to achieve its own death, we might say. That in this respect a hybrid series like *Justified* is closer to *Little Did I Know* than it is to a feature-length film helps to explain, perhaps, why in recent years such series have so often been more believable, have seemed more realistic, than most new movies. These cynical times have made us too skeptical to readily believe as movie audiences once did that it's a real possibility for anyone to walk a straight path that leads, without detours, directly to a once-in-a-lifetime, religious-conversion-like metamorphosis tantamount to death and rebirth. These days it's easier to believe, as did Emerson and Cavell, that to become the kind of person we wish to be, we must let an old self die so that a new self may be born not once but many times. We must let change be part of our everyday lives if, to paraphrase Bob Dylan, we wish to be busy living, not busy dying.

Notes

1. Stanley Cavell, *Cavell on Film*, ed. William Rothman (Albany: State University of New York Press, 2005), 96.
2. Cavell, *Cavell on Film*, 59.
3. Ibid., 63.
4. Stanley Cavell, *The World Viewed: Reflections on the Ontology of Film* (Cambridge, MA: Harvard University Press, 1976), 26.
5. Cavell, *The World Viewed*, 72.
6. Cavell, *Cavell on Film*, 72.
7. Cavell, *The World Viewed*, 64.
8. Cavell, *Cavell on Film*, 64.
9. Ibid., 72.
10. Ibid.
11. Ibid., 66.
12. Cavell, *The World Viewed*, 47.
13. Elmore Leonard, 'Fire in the Hole', in *When the Women Come Out to Dance: Stories* (New York: Harper Collins, 2002).
14. Leonard, 'Fire in the Hole', 109.
15. Cavell, *Cavell on Film*, 96.
16. Leonard, 'Fire in the Hole', 109.
17. Ibid., 78.
18. *Justified* Wiki, https://justified.fandom.com/wiki/Justified_Wiki (accessed October 3, 2022).
19. Ibid.
20. Stanley Cavell, *Little Did I Know: Excerpts from Memory* (Stanford: Stanford University Press, 2010), 4.
21. Ibid.

2

'You Get Paid for Pain': *Kingdom* and New Television

Martin Shuster

Introduction: The Importance of *Kingdom*

Let me put my cards on the table right away: I am convinced that Byron Balasco's *Kingdom* (Audience Network, 2014–17) is in fact one of the most sophisticated and self-conscious reflections on the medium of new television yet available.[1] I suspect that this claim will not strike most readers as much of anything, since they likely have never heard of or seen *Kingdom*, which is a shame, and exactly the reason I felt an imperative to write this chapter. I think *Kingdom* is an important show exactly because it both compels as a serious work of art and meditates in a remarkable way on the entire genre of new television.

Let's start with a brief synopsis and setup of the show, since even readers familiar with it may not be immediately convinced by the claims above. Or at least, I should say, may not be *fully* convinced; my sense is that anyone who has seen the show cannot fail to acknowledge its success as a work of art, riding in part on the minimalist but poignant script, and in part on remarkable performances by Frank Grillo (as Alvey Kulina), Jonathan Tucker (as his son, Jay Kulina), Kiele Sanchez (as Lisa Prince), and Matt Lauria (as Ryan Wheeler), among others such as Joanna Going (as Christina Kulina) and perhaps most surprisingly, Nick Jonas of pop music fame (as Alvey's other son, Nate Kulina). The premise of the show is that Alvey Kulina is a legendary, aging mixed martial arts fighter past his prime (I don't say 'washed-up' because this category, in many ways, is made irrelevant by the stance the show takes). Kulina owns, with his girlfriend, Lisa Prince, a gym called Navy St. Having fought all over the world, Kulina retired due to an injury, and now takes pride in his gym and in being a coach (whether to his own two sons or to fighters of varying skills and levels of success).

Martin Shuster, "You Get Paid for Pain': *Kingdom* and New Television' in: *Television with Stanley Cavell in Mind*. University of Exeter Press (2023). © Martin Shuster. DOI: 10.47788/LUXS1638

The show's plot initially revolves around the release from prison of Lisa's former fiancé, Ryan Wheeler, who was an accomplished fighter before being sent to prison (his nickname, still prominently tattooed across his chest, is 'Destroyer'). Part of the story revolves around the emerging love triangle between Kulina, Lisa, and Ryan; part around Kulina's life and working through his family situation and the unavoidable facts of aging (bound up with this element of the plot are certain facts like his eldest son, Jay, being a drug addict, as also his ex-wife, who additionally is a sex worker); and part of the story also revolves around Ryan's own relationship to his family and his own past. There are notable other plot developments, including the sexuality of Nate (whose homosexuality is incapable of being acknowledged, including by himself), the emergence of Lisa's pregnancy (with Kulina's child), and the various forms of addiction on display (ranging from alcohol to cocaine and crack cocaine, to steroids and growth hormone, to whatever else). What unites all of these seemingly disparate—and frankly, at best melodramatic, or perhaps, at worst contrived or hammy—elements is fighting.

For *Kingdom*, fighting is bound up with every aspect of human life, be it materially (it is literally how the characters make a living), or existentially (it is how ordinary life, familial and otherwise, proceeds; it is ultimately how life unfolds). Oftentimes this prioritization of fighting explicitly suggests that *every* subject in late capitalism is best understood as a fighter, as always fighting, and that late capitalism itself is best understood as a fight. What makes the show remarkable, however, is the subjective depth it manages to achieve through this conceit, for the characters of *Kingdom* also *love* fighting. To the extent that this emotional investment on screen connects to and affects our emotional sensibilities as viewers,[2] *Kingdom* intends for us to reflect on the plausibility of its portrayal of late capitalism as much as on the very status of desires within late capitalism (and notably this psychoanalytic theme is not a contrivance on my part, but rather continually referenced on the show, both in Alvey Kulina's remarkable sessions with his psycho therapist and with Jay's striking remarks on Freud). Thus, when Ryan Wheeler notes to Alvey that 'you get paid for pain', he intends the remark to register with us as much as anyone else; in late capitalism, we all get paid for pain. What makes the show even more remarkable, however, is that this complex exploration of the conditions of late capitalism is pursued at the same time in the context of an equally serious reflection on the entire genre of new television.

The Genre of New Television

To see how this is the case, note that in most ways *Kingdom* fits into what I have elsewhere termed the genre of new television.[3] What's striking about the show is the extent to which it also pushes against this genre, aims to reflect on it, serving as a compelling, serious, and successful instantiation of the genre as much as a reflection on the genre's negation.

Stanley Cavell once noted that a medium refers as much to 'the physical bases of various arts' as much as to particular 'modes of achievement within the arts'.[4] What unifies these two ideas is Cavell's thought that 'a medium is something through which or by means of which something specific gets done or said in particular ways'.[5] In this way, Cavell's first sense of medium refers to our common associations with the word 'medium' (say, painting, music, film, and so forth), while the second sense refers to the idea of a medium as a variation within a particular art (say, the blues, black metal, or funk within music). This is why Cavell highlights that a medium ultimately provides 'particular ways to get through to someone, to make sense; in art, they are forms, *like forms of speech*'.[6] Just as different forms of speech (say, an imperative or an interrogative, or, even more broadly, a reminiscence or an argument) serve particular functions within our life as language users, so do different media—both as physical or formal media and as genre conventions—serve particular functions within our lives as creatures with senses and a capacity for experiencing art. Art, then, among other things, is *also* a means of making sense and getting through, whether to ourselves or to someone else, or both. Cavell thereby notes that, 'to discover ways of making sense is always a matter of the relation of an artist to his art, each discovering the other'.[7] While there are deep questions here, especially about the distinctions and relations between media and about the status and possibility of modernism as a question of the possible crisis of media, they are beyond my scope in this chapter.[8]

Instead, let me elaborate on the genre of new television as I understand it. Here, too, there are important questions about the genesis of this genre—in other words, questions about the relation between this televisual genre and other media, most notably, earlier television (to the extent that new television participates in earlier televisual conventions), film (to the extent that new television shares properties with film), literature (to the extent that many of the chief works of new television art explicitly draw either from literary works or literary conventions), and so forth.[9] Again, these questions are beyond my scope, and I can only start with the fact of the genre itself, which on my account is defined by two features. While many focus on the qualities of new television (either its 'complexity',[10] its 'quality',[11] its 'cinematic style',[12] or countless other invocations), my suggestion is that new television is unified by a particular portrayal of authority and a particular solution or response to that state of affairs. (To be clear, my suggestion is *not* that these other elements are unimportant or not present in many instances of new television, but rather that they do not form its specific core, serving instead as a range of family resemblances, sometimes present, sometimes not, around the two genre features I am about to outline.[13])

New television perpetually exhibits, above all, a wholesale collapse of normative authority. Such collapse takes many forms, from illustrations of the failure of institutions to function properly (whether as intended or without the production of suffering), to the sorts of pathologies that appear within various forms of agency arising from the conditions created by such institutions and/or modernity more broadly. Regarding the kinds of institutions exhibited, note that examples range from a city (*The Wire*) to a legal system (*Damages*) to a police force (*Bosch*) to a frontier on the verge of incorporation (*Deadwood*) to a penitentiary (*Oz*) to a future apocalypse (*Battlestar Galactica*), to many, many others. On the possible forms of agency exhibited, note the complex psychological perspectives found in the protagonists of *Weeds, Breaking Bad, Justified, The Sopranos, Mad Men*, and so forth. What should be immediately obvious is that in all cases, the collapse of authority also runs concurrently with other genre conventions—from, for example, the gangster (*The Sopranos, Breaking Bad, Weeds*) to the Western (*Justified, Deadwood, Longmire*) to the apocalypse (*The Walking Dead, Snowpiercer, Falling Skies*), to, again, many others. Relatedly, we find a plethora of TV devices within these lists, from police procedurals (*The Wire, The Shield*) to court dramas (*Damages, Better Call Saul*) to sitcoms (*Weeds, Atypical*), and so forth. What's remarkable is that across all such diversity in content, form, style, network, and whatever other criterion might be brought to bear, these shows all appear to exhibit a world where there just is no normative authority: reasons simply do not make sense in these contexts—they lead to contradiction or destruction. There just is no stable normative basis, nothing *makes sense* for the agents screened to us.

Save with one exception: the family. Across times, places, genres, styles, and contexts of whatever sort, the one constant exception to the above exhibition of the complete loss of normative authority is the institution of the family, which is marshaled across shows that otherwise may be as different as *Six Feet Under* is from *The Sopranos*, or *The Americans* from *True Blood*. The family is exhibited as the last remaining site of normative authority, oftentimes presented by agents as a clear reason for actions of various sorts: *I was or am doing it for my family*. 'For my family' is the one constant refrain of new television (importantly, it must be noted that the invocation of family in such cases is not inherently conservative, and admits instead a range of possibilities, traditional and otherwise—more on this shortly).

These two criteria suggest that it is more accurate to call new television not a genre, but rather a *mode*, akin to a literary mode,[14] since it can stretch across disparate genres (the analogy here might be the gothic mode, which can admit of instantiations across genres, as in gothic humor, gothic horror, southern gothic, and so forth). As noted above, while the invocation of family in new television is not inherently conservative or traditional or regressive, it nonetheless always has political significance (in this way, new television participates in a tradition of Western philosophical reflection on the family as a site for political inquiry dating back to antiquity).

First, the invocation of family situates new television as a unique and powerful response to contemporary conditions. Although I cannot defend this claim here, it has been asserted by theorists of various stripes that authoritarianism is precisely not a byproduct of too much authority, but rather the opposite: authoritarianism becomes a compelling possibility for agents exactly when authority is absent or waning.[15] For this reason, it is striking that just exactly in the era that normative authority has waned more generally, evidenced by the palpable rise of authoritarianism globally,[16] new television has emerged as a dominant and global art form. The comparison, at a very high-level altitude, might be to the way in which György Lukács envisioned the function of the novel in the last century, as an aesthetic response to that historical moment.[17] Relatedly, new television functions similarly to how Cavell diagnoses film as functioning, as when he writes that film comes to embody 'segments of the experiences, the memories, of a common life'.[18] The challenge, and the continuing importance of criticism, as Cavell notes, is 'the difficulty of assessing' films, which remains equally true for new television.[19]

Second, family can be deployed and conceptualized in a regressive way, signaling, expressing, or serving as a placeholder for forms of racial thinking and/or nationalism.[20] This is exactly the case for so much of new television, which certainly does perform such a regressive—ideological—function, reinforcing existing (and future) systems of domination. At the same time, though, there are invocations and conceptualizations of the family within new television that serve as examples of a different way of understanding the family, not as a natural, regressive way of grounding our ties to one another, but rather as a political marker, a sort of 'summoner' if we might speak with Plato,[21] wherein we are invited to see the family as an open space that makes possible the production of something entirely new. The analogy here would be to Hannah Arendt's notion of natality as the introduction of something new into the world.[22]

The Genre of New Television and Its Negation

Operating once again at a high level of altitude, there are interesting points of connection between the way in which the genre of new television as I have sketched it functions, and the way in which remarriage comedies as sketched by Cavell function. At one point in *Pursuits of Happiness*, Cavell highlights the power of the films he discusses under the rubric of remarriage comedies, noting that the artistic impact of this genre is as 'a search for reaffirmation ... not merely an analogy of the social bond, or a comment upon it', but rather 'a further instance of experimentation in consent and reciprocity'.[23] Remarriage comedies, according to Cavell, thereby comment on the social bond, and, as Cavell stresses in his remarks on the genre in 'More of the World Viewed', these films are also concerned with authority and thereby normative breakdown.[24] The scopes of the genre of remarriage comedy and the genre of new television, are, of course, quite different, with the normative breakdown exhibited in remarriage comedies being much narrower, where the question is 'about the search for society, or community, outside, or within, society at large'.[25] At the same time, even Cavell himself acknowledges that elements of remarriage comedies may be found in other places and in contexts broader than the structures of remarriage narrowly conceived. He mentions, for example, 'a recent group of interesting films exploring the limits and desire for what may be understood *as an improvised family*, which includes the *philia* of friendship and of marriage within it'.[26]

My point is not to push the analogy, but only to flag it—again at a very high level of altitude—in order to make plausible certain claims about *Kingdom*. *Kingdom* bears a strong internal relation to the genre of new television, but it is a relation that requires elaboration, for *Kingdom* is not merely an instantiation of the genre. The analogy to Cavell's discussion of remarriage comedies is worthwhile to the extent that Cavell himself also develops an analysis of another genre, the melodrama of the unknown woman, which he views as intimately connected to the genre of remarriage comedies, except as a sort of 'negation of the features of the comedies by the melodramas'.[27] *Kingdom* evinces a *formally similar relationship* to the genre of new television (and this is only as far as the analogy can be pushed). The melodrama of the unknown woman negates the category of 'marriage itself', so that remarriage can no longer be 'a route to creation, to a new or an original integrity', and so that ultimately the entire category is 'transcended' according to Cavell.[28] *Kingdom* performs a similar function on the genre of new television, and an analysis of *Kingdom* can thereby serve as an important first step in the construction of an emerging related genre to new television, one that also somehow negates it. Cavell notes that 'there must exist a genre of film … adjacent to, or derived from, that of remarriage comedy, in which the themes and structure of the comedy are modified or negated in such a way as to reveal systematically the threats (of misunderstanding, of violence) that in each of the remarriage comedies dog its happiness'.[29] The same, it seems, is true of new television, at least formally.

In *Kingdom*, a central characteristic of the genre of new television is also negated, but in a way distinct from the negation that Cavell diagnoses in the melodrama of the unknown woman. Where the latter works through or around threats to remarriage, elements that, in Cavell's words, 'dog' its possibilities for happiness, *Kingdom* negates the family, thereby closing off the possibility for either a conservative orientation towards the family, or one committed to the prioritization of human possibility through reference to natality.[30]

Kingdom and the Family

It's undeniable that *Kingdom* participates intensely in the genre of new television, at various points highlighting the family as the thematic core unifying all its diverse features, the motivations of its characters, and (thereby) the parameters of its aesthetic accomplishment(s). Let me note a few:

   a. The relationship between Ryan and his father, Rick (M.C. Gainey), whom he assaulted during his first foray into fighting. This is the relationship that leads to his prison sentence for attempted murder. Embroiled in addiction at the height of his fighting career, during a confrontation with his father, Ryan cripples him through a brutal assault. The guilt that follows Ryan, as well as his respect for his father, who he notes during an interview is his 'idol',[31] continues to orient his psychic life even after their rapprochement. In this way, the relationship between Ryan and his father is an initiation into a form of life—fighting—but one that is understood as much as a sort of spiritual quest as a career. In addition to describing the sort of virtues that his tutelage in fighting built, his father stresses how fighting is central to Ryan's initiation into the capitalist form of life; it is Ryan's father who cultivates Ryan's skills as a means of making a living. As Rick notes, 'it was freshman year of high school, when it first became clear that this was a *path* for Ryan'.[32] Ryan highlights this feature not only when he speaks of the centrality of his father in his own understanding of himself ('I've always looked up to my dad'), but also when he recites the central capitalist creed of competition, noting that what he took away from his father was, above all, the idea that 'getting by is not an option if you can be exceptional'.[33] The deep link between certain virtues and capitalism, has, of course, long been a mainstay of theories of capitalism,[34] but it nonetheless remains an impressive aesthetic accomplishment to see it so vividly on display.

b. There are also the aforementioned relationship(s) between Alvey Kulina and his sons, Jay and Nate, and then between Alvey Kulina and his fighters, notably Ryan and Alicia Mendez (Natalie Martinez), the latter of whom, for example, is brought to tears when Alvey tells her in an episode that he is proud of her.[35]

c. Also explored extensively is the relationship between Christina and Alvey, which bears the devastation that Alvey's career leaves in its wake, leading ultimately to Christina's turn to drugs and sex work. The show explores this relationship from several angles, at times engaging the husband–wife relationship, at others the mother–son relationship, and at others yet, the sort of surrogate motherly relationship that Christina established with the various sex workers that came under her care in the business.

d. There are other configurations of familial life explored, from Jay Kulina's destructive fling with Ava Flores (Lina Esco), Alvey's failed relationship with Lisa Prince and then with Roxanne Dunn (Grillo's one-time real life wife, Wendy Moniz-Grillo), and then also Lisa's (and Alvey's) relationship with her parents, not to mention Jay Kulina's short-lived marriage coupled with his desire to be a father to his daughter.

I mention these in order to highlight the centrality of familial life to the show. To put the point another way, it does not seem at all obvious why a show revolving around mixed martial arts should be so focused on family. Furthermore, *Kingdom* explicitly explores family as the site where the human form of life—and for its purposes, especially the capitalist form of life—creates and recreates itself. In an episode in the second season, *Kingdom* exhibits this feature of its approach by means of a discussion that Alvey has with his therapist where he muses about his dad. In response to the therapist's question about Alvey's alcohol use, Alvey recalls: 'Guys like my father, my old man. A fifth of vodka every day … but hand—steady as a surgeon. Vicious man. Never stopped. Up at the crack of dawn every day. Perfect Windsor knot in his tie. […] Why are we having this conversation? My drinking? Alcohol is not my problem, doc.' The therapist follows up, pointing out that, 'when you feel pain, you reach out for external coping mechanisms: alcohol, women, fighting'.[36] Alvey is completely flabbergasted. He responds simply with, 'Isn't that how people fucking live?'

Kingdom's suggestion is that, in one way or another, in late capitalism, this is how we all live (and to say that this scene is a commentary on the moralism of therapeutic culture is not thereby to deny this point, but rather to specify it even more). To bring this point into sharper focus, it is worthwhile to invoke here a certain tradition of critical theory, exemplified by the Frankfurt School, especially in the early work of Erich Fromm and Max Horkheimer. Central to their work is a particular inheritance of Freud's project and a subsequent attempt to fuse that inheritance to elements of Marx's project. A key feature of their account, unlike for many critics of Freud then and now, is the extent to which they find Freud's early drive theory central and compelling. That theory claimed that the human psyche is best understood as consisting of two kinds of drives: self-preservation and libido. The latter, sexual drives can always be postponed, repressed, and ultimately satisfied in a variety of ways (such drives can be *occupied* with a range of objects, real or imaginary).[37] Fromm stresses that: 'Freud recognized the biological and physiological influence of the instincts; but he specifically emphasized to what degree these instincts could be modified, and he pointed to the environment, social reality, as the modifying factor.'[38] The social (and thereby historically variable) structure of these drives, however, is not formed by society directly, but is rather formed mediately, by means of the subject's early experiences of familial life. In this way, on one hand, the early Frankfurt School followed Freud, acknowledging that the 'beginnings of … [the] development' of the libidinal drives is discovered 'in a narrower circle … that of the family'.[39] On the other hand, unlike Freud, they stressed an aspect of Freud's early drive theory that he ignored for the most part, that 'the family itself, all its typical internal emotional relationships and the educational ideals it embodies, are in turn conditioned by the social and class background of the family'.[40] In this way it is possible to speak of a synthesis of Freud and Marx, the former providing the drive theory, and the latter providing the context for how that theory is concretely instantiated. No less important in this context is the claim by some members of the Frankfurt School (most notably Theodor W. Adorno) that such drive theory also allows for conceptualizing a distinction between the sorts of non-teleological possibilities that biologically conditioned drives offer, and the sorts of teleology that desires conditioned by late capitalism evince. It is this theme—of the ways in which late capitalism can (com)modify desire—that unifies the interests of *Kingdom* and the early Frankfurt School.

What *Kingdom* does, in a symbolic and aesthetic move, is to distill late capitalism into its alleged core feature: fighting. If I may try to unpack the orientation suggested by the show, it seems to be something like: fighting—whether as competition or as combat, wage labor or class struggle—can symbolically be understood as the central feature of (late) capitalism. Part of the aesthetic and political significance of the show is the extent to which it is seriously able to explore such symbolism through its three seasons. On such a view, fighting is the great leveler: everything solid melts into air, melts into a fist, into a fight. Alvey Kulina, in an incredibly intimate discussion—but also one where he is incredibly drunk and thereby in a state where his unconscious drives can more easily come to the fore—relates to a character known simply as the Hotel Owner (played by the incredible Andre Royo of *The Wire* fame). Alvey recounts how he, as a 'coping' mechanism, destroyed his office to deal with his rage. He notes in an incredible moment of insight, 'I put my fucking fist through a glass cabinet, right? I fucking destroyed my office. I destroyed it.' Then he continues, pointing out, however, that 'I wasn't really that mad. You know what I mean? I mean I just figured that's something I should do. But as far as the pain is concerned. I never fucking felt any pain.'[41] *Kingdom* suggests this is the case for all emotions in late capitalism; everything is already always modulated by the market, by *fighting*.[42] We get paid for pain as a way to make the pain something else, something we don't feel as pain. Again, Alvey makes this point to his therapist: 'Doing what I'm doing is fucking me. Same shit. Day in, day out. I destroy myself. And I peel myself off the floor. I keep it up. And I work it out. […] I fuck myself up over and over again. I can't stop. I can't. The truth of it is, I think it's keeping me alive.'[43] This is why Alvey's advice to everyone is always the same, on display, for example, in his remark to Alicia when she needs advice most: 'just keep doing what you're doing'.[44]

A central category here, but one that is not thereby necessarily or immediately available to the agents we see on the screen, is alienation. While in symbolic form prioritizing Marx's account of class struggle and competition, *Kingdom* proceeds by leveraging the subjective effects produced by the same. Think here of Marx's discussion in his '1844 Manuscripts', where he moves through various forms of alienation under the regime of commodity exchange under capitalism, noting that the worker is alienated from the products of their labor, from the labor itself, and from themselves as a subject (whether a mind or a body). Marx notes that the same is true when the subject confronts other subjects in such a world, where 'within the relationship of alienated labor each man views the other in accordance with the standard and the relationship in which he finds himself as a worker'.[45] According to *Kingdom*, such alienation becomes so omnipresent and so supreme that pain comes to be the norm rather than the exception, and can thereby only be seen as the way station to or the byproduct of something else (think, for example, of the boxing adage that 'pain is just weakness leaving the body', equally applicable as a capitalist virtue or ethos).[46]

Keeping these points in mind, let me note that *Kingdom* harnesses these features to exhibit a fundamental tension and ambivalence towards the family.

On one hand, *Kingdom* participates in the standard trope of the new television genre: while the market has a sort of normative authority, it is one that is inconstant, volatile, perpetually subject to crisis and shock. In *Kingdom*, it is literally combat, oftentimes to the death. The 'solution', as with all instances of new television, is the family. While this is implied throughout, Alvey makes this explicit in the second to last episode of the show. Speaking to Nate after Alvey's mother dies, he says, 'We gotta stick together. We've got to stick together. Women, and fucking friends, they come and they go. In the grand scheme of things, they don't mean a fucking thing. Do you understand? You stay close to me, you stay close to him, that's it. My mother wrote one note, Nate. One note. To me. No one else left. That's it.'[47] The implication, of course, and it is a point that is made explicit throughout the show, is that family is the last refuge; *that* institution still makes sense. In fact, it's all there is. *That's it*.

On the other hand, *Kingdom* also undermines that invocation, both in how it presents the family and how the family in fact functions. The family is that very thing that infuses every individual with the ills of capitalism; it is the mechanism of delivery, the shot that brings the poison home. As noted already, this is a core feature of the show on display throughout, but to spare the viewer any confusion, the show also makes the point explicit in its final season. For example, Jay explicitly states in the finale that 'we're not going to get through this as a fucking family, because that is not what we are. Nate was the only one that gave a shit.'[48] Of course, as viewers, we are meant immediately to recognize the lie even in this, for not only was Nate himself highly ambivalent towards his (the) family, but we know—in a way that he perhaps did not—that his ambivalence towards the family exactly mirrors his closeted ambivalence towards himself, towards his own sexuality. Furthermore, exactly when he relies on his family—finally reveals his sexuality to his father, Alvey, and thereby admits to himself a feature of who he is and his desires—he is killed. The tragic logic of this sequence is thereby meant to suggest that the family offers no more refuge than any other institution; in fact, it seems to serve as the genesis for the ills of late capitalism, recreating them again and again in the subjugation of every child to their family. To this extent, we should not overlook the intimate links between capitalism and the production of sexuality, including homophobia,[49] and also the constant references throughout the show to Oedipal themes around killing one's father, no more prominent and pronounced than in Ryan being forced—by means of his guilt around his earlier assault—to assist in his father's suicide (i.e., kill his father).[50] Ryan thereby makes concrete this link, ultimately guaranteeing his destruction both as a fighter (to the extent that all violence will now always bear the mark of this act towards his father) and as a human being (to the extent that this is just the latest atrocity he's forced into). In this context, Ryan's subsequent turn to religion in the later episodes of the show is exactly, with reference again to Marx, an 'opium', here the treatment for 'the sigh of the oppressed creature'.⁵¹ In short, then, there is on display in *Kingdom* a negation of the genre of new television through the rejection of the family as a site for normative authority.

It is worth pausing here to make clear what I am suggesting. After all, there are other shows that exhibit the collapse or breakdown of a family (for example, *Breaking Bad*). The difference between *Kingdom* and such shows is that *Kingdom* explicitly negates this genre convention. Thus, while Walter White *loses* his family in *Breaking Bad*, this loss is a *byproduct of* his continuing commitment to his family. *Breaking Bad* thereby suggests the dangers of a certain kind of *inflection* towards this commitment, but it does not *negate* that commitment (the suggestion is that Walter White's destruction was guaranteed by his becoming a kingpin, not by his having become a father). Another way to put this point is just to acknowledge that the genre of new television always admits of the possibility of tragedy, but it also thereby always suggests the possibility of a *certain kind* of family life as succeeding as a bulwark against late capitalism. With respect to the family and new television, things *need not* end in tragedy—not so for *Kingdom*.

Conclusion: *Kingdom* and Its Negativity

What's different in *Kingdom* is that the category of the family is entirely negated, a point nowhere more obvious than in the one great event that I have not yet mentioned: Lisa losing the child she was to bear as the fruit of her relationship with Alvey. It is this loss that breaks her and that tears apart their familial structure; it is also this loss that is meant exactly to symbolize the rejection of family. This sequence of events is also intimately connected to the rejection of Ryan's familial life, a point highlighted in the finale of the second season, where Ryan and Lisa finally come to talk about her pregnancy. Ryan quickly gives her his newly adopted religious spiel, noting that the death of his father was a blessing (lying thereby about how it occurred as a bit of assisted suicide) and telling Lisa that he thinks 'that God gives people as much as they can handle'.⁵² After Lisa expresses skepticism, their conversation takes an interesting turn, turning to their desires. In response to being asked whether she considered suicide after the loss of the baby, Lisa replies, 'Killing myself? No. But I do fantasize about being dead with my son.' She continues, saying, 'Sometimes, I think I caused it. [...] I didn't want him. I thought he was someone Alvey stuck me with. He was going to ruin my life. I swear to God he felt that. I know he did. And it kills me. But then when we got to San Francisco, it all changed. It was just him and me. I fell so in love.' We see here the alleged possibility of a life and an economy of desire distinct from the vicissitudes of capitalism, symbolized by her departure from Alvey and exactly the capitalist ethos he represents. Lisa then continues, exuding joy, 'I thought about our whole life, and the way that he would look at me.' This moment of something distinct from everything else, of course, was not to be, and Ryan chimes in, claiming, affirming: 'No reason.' (And, of course, it is equally plausible to say here that this moment of utopia was at best an illusion, just another means by which late capitalism affects the desires of women in order to extract domestic and other labor from them; with either reading, the point that follows stands.) Lisa then responds, all joy gone, replaced by a smile that is obviously contrived, 'I know. It just is.' This encounter leads to a rapprochement between Lisa and Ryan (it would not be too much to say a—sort of—remarriage). This is short-lived, however, and it is striking that despite all of the other balls *Kingdom* is juggling in its final season (Nate's death, the fights, Jay's destruction, and so forth), the show makes sure to double back to this relationship in order to show conclusively how it simply cannot be, and offers no way out.[53]

Indeed, nothing offers a way out: not killing your father, not family, nothing. Put in these terms, natality and the production of novelty cannot do what it does in the most progressive instances of new television—instead, it comes literally stillborn. Like the early Frankfurt School, *Kingdom* shows a thoroughgoing suspicion towards familial life as *any* kind of response to capitalism (even a failed one, say).[54] Drugs, religion, and even violence also offer no way out; this is the great symbolic meaning of Ryan's drug-fueled attempted murder of his father. At the same time, family offers no way out either, since it is his father who initiates Ryan into the capitalist form of life. *Kingdom*'s claim, on this front, and thereby its complete negation of the genre of new television, is that there is no way out, not in *any* kind of family. In fact, in the end, there is only what Ryan says there is in the finale: 'you get paid for pain'.

Coda

Where do things stand, then? What is the ultimate significance of this negation of the genre of new television? The answer to these questions depends entirely on how one understands the extraordinary sequence that concludes the show.

After winning the fight he has been training for since the beginning of the season—a fight which will give him financial stability beyond his wildest dreams—Alvey is given the champion's belt and asked about the fight, to which he responds, 'This fight is for my son Nate. I miss you and I love you.'[55] The camera moves across the arena, lingering for a moment on Christina, Lisa, and Jay, registering the deep ambivalence on everyone's faces (their faces evince sadness and yet grudging respect for Alvey's words). Everyone is broken. Alvey then lumbers out of the ring, belt around his waist, utterly bloodied, brutally bruised, drenched in blood and sweat and spittle. The crowd goes wild, but he walks on unfazed. The Fratellis' 'Slow', a haunting acoustic piece about loss and time, plays in a long sequence as the camera follows behind Alvey, seemingly walking step for step with him. We focus on his back, hesitantly following him. At first he jogs, but then a limp emerges. He's eventually struggling to walk. *Slow*, as the song highlights. He walks into the locker room, and the music is suddenly cut. There is first the silence of being alone. Then we hear Alvey's uneven steps and his labored breathing. His back is still to us. He's now completely alone in the showers. He drops to his knees, no longer able to stand. He sits. Finally, he turns to the camera, staring at us, exhausted, utterly spent. There's a pause. And then the screen fades to black, the viewer left only with the sound of Alvey's labored breathing. The entire sequence I've just described lasts a remarkable two minutes. As we stare at the black screen, we can't help but recall that as Alvey was sitting, the camera lingered on his belt. We know he is the champion, we know he's wealthy, we know he has won. But amidst the darkness of the screen, we cannot help but ask and be asked: was it worth it?

My sense is that it is impossible to watch this last sequence and think that the answer to this question is, 'Yes.' If my assumption is correct, then the negation of the genre of new television in and by *Kingdom* is the negation of the capitalist prioritization of commodity exchange itself, for *Kingdom* seems to be saying: this is its telos—beware.

And to the extent that the genre of new television has now exclusively and perhaps solely become a commodity, with new shows produced at a breakneck pace and by means of algorithms and analyses of the market, it may be that the negation of the genre responds as much to late capitalism as to the material facts of the genre as it now stands. Such a negation may be the only way out. It may be the only forward for new television, for the genre itself.

Notes

1 I am grateful to Daniela Ginsburg, Ada Jaarsma, and Larisa Reznik for profound discussions about *Kingdom* and especially to Larisa for extensive comments on an earlier draft of this chapter. I am also grateful to the questions and comments I received at the conference "Stanley Cavell: Philosophical, Literary, and Cinematic Skepticism" at Binghamton University in 2022 (where an earlier draft of this chapter was presented). Thank you to Jeroen Gerrits for the invitation to present there. The comments of the anonymous reviewers were also useful.

2 To quote Martha Nussbaum: 'Moral communication, too, both here and later in the scene, is not simply a matter of the uttering and receiving of general propositional judgments. Nor is it any sort of purely intellectual activity. It partakes both of the specificity and of the emotional and imaginative richness of their individual moral effort.' See Martha Nussbaum, '"Finely Aware and Richly Responsible": Moral Attention and the Moral Task of Literature', *Journal of Philosophy*, vol. 82, no. 10 (1985), 521. Nussbaum is discussing literature, but many of the same points can be explored in the context of new television. I focus on this point in the context of the spectatorship of viewers of new television in Martin Shuster, "Dig if You Will the

Picture ...": New Television, Myth, *Black Monday* and the 1980s', *Revue Internationale de Philosophie*, 2022/3 (No. 301), 105–19.
3   Martin Shuster, *New Television: The Aesthetics and Politics of a Genre* (Chicago: University of Chicago Press, 2017).
4   Stanley Cavell, *The World Viewed: Reflections on the Ontology of Film, Enlarged Edition* (Cambridge, MA: Harvard University Press, 1979), 105.
5   Cavell, *The World Viewed*, 32.
6   Ibid. Emphasis added.
7   Ibid.
8   For the former, see Diarmuid Costello, 'On the Very Idea of a "Specific" Medium: Michael Fried and Stanley Cavell on Painting and Photography as Arts', *Critical Inquiry*, vol. 34, no. 2 (2008), 274–312; Diarmuid Costello, 'Automat, Automatic, Automatism: Rosalind Krauss and Stanley Cavell on Photography and the Photographically Dependent Arts', *Critical Inquiry*, vol. 38, no. 4 (2012), 819–54; Diarmuid Costello and Dawn M. Phillips, 'Automatism, Causality and Realism: Foundational Problems in the Philosophy of Photography', *Philosophy Compass*, vol. 4, no. 1 (2009), 1–21. On the latter, see *Understanding Cavell, Understanding Modernism*, ed. Paola Marrati (London: Bloomsbury, 2023).
9   I detail some elements of this in Shuster, *New Television*. Other discussions include Ted Nannicelli, *Appreciating the Art of Television: A Philosophical Perspective* (London: Routledge, 2016); Martha P. Nochimson, *Television Rewired: The Rise of the Auteur Series* (Austin: University of Texas Press, 2019); Sarah Cardwell, 'Television Amongst Friends: Medium, Art, Media', *Critical Studies in Television: An International Journal of Television Studies*, vol. 9, no. 3 (2014), 6–21; and Jason Mittell, *Television and American Culture* (Oxford: Oxford University Press, 2010).
10 Jason Mittell, *Complex TV: The Poetics of Contemporary Television Storytelling* (New York: New York University Press, 2015).
11 Janet McCabe and Kim Akass, *Quality TV: Contemporary American Television and Beyond* (London: I.B.Tauris, 2007).
12 Deborah L. Jaramillo, 'Rescuing Television from "the Cinematic": The Perils of Dismissing Television Style', in *Television Aesthetics and Style*, ed. Jason Jacobs and Steven Peacock (London: Bloomsbury, 2013); Brett Mills, 'What Does It Mean to Call Television "Cinematic"?', in ibid.
13 For a discussion of the term 'family resemblances', tied closely to Wittgenstein's work, see Hans Sluga, 'Family Resemblance', *Grazer Philosophische Studien*, vol. 71, no. 1 (2006), 1–21.
14 On this point, see Alastair Fowler, *Kinds of Literature: An Introduction to the Theory of Genres and Modes* (Cambridge, MA: Harvard University Press, 1982). See also my earlier discussion in Shuster, *New Television*, 170–74.
15 Powerful arguments to this effect can be found in Hannah Arendt, 'What Is Authority?', in *Between Past and Future: Eight Exercises in Political Thought* (New York: Penguin, 2006); Max Horkheimer, 'Authority and the Family', in *Critical Theory: Selected Essays* (New York: Herder and Herder, 1972); and Theodor W. Adorno, 'Freudian Theory and the Pattern of Fascist Propaganda', in *The Culture Industry: Selected Essays on Mass Culture*, ed. J.M. Bernstein (London: Routledge, 2001). See also Karen Stenner and Jonathan Haidt, 'Authoritarianism Is Not a Momentary Madness, but an Eternal Dynamic within Liberal Democracies', in *It Can Happen*

Here? Authoritarianism in America, ed. Cass R. Sunstein (New York: Harper Collins, 2018).

16 See Wendy Brown, Peter E. Gordon, and Max Pensky, *Authoritarianism: Three Inquiries in Critical Theory* (Chicago: University of Chicago Press, 2018).

17 The 'high level of altitude' constraint is important to the extent that it highlights that Lukács' theory required a much more substantive and robust assessment of the conditions of modernity to which the novel served as a response. See György Lukács, *The Theory of the Novel: A Historico-Philosophical Essay on the Forms of Great Epic Literature*, trans. Anna Bostock (Boston: MIT Press, 1971).

18 Stanley Cavell, *Pursuits of Happiness: The Hollywood Comedy of Remarriage* (Cambridge, MA: Harvard University Press, 1981), 41.

19 Cavell, *The World Viewed*, 215.

20 Étienne Balibar, 'The Nation Form: History and Ideology', in *Race, Nation Class: Ambiguous Identities*, ed. Étienne Balibar and Immanuel Wallerstein (London: Verso, 1991), 100ff.

21 See for example 524d of *The Republic* in *Plato: Complete Works*, ed. John M. Cooper (Indianapolis: Hackett, 1997). The Greek is παράκλητιος and this is a central notion for the latter idea of a Paraclete in Christian theology.

22 On Arendt's notion, see Patricia Bowen-Moore, *Hannah Arendt's Philosophy of Natality* (New York: Macmillan, 1989). For an understanding of the family in new television in this way, see Shuster, *New Television*, 167.

23 Cavell, *Pursuits of Happiness*, 182.

24 See notably *The World Viewed*, 214f. I further detail these points of comparison between new television and remarriage comedies in Shuster, *New Television*, 159–69.

25 Cavell, *The World Viewed*, 176.

26 'The Incessance and the Absence of the Political', in *The Claim to Community: Essays on Stanley Cavell and Political Philosophy*, ed. Andrew Norris (Stanford: Stanford University Press, 2006), 300. Emphasis added. Cavell is here discussing films like *About a Boy*, *Flawless*, *Daddy and Them*, and others.

27 Stanley Cavell, *Contesting Tears: The Hollywood Melodrama of the Unknown Woman* (Chicago: University of Chicago Press, 1996), 5.

28 Cavell, *Contesting Tears*, 6. Again, the 'high level of altitude' constraint is important here also, as there are many more significant details in the connection between these two genres for Cavell (he importantly says that the category is 'transcended *and perhaps reconceived*' [emphasis added]). For more on the melodrama of the unknown woman and these broader connections, see Robert Sinnerbrink, 'Between Skepticism and Moral Perfectionism: On Cavell's Melodrama of the Unknown Woman', in *The Thought of Stanley Cavell and Cinema: Turning Anew to the Ontology of Film a Half-Century after* The World Viewed, ed. David LaRocca (London: Bloomsbury Academic, 2020).

29 Cavell, *Contesting Tears*, 83.

30 Larisa Reznik has pushed me to differentiate these two options more forcefully. What if the latter is just a variation on the former? In this vein, we might especially cite the work of Lee Edelman and his claims about reproductive futurism—see Lee Edelman, *No Future: Queer Theory and the Death Drive* (Raleigh: Duke University Press, 2004). I have addressed this point briefly in the conclusion of Shuster, *New Television*. There is, however, more to say, but it is not within my scope here to

respond to this line of inquiry in the detail it requires. I note that the analysis that follows works even if this second option does not exist; at the same time, I do think it is important to tackle this question and so leave it for a future, more extensive discussion.

31 See *Kingdom*, Season 2, Episode 7, 'The Demon Had a Spell'. Written by Byron Balasco. Directed by Michael Morris.
32 Ibid. Emphasis perhaps added (or more perhaps in the original). The viewer will have to judge for themselves.
33 Ibid.
34 See, of course, Max Weber, *The Protestant Ethic and the Spirit of Capitalism: And Other Writings*, trans. Peter Baehr and Gordon C. Wells (New York: Penguin, 2002). More recently, see Eugene McCarraher, *The Enchantments of Mammon: How Capitalism Became the Religion of Modernity* (Cambridge, MA: Harvard University Press, 2019). In this context, it is important to note also Ryan's growing religiosity as the show progresses; this is not accidental.
35 *Kingdom*, Season 2, Episode 11, 'Lay and Pray'. Written by Byron Balasco. Directed by Gary Fleder.
36 *Kingdom*, Season 2, Episode 14, 'Do Not Disturb'. Written by Byron Balasco and Patrick Aison. Directed by John Dahl.
37 Central accounts include Benjamin Y. Fong, *Death and Mastery: Psychoanalytic Drive Theory and the Subject of Late Capitalism* (New York: Columbia University Press, 2016); Martin Jay, *The Dialectical Imagination: A History of the Frankfurt School and the Institute of Social Research 1923–1950* (Berkeley: University of California Press, 1973), 86–113; Joel Whitebook, *Perversion and Utopia: A Study in Psychoanalysis and Critical Theory* (Cambridge, MA: The MIT Press, 1996); Joel Whitebook, 'The Marriage of Marx and Freud: Critical Theory and Psychoanalysis', in *The Cambridge Companion to Adorno*, ed. Tom Huhn (Cambridge: Cambridge University Press, 2004); and John Abromeit, *Max Horkheimer and the Foundations of the Frankfurt School* (Cambridge: Cambridge University Press, 2011), 185–227, 336–49.
38 Erich Fromm, 'The Method and Function of an Analytic Social Psychology', in *The Crisis of Psychoanalysis: Essays on Freud, Marx and Social Psychology* (New York: Holt, Rinehart, and Winston, 1970), 116.
39 Sigmund Freud, *The Standard Edition of the Complete Psychological Works of Sigmund Freud*, trans. James Strachey, Anna Freud, and Alan Tyson, 24 vols. (London: Hogarth Press, 2001), 18:70. Fromm quotes this in Fromm, 'The Method and Function of an Analytic Social Psychology', 116.
40 Fromm, 'The Method and Function of an Analytic Social Psychology', 116.
41 *Kingdom*, Season 2, Episode 11, 'Lay and Pray'. Written by Byron Balasco. Directed by Gary Fleder.
42 Once again, there are potential formal analogies and lines of salience to be pursued here to other works of critical theory, like, for example, those of Guy Debord.
43 *Kingdom*, Season 2, Episode 14, 'Do Not Disturb'. Written by Byron Balasco and Patrick Aison. Directed by John Dahl.
44 *Kingdom*, Season 2, Episode 13, 'Woke Up Lonely'. Written by Byron Balasco and Alex Metcalf. Directed by John Dahl.
45 Karl Marx, 'Economic and Philosophic Manuscripts of 1844', in *The Marx–Engels Reader*, ed. Robert C. Tucker (New York: Norton, 1978), 77. Translation modified.

46 There are, of course, a range of other issues here. In the case of Adorno, this is intimately tied to his exploration of a 'new categorical imperative' that aims to respond to such instances of raw suffering. For an assessment of this idea, see especially J.M. Bernstein, *Adorno: Disenchantment and Ethics* (Cambridge: Cambridge University Press, 2001), 330–415; and Martin Shuster, *Autonomy after Auschwitz: Adorno, German Idealism, and Modernity* (Chicago: University of Chicago Press, 2014), 71–134.
47 *Kingdom*, Season 3, Episode 9, 'Cactus'. Written by Byron Balasco, Enzo Mileti, and Scott Wilson. Directed by Padraic McKinley.
48 *Kingdom*, Season 3, Episode 10, 'Lie Down in the Light'. Written by Byron Balasco, Enzo Mileti, and Scott Wilson. Directed by Padraic McKinley.
49 On this point, see especially Christopher Chitty, *Sexual Hegemony: Statecraft, Sodomy, and Capital in the Rise of the World System* (Raleigh: Duke University Press, 2020). See also Balibar, 'The Nation Form: History and Ideology', 102ff.
50 *Kingdom*, Season 2, Episode 10, 'Traveling Alone'. Written by Byron Balasco. Directed by Sidney Sidell.
51 Marx, 'Contribution to the Critique of Hegel's *Philosophy of Right*' in *The Marx–Engels Reader*, ed. Robert C. Tucker (New York: Norton, 1978), 54.
52 *Kingdom*, Season 2, Episode 20, 'No Sharp Objects'. Written and directed by Byron Balasco. The references in the rest of this paragraph are to this episode.
53 *Kingdom*, Season 3, Episode 10, 'Lie Down in the Light'. Written by Byron Balasco, Enzo Mileti, and Scott Wilson. Directed by Padraic McKinley.
54 This theme has been explored most forcefully recently in Robyn Marasco, 'There's a Fascist in the Family: Critical Theory and Antiauthoritarianism', *South Atlantic Quarterly*, vol. 117, no. 4 (2018).
55 *Kingdom*, Season 3, Episode 10, 'Lie Down in the Light'. Written by Byron Balasco, Enzo Mileti, and Scott Wilson. Directed by Padraic McKinley. All the references in this paragraph are to this episode.

3

To See and to Stop: The Problem of Abdication in *Succession*

Elisabeth Bronfen

A Shakespearean Pitch

When critics call a contemporary TV drama 'Shakespearean', it is not immediately clear to what exactly they are attributing this label. Is it merely the citation of famous passages, taken out of context and reused? Is it the screenplay, blending poetic language with verbal wit? Is it the constellation of a large group of characters, divided into main players and minor ones supporting them? Is it the parallel development of several plotlines? Is the reference meant to draw attention to thematic constellations that a particular television show shares with Shakespeare's own preoccupations—such as the ambiguity of power, the violence of ambition, and the treachery of desire? Or does this attribute speak to a shared self-reflection on theatricality, a sense that all the characters we encounter on screen are presented as players on a stage, moving towards a closure we anticipate from the beginning, even if it is deferred not for several acts but several seasons?

If, as Douglas Lanier points out, the designation 'Shakespearean' refers not only 'to qualities and themes regarded as being essential to his plays', but also to a cultural authority that lends legitimacy to whatever the name is applied to, the question becomes, how far are we willing to extend it?[1] Whether the screenplay explicitly cites these plays, or whether the reference is in the eye of the reader/critic, in either case at issue is a two-way dialogue. The attribute 'Shakespearean' gives a touch of weightiness to serial TV drama even while the cultural authority of this oeuvre is reasserted. Although we access Shakespeare through theatrical and cinematic appropriations, these reworkings are the sites where he, conceived as an active participant in the exchange, returns to take hold of us. Any contemporary revisitation of his oeuvre thus not only means straddling the past with the present. It also

Elisabeth Bronfen, 'To See and to Stop: The Problem of Abdication in *Succession*' in: *Television with Stanley Cavell in Mind*. University of Exeter Press (2023). © Elisabeth Bronfen. DOI: 10.47788/ZIFG7093 means looking at this past with the subsequent interpretations of these plays in mind, at different historical moments and in different media, including that of the philosophical essay.

In the following crossmapping between *King Lear* and *Succession*, my concern is not only noticing the way the creator of the TV drama, Jesse Armstrong, draws on our ability to detect a Shakespearean pitch in his screenplay. I am equally concerned with the reading that becomes possible only once Shakespeare's presence has been detected. At the same time, the particular line of correspondence between these two distinct texts that I will seek to draw out brings a third perspective into play, namely Stanley Cavell's reading of *King Lear* in his essay 'The Avoidance of Love'.[2] As I have argued in *Serial Shakespeare*, crossmapping entails a self-consciously operative hermeneutic process.[3] By surmising connections between these three texts, the reading I will offer in what follows performs the proposed encounter. It seeks to draw out the reciprocity at issue in charting the superimposition of an early modern play with a philosophical meditation and a television appropriation. The heuristic gain in proposing such a transhistorical dialogue, in turn, is both the discovery of similarities as well as the apprehension of dislocations and transformations, which Shakespeare's tragedy has been afforded in the process of its cultural afterlife. At issue, in other words, is not only what has been retained, but also what is left out, what is re-encoded, refigured, and aesthetically transformed to transmit a different narrative, to sustain a different philosophical outlook, to broadcast a different ideology. Which is to say, while the parallels and connections to be mapped are provided by each of the texts, the meanings that are discovered in the process of the following crossmapping are also the effect of my reading.

Let's begin by asking how Shakespeare explicitly resurfaces in Jesse Armstrong's satirical melodrama about the vicissitudes of fortune in the family of the powerful global media mogul Logan Roy (Brian Cox). As Christina Wald has shown, when the first season of *Succession* aired, TV critics were not the only ones to call it an updated version of *King Lear*.[4] Tapping into a Shakespearean legacy was also part of the overall promotion strategy of the show. In several interviews, Brian Cox explicitly spoke to the similarity between his performance of the regal paterfamilias in *Succession* and Shakespeare's control-hungry king, whom he had already played several times, including in the production by the National Theatre in 1990, directed by Deborah Warner. The dialogues, in turn, explicitly cite Shakespeare over and again. Frank Vernon (Peter Friedman), the COO of Waystar Royco and oldest confidant of Logan, is demoded early in the first season because Roman, one of the sons vying for the position of successor to his father's throne, insists on being given his position. When Kendall (Jeremy Strong), his older brother, brings him back in after his father has had a stroke, Frank says of himself, 'I am just an attendant lord, here to swell a scene or two.'[5] He is referring to T.S. Eliot's gesture towards Shakespeare in 'The Love Song of J. Alfred Prufrock': 'No, I am not Prince Hamlet, nor was meant to be / Am an attendant lord, one that will do to swell a progress, start a scene or two'. Early in the second season, Roman (Kieran Culkin), in turn, will offer his own skewed reference to *Hamlet*. Describing his vision of how he might supersede his older brother, he explains: 'I land the deal. I kill Kendall. I'm crowned the king. Just like in *Hamlet*. If that is what happens in *Hamlet*, I don't care.'[6]

When it comes to *King Lear*, in turn, the script self-consciously fragments and reassembles the character constellations and thematic concerns, and yet it is telling that there is only one direct quote that has, to date, migrated to *Succession*. During an emergency meeting with his general advisors in the second season, Logan calls his daughter Shiv (Sarah Snook), another contestant for the position of successor. He has found out that *New York Magazine* will be doing a piece on the sex scandals and suicides that happened a few years back on the cruises which Wayco Roystar runs. While Shiv's advice is to find a way to placate the editors, claiming, as a woman, to have more authority than her rival brother, Kendall vehemently offers his counter-strategy of relentless attack: 'Just fucking kill, kill, kill.'[7] An astute ear will hear King Lear in act 4, scene 2, who, coming out of his bout of madness after being exposed to the storm on the heath, confides in Gloucester his stratagem for hitting back at those whom he feels have betrayed him: 'When I have stolen upon these sons-in-law, / Then kill, kill, kill, kill, kill, kill!' (IV.6.183). That Kendall should ventriloquize the moment when Shakespeare's king, having regained his wits, also rediscovers his venomous desire for revenge, is not merely a further indication of the free-floating nature of Shakespearean citations in this TV drama. Rather, it uses this son's particular claim on Shakespeare to articulate his claim on Logan Roy's position as well. After all, Kendall not only speaks in the voice of the reawakened king. He also relegates his father, still presiding over Wayco Roystar, to the position of the blinded Gloucester.

Two entangled concerns regarding the question of succession thus ground the crossmapping this essay proposes: While Jesse Armstrong's TV drama self-consciously taps into the legacy of Shakespeare in contemporary media culture, proposing itself to be a valid heir, the narrative it unfolds itself revolves around the fraught moment of transition it has appropriated from *King Lear*. The point of departure for both texts, after all, is a ruler who goes through an abdication without abdicating. In both cases the division of his kingdom, which he proposes, engenders a fatal division among his children. In Shakespeare's tragedy, the competition in the opening scene, in which each daughter is called upon to declare her love for her father in public, leaves the favorite, Cordelia, dumbstruck. She would rather stay silent and say nothing. Forced to speak nevertheless, she does not follow her sisters' suit and, instead, defies her father's demand. This results in her banishment, along with the loyal courtier Kent, who dared to criticize his sovereign for his folly.

The internal dramatic repetition of Shakespeare's tragedy is such that Lear himself comes to be banished, and twice—first by Goneril and then by Regan. Both fear that the presence of his riotous retinue in their respective castles will destabilize their own political power. If, when exposed to the harsh elements on the heath, the old king loses his wits, this 'tempest in his mind' is to be taken as a transformation of his previous mad anger. Though Kent, albeit in disguise, has accompanied him throughout the storm, Lear will only regain his sanity upon encountering his double, the blinded Gloucester, the other father in the play, who pits his two sons against each other only to find himself banished as well. Then, when the estranged members of the family finally come to be reassembled on the battlefield close to Dover, death ensues all round. Cordelia, now Queen of France, has returned to fight for her father in the war her two sisters have unleashed, by first scheming together and then against each other, in their bid for absolute power. Neither of these two rivaling sisters will survive, nor will Gloucester's bastard son Edmund, their mutual paramour. While Lear's Fool simply disappears after act 3 and a servant kills the Duke of Cornwall to punish him for blinding Gloucester, Lear dies after carrying the corpse of his favorite daughter back onto the stage. Indeed, it is Cordelia's death that is most shocking, yet also seemingly inevitable. It leaves the regained peace in a gutted nation to three inconsolable characters: Kent, who hopes to follow his master into death; Edgar, who during the long journey to Dover staunchly refused to expose his identity to his blind father; and Albany. Though, throughout the play, this duke never sided with his wife Goneril in her hunger for power, he is now the one left to succeed the dead king. As so often in Shakespeare's tragedies, the dramatic resolution in the final scene of the final act is ambiguous. Whether, by declaring to Edgar and Kent, 'Rule in this realm and the gored state sustain' Albany is offering the crown, over which there has been such fatal ado, to Edgar, or whether he is asking Gloucester's son to join him as sovereign remains an open question.

Noteworthy regarding the mapping of this character constellation onto *Succession* are the transformations. The creator, Jesse Armstrong, changes the family dynamics by not only adding an elder son, Connor (Alan Ruck), who has no interest in being part of his father's company and, instead, is preparing his campaign for the presidency of the United States. Regarding the three siblings vying for Logan's succession, Cordelia's part is taken up by the second son Kendall. He is not only the favored one. Like Cordelia, he also defies his father's demands precisely because of his love for Logan and is banished from the company. It is part of the serial logic of TV drama that this should happen several times—first when, acting as CEO after his father has suffered a stroke, Kendall sells part of the company to his friend Stewy (Arian Moayed), hoping to salvage their debt through private equity. Then, when he proposes a vote of no confidence to the board because he feels his father is no longer capable of making the right decisions regarding the changed media situation. And, finally, when he designs a hostile takeover of the company by his father's long-standing enemy Sandy. That Kendall should repeatedly be called back as COO is part and parcel of this serial logic, much like the fact that he is both his father's staunchest critic and his most adamant supporter.

The twins Shiv and Roman, in turn, can be seen as contemporary refigurations of the other two daughters. They both repeatedly ingratiate themselves with their father, hoping he will declare them to be the 'next one' even while, in their effort to oust Kendall, they both scheme together and also against each other. All these shifting alliances show how the struggle for succession within a powerful family is invariably entangled with the financial survival of their media kingdom, and the political power this represents. Comparable to Lear's daughters, all three siblings serially engage with the way their father instrumentalizes them to remain in power despite but also because he realizes his absolute sovereignty is about to end. Significant, of course, is the absence of any hands-on fighting. What in *King Lear* turns into civil war, in *Succession* becomes a series of hostile media takeovers, during which Logan fires half of his board and restructures it in the hope of retaining his power, even while the bid against his firm by his adversaries as well as the mounting cruise ship scandal leads him to fear that his stockholders will vote him out.

Succession also makes use of the parallel plot involving Gloucester and his two sons, Edgar and Edmund, so as to draw into focus the cruelty that ensues from a father's unwillingness to cede control. In Logan Roy, Lear comes to be conflated with his loyal counsellor. By being condensed into one character, Gloucester's blindness towards both sons, as well as the abuse he subjects them to, is thus enhanced. Further transformations become noticeable when filling out the rest of the map of the dramatis personae. The counsellors are multiplied. While Logan's oldest confidant, Frank Vernon, is repeatedly banished and recalled, and as such plays Kent to Kendall's Cordelia, the general counsel, Gerri Kellman (J. Smith-Cameron), as well as the chief financial officer, Karl Muller (David Rasche), remain by Logan's side, wily yet cautious enough to protect their own interests, and their own skin. Noticeable also is the fact that there are no real outcasts like the bastard son Edmund, even if Roman comes up with a series of intrigues pitted against the brother who, like Edgar, is his father's preferred successor. While Kendall's estranged wife Rava (Natalie Gold) has no significant place on such a map, Shiv's husband Tom Wambsgans (Matthew Macfadyen) is comparable to Goneril's Albany. Abused by his wife in her power games, he too will ultimately shift his alliance to the old media mogul. Which leaves one to account for the Fool, who holds up the mirror to Lear's folly. Logan's step-nephew Greg (Nicholas Braun) plays the part with his bemused comments that debunk the power games he is himself entangled in. Of him, too, one might say that he is 'not altogether fool', even if it remains unclear how aware he is of his own insight.

Such a crossmapping draws into focus the shared premise between *King Lear* and *Succession*. A sovereign's failed abdication puts into peril the very issue of succession, on which the stability of a nation or a company within an ever-changing political landscape is predicated. As such, it undermines the very thing that would ascertain the continuation of the line—as though, by hesitating, or rather reneging on an initial promise, each of these sovereigns were ruled by a death drive; not only uncertain who the best heir would be, but also uncertain whether they even want an heir to continue what, given their own mortality, they will invariably be forced to relinquish, even if not quite yet. The unwillingness or sheer inability to cede to the next generation engenders an internal battle that transforms renunciation of power into paternal sacrifice, or at least the threat thereof. In both cases, the sovereign, unwilling to step down, not only initiates the rivalry among the children, but plays with it. Logan, after recovering from his stroke, never actually leaves his realm; he is more apt at putting his children to the test than his Shakespearean predecessor. Over and again he re-poses the love test with which *King Lear* begins. Giving and withholding praise, cruelly pitting them against each other, keeping some in the loop and others in the dark—all this is Logan's way of figuring out which of his children would, indeed, be the fittest to take his place. He senses that a perfect replacement, predicated as it is on being exactly like him, is also his annihilation and it is this conundrum that drives the serial logical of *Succession*. Faced with the knowledge of his inevitable death, he struggles against the very symbolic death he can't avoid taking into account. What he avoids instead, as my discussion of Cavell's reading of *King Lear* will suggest, is love.

The reflection on the theatricality of politics so quintessential to Shakespearean drama is, thus, not limited to the way *Succession* comments on the politics of the news and entertainment business. Much like Lear, who stages his demand for his daughter's love publicly in his court, Logan commands his world as though it were a stage. On it, all his children are compelled to play the parts he assigns to them, even if they invariably improvise while performing in the interwoven and mutually implicated storylines their father has devised. There are, however, two significant transformations that need to be taken into account. Firstly, while *King Lear* makes use of internal dramatic repetition regarding the banishment of family members and their reunion, as serial drama, *Succession* even more explicitly tarries with the abdication scene, repeatedly playing through its consequences. Logan's coma after his stroke is comparable to Lear temporarily losing his sanity while out on the stormy heath, not only because, in this state of bodily incapacitation, we are made aware of the tempest in Logan's mind. It also draws into focus the vulnerability which, once he has recovered, he will subsequently seek to ward off with his rage. Armstrong's media mogul, however, is never unsheltered, never reduced to bare life. After Logan recovers his wits, he, in contrast to Lear, himself heads the armada against his adversaries, even if, having enlisted his children to join him in battle, they at times deploy subterfuge against each other.

Secondly, while, after Logan's stroke, the end of his reign is something everyone is called upon to reckon with, there is no death in *Succession*; nothing like Cordelia's corpse being brought back on stage by her bereaved father. Fatality is relegated to the margins, or to be more precise to the abused sex worker on the cruise ship, whose suicide is at the heart of the media scandal and the Senate investigation. *Succession* is not a tragedy, but a serial melodrama, so that any anticipation of the end of a dynasty and the beginning of another must necessarily be deferred. Furthermore, there is no innocence in *Succession* to resemble that of Cordelia. All characters, especially Kendall and Shiv, are implicated characters. They actively perpetrate the very cruelty that has made them wounded individuals in the first place. There are no scapegoats and there is no redemption. So the question that has concerned so many readers of *King Lear*, namely why Cordelia must die, has to be rephrased. Why do these children allow their father to assign parts for them to play in a world he inhabits as though it were a stage? Why do they betray, rather than trust each other? Indeed, why do they continue to do what is so hurtful to them, why do they continually allow themselves to be abused and abuse others in turn? To seek answers for these questions, it is useful to now turn to the third text I propose for my crossmapping.

Stanley Cavell's *King Lear*

The most controversial problem that, according to Stanley Cavell, Shakespeare's tragedy raises is the nature of Lear's motivation in the opening scene and Cordelia's response to it. Approaching the text from the perspective of ordinary language philosophy, Cavell relates the puzzling psychological disposition of the king and his favorite daughter to the problem of knowing the other in relation to the words someone uses to express themselves. The issue isn't only that people sometimes cannot say what they mean for lack of a clear insight into their situation, but 'that for various reasons they may not know what they mean, and that when they are forced to recognize this they feel they do not, and perhaps cannot, mean anything, and they are struck dumb'.[8] Given the prominence of eyes, of blindness, and of seeing in *King Lear*, the issue of lacking insight into what one means is directly linked to the psychological dimension of eyesight. By taking Cordelia at her word when she claims that she has nothing to say to his demand, Lear does not see his youngest daughter, although she is in his presence; he does not recognize her for what she is over and beyond what he wants and expects of her. The same can be said of Gloucester, who doesn't see through Edmund's intrigue, doesn't see Edgar's loyalty until he is blinded as a consequence of this lack of insight. For Cavell, seeing is thus more than visual perception. It is a form of acknowledgement, while a refusal (or inability) to see the other is a form of repudiation.

If, then, these children are not recognized by their fathers, this is because they are not visible to them as separate individuals, as the next generation who, in one way or another, will succeed their fathers, even if they do not become their heirs. Instead, they are treated as though they were nothing more than an extension of both fathers' self-vision, which is to say the way both Lear and Gloucester do (or do not) know themselves; the way they can (or cannot) articulate their desires.[9] In so far as the question the opening scene poses revolves around something that Lear stops himself from doing, namely seeing Cordelia, this brings in a further aspect of avoidance. At issue is not just an inability to know what one means, but a refusal to let someone else see this epistemic fallibility. As Cavell puts it, 'if the failure to recognize others is a failure to let others recognize you, a fear of what is revealed to them, an avoidance of their eyes, then it is exactly shame which is the cause of [Lear's] withholding of recognition'.[10] The distinction between shame and guilt is crucial. While the latter seeks to avoid the discovery of a deed, the former serves as a cover up of oneself.

If recognizing a person depends upon allowing oneself to be recognized by them, the question *King Lear* like *Succession* poses leads to a second set of questions. Why should this be so difficult? Why do characters so staunchly choose not to reveal themselves to others? What kind of avoidance is this? It is, however, important to note: The refusal to be seen and subsequently to see is not relegated to the confused fathers. By having recourse to the word 'nothing' rather than say what she feels, Cordelia herself avoids being recognized, namely in her own confusion at her father's demand for a public display of intimacy. The same is true for Edgar, who pointedly avoids exposing his identity to his blinded father throughout their journey to Dover. The tragic consequences of the play thus hinge on the psychic and physical cruelty that this refusal to see and, in so doing, to acknowledge both the other and oneself, engenders. As Cavell notes, 'there are no lengths to which we may not go in order to avoid being revealed, even to those we love and are loved by. Or rather, especially to those we love and are loved by.'[11] At the same time, this refusal to see is also what the internal seriality of this play, which keeps returning to the aftereffects of a failed abdication, is predicated on. There are no lengths to which certain characters will not go to do something, instead of stopping, and seeing. The dramatic repetition compulsion is such that several characters go on doing the very thing that needs making up for—which is to say, they continue to harbor a blindness towards themselves and towards others. And this, in turn, sustains the drama of abuse—and therein lies one of the more pertinent lines of connection between *King Lear* and *Succession*—shown to be a consequence of their refusal to see.

For Cavell, the tragedy's opening scene thus boils down to three mutually entangled motivations: the attempt to avoid recognition, the shame of exposure, and the threat of self-revelation. Though it remains unclear what King Lear is ashamed of, or rather what revelation he is afraid of being shamed by, the symptom of this avoidance of love is the bribe he offers to his three daughters. Regan and Goneril accept the bribe and, in exchange for their premature inheritance, offer a public declaration of a love that has more to do with loyalty than affection. They understand this to be political theatre and accept the part their father assigns to them. Cordelia refuses to go along with this confusion of politics and love. The 'nothing' (I.i.87) she utters when called upon to speak is her own way of avoiding something shameful, namely the interpenetration of public display by an appeal to an intimacy a father and daughter should only share in private. Yet if, as Cavell suggests, Lear's bribe reflects his terror of being loved, the timing is also decisive. The moment at which he avoids being seen by his daughters, hiding behind his bribe, is also the moment when, proposing to divide his kingdom, the reality of lost power comes over him. The dilemma is of his own making. There was no need for him to abdicate. The love test he poses to his three daughters is really a self-test. Warding off the knowledge of his own vulnerability on the one hand and, on the other, warding off being loved proves to be two sides of the same coin. Both are a testament to his refusal to show himself as other than the omnipotent figure of sovereign power and authority he wants to believe himself to be, even though he knows this not to be the case. After all, to show himself willing to abdicate means accepting the end of his reign—indeed, to choose it.

In other words, if instigating a scene of premature abdication signals that he recognizes his unavoidable mortality, reneging on this promise is a sign that he cannot acknowledge what he knows. Instead, he undermines the very power which he, as sovereign, seeks to sustain. As Cavell notes, '[Lear] feels powerless to appoint his successor, recognized as the ultimate test of authority. The consequence is that politics becomes private.'[12] Indeed, it becomes a family affair in which the public and the private become fatally entangled. As such, Lear abdicates his responsibility in a double sense—towards his children and towards his subjects. The angry fury, the cursing, and finally the temporary madness that ensues: all these passions are part of the avoidance of being seen, of exposing himself to the one daughter who, at the onset, he possessively called 'our joy' (I.i.82) in the first act of the play. The tragic consequence of his refusal to be seen, and to see, is that Lear would rather cede the very authority he has done everything to maintain than be recognized in his fallibility by the one he loves most. Part of the internal dramatic repetition of the play, in turn, is that the avoidance, performed at the beginning of the play, is sustained throughout the ending. As Cavell argues, 'the final scene opens with Lear and Cordelia repeating or completing their actions in the opening scene: again Lear abdicates, and again Cordelia loves and is silent'.[13] At this point they have become prisoners of war and Cordelia asks her father, 'Shall we not see these daughters and these sisters?' (V.iii.7) His resolute 'no', repeated four times, suggests not only that he cannot face what he has done, namely produce division amongst his children. It also cements the very avoidance that has initiated and then sustained all the dramatic cruelty. In the face of this refusal, Cordelia is, once again, dumbstruck, and taken away by soldiers before she can respond.

Cavell contends, 'Lear's opening speech of this final scene is not the correction but the repetition of his strategy in the first scene, or a new tactic designed to win the old game; and it is equally disastrous', only to add 'and this means what it always does—he can't bear being seen'.[14] Instead, Lear imagines a scene of mutual imprisonment: him and Cordelia alone, telling old tales and laughing together, commenting on the trials and tribulations at court from a distance, as though they were God's spies. Lear thus not only gets himself and his daughter locked up in a prison cell but actually locks Cordelia up in his final fantasy of regal power. To the end, he cannot recognize her for what she is, a woman, separate from any self-projection and any claims to possession. Cordelia's death, one might surmise, is necessary, because Lear would rather have her dead than expose himself to her in all his vulnerability. This would be tantamount to acknowledging her separateness, which to avoid he had come up with the scheme of a false abdication in the first place. But there is something else he cannot bear—namely, to acknowledge that any one of his daughters, especially the one he enjoys most, will succeed him after a demise he knew from the start to be inevitable. To avoid this, the question of succession must be kept afloat at all costs, as a question still to be answered, to be posed over and again, not as a final decision to be made. Even if it means dying in the process.

Lear's staunch avoidance of recognition, coupled as it is with the shame of exposure, touches on a particularly salient theme of tragedy, namely the way actions can have consequences that outrun all bad, or good, intentions. What Cavell discovers in Shakespeare's reworking of this old theme is a way out of the conundrum this poses: 'For what it shows is that the *reason* consequences furiously hunt us down is not merely that we are half blind, and unfortunate, but that we go on doing the thing which produced these consequences in the first place.' The seriality inscribed in the internal dramatic structure of *King Lear* thus offers up two different courses of action: 'What we need is not rebirth, or salvation, but the courage, or plain prudence, to see and to stop. To abdicate. But what do we need in order to do that?'[15] The refusal to abdicate, in turn, is tantamount to a refusal to stop not seeing the other, not acknowledging the other—be it one's parent, one's child, or one's loyal friend. Cavell's point is that this is a conscious refusal, not something imposed by fate; it is something each of the characters in the play continues to do rather than doing something else. There is an alternative, but for some reason, to stop does not appear to be an option. All the raging, madness, jealousies, betrayals, and brutalities are preferable to that.

What then would it mean to see and to stop? The opposite of avoidance. Accepting the need for succession as this is predicated on acknowledging the other—and ourselves—in our separateness. As the opposite of avoiding exposure, to see and to stop would entail learning to reveal oneself, allowing oneself to be seen. It would mean putting oneself in the presence of another instead of keeping oneself in the dark, instead of treating the world as a great stage of fools where everyone plays their designated part. Lear's inability to stop turning his demands and deeds into theatre, however, also allows for a self-reflexive moment to be discovered in the play. His failure to see and to stop reveals the motivation on which the proclivity to theatricalization is predicated—namely the need to remain hidden and isolated, unwilling (or unable) to accept the suffering of others. One is safe from them because what is happening to them is conceived in terms of a theatrical performance. To see and to stop would, thus, require a perception of the other not as a player in a drama of one's own making, but rather as separate from oneself; it would mean accepting their alterity, putting oneself in their presence so as to truly face them, rather than keep avoiding their eyes.

The point, then, is that there is a way to avert tragedy. It isn't necessary to keep repeating actions which will have fatal consequences. This is a choice the characters make, and we are called upon to take notice of this. Lear need not have chosen to sacrifice either his daughter or the lives of his subjects. The fact that he does so suggests that choosing destruction is preferable to seeing and, subsequently, putting an end to the cycle of repetitive violence. This, in turn, is a question of interpretation. As Cavell notes, 'Tragedy grows from the fortunes we choose to interpret, to accept, as inevitable', which is to say from our desire to comprehend the world in terms of events repeatedly succeeding other events based on causation.[16] So the question is not just why characters subject themselves to paternal cruelty, but also why they accept that the serial repetition of abuse is inevitable. Why does the figure of paternal authority not abdicate from this fateful repetition when legitimate succession is the only promise that a nation (or a company) has if it wants to survive?

In part this involves epistemological avoidance. We prefer to anticipate the future, prefer to believe that an outcome of a series of events must be necessary, that the wheel inevitably comes full circle, rather than accept that the result of one's actions cannot be known with certainty. In part this involves the necessity of narrative succession as the driving force of any drama, and the distinction between stopping and ending on which this force is predicated. What goes on to happen after the opening of a play is not inevitable, even though each subsequent event bears the marks of what has happened before—much as all previous events may not have been inevitable, even if, once they have happened, the marks they leave are indelible. As Cavell points out, many of Shakespeare's plays 'close with the promises of words and understanding to come; as if to say, what has happened has stopped but it has not come to an end; we have yet to come to terms with what has happened; we do not know where it will end'.[17] Closure must be found, but from both a dramaturgic and an epistemological point of view, this leaves us at a crossroads. This is as true for the ending of *King Lear* as it is for Jesse Armstrong's appropriation of this tragedy.

Succeeding to *King Lear*

As I have argued in *Serial Shakespeare*, to look for Shakespeare's resilient legacy in contemporary TV drama means taking seriously the open-endedness of the dramatic resolutions he offers, when, returning to the point of departure, his plays re-pose the problems that set the dramatic action into motion in the first place. Let us, therefore, return once more to *Succession* and reconsider the crossmapping I propose through the lens of Cavell's discussion of the avoidance of self-revelation, as this plays itself out as a serial repetition of failed abdication. As in *King Lear*, the controversial problem raised by Jesse Armstrong's TV drama also resides in the nature of the conflicted motivation of his paterfamilias, introduced in the very first moments of the pilot of the show. 'Celebration' begins with Logan Roy snoring, grunting, and panting in his sleep. Upon awakening, he gets out of bed and gropes around in a room he doesn't recognize. The camera shows him to be both literally and figuratively in the dark. Confused, he whispers, 'Where am I?' and, continuing to move around though unable to see, repeats this question. The heartbeat on the soundtrack underscores his distress until he finally relieves himself. Only the appearance of his wife Marcia (Hiam Abbass) brings light to the scene, and both he and the audience realize that he has pissed on the floor of his bedroom, close to one of the walls. Still confused, he asks for the third time, 'Where am I?' and, to reassure him, Marcia explains, 'We're in the new place.'[18]

In contrast to Lear, who, after having been thrown out by his eldest daughter Goneril, asks, 'Who is it that can tell me who I am?' (I.iv.138), Logan's uncertainty pertains to place. The question is not who but rather where he is, and yet the answer that the Fool gives to the outraged king befits Logan's position as well. He is his own shadow. Marcia has organized a celebration for his eightieth birthday and all his children are about to assemble in this new home, where he has promised to announce Kendall as his successor. However, when he wanders into the living room a few hours later, still slightly disoriented, he picks up an issue of *Forbes Magazine* lying on the table in front of the mantlepiece. The title on the cover calls Kendall 'The Heir with the Flair'. Seeing his son in the symbolic place he still occupies, and thus as his nemesis, he is suddenly fully awake. He angrily tosses the magazine away and, with this gesture, signals that he is about to do the same with his favored son.

A few hours later, Logan calls his children to a private meeting in the room adjoining the dining room where the table has been set for an elegant lunch. He has an announcement to make, but not the one they expect. 'On the family trust, which will decide the situation in the event of my unlikely demise, I'm going to add Marcy to myself and you four', he explains, 'and my seat also to go to her on my death.' The camera captures his facial expression as he cunningly watches his children hesitate. He then adds, 'this is the present I really want', before finally coming out with the audacious declaration he has been working up to: 'despite the chatter and all things considered, I'm going to give it a couple of years ... I'll stay in situ, as chairman, CEO, head of the firm.' The camera work, using both rack shots and forward jumps, underscores the surprise on Kendall's face. Unable to find the right words to express his dismay and disappointment, he begins to stutter, but his attempt at responding is immediately interrupted. Signaling that he wants no further discussion, Logan calls out to all of them, 'Okay, come on, let's eat'. It is the beginning of a long series of attempts at avoiding recognition. Like Lear, he will not reveal himself to his son, which is to say he won't acknowledge him other than as a player in a drama, which he insists he is still directing.

By reversing the original sequence of events in the play, showing Logan's disorientation before the reneging of his promise, *Succession* draws into focus how this avoidance is predicated on shame. Logan is aware of his frailty, even names it explicitly by invoking both his 'unlikely demise' and his 'death', yet does so as a legal issue, which, furthermore, by not stepping down, he can prevent from happening, or at least stall. If, in the series of dramatic events that follow, he refuses to name which child will be next, then it is not only because he is testing all three of them over and again, to see which could best play the part. What is also rendered visible is that Logan feels powerless when it comes to appointing his successor because this would mean revealing his fallibility, to himself and to others. Assuring a smooth transition of power may be the ultimate test of his authority as head of the company, but not as a father. Tantamount to abdicating his symbolic body would be the foregrounding of his natural body, and that, in turn, would mean exposing what he is ashamed to reveal—the man behind the figure of power he has always performed for them, and of whom they are in such awe.

The discussion among the four children that sets in once Logan has left the room also sets the pattern for the serial intrigues to follow. With Kendall's succession suddenly uncertain and Marcia about to get a double vote on the trust, only the eldest son, Connor, staunchly walks out on his siblings, thus bodily underscoring his refusal to play his father's game. Both Shiv and Roman recognize this change in fortune as a golden opportunity, convinced that the one who succeeds in pleasing their father most will be the 'next one'. Yet if, in contrast to *King Lear*, the *mise-en-scène* places Logan's rebirth as sovereign in the very first episode of *Succession*, it is also here that the experience of bare life so seminal for Lear's return to his kingship is staged. In the family drama that Logan performs with his children, his assertion of absolute power emerges as his cover for the shame of self-exposure. When, at the end of 'Celebration', the twins, Shiv and Roman, have deferred signing the new trust that would give power to their unloved stepmother, Logan interprets this as a slight comparable to being thrown out of their respective homes. The stroke he has is his response. In *Succession*, the heath to which Shakespeare's king flees thus transforms into the coma into which Logan subsequently falls. During the brief interim that leaves him suspended between life and death, the son he has accused of being too soft to run the company tries to assert his prowess, but once Logan reawakens at the end of the second episode, he goes on doing the very thing which has produced the series of consequences that threaten the safety of his company—namely Waystar Royco's uncertain financial future as well as the cruise ship scandal.

It is telling that the latter hinges on a cover-up. Logan refuses to see, and to stop. Instead, aware of his frailness yet resiliently holding onto his power, he keeps replaying the failed abdication scene over and again. He hints at a future that will inevitably happen, namely his demise as CEO, even while refusing to specify what exactly it will look like to his children and the bevy of counselors that have also readily assumed their parts in his play. Part of the serial return to the love test in *Succession* involves a repeated public display of emotions on the part of the children, competing on screen against each other in performing their affection for their father at various lavish rituals, including a commemorative ceremony for Logan in his hometown in Scotland. Another part of this serial return is the *fort-da* game he plays with his children. Kendall is not alone in being banished from the company only to be recalled. Logan also brings Shiv into the company by promising her that she will be the next one, only to keep her in the dark regarding key decisions and then, when he feels he needs her advice, asking for it nevertheless. This indecision is comparable to the confusion Lear instigates when he divides his kingdom while wishing to retain his retinue. In Logan's case, however, one might say that he is also playing *fort-da* with himself—as though he were enjoying the mastery that continually playing at abdication in an open-ended sequence of events affords him. Tossing away and retrieving not only his children but also, albeit in fantasy, himself, is his way of confronting the tempest in the mind that he experienced in the opening scene of 'Celebration', by repeatedly covering it up. Even while, or rather by constantly anticipating the possibility of this ending, he can also prevent his demise as CEO from taking place.

The shame of exposure, which this game allows him to avert, is also the driving force behind another aspect of avoidance on which the *mise-en-scène* thrives, namely the avoidance of conversation. Throughout the first two seasons of *Succession*, not only Logan but also his children avoid revealing themselves to each other. Instead, they often respond to something they are told with Brian Cox's idiosyncratic 'uh, huh'. Culkin's, Snook's and Strong's performances renders visible how these siblings, like their father, hide behind a façade—be it Roman's joking, Shiv's elusiveness, or Kendall's earnestness, regardless of whether he is trying to oust his father (in the first season), robotically following his command (in the second), or once again trying to oust him (in the third season). These children have inherited Logan's wish to keep what he means to himself. This sustained practice of withholding not only holds the family together but also continues to produce the awe and terror all three feel for their father. Thus, while Logan keeps his children in the dark regarding his motivations and, instead, compels them to play parts on a stage he has devised for them, they also willingly (or unwittingly) do the same. By interrupting each other, by turning their attention away from others, as though distracted by something more important, which is to say by refusing to put themselves in the presence of those they should face, they are repeating their father's proclivity to avoid acknowledgement. They, too, treat each other as though they are always on stage, even in the most intimate encounters. If they can't perceive themselves as separate from their father because of the failed abdication he sustains, they also can't perceive others as separate from them. As such, they are all caught up in repeatedly doing what brought about their filial dilemma in the first place. Tossed away and retrieved over and again by their father, they can only resign to being players to his whims, so poignantly demonstrated in Brian Cox's performance of paternal mastery.

The *mise-en-scène* produces a particularly painful performance of shame during the commemorative ceremony in Scotland, and this is the one that fatefully ties Kendall to his father, compelling him to stand by him with a blind loyalty comparable to Cordelia's. In 'Nobody is Ever Missing', the final episode of season 1, Kendall's co-conspirators pressure him into announcing the takeover of Waystar Royco by competitors, which would finally force Logan to step down as CEO.[19] Kendall's sense of guilt after having delivered the 'bear hug' letter compels him to go in search of some cocaine, and this sets into motion a series of contingent events which he chooses to interpret as having been inevitable. The young man who is willing to supply him with drugs is himself already high and ends up driving his car into a lake. Kendall is able to save himself, leaving the other man to drown. But this also leaves him completely dependent on his father, who, because he is in cahoots with the local police, can cover up this irresponsible deed. The tears Kendall sheds during this meeting recall their confrontation in the first episode. Once again, Logan thwarts his son's hope that he will step down. Instead, the shame of having his deed exposed (as well as the legal consequences) compels Kendall to extricate himself from the hostile takeover. And once again, Logan refuses to see his son. Rather than forging an affective bond, based on compassion, he instrumentalizes Kendall even further in his effort not to cede power. The sad lethargy on Strong's face foregrounds how he has been forced into the role of robotic right hand to his father, seemingly willing to carry out all commands in a battle in which salvation will ultimately require a sacrifice.

In the face of the Senate hearings into the wrongdoing at Waystar Royco and its cruises, one of the lead shareholders suggests to Logan that he should be the one to take the fall. With this imminent threat of a forced abdication, the wheel does, indeed, seem to have come full circle. The financial fortune of the company now hangs on pure chance. This brings us once more to the beginning of this TV drama, with Logan and Kendall repeating and completing their actions in the opening episode. While in Shakespeare's tragedy, as Cavell puts it, again Lear abdicates and again Cordelia loves and is silent, *Succession* is aware of its serial needs, and thus gives a new spin to this dramaturgic inevitability in 'This Is Not for Tears'.[20] Once more united, as they were during the eightieth birthday party, all the members of the Roy family along with the counselors are waiting for an announcement. This time it is not the name of the successor they want to hear, but that of the scapegoat. It is clear to all that Logan, though the obvious choice for the shareholders, is not an option. After presiding over a public discussion in which everyone is called upon to say who they think would make the best fall guy, and in the process publicly tear each other apart, Logan calls his prodigal to a private audience. In this final confrontation, Kendall accepts his role without offering any resistance. He does, however, ask his father whether he ever thought he could have been his successor. In a final act of disavowal, Logan replies, 'You're not a killer. You have to be a killer.' That he only unwillingly allows Kendall to kiss him is again telling. Logan's shame of exposure is still well in place.

The unanticipated turn of events at the subsequent press conference can be read as a dramaturgic refiguration of Lear carrying Cordelia's corpse on stage; if, that is, we read this as the satisfaction of the desire behind his demand in the first scene of the play. If Lear could not bear Cordelia's separateness, then we might take this fusion in death to be the logical consequence of his previous fantasy about the bliss of joint incarceration—as an abdication from all abdication. In Kendall's case, he walks onto the stage with everyone expecting that he will publicly slaughter himself. He has been given a speech to read, in which he is to admit having directed a cover-up that never went any higher than himself. Opening his self-revelation by admitting that he would be a suitable figure to absorb the anger and concern regarding wrongdoing at Waystar Royco, he undermines the promise he made to his father, turning the wheel of fortune in his own favor. The camera repeatedly captures him in a close-up while he is addressing the journalists who have gathered in the room. Now fully self-confident, he proceeds to call his father a bully and a liar, who was fully aware of the events and their subsequent cover-up.

The parallel editing, in turn, draws into focus how fully he finally has his father's attention, who is sitting in front of the TV on the yacht. Utterly spellbound, Logan forbids either of the twins, who have joined him, to say a word during Kendall's public display of an intimacy that was meant to remain private. 'My father keeps a watchful eye over every inch of his whole empire', Kendall confesses with aplomb, 'and the notion that he would have allowed millions of dollars in settlements and compensations to be paid without his explicit approval is utterly fanciful.' Then, looking directly into the television camera, he performs the act of abdication for his father, declaring: 'This is the day his reign ends.' The parallel editing is such that in the reverse shot we see him gazing directly at Logan. He has finally produced a situation in which his father can no longer avoid his eyes, albeit through the medium he commands—the television screen. That this speech act satisfies Logan's desire is something we are asked to surmise. Enigmatically, Brian Cox smiles.

The open-endedness that this dramatic resolution affords returns us to the point of departure. Reborn is the son who, like Cordelia, defies his father. This does not, however, only re-pose the controversial problem that set the dramatic action into motion. Condensed in this final shot of Kendall, looking directly at his father from a TV screen, and Logan looking back, is also the conundrum of closure. In Kendall's face our knowledge about what had happened previously overlaps with our anticipation of the effect this will have, when the third season once more returns to the question of abdication. This time, Waystar Royco is compelled to fuse with another company and the TV drama thus returns to the failed abdication of the first act in *King Lear* with yet a further dramaturgic twist. Once more Logan betrays his promise to his children, this time drawing their mother into the game. She is about to be married again, which is why the entire family has convened in Tuscany. It is there that the children discover that their parents have decided to sell the company without asking for their consent, which again puts their succession into jeopardy.

In 'All the Bells Say', they bond together for the first time and with false confidence confront their father in the villa, where he has set up his war room.[21] To their surprise they discover that someone has already informed him of their battle plan. The *mise-en-scène* is such that Brian Cox, sitting on the arm of one of the sofas, is clearly in control, mocking the children who have come to battle with him. The handheld camera that moves between the characters, capturing them in medium shots and close-ups, underscores the emotional confusion. In the background, the two advisors Gerri and Frank quietly watch as Logan plays his trump card. Defiantly placing his cell phone on the table that separates him from his children, he tells their mother that she is on. Her disembodied voice makes them realize the extent to which they have been betrayed. A series of abruptly spliced together close-ups, as well as handheld shots that connect the various players to each other, visually underscore how the change in the divorce contract between the parents has left the children powerless.

Then, as in 'Celebration', when Logan had initiated his refusal to abdicate, he simply walks out on his children, signaling that he continues to avoid facing the emotional consequences of his paternal treachery. As he walks into the dark hall, he is met by Shiv's husband who has just arrived, and pats him on the shoulder. In the reverse shot, we see the bemused Shiv, gazing at this gesture. She suddenly realizes who has betrayed them, yet as Tom walks towards her and her siblings, she says nothing. The camera captures her as she walks away from him, panting in quiet despair, while he follows her and kisses her on the back of her head. This is a more complicated betrayal than the previous ones performed in *Succession* because it not only involves the mother—absent in Shakespeare's tragedy—but also the husband, who, like Albany, has now bonded with Logan against his wife. The three siblings, in turn, have become a 'Cordelia conglomerate', a significant refiguration of the sacrificial corpse that Lear carries onto the stage in the final act of the play, berating himself that he might have saved her. Having walked out on these children, Logan, however, does not berate himself. Instead, he signals that saving his children is precisely what he does not wish to do. Still unable to face his own shame, Armstrong's media king shames his children instead. As at the close of *King Lear*, we are at a crossroads, called upon to realize that here, too, the resolution the third season offers is provisional.

Shown on screen is again what it means to see, but not to stop. To continue. Despite the insight. Or perhaps because of it. That is the wager of complex TV drama.

Notes

1. Douglas Lanier, *Shakespeare and Modern Popular Culture* (Oxford: Oxford University Press, 2002), 9.
2. Stanley Cavell, 'The Avoidance of Love: A Reading of *King Lear*', in *Disowning Knowledge in Seven Plays of Shakespeare: Updated Edition* (Cambridge: Cambridge University Press, 2003).
3. Elisabeth Bronfen, *Serial Shakespeare: An Infinite Variety of Appropriations in American TV Drama* (Manchester: Manchester University Press, 2020).
4. Christina Wald, *Shakespeare's Serial Returns in Complex TV* (Cham: Springer / Palgrave Macmillan, 2020), 84f.
5. 'Shit Show at the Fuck Factory', s1:e2; dir. Mark Mylod, writ. Terry Roche, HBO 2018.
6. 'Hunting', s2:e3; dir. Anfrij Parekh, writ. Tony Roche, HBO 2019.
7. 'Argestes', s2:e6; dir. Matt Shakman, writ. Susan Soon He Stanton, HBO 2019.
8. Cavell, 'The Avoidance of Love', 42.
9. For a discussion of how treating one's child as an extension of oneself means there is no separateness, see Emily Sun, *Succeeding King Lear: Literature, Exposure and the Possibility of Politics* (New York: Fordham University Press, 2010). As Sun notes, all the corpses at the end of the play indicate how vehemently these fathers want to make sure that there will be no succession, at least not by their natural-born children.
10. Cavell, 'The Avoidance of Love', 49.
11. Ibid., 56.
12. Ibid., 68.
13. Ibid., 68.
14. Ibid., 68. If *Succession* seems stuck in the first act of Shakespeare's tragedy, Claire McEachern's point that *King Lear* seems to begin again and again is, in itself, poignant. In *Believing in Shakespeare: Studies in Longing* (Cambridge: Cambridge University Press, 2018), she notes that Lear fights first with one daughter, then with another. The Fool keeps reminding him of what he has done. Kent tries throughout to put his king back on the throne. Cordelia tries to restore her father to his senses. 'Despite all the schemes', McEachern concludes, 'the action never seems to move forward from the mire of the initial scene; it just replays it over and over again' (245).
15. Cavell, 'The Avoidance of Love', 81.
16. Ibid., 89.
17. Ibid., 113.
18. 'Celebration', s1:e1; dir. Adam McKay, writ. Jesse Armstrong, HBO 2018.
19. 'Nobody Is Ever Missing', s1:e10; dir. Mark Mylod, writ. Jesse Armstrong, HBO 2019.
20. 'This Is Not for Tears', s2:e10; dir. Mark Mylod, writ. Jesse Armstrong, HBO 2019.
21. 'All the Bells Say', s3:e9; dir. Mark Mylod, writ. Jesse Armstrong, HBO 2020.

4

When TV is on TV: Metatelevision and the Art of Watching TV with the Royal Family in *The Crown*

David LaRocca

While there is a range of compelling cases in which television shows reference other television shows (e.g., by stylistically imitating them, such as in *WandaVision* [2021–], explored in this volume by Stephen Mulhall), my focus here is on the literal presence of television (e.g., a television set or the display of television footage, whether archival or ersatz) in a television show, namely *The Crown* (2016–). Thus, in the lexicography of metamedia, I am turned less towards reference and more towards reflexivity: not TV as TV, but TV in TV, or TV on TV. Reference typically highlights a creator's cultural frames of reference (e.g., other media texts), while reflexivity generates an often-vertiginous *mise en abyme*; in the latter case, and in our case in what follows, for instance, we are invited to watch TV in company with those who are watching TV—and in *The Crown*, this means the Royal Family, including the Queen herself. Instead of being an audience for the Queen, we are an audience with the Queen. Moreover, in Garrett Stewart's innovative parlance, we are implicated in 'apparatus reading', which not only aligns our interest with the presence of television (e.g., the TV set) but also, in a highly complementary fashion, heightens the stakes of 'medial immanence'.[1] Metatelevision, as we find it in *The Crown*, puts us in a shared position as viewers, as listeners, thus amplifying the Queen's humanity (as a fellow viewer of history on screen) and as a person with whom we can share company; by these reflexive techniques, the radical asymmetry of monarch and subject is flattened.[2] Like us, the Queen is just another (often solitary) viewer, even as we—from this imagined distance, looking over her shoulder—share in the phenomenology of her relation to the screen.

David LaRocca, 'When TV is on TV: Metatelevision and the Art of Watching TV with the Royal Family in *The Crown*' in: *Television with Stanley Cavell in Mind*. University of Exeter Press (2023). © David LaRocca. DOI: 10.47788/WIGS5588

As many viewers of *The Crown* know, Peter Morgan, the show's creator and head writer, had earlier demonstrated his proclivity to draw from archival television footage in *The Queen* (2006)—written by Morgan, directed by Stephen Frears—a habit that he sustains in his television series (strikingly, for instance, from the first frames of 'Fagan' [s4:e5]). Yet he has also expanded and innovated upon this approach so that the show's repertoire includes faux television footage (for example, see the memorable framing of 'Dear Mrs Kennedy' [s2:e8], which begins and ends with footage of actor Jodi Balfour playing Jacqueline Kennedy; or 'Vergangenheit' [s2:e6], which starts with the Queen and the Queen Mother watching television coverage of the arrival in England of American pastor Billy Graham; or look to the initial narrative characteristics of the show—for example, the first season's 'Hyde Park Corner' [s1:e2], in which a proud father, King George VI, played by Jared Harris, watches his daughter, Elizabeth, on television as she and Philip undertake a four-continent Commonwealth tour).[3]

In other, related research I have explored the presence of the home movie—including the camera itself, the projection of the contained film, and the adoption of a home movie aesthetic in the containing film.[4] And I have articulated the prominent and evolving domain of metacinema.[5] In the present study of *The Crown*, I presume an appreciation for the role of the home movie camera (since it too is a hallmark of the early seasons of the show) and the traits of metacinema, while amplifying our attention to the television set and the broadcasting of live and pre-recorded sounds and images in the context of a dramatic TV show's narrative; following Stanley Cavell, then, a preoccupation with the meaning of film as '*a succession of automatic world projections*' is complemented by an interest in television as '*a current of simultaneous event reception*'.[6]

With metacinema in mind (how could it not remain relevant in such a case as the cinematically lush Netflix-produced drama?), I consider how metatelevision is a kindred phenomenon (perhaps at a time when streaming production houses have drawn seriality into conversation with the cinematic) and yet, to be sure, how it offers its own distinctive traits and illuminating tendencies. Attention to the formal nature and achievements of metatelevision such as *The Crown* is accompanied, in turn, by a consideration of content (again involving apparatus reading). Indeed, an underlying claim for metaworks, especially accomplished instances, is the degree to which they make form and content interdependent and mutually reinforcing: formal innovation teaches us about content, and in turn, content tutors us about the significance of form.

There are, of course, many exemplary works of preexisting scholarship that bear directly on remarks in this chapter—some stretching back decades, some fresh from the critic's keypad, all germane to these deliberations. I have drawn a few examples out from the endnotes, since the select labors of John Thornton Caldwell, George Wilson, and Murray Pomerance contribute so much to the pre-history and ongoing negotiation about what we mean by metacinema, and more particularly on this occasion, what we notice when such traits familiar to moving pictures arrive under the aegis of television. (And the list, of course, goes on: V.F. Perkins, Gilberto Perez, George Toles.) For instance, Caldwell's innovative work on televisuality in the 1990s looks back at the evolution and 'crisis of network television' in the 1980s *and* anticipates changes in the medium on the near horizon at the turn of the twenty-first century.[7] Caldwell emphasizes how televisuality cultivated, among other things, a 'stylizing performance' that countered the moribund state of much existing network television. Before theories of 'cinematic television' could be applied to *Sopranos*-and-after endeavors, Caldwell's videographic televisuality offered a matrix of instances that could be tracked along formal, authorial, generic, and historical axes. Moreover, Caldwell's deep focus on the history of television yields discoveries and reminders such as '*Leave It to Beaver* was no stranger to self-consciousness and aesthetic reflexivity.'[8] With an episode like 'Beaver on TV' (1963, s6:e22), we are given to remember the extent to which the metatelevisual was an accessible and cleverly deployed formal property decades before its widespread presence in the current era.

Another set of crucial contributions to our thinking about metatelevision can be found in George Wilson's *Narration in Light*, which incarnates 'studies in cinematic point of view'.[9] Wilson's coupling of narration and point-of-view transforms our understanding of how aesthetic features of *mise-en-scène*, for instance, may underwrite structural aspects of storytelling, and indeed, how cinema is an art—as Cavell has also emphasized—insistently, pervasively 'concerned' with its existence as an art (the scare quotes are in place to admit the inescapable anthropomorphism on this point).[10] Moreover, cinema as art transforms the very possibilities of philosophy (another intermedial illumination—since, as Cavell said, film was as if made for philosophy, a veritable, perceptible embodiment of philosophy's accumulated, if still-contested, claims, lessons, and convictions).[11] Self-aware cinema and the human awareness of thinking (these tandem reflexivities) feel perpetually pertinent to one another. Wilson's observations on 'self-conscious narration' thus highlight the many ways in which filmmakers call attention to 'the boundaries of the frame, the recording presence of the camera, or the visual discontinuities the editing imposes'.[12] The syntagma 'cinematic thinking' suddenly seems a profound pun, a confirmation of an undeniably double status. Such strategies have been readily imported to televisual narration and the stylistics of point-of-view on the small screen, and how could they not be when the likes of Michael Mann are given the reigns of *Miami Vice* (1984–89)? Murray Pomerance brings home this point in the opening salvo of *Uncanny Cinema*, where he begins a book largely about movies by discussing *The Crown*. Given Pomerance's devotion to studying scores of films, it is a testament to the signal importance—the 'cinematic' vitality—of *The Crown* that it stands as an inaugural specimen.[13]

With these and related touchstones at hand—and in the context of the volume's aspirations more generally—Cavell's remarks on the ontology of television and moral perfectionism also activate and enrich any approach to the formal and the content-specific as it is enframed, narrated, and projected. Watching television with Stanley Cavell in mind means one can illustrate what is at stake in parsing medial differences and alignments (with respect to cinema and/or/as television), and how such observations productively enhance our appreciation of metatelevision—and more generally of what it is TV series do, what they achieve.

* * * *

The Crown is a multi-season historical drama television series created by Peter Morgan and produced by Netflix that focuses on the Royal Family of Great Britain, centered on events populating the life and reign of Queen Elizabeth II (1926-2022). The series is pre-dated by two other related works by Morgan: the feature film *The Queen* (2006, dir. Stephen Frears), more tightly conscribed around the death of Princess Diana and the aftermath as handled by Elizabeth circa 1997; and the stage play, and more immediate inspiration for the show, entitled *The Audience* (2013), focused on weekly meetings ('audiences') with the Queen. The titles of the film and play offer bold relief to two major elements in *The Crown*, namely depictions of the Queen's opinions, decision-making, personality, and personal life, and the way these are discovered or expressed in a series of private encounters she has with a range of people—from prime ministers (such as Winston Churchill) to family members, from household staff to trespassers.[14] Morgan's decades-long commitment to the depiction of the Royal Family, and especially Elizabeth—and across three major types of art (film, theatre, and television)—provides a rich site for the exploration of intermedial traits, already a gesture of any meta-investigation. What is more, Morgan has exhibited, first in Frears' *The Queen* and now in *The Crown*, a special talent for representing perspectivism: that is, scenes in which we, 'the audience', are presented as an audience to the Queen as she, in her presence on screen, receives an audience.[15] The presence of a TV set, however, amplifies yet another facet, one in which the Queen herself is made audience to the screen in her midst.

Because of the temporal longitude of the reign of Elizabeth II, the series covers a vast swath of time, which provides Morgan an opportunity not merely to acknowledge evolving, emerging, and sometimes eclipsed technologies of representation as he tells one story and the next, but also a chance to put them to use aesthetically in the diegesis of the work—and not just as props but as machines that generate content (e.g., portable motion picture cameras) or display it (such as broadcast television). In an effort to ground the philosophical treatment of Morgan's achievements, let us integrate close analysis of these varied technologies in the context of specific scenes, plotlines, characterizations, dialogue, *mise-en-scènes*, and much else—especially those moments in which television is featured or otherwise transformed *on* television, i.e., on the show we call *The Crown*. When coupled with Cavell's remarks on media ontology, television as situated with or beside cinema, and perfectionist traits as found in narrative art, we are poised to better appreciate the specific metatelevisual achievements of *The Crown*.

Looking and listening to the series itself, a necessarily selective, and therefore incomplete, catalogue of conspicuous and fascinating instances will afford the chance for deep dives into a few wonderfully fractal scenes. We pick up at the point when Philip (Matt Smith), by dint of timing and insight, appears to have created the ground zero of the modern television age: his hectoring plea to his wife, Elizabeth (Claire Foy), that she allows her coronation to be televised live—and globally. What at first blush may seem a stunt, a bit of vanity, even a foolish moment of self-inflicted harm, turns out to be a visionary turning point in television history. In an uncanny, if informed, echo of such familial media savvy and innovation, on the occasion of his inheritance of the crown from his just-deceased mother, King Charles III chose to telecast his inaugural address as sovereign, and soon after—shifting from clandestine to revealed—the proclamation of the new sovereign's accession before the Ascension Council at St. James's Palace was also televised live. A double-impulse—to make the private public via broadcast and also to retain, or reclaim (as if to rescind), privacy in the face of 'overexposure' by the same means—remains a leitmotif of the House of Windsor. While much 'coverage' of the Royal Family tends to trade in the lexicon and dramatic arcs of scandal, Elizabeth was aware, sometimes playfully, of the *fort-da* of concealment and revelation: 'When a courtier suggested that she was giving TV cameras too much access to her private life, she retorted: "I have to be seen to be believed!"'[16]

In the first season's 'Smoke and Mirrors' (s1:e5), television makes its most elaborate debut in the series, as it did in the lives of the characters and indeed, the world at large. David, Duke of Windsor and the former King Edward VIII, who abdicated in 1936, hosts a soirée in which a small black-and-white television set is the star of the occasion—along with the new Queen being sanctified on screen.[17] This was June 1953. Cavell suggests that 'television's first major accomplishment can be dated to no later than 1953', but he has in mind the coverage of Dwight D. Eisenhower's presidential inauguration in January of that year.[18] Either way, the broadcast—or better, global simulcast—of live footage of such events marked a turning point in the human experience of, and thus thinking about, the 'sheer fact that television exists', an 'existence' Cavell tells us that remains 'among the most obvious and the most mysterious facts of contemporary life'.[19] It also transformed the presence of television into a global phenomenon; the *New York Times* declared that the broadcast 'marked the birth of international television'.[20] Ever after, television's ubiquity would be partner to its mystery.

As with the radio, telegraph, phonograph, telephone, cinema, and other medial technologies, what at first seems like a tool or 'appliance'—indeed, in the early days of television, a veritable piece of furniture—in turn, in time, becomes a site for art. For a quick analogue, consider how significantly the notion of 'phone' has transformed between 2007 and the present—since now 'phone' means, well, everything: telephony, texting, camera, video, video telephony, email, web browser, maps, calendar, social media, and a billion bespoke apps. Still, the strangeness of televisual reality may go unrecognized precisely because of its ubiquity; in addition to the 'phone', or in league with it, consider how seamlessly and invisibly the internet circulates through our lives, prompting our notice principally when the signal drops and we are blocked from our immersion in 'the portal'.[21] We are caught between recommendations that the internet be treated like a utility and others that find it an occasion for the exploration of computational art.[22] By comparison, television per se may seem quaint—a familiar holdover from an earlier age that is finding new traction as it becomes, somehow, more 'cinematic' (or simply cinematic, full stop), a shift that has underwritten the pliable notion, and thus ongoing phenomenon, of 'prestige TV' and its heirs in the age of streaming platforms and 'on demand content'.[23]

What Cavell called the 'aesthetic possibilities of a medium' in cinema, then, have taken time to announce themselves in television (along an arc traceable to at least 1953), and we must place ourselves in a position to take such possibilities seriously if they are to become sensible to us.[24] To begin with, and more on this below, Cavell postulates that a shift from singular work (say, a film) to the serial and episodic (what we call 'the series' or 'the show', what Cavell calls 'the program'[25]) offers an 'ontological recharacterization' that 'should be of essential aesthetic concern';[26] indeed, this description is one of the core nerves on which the present investigation presses. And with even more pressure applied, we look to the ways in which the *internalization* of television within a TV show—a kind of digestion of the medium by the medium—heightens the interplay between ontology and aesthetics. With *The Crown*, and kindred metatelevision, the expression of televisual ontology—experimenting with its possibilities—becomes its own bona fide aesthetic, one that can be traded across genres. Just as it was a 'guiding thesis' of Cavell's *The World Viewed* 'that major films are those in which the medium is most richly or deeply revealed', we are positioned to explore how major works of television, such as *The Crown*, provide access not simply into the evolution of storytelling (across media types), but a special glimpse of the potentialities of television in its once and evolving nature—indeed, in something that may pass for 'maturity'.[27]

Cavell was, way back in the 1970s and in the early 1980s, when 'The Fact of Television' appeared in the immediate wake of *Pursuits of Happiness*, already prepared to say that 'masterpieces among movies reveal the medium of film' by means of 'individual works' (and as such 'these works have a status analogous to traditional works of art'); thus, *Citizen Kane* is 'individual' in the way its duration is at once enclosed (viz., running time) and foreclosed (e.g., there is no sequel, no companion piece to follow). A different logic applies to television, a logic imposed by the medium and how it is used: what is 'memorable, treasurable, criticizable', Cavell says of what he sees on television, 'is not primarily the individual work, but the program, the format, not this or that day of *I Love Lucy*, but the program as such'.²⁸ As noted, let us update the terminology by way of cognates: for 'the program, the format', we can read 'the show', 'the series', 'the platform', and similar. Thus, when Cavell remarks that television's 'value is a function of its rule of format',²⁹ he is thinking of how the medium has evolved to speak of 'seasons' and 'episodes'.

In the present engagement with *The Crown*, I mean not only to find ways of taking the show seriously (as serious television), but, in the light of Cavell's work, to conjure reflections 'intended as something like experiments to test' intuitions about the 'aesthetic range of the phenomenon we know as television'.³⁰ Cavell's frontier metaphor serves the medium well, since it affords television the diversity of expressions it clearly demands of us: the mini- and limited series, the multi-year season-based serial, the tent-pole franchise and its spin-offs (sequels, prequels), live entertainment and cultural events, sports, weather reports, game shows, talk shows, sitcoms, news, documentary, commercials, social media incarnations and hybridizations with TV, and the way all of these modes, among others, interact with distribution on platforms and make contact with viewers via a range of devices (no longer just the 'TV set'). Cavell, of course, lists movies too—since television as a mode of scheduled repertory and revivalist screenings was familiar to his age, less so ours; we have become accustomed to 'streaming' and 'on demand', which afford viewers unrehearsed access as well as control over playback (e.g., pausing, rewinding, etc.).³¹ And we have been dealing with devices and platforms all along, which is one of the many things *The Crown* provides an accomplished glimpse of: there is King George VI watching a newsreel, there is Philip documenting his travels on film, there is Margaret leading a news conference, there is Charles giving a televised speech, there is the Queen watching a television set, and so on.

The aggressive referentiality of *The Crown* stirs an awareness of the medium (as befits Morgan's accomplished meta-methodologies), yet the references are, for the most part, enlisted in the service of the plot; in this way the fabula is furthered by each subsequent reference. *The Crown* deploys TV as a prop, but as one that gives shape and meaning to the narrative—that is, television in such instances is most keenly deployed as an expository device. Though we have seen it before, broadcast TV as depicted in *The Crown* is especially oracular: it announces the historical world to the fictionalized realm we recognize as the mythologized history of the British Royal Family of the twentieth century. History makes contact with fiction and television is the interface between them. The episode 'Moondust' (s3:e7), for instance, dramatizes the way in which a family—any family, even a royal one—finds its life consequentially entwined with television. In this case, Philip, like the Queen, has the power, as it were, to reach through the television to summon the Apollo astronauts to an audience of his own. Philip's passionate monitoring of the moon landing in 1969—televised live—mobilizes a euphoric effect in him; yet when he speaks in person with John Glenn and crew newly back from spaceflight, his stratospheric enthusiasms for their achievement are brought crashing down, figured perhaps most casually in the sniffling noses of the 'otherworldly' creatures before him.

Philip, it turns out, sits at the inflection point of many technologies of display, especially as they affect the life of the family. Consider how the home-movie-camera-cum-documentary-camera, of which Philip inadvertently became a savvy practitioner, could also be used to serve the desires of a major television network such as the BBC. Thus, when a documentary production is pitched to the Royal Family, Philip is defensive and put out, especially because it means risking renewed attention to his origins, including the existence of his dying mother, herself an exiled aristocrat. In an episode entitled 'Bubbikins' (s3:e4), the mother's affectionate nickname for her son, Philip, the film is rolling and the pressure on the family is felt in a range of responses—from knowing performativity to reluctant noncompliance to brilliantly self-aware meta-commentary in the last case, when the Queen's sister, Margaret (in this season played by the incomparable Helena Bonham Carter) says: 'We are being filmed watching television. The people might watch us watching television on their own television sets at home. This really is plumbing new depths of banality.'[32] And to plumb them further, of course, we—Netflix viewers—are watching the Royal Family watching television, the BBC documentary film of which might be seen by 'the people', and so on (including a glimpse of what they, the Royal Family, are watching—namely, a documentary about the coming computer revolution, with voice-over announcing: 'Europe's first home computer terminal. They're simple to operate, and experts predict that in twenty years' time all new houses will be built with special computer points and that terminals will be cheaper to rent than today's telephones.') The *mise en abyme* here is at a nadir, and presented with accomplished intensity, which makes the scenes—and the narrated, self-conscious commentary—all the more emblematic for the coursings of *The Crown*, a show that undertakes a rehearsal of such 'documentary' instincts and observations in every frame (again, stepping back to see the entire show, *The Crown*, as an elaborately staged home movie, if presented in the key of reenactment—along with varying degrees of evocation and impersonation). In short, the implied gimmick of the undertaking requires not just that familiar demand for a 'willing suspension of disbelief', but a kind of *participation* in the stakes of the artifice: what we do as viewers is dive headlong into the abyss, joining the nested figures, one atop another.

It is, of course, ironic—and splendidly so—that one of the most celebrated television shows of the decade announces the 'banality' of offerings from the medium it finds itself contributing to, somehow managing to make vacuity interesting by means of dramatic tension and the particular powers of reflexivity. Distracted by *our own interest* in the interest characters are taking in their experience (e.g., fear, boredom, frustration, confusion, etc.), suddenly the scene that is called out for its lack of drama becomes overdetermined by its overflowing abundance of it. Philip standing off screen from the documentary crew—presiding over all the seated family members being filmed—is, to be sure, watching the watchers, even as we are positioned behind him, watching him, and so on. A frame such as we find at 00:32:53 captures the metatelevisual at a moment of formidable artistry, but not without *also* presenting to us a picture of our contemporary predicament with respect to seeing and being seen, and that cruel burden gifted by photography: the ever-present tension between 'recording' and 'experiencing'. This frame offers a tableau of modern life as we know it on screen and off, part of the willing (if occasionally conflicted) self-surveillance that began with the Kodak Brownie, went animated with the 8mm home movie camera, and has continued its march through Polaroids, VHS camcorders and mini-DV recorders, Flip cameras, and now GoPro units, iPhones, and Zoom; the active uploading of audiovisual content to the internet, including YouTube, TikTok, and other public-facing social media websites; and, we are told, will evolve yet again in the metaverse.[33]

Cavell, as if picking up the strain of Margaret's sentiment, observes how television—in the aftermath of World War II, the Holocaust, atomic annihilation (and the specter of more devastation to come), the threat of subsequent wars, a rise in criminal activity, economic crisis, the diminishment of social cohesion, and the general degradation of the natural environment—contributed to 'producing the present world of shut-ins'.[34] Consider the number of times in *The Crown* that we TV viewers are presented with a scene of the Queen watching (her own) TV—in solitariness, or with one or two others for company. (And yet another long list would find other characters watching films and TV on their own screens.) Elizabeth, in such moments, is an avatar for the postwar shut-in, a status that remains fully intact (and perhaps especially pronounced at moments of crisis: heat waves, snowstorms, and of course, most saliently in recent memory, a global pandemic that for the privileged entailed baking bread and bingeing TV, which in their ways gave shape to days, weeks, and months of quarantine). Well before *The Crown* emblematized the scenario, Cavell noted:

> what [television] monitors, apart from events whose existence preceded its own (cultural coverage, sports, movies), are so often settings of the shut-in, a reference line of normality or banality so insistent as to suggest that *what* is shut out, that suspicion whose entry we would at all costs guard against, must be as monstrous as, let me say, the death of the normal, of the familiar as such.[35]

No doubt, Margaret would approve.

One of the most obvious yet strange facts of royal TV watching as we see it portrayed on *The Crown* settles on the fact that they watch (live and pre-recorded) news and nonfiction coverage (a holdover from the earlier film newsreels and home movies that tracked the first two seasons). Not shows. No *Bewitched* or *All in the Family*, no *The Cosby Show* or *Seinfeld*. In fact, the television broadcasts we see in *The Crown* are seldom merely background—offering a familiar sonic landscape of the indecipherable or inaudible—but rather the main event, or part of the principal action of the scene. Moreover, TV in these myriad instances becomes more than a cleverly deployed expositional conceit, and instead a character in its own right, projecting a world into the diegesis (much as, at present, the smartphone has become a character, displacing the hegemony of the TV as a point of reference; and relatedly, frequent display of text messages over the action is now part of the larger repertoire, as seen for example in *Sex Education*, *Emily in Paris*, and *Deadwind*, among others). Actors, then, respond to historical verities, absorbing and contending with them as if they were contemporaneous with the event itself. Similar to films that use news content—including genuine news footage, such as *The Queen*—we see how this technique in *The Crown* underwrites the reality credentials of the show. From newsreels to real news, the approach not only provides elegant, concentrated exposition, it also heightens the stakes of the drama by tying it to a shared historical world (of which, it turns out, *The Crown* is now a part). Where the first is a clever propellant for plotting, the latter is a trick that usually goes unnoticed (and the same goes for the inclusion of home movie footage).[36]

Given the conceptual layering and reflexivity at work in *The Crown*, it should not come as a surprise—especially for admirers of the show, and those who enjoy the challenges of making sense when ontology interacts with aesthetics—that Morgan's metatelevision activates human metacognition. The show courts us to notice our awareness of awareness. It is, therefore, a testament to Morgan's art and those of his creative accomplices, that metacognition *enriches* the experience of watching *The Crown* rather than defeats it. The show is not a self-sabotaging curiosity, much less a chagrining group portrait—for instance, as in the key of Caveh Zahedi's *The Show about the Show* (2015–21). In Zahedi's hands, metacognition leads to confounding logic, persistent anxiety, and (thus) narrative frustration for him and his viewers alike. By contrast, Morgan and his team have found ways of making an awareness of *mise en abyme* an asset that both clarifies narrative sense and adds genuine philosophical depth.

At a fundamental level of media archaeology (reaching back to the very first frames of moving pictures), we are faced with the experience of watching human behavior—initially the movements of bodies, then, some decades later, what these people say, how they sound, how they interact through speech, and including the sounds of the natural or built environment. There is something strangely ethnographic about the serial scenes of the Queen—and the Royal Family—watching TV: as if, despite pedigree and privilege and the power to meet with anyone on earth, these humans are, like us, shut-ins framed by a radical isolation that also, somehow, offers the comfort of company. Paradoxically, alone in a room watching TV, one may seldom feel alone. And the Queen herself appears duly aware of such effects: in her annual Christmas message, delivered during the rapid spread of the Omicron variant, she aimed to offer comfort, perspective, and a reminder of where to find both: 'While covid again means we can't celebrate quite as we may have wished, we can still enjoy the many happy traditions', the Queen said. 'Be it the singing of carols, as long as the tune is well known; decorating the tree; giving and receiving presents; or watching a favourite film where we already know the ending'.[37]

Still, Buckingham Palace makes for a peculiar homestead. Its royal inhabitants can seem to be imprisoned there as much as housed—these televised glimpses offering a view of a largely alien world beyond the gates, even as most outsiders are alien to Buckingham Palace. The Queen, it turns out, lives in a giant, fortified spacecraft permanently landed in central London. Inside, it could still be 1925 or 1955, 1975 or 2000. TV—as technology and as a mode of communication—is among the few most salient attributes of this hermitic realm over the course of Elizabeth's reign from 1952 to the present. And given the uncanny time horizon (namely, that her reign coincides with the entire existence of television), could it be that Elizabeth was the world's oldest living and most long-standing (television) celebrity—and yet perhaps among its least known? Her fame reached its fitting apogee during 'Her Majesty's last broadcast', when her funeral was beamed live to billions across the earth. As James Poniewozik put it, the broadcast 'felt like a capstone to the mass TV era that defined her reign', a reign 'marked by unprecedented visibility'—especially as it was made possible via television.[38] On this occasion, as on so many others, the 'camera's vigil was constant'. And TV coverage of the funeral marked yet another first for the Queen, which is to say, her last first: allowing television access to the otherwise private ceremony, including the rituals of her entombment at Windsor Castle.

Many of us today watch TV for company—for its positive parasocial effects. We get involved in the lives of others, even though the prospect of participation or interaction is mechanically impossible (as Cavell noted long ago about film).[39] With film, 'the stars are only to gaze at, after the fact, and their actions divine our projects'.[40] We know them, but they do not know us; and yet, the intimacy of television—first in our living rooms, and now in our beds, in our pockets—creates the impression, a deep and abiding one, that we are, indeed (somehow), implicated in these lives. Or better, these lives live in us. With the Queen, by contrast, her observation of television functions more like the receipt of a letter: she often can or must respond to the events she sees on her screen (e.g., news coverage of this or that crisis, some of them involving her and her family). The Queen, like others in power and unlike most of us, can go a step further 'into' interactivity with the medium. She is *on* the news, yes, as if passively; yet she can also, in turn, actively participate in its creation. Hence a royal take on 'media relations', which no doubt began in earnest when Philip caught sight of television's radical potential—one that can cut both ways.

Because metatelevision intensifies our intimacy with worlds (on screen and off), it must also increase our sense of moral obligation to the lives we are made privy to (again, on screen and off). It may be unsurprising, if still mysterious, to discover that the cumulative effect of such extended close proximity to the Queen and her family would resolve itself into a fan's posture of committed monarchism. Metatelevision implicates viewers—makes them complicit—in ways that standard narrative does not cultivate, does not require. Though we remain divided from the diegetic space (as all encounters with television, meta or otherwise, insist), the sustained reflexivity of the *mise en abyme* inscribes our place as watchers—as monitors to these scenes of monitoring. As voyeurs caught—and caught up—by our meta-relation to the characters and their historical referents, to the television within the frame and to our own televisions, we watch nervously, knowing that we are ethically beholden one to another, to those on screen and those who address it. Unlike a *Verfremdungseffekt* that would alienate us from what we see and hear, our awareness of ourselves watching *The Crown* achieves the obverse. We are implicated, imbricated in scenes, summoned time and again to an audience with the Queen and her royal retinue—called to acknowledge and to be acknowledged.

Notes

1. Garrett Stewart, *Cinemachines: An Essay on Media and Method* (Chicago: University of Chicago Press, 2020), 3–4.
2. Deliberation on the nature and meaning of metatelevision has been sporadic, but there are usefully orienting dispatches. For a recent engagement, see Jen Chaney, ''When Did TV Get So Meta?', *Vulture*, February 10, 2017, and a more formative one, Scott R. Olson, 'Meta-Television: Popular Postmodernism', *Critical Studies in Mass Communication*, vol. 4, no. 3 (1987), 284–300. See also my *Metacinema: The Form and Content of Filmic Reference and Reflexivity* (Oxford: Oxford University Press, 2021), 6, 27n22, and 312.
3. Elizabeth and Philip are also the names of the principal pair in *The Americans* (2013–18), another show that has an ostensive topic (espionage) and then less overt but even more impactful sets of subthematics (among them, marriage and parenting). See my '"You Must Change Your Life": *The Americans*, (Concepts and Cults of) Authenticity, and EST', in *The Americans and Philosophy*, ed. Robert Arp and Kevin Guilfoy (Chicago: Open Court, 2018); and 'Of Mothers and Motherlands: Figurations of Parenting and Patriotism in *The Americans*', in *Cold War II: Hollywood's Renewed Obsession with Russia*, ed. Tatiana Prorokova-Konrad (Jackson: University of Mississippi Press, 2020). See also Chapter 14 of this volume: Sandra Laugier, 'Love, Remarriage, and *The Americans*'.
4. See my 'On the Aesthetics of Amateur Filmmaking in Narrative Cinema: Negotiating Home Movies after *Adam's Rib*', in *The Thought of Stanley Cavell and Cinema: Turning Anew to the Ontology of Film a Half-Century after* The World Viewed, ed. David LaRocca (New York: Bloomsbury, 2020).
5. See LaRocca, *Metacinema*.
6. Stanley Cavell, *The World Viewed: Reflections on the Ontology of Film* (Cambridge, MA: Harvard University Press, 1971; Enlarged edition, 1979), 72; Stanley Cavell,

'The Fact of Television', in *Themes Out of School: Effects and Causes* (San Francisco: North Point Press, 1984), 205. Italics in original.
7   John Thornton Caldwell, *Televisuality: Style, Crisis, and Authority in American Television* (New Brunswick: Rutgers University Press, 1995). See especially chapter 1, 3–31.
8   Caldwell, *Televisuality*, 40.
9   George M. Wilson was among the earliest reviewers of *The World Viewed*; see *The Philosophical Review*, vol. 83, no. 2 (April 1974), 240–44.
10 George M. Wilson, *Narration in Light: Studies in Cinematic Point of View* (Baltimore: Johns Hopkins University Press, 1986). See especially chapters 1 ('Film, Perception, and Point of View') and 7 ('On Narrators and Narration in Film').
11 See also *The Thought of Stanley Cavell and Cinema* and Robert B. Pippin, 'The Idea That Films Could Have a Bearing on Philosophy', in *Inheriting Stanley Cavell: Memories, Dreams, Reflections*, ed. David LaRocca (New York: Bloomsbury, 2020).
12 Wilson, *Narration in Light*, 141.
13 Murray Pomerance, *Uncanny Cinema: Agonies of the Viewing Experience* (New York: Bloomsbury, 2022).
14 For the trespasser, see 'Fagan' (s4:e5).
15 See *Voir*, season 1, 'Film vs. Television' (13:40–16:29), which uses *The Queen* and *The Crown* to explore the relationship between the two historically situated categories.
16 See Sally Bedell Smith, *Elizabeth the Queen: Life of a Modern Monarch* (New York: Random House, 2012), 494. See also Elizabeth Longford, *Elizabeth R: A Biography* (London: Weidenfeld and Nicolson, 1983), 5.
17 'Smoke and Mirrors' (s1:e5), 00:41:41.
18 Cavell, 'The Fact of Television', 238.
19 Ibid., 235–36.
20 Jack Gould, 'Coronation Marks Birth of World TV', *New York Times*, June 3, 1953.
21 I am invoking Patricia Lockwood's sobriquet for the internet. See her *No One Is Talking about This* (2021).
22 Dave Yost, 'Let's Make Google a Public Good', *New York Times*, July 7, 2021; and Kevin Roose, 'Buy This Column on the Blockchain!', *New York Times*, March 24, 2021.
23 See Angelo Restivo, *Breaking Bad and Cinematic Television* (Durham: Duke University Press, 2019).
24 Cavell, *The World Viewed*, 31. See also *The Thought of Stanley Cavell and Cinema*, 29, 39n15 (Garrett Stewart); 47–48 (Noël Carroll); 68 (Kyle Stevens); 89–91 (Stephen Mulhall); 217–18 (Sandra Laugier); and 249 (LaRocca). See Sandra Laugier, 'The Importance of Stanley Cavell for the Study of Film' and my 'The Seriousness of Film Sustained', in *Movies with Stanley Cavell in Mind*, ed. David LaRocca (New York: Bloomsbury, 2021). See, moreover, Cavell, 'The Fact of Television', 239–41, where 'seriousness' is an issue vis-à-vis Leslie Fiedler's take on television, in Cavell's surmise, as providing 'a relief from art'.
25 Cavell, 'The Fact of Television', 239.
26 Ibid., 241.
27 Ibid., 239, 237.
28 Ibid., 239.
29 Ibid., 240.

30 Ibid.
31 Ibid., 252.
32 'Bubbikins' (s3:e4), 00:32:53.
33 See my 'Shooting for the Truth: Amateur Documentary Filmmaking, Affective Optics, and the Ethical Impulse', *Post Script: Essays in Film and the Humanities*, vol. 26, nos. 2 and 3 (Winter/Spring/Summer 2017), 46–60 and 'A Photograph as Evidence of Itself: Representation, Reflexivity, and Tautology in Light-Based Art', *Social Research*, vol. 89, no. 4 (Winter 2022), 915–45. See also *The Philosophy of Documentary Film: Image, Sound, Fiction, Truth*, ed. David LaRocca (Lexington: Lexington Books of Rowman and Littlefield, 2017).
34 Cavell, 'The Fact of Television', 267.
35 Ibid.
36 In other, related work I explored the presence of the home movie—including the existence/depiction of the camera itself, the projection of the contained film, and the adoption of a 'home movie aesthetic' in the containing film. See my 'On the Aesthetics of Amateur Filmmaking in Narrative Cinema'. The present study of *The Crown* shifts from the home movie camera—which, in fact, functioned in early seasons—to the television set and the broadcasting of (mostly live) sounds and images.
37 Queen Elizabeth II, 'Christmas Message', December 25, 2021.
38 James Poniewozik, 'Her Majesty's Last Broadcast', *New York Times*, September 19, 2022.
39 Cavell, *The World Viewed*, 25–26.
40 Ibid., 29.

PART II
BIG PERFECTIONISM ON THE SMALL SCREEN

5

It's My Party and I'll Die Even If I Don't Want To: Repetition, Acknowledgement, and Cavellian Perfectionism in *Russian Doll*

Michelle Devereaux

In his late-career exploration of moral perfectionism and cinema, *Cities of Words*, Cavell writes: 'We have to reverse our lives, reconsider the magnitude of our claims upon the world, and its (consequent) claims upon us.'[1] This is done, according to Cavell, through 'a reassessment and reconstitution of one's life' brought on by a crisis in its direction.[2] Such a crisis allows for 'a new day creating and created by a new human being', a 'new ordinary' that leads to 'a reconception and achievement of a genuine future'.[3] The idea of going backward to move hopefully forward is a curious one, but if we view it through the lens of repetition, it makes sense. It's through an examination of the dailiness of existence that we alter our perspectives on ourselves and on our world, if we can only commit to viewing the quotidian realities of our lives through the prism of adventure, improvisation, and endless possibility. Importantly, this examination is sourced in confrontation and conversation, a 'moral exchange' found in friendship.[4] Cavell sees a commitment to perfectionism as 'the moral calling of philosophy', signifying a 'redemption of … the ordinary' from the discipline's tendency to reject it.[5]

In season 1 of the Netflix series *Russian Doll* (Lyonne/Headland/Poehler, 2019),[6] cynical video-game designer Nadia Vulvokov (Natasha Lyonne) fancies herself as something of a philosopher. But unlike Cavell, her philosophy has the tendency towards an abstract, sceptical disengagement from ordinary life. 'Fun is for suckers—staring down the barrel of my own mortality always beats fun', she replies when, in her first few minutes on screen, someone asks if she's enjoying her thirty-sixth birthday party (s1:e1). This is the kind of philosophy Cavell sees as far too commonplace, making specific reference to Wittgenstein's lamentation of 'philosophy's aspirations to purity as stranding human desire in a field of ice'.[7] From the outset, it's clear that Nadia values her uniqueness and sense of personal freedom above all else, even her own happiness. When she informs her friends Maxine (Greta Lee) and Lizzy (Rebecca Henderson) that her cat, Oatmeal, has gone missing, Lizzy suggests she keep the cat exclusively indoors, safe from the mean streets of New York City's East Village. 'I don't believe in dictating the boundaries of a sentient being's existence', she retorts. 'For you, it's safety. For me and Oatmeal, it's a prison' (s1:e1).

This sentiment might seem to embody both Emerson's and Cavell's notion of a perfectionist life, the desire for self-reliance and liberation from societal conformity. Living a seemingly carefree, bohemian existence and answering to no one but herself, Nadia has constructed what many would consider an enviable life, and she herself contends she has it all figured out. Single since a messy break-up from her married ex-lover, John (Yul Vazquez), her view on finding a romantic partner so she won't 'die alone' is 'to wait until my late sixties and then seal the deal'. (She figures that with the amount she abuses her body, she will live until her 'early seventies, tops' [s1:e1].) But her desire for freedom has perversely led her to construct her own personal cage in order to exclude others from entering to potentially impinge on that freedom. She is, in essence, afraid of the change true confrontation might bring, afraid of finding her next self through an encounter with the other.

That cage is rattled (really, its doors are blown off) when, after dying in a street accident on the night of her birthday, Nadia is mysteriously resurrected, waking up several hours in the past to relive the same moments of her party all over again. Initially believing this to be some kind of hallucinatory drug trip, or that she might be 'crazy' (her deepest fear), she soon realizes she's trapped in a time loop, seemingly destined to die over and over in order to eternally relieve this same night and the day following. 'The universe is trying to fuck with me, and I refuse to engage!' she yells to no one in particular (s1:e1). But the carefully constructed fortress she has built for herself cannot protect her from this existential nightmare, and as a result she feels hopelessly unmoored, painfully exposed.

Forced to navigate the circumscribed boundaries of her new existence—one that can end with a horrible death and begin anew at any moment—Nadia finds herself, perhaps for the first time in a long time, at a loss. Such a sense of loss is the place, according to Cavell (via Wittgenstein) where philosophy *truly* begins: 'The question we have been brought to ask, that we did not know we were asking, produces the sense of illusion, of reality passing us by, that demands philosophizing.' For Wittgenstein, 'a philosophical problem has the form "I do not know my way about".'[8] This place of confusion and loss, in which the ground of reality itself is in question, will lead Nadia down a truly perfectionist path through an engagement with a new everyday reality, one that offers the possibility of moving forward by literally going back.

'A Base Instinct for Suckers and Mediocres': Marriage, Friendship, and Genre Hybridity

The films Cavell discusses in *Cities of Words* all feature ongoing perfectionist journeys to a 'next self'.[9] They relate to two genres, as Cavell conceives them. The first, dubbed the 'comedies of remarriage' in his 1979 book *Pursuits of Happiness*, features couples who divorce (either literally or metaphorically) only to come together again in a new-found commitment to conversation, acknowledgement, adventure, and mutual education through 'one soul's examination of another'.[10] According to Cavell, in films such as *Bringing up Baby* (Howard Hawks, 1938), *Adam's Rib* (George Cukor, 1949), and *The Awful Truth* (Leo McCarey, 1937), the man of the central couple is responsible for the 'new creation of the woman' by teaching her to identify and articulate her desire in order to emerge as an 'autonomous human being'.[11] His education, in turn, rests on his learning to respond to that desire.[12] The resulting happy marriage becomes an everyday commitment to 're-marriage', as marriage receives its continual ratification through the man and woman finding joy and adventure in their everyday existence with each other. Cavell sees in these comedies of 'dailiness' a legitimation of democratic society allegorized through the legitimacy of marriage, as both require ongoing consent in order to function properly. He refers to them as 'comedies of equality', but he also insists that the 'consciousness women hold of themselves ... is developed in relation to the consciousness men hold of them'.[13] We might be tempted to ask how the woman can be considered newly 'autonomous' and equal if her self-consciousness is solely related to how the man in her life perceives her, a paradox even Cavell admits to.[14]

In Cavell's 'melodramas of the unknown woman', the women in question reject marriage on the grounds that their husband/object of affection cannot provide such an education. Cavell calls this 'the collapse of the fantasy of remarriage', an inversion of the remarriage comedies.[15] Instead, the heroines of films such as *Stella Dallas* (King Vidor, 1937), *Now, Voyager* (Irving Rapper, 1942), and *Gaslight* (George Cukor, 1944) must set out on a journey to create *themselves*, offering a declaration of the 'proof of their existence' through irony, the negation of conversation, and the finding of their voice outside the union of marriage.[16] Time, memory, and repetition are viewed antithetically in Cavell's two genres: in melodrama, 'time is transient, closed, and repetition signals death',[17] while in the comedies, dailiness is celebrated through improvisation in repetition, in the willingness to meet each day with an openness to change, and the continual creation of a new, better society and new, better selves.

In both of these genres, then, Cavell connects moral perfectionism with marriage, with its success or failure. But is a perfectionist journey not possible outside the bonds of matrimony? If it requires a friend—'a figure that may occur as the goal of the journey but also as its instigation and accompaniment'—for Emerson, such a friend is epitomized by two figures, 'the true man and the boy'.[18] Presumably Emerson and Cavell have in mind the ideal of male friendship here, so it would seem moral perfectionism is attainable outside of a romantic relationship. Beyond Emerson's rubric, Cavell proposes a 'third image of moral exchange' found in the remarriage comedy, the only one of the three that seems open to women.[19] But why does the articulation of a woman's creation have to be sourced in a discovery of her sexual desire by and for a man and her subsequent embrace or rejection of that man? Cavell concedes that in order to remain pleasurable, romantic comedy needs to evolve with our increasing cultural sophistication, particularly in relation to (female) sexuality: 'we are going to require narratives that do not depend on the physics of virginity but rather upon the metaphysics of innocence'.[20] Such a metaphysics is related to identity, which on film is expressed 'through the concept of difference—either the difference between men and women, or between innocence and experience, or between one person and another'.[21]

Indeed, Cavell himself speaks of marriage in these films as an allegory for Aristotelian friendship, but later cautions that the 'issue of friendship between men and women remains controversial, namely in posing publicly the role of the erotic in friendship'.[22] What is so controversial about the erotic in friendship? For that matter, why must friendship between a (heterosexual) man and woman be classified as 'erotic' at all? Finally, we may also ask why the woman cannot play the role of this teacher/friend in a perfectionist relationship. In such a relation, the friend becomes an idealist symbol of the next 'best self',[23] so there is more than a healthy dose of paternalism at work in Cavell's equation. According to Catherine Wheatley, Cavell is 'unforthcoming' about how perfectionism might be gendered, but for him, 'It seems that in perfectionism, as in the overcoming of scepticism, the "creation of woman" remains the "business of men".'[24]

Russian Doll engages with many of Cavell's notions of moral perfectionism, including its relation to gender, friendship, community, and the journey from paralysing doubt to a quotidian intimacy with the world. The narrative renders 'perfectionist perceptions of the way we live—the sense of personal crisis given a social projection'.[25] That is, Nadia's personal crisis—her doubts about her worthiness to be happy after 'abandoning' her mentally ill mother, Lenora (Chloë Sevigny), who died just before her own thirty-sixth birthday—profoundly alters her relation to the world, so much so that she becomes stuck, literally unable to move forward in time. The world of *Russian Doll* creates a kind of thought experiment for its protagonist, one that she actually has to *live*, externalizing her internal sceptical crisis and providing the fertile ground for her to grow her way out of it.

For Cavell, scepticism is antithetical to moral perfectionism's guiding principle of 'recognizing the extraordinary in what we find ordinary, and the ordinary in what we find extraordinary' in everyday life.[26] 'Skepticism breaks into that life, with a surmise that I cannot live with, that the world and

I and others are radically unknown to me. I *must* find a way to put this doubt aside'.[27] Nadia finds herself in a world where the ordinary is under attack, and she attempts to solve the ultimate mystery of her fate. Eventually she understands that her 'epistemological problem of knowledge' is unanswerable,[28] and the only way out of her crisis is to meet the world halfway by agreeing to participate in it fully. For this, she requires not knowledge, but faith—something akin to what Cavell calls the 'miraculousness of the everyday' in the form of the 'secularization of the transcendental'.[29]

A 'comedy of dailiness',[30] wherein death signals repetition—with that repetition offering the key to finding a way out of stagnation—in many ways *Russian Doll* is an amalgam of Cavell's two film genres, featuring a tonal and thematic blend of comic absurdism and Freudian melodrama. The series is an early example of a genre I call (taking generous inspiration from Cavell) the 'comedies of reconstruction', one of several recent (post-2019) broadcast television and online streaming series from the US and UK that explore a central woman character undergoing a sceptical crisis—a 'fantasy ... of exposure'[31]—that leads to a journey of self-discovery and, hopefully, self-improvement.[32] Like the remarriage comedies, *Russian Doll* features a central relationship between a man and a woman indicative of moral perfectionism, but here it is (almost entirely) based on friendship. And while marriage plays a thematic role, it is never equated with the perfectionist relationship: Nadia refers to marriage as a 'base instinct for suckers and mediocres' (s1:e6) and rejects John's proposal to get back together out of her desire, in unknown-woman fashion, for more than just 'a warm body' (s1:e3). Similarly, *Russian Doll* flips the gender script of remarriage comedy. Here, it is principally the woman who 'creates' the man, although through the experience of that education and creation, she learns to acknowledge her 'desire for the attaining of a self that is [hers] to become, the power to act on behalf of an attainable world [she] can actually desire'.[33]

Conversely, Nadia's quest mirrors the narrative drive of the unknown woman melodrama, namely the woman's 'search for the mother'.[34] In the melodramas, the woman's mother becomes a key figure in her struggle for perfectionist self-reliance.[35] Although Nadia's own mother is long dead (for unnamed reasons, although likely the result of suicide), her spectre looms so large that it informs nearly every action of Nadia's daily existence. Through a 'melancholic' identification with her,[36] Nadia suffers a sense of being doomed to re-enact her mother's mental disintegration and eventual destruction, perhaps out of a perverse sense of desired reunion. Her copious drug use ('who loves drugs more than me?') (s1:e2) and other risky behaviours speak to a woman resigned to her fate—as Ruth (Elizabeth Ashley), a therapist and surrogate mother figure, says, she is 'chasing down death at every corner' (s1:e7). Like the unknown women, Nadia's journey eventually culminates in an 'aria of divorce',[37] not from her husband, lover, or her own child, but from the child she once was, who suffered so keenly, and from a mother whose hold on her is so intense it transcends death.

Russian Doll's hybridity is also medium-specific. It slyly plays with contemporary notions of the heavily serialized 'prestige' television series, wherein the story often becomes so convoluted, its breadth and mythology so expansive and deep, that it can become a struggle to even follow the significance of what's occurring at any given moment.[38] Here, the serialized story becomes cheekily episodic, 'resetting' to zero yet also propelling itself forward with significant bursts of narrative momentum. For Cavell, 'film is a dream machine' and television an 'information machine',[39] but *Russian Doll* demonstrates that television is also capable of rendering dreamlike the realities of existence. Arguably, streaming series designed to be 'binge-watched' offer potentially even more of a sustained immersion in the 'life and death struggle with unconsciousness' than cinema does.[40] The uncanniness of its repetition lends *Russian Doll* a nightmare-like quality, but its variations in repetition also attest to the exhilaration of a dream in which anything can happen, even as the same things happen over and over again: Nadia dies, wakes up in Maxine's bathroom staring at herself in the mirror, comes face to face with the abyss-like, glowing gash shaped into the bathroom door, and opens the door with a *click* of the trigger on its gun-shaped knob, all to the ironically cheerful strains of Harry Nilsson's 1971 tune 'Gotta Get Up'. In the kitchen, Maxine waits for her with a joint laced with cocaine ('like the Israelis do it') and a 'birthday chicken'. 'Sweet birthday baby!' she coos, blithely unaware that Nadia has heard and seen it all before.[41]

Nadia initially seems to be the only one subjected to her peculiar plight—every time she dies, life (along with time) goes on for everyone else. But she isn't trapped in this nightmare alone, as she soon discovers: a nervous young man named Alan Zaveri (Charlie Barnett) is also experiencing the same seemingly endless death/rebirth scenario. Initially adversarial, Nadia and Alan's friendship eventually becomes a life-changing relation of equals, one whose equality is rooted in both sameness and difference just as the relationships of the remarriage comedies are.

Her Boy Friday, or *The Aristocrat and the Peasant*: A Perfectionist Journey

We are officially introduced to Alan in the appropriately titled 'Alan's Routine' (s1:e4), when he is resurrected, like Nadia, in front of a bathroom mirror. With a vaguely robotic precision of movement, he awakes, turns off his bathroom tap, and kills a nearby fly with expert aim. In his grey-walled bedroom, he commands his computer to play 'affirmations for success' before emptying a meticulously packed suitcase. He parrots the recording's droning mantras—'I am beautiful. I am loved and deserve love. I am in control'—as he retrieves a ring box from the suitcase and opens it with a slight smile; it houses what looks like an engagement ring. After efficiently feeding his fish, he waits expectantly just behind the door inside his building's lobby, opening it just in time to let in an elderly neighbour. Clearly, Alan has done this all before. (His first word to himself after resurrecting, 'Ten', suggests he has been keeping track of how many times.)

What isn't clear is why Alan, unlike Nadia, should be meeting such extraordinary circumstances with such serenity, even optimism. This is, after all, a man who has died close to a dozen times in the span of a day. Yet he comports himself as if experiencing a pleasant, lucid dream, not a horrible existential nightmare. For Alan, being trapped in the 'worst night of [his] life' (s1:e6)—the night he finds out his girlfriend of nine years, Beatrice (Dascha Polanco), is having an affair after she turns down his marriage proposal—gives him a chance to 'correct' that life. But for him, this doesn't mean a correction of perspective. Rather, it's a chance to wear his life down into such a groove it becomes perfectly smooth, shorn of all surprises. Alan uses his strange situation as a chance to perfect his every reaction to this limited range of events, finding the perfect retort to Beatrice when she dumps him, rather than improvising a way out of his Sisyphean plight. 'Routine is an incredible thing, Beatrice', he tells her. 'We become what we repeatedly do' (s1:e4). Alan would like to become one with pure order, to align the universe with his need for everything to go according to plan. In many ways, he is the personification of Emersonian conformity, in which 'most people who have some choice in their lives are as afraid to insist on their own desires as they are unable to determine their duties by discounting those desires. Instead they quote, imitate, *they go along*'.[42]

It would seem the universe is trying to tell Nadia and Alan that they are special, and that, like the couples of the remarriage comedies, they are 'made for each other'.[43] But what could these two possibly mean to each other? On the surface, they seem to have nothing in common. Alan does what is expected of him (by whom, it's uncertain) by participating in his own perpetual humiliation, mechanically quoting his self-help tapes, waiting for things to improve. His is the opposite of perfectionist ambition. Nadia, meanwhile, exists by a code all her own, often striving to do what is least expected of her. In the opening episode, 'Nothing in This World Is Easy', Mike (Jeremy Bobb), a pompous literature professor we eventually learn is Beatrice's duplicitous lover, delivers one of a series of self-satisfied lectures in the form of small talk. 'It's like John Updike said, "Every marriage seems to consist of an aristocrat and a peasant, and a teacher and a learner"', he smugly proclaims (s:1e:1). (Mike, the series' ultimate philosophical villain, is suspiciously fond of quoting others.) He, and Updike, could be referencing Cavell's relation of marriage to perfectionism, in which a 'philosopher-sage' or 'natural aristocrat', such as *The Philadelphia Story*'s C.K. Dexter Haven (Cary Grant), provides vigorous lecturing to his heroine—in Dexter's case, Tracy Lord (Katharine Hepburn)—affording her the education to become a 'first-class human being'. In *Russian Doll*, Nadia primarily occupies the role of the sage, while Alan is principally the learner. But the series also complicates this dynamic, just as it challenges the gendered dynamics of remarriage comedy (or, rather, Cavell's view of them).

If, in remarriage comedy, marriage is an allegory for friendship, it's tempting to view Nadia and Alan's relationship as an allegory of remarriage, if only because several of Cavell's remarriage comedies are allegorical themselves. Alan and Nadia did, in a sense, 'grow up together' as the remarriage couples did—not literally, like Alan and Beatrice, but they *did* first meet shortly after being (re)born. Like these couples, they have a kind of private language that isn't understood by outsiders, in their case due purely to external circumstances. Nadia and Alan have a solitary sexual liaison, when a drunken, debased Alan feels the need for some compensatory affirmation after confronting Mike. The narrative climaxes in a 'divorce', when Alan decides to leave Nadia to make things right with Beatrice.[44] They are reunited in their eventual gambit to escape the time loop by helping convince their 'old' selves to change their attitudes and thus their actions. The series essentially articulates the journey of the remarriage comedy, which features a central couple 'overcoming internal obstacles' through the 'revision and transfiguration' of their way of life.[45]

But *Russian Doll* doesn't concern itself with the articulation of the woman's sexual desire, nor with the man's identification of it. This single woman is no Charlotte Vale–esque spinster waiting for a man to teach her to become more herself. From the first episode, when she invites Mike back to her place shortly after meeting him, it's clear owning her sexuality isn't Nadia's problem. Rather, her issue is one of relating to the other in true friendship, a perfectionist friendship that challenges her out of her stasis. Her primary friendship, with Maxine, is rooted in competitive one-ups-(wo)manship ('I love that you're a cunt', Maxine says, 'It makes me feel morally superior') (s:1:e5) and her relationship to Ruth revolves around the need to feel mothered.[46] While Nadia is gregarious with strangers and has no problem saying she loves both Lizzy and Ruth, these actions feel compensatory. She comports herself as if the queen of the neighbourhood, benevolently ruling over her subjects. Rather than truly reach out, Nadia tends to fall back on ironic detachment. This is a woman, after all, who owns a framed poster of William S. Burroughs featuring the phrase 'Life is a killer'. When such conclusions are foregone, it's better not to get too attached.

It's surprising, then, that Nadia enlists Alan's help in extracting her from her nightmare, insisting they are 'in this together' (s1:e4). But like any good sceptic, her desire is primarily rooted in her need to control the narrative, solve the mystery, and gain the knowledge—to fix the 'bug in the code' (s1:e7), as she so expertly does in her work meeting. (There is a brief running gag regarding Nadia's ludicrous theory that she and Alan might be the same person, a perfect encapsulation of Cavellian scepticism if there ever was one.) Alan, however, sees Nadia as a 'carcinogenic siren' for wanting to upset his carefully proscribed, seemingly infinite routine (s1:e7). It's up to Nadia to school Alan, whom she refers to as 'a child that the universe has tasked me with babysitting' (s1:e5), in the rewards of risk-taking and the rejection of empty moralism. She calls Alan's theory that they are being punished for unnamed transgressions 'morally simplistic and narcissistic'. 'The universe is moral, but it shares your views on morality?' she asks derisively (s1:e5). It's clear who is the wizened sage and who is the innocent naïf in this relationship. Nadia is, in many respects, a sort of 'philosophical genius', however frozen in ice her philosophy may be. She epitomizes what Nietzsche calls 'free manliness of character, early knowledge of mankind, no scholarly education, no narrow patriotism, no necessity for bread-winning, no ties with the state—in short, freedom and again freedom'.[47] This 'manliness of character' aligns her with Grant's famous portrayals of comedic 'natural aristocrats', namely Dexter and *His Girl Friday*'s scheming newspaperman Walter Burns.

Lyonne's performance, and her star persona in general, could be classified as 'masculine': clad mostly in mannish suit jackets and coats as Nadia, with a genetically gifted whisky-and-gravel voice enhanced by years of copious smoking, her attitude is generally brusque, often brazenly contemptuous of others, and forthrightly challenging of authority. Even her mass of fiery red hair seems defiant and unruly. She is, in short, 'unladylike'. But she also radiates an ageless, timeless, genderless wisdom and world-weariness unmatched among her peers. Like Grant, Clark Gable, Spencer Tracy, and James Stewart in the remarriage comedies, who are 'given authority by their experience', she is able to 'risk a certain standing in the world', i.e., that authority, by making herself look foolish.[48] Cavell writes of Grant's 'photogenic tendency to thoughtfulness',[49] and we can see echoes of this in Lyonne. We get the sense that she is the smartest person in the room, that she knows it, and that she views it as simultaneously a burden and an opportunity. Like Grant, this imbues her with a sense of privacy, of being 'spiritually inaccessible to those around [her]' despite the fact that she can rarely keep her mouth shut.[50] As Nadia, Lyonne talks and talks, but she rarely reveals. Her 'thirst for talk', unlike Grant's Dexter Haven, is not so much a 'quest for self-knowledge' as it is a deflection from it.[51] She is really more a goddess of sardonicism, having turned herself to stone like Tracy Lord, motivated by 'the *fear* of living inside out, of being exposed'.[52] This is extremely shaky ground from which to conduct any lecture on moral perfectionism. Seemingly compelled exclusively by her own desires and situating herself above the fray, she also fails the perfectionist test. Both Nadia and Alan, then, are surprisingly, fundamentally alike.

So, in turn, it's up to Alan to confront Nadia with her own selfishness, her impossible standards for other people and herself, and her inability to truly reach out to another. This is mainly accomplished obliquely, through Nadia's acknowledgement of the otherness of the other via Alan, as she accepts responsibility for helping him out of his suicidal spiral. In this way, Nadia and Alan occupy both the teacher and learner positions at various moments; they are, then, both aristocrats and peasants. Could this be a solution to Cavell's seeming paradox about equality between the genders in a perfectionist relationship? Likely not, as the remarriage comedies posit the same general reciprocity: for every man lecturing a woman on humanity, we find a woman humiliating a man trying hopelessly to maintain his position of authority. (This is part of, for Cavell, remarriage comedy's 'questions and exchanges of gender roles'.[53]) But by placing Nadia in the role of principal 'creator', *Russian Doll* questions Cavell's gendered assumptions about agency. This is, narratively speaking, a show about Nadia, *not* about Nadia and Alan's relationship, which goes some way to explaining why that relationship is never romantic. As the title *Russian Doll* makes clear, it is primarily an exploration of identity within the nested layers of one woman's unconscious—a woman whose Russian name, as the eponymous heroine of André Breton's 1928 surrealist memoir *Nadja* notes, is 'the beginning of the word hope, and … only the beginning'.[54] In order to get past the seemingly never-ending beginning, Nadia will need to ask herself the question Breton poses in *Nadja*'s first line: *Who am I?*

'All My Mother Gave Me Was a Subway Token and an Eating Disorder': Identity, Faith, and Escaping the Abyss

Cavell opens *Cities of Words* by underlining perfectionism's relation to personal identity: '[E]ach of the thinkers and artists we will encounter in the following pages may be said to respond to some such insight of a split in the human self, of human nature as divided or double', he writes.[55] Such a divided self—'providing a perspective of judgment upon the world as it is, measured against the world as it may be'— can kindle a desire for 'reform or transfiguration' indicative of moral perfectionism.[56] He relates perfectionism to the occult concept of metempsychosis, the transmigration of souls, wherein one is 'reborn' to a further life, choosing 'its (own) altered body again'.[57] His description of 'differences, as we might put it, of each human being from itself, torn from itself, repaired by itself, comically or tragically, as perfectionism insists in reminding us' is reminiscent of Matryoshka nesting dolls: each smaller copy hidden inside the larger, each larger copy representing incremental growth—the same yet different.[58] Being stuck in a time loop against her will, Nadia's predicament operates as a parody of metempsychosis, a literalization of rebirth that refuses change, of moving forward, itself. It is up to her to rebirth her soul in accordance with her new, and perpetually renewed, body. To do that, she has to open herself up and reveal what's nested inside.

In the season's penultimate episode, 'The Way Out' (s1:e7), Nadia finally fulfils her promise to meet John's young daughter, Lucy (Tatiana E. Rivera), for breakfast. She gives her a copy (her own copy) of *Emily of New Moon*, the book she most loved as a child of Lucy's age, the same age she was when torn from her mother. *Emily* concerns a young orphan girl shipped off to live with hostile relatives, a girl who often retreats into a vivid fantasy life to escape dark realities and thoughts. She receives what she calls 'flashes', ecstatic glimpses into another brilliant world adjacent to our own that remains largely unseen due to a lack of proper perspective. This is Cavell's (and Emerson's) brave new 'next' world, a world of ordinary extraordinariness. But it can also be seen as a 'magical hallucinatory gesture ... characteristic of early childhood' that signals an inability to properly articulate real experience.[59] For Nadia, the loss of her mother is the one life event she can't successfully express, can't incorporate into her psychic identity, so it finally manifests in a burst of surreal physicality, a fantasy in which 'the girl puts her mother's body inside her own' in an attempt at maternal reunion.[60] In her own form of terrifying flash, Nadia sits across from Lucy and begins to choke, coughing blood all over the young girl's face as she sits impassively. 'She's still inside you', Lucy flatly states. Nadia rises and reaches into her bloody mouth to extract a shard of jagged mirror. This is a psychic artefact, a remnant from her mother's crazed tirade in Nadia's youth, seen in flashback, in which she smashes all the mirrors in Ruth's house. Lucy then transforms into Nadia as a young girl, as Nadia collapses on the floor. Young Nadia (Brooke Timber) looms over her. 'Are you ready to let her die?' she asks. 'This is the day we get free.'

Mirrors are associated with *mise en abyme*, or 'placement in abyss', infinitely reflecting their own image when facing one another. 'I think of this as endless displacement', writes Cavell.[61] By removing the mirror shard, Nadia frees herself from her mother's emotional grip, but also from her own sense of being displaced, a mere reflection of her mother. Earlier John tells Nadia that she *is* 'the abyss', an insult that sends her reeling. In episode 1, she discusses Maxine's renovation of her bathroom door, the one that confronts her after each resurrection. 'Congrats, it's terrifying', she quips (s1:e1). The crystalline carving on the door is indicative of the abyss itself; rendered in a baroque, amoebic shape and underlit in a frosty pale blue, it's an icy chasm that radiates doom. Yet it's also ethereally beautiful, as if beckoning the beholder to the sweet release found only in oblivion. This is why Nadia is afraid of it; it is too seductive. Her name might be a shorthand for hope, but it's also perilously similar to *nada*—that is, *nothing*. And yet, *nada* is derived from the Latin *nata*, a 'situation, circumstance, literally, a thing come into being'. To extract herself from the abyss's glamourous pull, then, Nadia will need to embrace her circumstances and facilitate that becoming.

In order to do *that*, she must reflect on what caused her to become stuck in the first place by viewing her past (and present) through new eyes. But she must also commit to change, to genuinely recommit to a life and a future. This is first and foremost a spiritual exercise, what Cavell refers to 'as a rubric ... a spiritual American might give to the empiricism practiced by Emerson and by Thoreau'.[62] The spiritual checking of experience relates the past towards the future, for if perfectionism 'depend[s] on a faith in something that is always happening, day by day', it also 'requires a reconception and achievement of a genuine future, one not merely a continuation of the outworn past'.[63] At times, Nadia appears to be such a spiritual American, but that spirit is trapped inside the consciousness of a woman too sceptical to have faith in anything but her own wits. A self-professed hater of organized religion, shortly after her first resurrection she exhibits misgivings about using Maxine's cavernous apartment, a former yeshiva, for parties and other general debauchery. 'This was once a sacred place', she intones with new-found awe and respect (s1:e1). This respect, however, is initially rooted in fear and superstition more than faith. Later, she visits a Jewish congregation in order to get clues about the building's past, wondering if perhaps it might be haunted (s1:e3). She asks the rabbi's receptionist to say a prayer of protection over her, as John—pretending to be her husband because the rabbi won't talk to a 'single woman off the street'—grills the rabbi on Nadia's behalf. 'You can only reach certain wisdom through surrender', he tells John. 'Buildings aren't haunted. People are haunted.'

For Cavell, modern (post-Cartesian) philosophy 'has retained the skepticism' of Descartes 'but lost the route to God, making the existence of the world a persistent, epistemological problem of knowledge perpetually unjustified'.[64] He supposes something he calls 'psychological or spiritual virginity', for which biological virginity becomes a 'trope'.[65] Could this waking up to a world beyond her normal perception be the moment of Nadia's (excusing Cavell's rather queasy terminology) 'spiritual defloration'?[66] Her conversion is better viewed as an opening up to the very *possibility* of faith. Such a possibility leads to a new, or renewed, intimacy between self and world—the world becomes no longer a problem of knowledge to be gained as it is one of perspective to be found. A yeshiva is a place of knowledge, but the knowledge shared there is spiritual, a knowledge of faith. Like Félicie in Éric Rohmer's *A Winter's Tale*, discussed at length in *Cities of Words*, Nadia's scepticism is 'overcome by something that resembles faith but that is also to be distinguished from what we may expect of faith'.[67] Both Nadia and Félicie are unbelievers who still ultimately recognize faith, characterized by what Cavell sees in Rohmer's work as 'a transcendental moment, a declaration that the world we are given to see, like the words we are given to mean, is not all the world there is, and not all we mean'.[68] Nadia's transcendental moment—her flash—doesn't arise from her literal death and resurrection. It comes from 'the death and revival ... of *feeling*'.[69] But how does this revival of feeling relate to the world in which she finds herself?

'Being a Person Is a Fucking Nightmare': Communal Despair, Precarity, and Creating the Good City

Cavell sees the perfectionist journey as one that signals not only the desire for personal growth, but societal growth as well: it evinces 'the vision of the demand for a transfigured future, expressed as a sense of the exhaustion of present culture, perhaps accompanied by a demand for the renewal of culture, call it a vision of modernity'.[70] The crisis of perfectionism spurs a utopian engagement with the world and a commitment towards its continual improvement—something particularly essential in a democracy, in which personal despair becomes 'a political emotion'.[71] The New York of *Russian Doll* appears in the throes of a sort of communal despair. Doubt, suspicion, paranoia, and a general lack of compassion permeate its denizens. Horse, a conspiratorial homeless man Nadia meets in the park, claims to have invented the dark web and calls himself a 'shadow'(s1:e6).[72] Alan gets pepper-sprayed by two women for simply getting too near them while walking down the street (s1:e5). The distributor for Maxine's drug dealer, who operates out of the psychedelic, underworld-like bowels of a local bar (seemingly part of the same icy-blue abyss as Maxine's bathroom door), refers to ketamine as a 'breakthrough depression medication' (s1:e2). Ruth's patient exclaims through tears that he just wants his wife to talk to him (s1:e2). After Beatrice confesses her affair with serial cheater Mike, Alan observes his fish tank, muttering to himself, 'If there are two, one kills the other' (s1:e4) Then the city begins to literally rot, erode, disappear, in a physical manifestation of this despair. Fruit moulds, flowers wither in fast-motion, people simply vanish. When Nadia finds Maxine dancing alone in her hollowed-out apartment, she begs her to leave with her. 'I can't', Maxine replies meekly (s1:e7).

If this is not exactly the 'black world' of *His Girl Friday* (Howard Hawks, 1940), it is at least adjacent. But while that film was characterized by its hardness, its lack of sympathy and fellow feeling, the world of *Russian Doll* is defined by its sense of precarity, despite its use of repetition. It operates in a mode of crisis-as-normalcy. In *Cruel Optimism*, Lauren Berlant writes of the 'precarisation' of Western neoliberal societies, referring to the 'fraying' fantasies of 'upward mobility, job security, political and social equality, and lively, durable intimacy'.[73] For Berlant, this precarity, on the rise since the Reagan era and exploding in the twenty-first century, has led to a 'waning of genre', a loss of the sense that we can make coherent stories of our lives.[74] Within this new paradigm, Berlant claims, it isn't just the economic underclass who suffer. Instead, now the 'relatively privileged' experience nearly the same feeling of precarity as the financially insecure.[75]

This sense of precarity could explain why in *Russian Doll* clearly defined genres break down and marriage no longer allegorizes the perfected human community. Scepticism about public institutions causes marriage's union of public and private to feel irrelevant to daily life, and 'the question of America, or whether America has achieved its new human being' has become moot.[76] In *Russian Doll* there is no mention of 'America', as a concept or a country. Instead, it focuses on what Berlant calls the 'impasse', in which the 'unbound temporality' of the present 'demands activity'.[77] This active response can lead to both positive and negative outcomes, of 'being-with in the world as well as of rejection, refusal, detachment, psychosis, and all kinds of radical negation'.[78] It can provide a radical rethinking of what happiness is—whether it is simply a neoliberal, late-capitalist commitment to the 'good life' or something else. For Berlant, it represents a new *genre of time*, in which 'the world is at once intensely present and enigmatic' and 'the activity of living demands both a wandering absorptive awareness and a hypervigilance that collects material that might help to clarify things'.[79] If anything, the precarity Berlant sees in contemporary society points to an *intensification* of the perfectionist crisis. *Russian Doll* isn't about economic precarity—most of the people we meet, aside from Horse and his gang, are financially stable; some even seem independently wealthy. Instead, it tells a story of collective emotional and spiritual precarity, an impasse of the *soul*.

For Berlant, 'conventions of reciprocity that ground how to live and imagine life are becoming undone in ways that force the gestures of ordinary improvisation within daily life into a greater explicitness affectively and aesthetically'.[80] The impasse is intimately linked with what she calls 'crisis ordinariness', in which crisis (the extraordinary) becomes embedded in the ordinary; the ordinary as a perpetual state of crisis. Perhaps (optimistically speaking) developing the improvisatory skills needed to deal with such perpetual crises can lead to a perfectionist-minded state of becoming, not just to 'scrambl[ing] for modes of living on'.[81] The sense of physical and psychological 'stuckness' in the present can lead to radical transformation, both for the individual and the collective.

This transformation-through-crisis plays out in microcosm in *Russian Doll*'s ingeniously executed season 1 finale, 'Ariadne' (written and directed by Lyonne),[82] in which Nadia and Alan are finally able to escape the labyrinth of their new realities and take a brave leap into a genuine future by engaging with the past—not their *own* pasts, but the pasts of each other (s1:e8). In the episode's opening scene, we see both their resurrections simultaneously in a split-screen effect. The split is visualized in a bird's-eye view of the false ceiling of each individual set, as if they are directly beside each other in space and time, suggesting their fates are inextricably bound. (Alan's fly even travels through the wall into Nadia's room.) While their world has been repopulated again, much to Nadia's exultant relief, there is now a new bug in the code. The new, transformed Nadia has resurrected into a timeline with the 'old' suicidal Alan, and the 'new' Alan has awoken in the world where only the 'old' sceptical Nadia exists. This is revealed through cross-cutting between two scenes in the same location, in which the screen eventually splits into quadrants featuring the mismatched pairs, indicative of Cavell's notion of split identity. If they are going to be able to move forward in time and stop their endless deaths, Old Alan must accept New Nadia's help, and Old Nadia must acknowledge New Alan. Through 'rewriting' their initial almost-meeting in the deli, they must become the teacher/friend for each other in a final test of their perfectionist bona fides.

They pass the test, in Cavellian fashion, through confrontation and conversation, by making themselves intelligible to one another.[83] Alan lures Nadia away from Mike—the true abyss, 'the hole where the choice should be'—by claiming he owes her $152,780.86. Earlier she had revealed to Alan this was the exact value of her 'college fund', the gold Krugerrands she should have inherited from her Holocaust-surviving grandparents, which her mother supposedly sold off long ago (s1:e6). Nadia wears the sole remaining coin on a heavy chain around her neck like an upscale noose; Alan transforms it into a point of positive connection. In the parallel timeline, New Nadia tells Old Alan a story about 'the broken man and the lady with a death wish': she 'caught him in her crazy hair, like it was a dolphin's net ... And then one night, something miraculous happened—they made it through alive.' Their final conversation on the roof of Alan's building, as Old Alan contemplates ending his life by jumping, is as succinct an encapsulation of the perfectionist journey in friendship as one is likely to find:

> Alan: 'You promise if I don't jump, I'll be happy?'
> Nadia: 'No man, absolutely not. But I can promise you that you'll not be alone.'
> Alan: 'Okay, what now?'

Rather than expressing the personal and social stuckness of the present and waning of the future, as in Jean-François Lyotard's 'and what now?' feeling,[84] Alan's, and *Russian Doll*'s, 'what now?' involves movement from temporal and spatial disjunction to new-found clarity, an expression, for Cavell, of moral reasoning.[85] It is not an expression of stasis, but rather signifies the possibility of what's *next*. It can also be classified as what Berlant sees as the 'tiny optimism of recuperative gestures in the middle of it all, for those who can manage them'.[86]

Such a recuperative gesture turns triumphant in the season's final scene, which can be seen as an aesthetic representation of moral perfectionism. As it begins, the two couples of Nadias and Alans stride along the street, again shown in split screen, before encountering a riotous costumed parade populated by the homeless revellers from the park, led by Horse, who brandishes a broken mirror like a torch. When the two Alans approach the centre of the split frame, they disappear. A jump cut into a closer shot of the parade follows. When it cuts back to what we assume is the previous shot, two Nadias continue walking towards the parade, but these now appear to both be Old Nadias, identifiable from their grey coats. After another confusing jump cut, which lends the impression that the camera has rotated 180 degrees, the next shot bypasses a few seconds of narrative time. We now see (New) Nadia, dressed in black and white, walking towards the camera with the parade, as the two Old Nadias, with their backs to the camera, walk in the opposite direction. New Alan (recognizable from his recently acquired scarf) walks alongside New Nadia, whooping ecstatically and jumping up and down as the parade moves through a tunnel, the camera craning up in a gesture of triumph as they exit.

Lasting fewer than two minutes, the dizzying scene provides the viewer with a feeling of 'I do not know my way about' before establishing a new dramatic paradigm. With the presentation of three Nadias—two 'old', one 'new'—it creates a visual metaphor for Nadia moving on to her 'next' self. She, and this makeshift community of misfits (including Alan), walk towards the camera in concert, *towards* the future and 'an attainable next self in an attainable further society'.[87] Such a euphoric, utopian gesture of solidarity in everyday life speaks to perfectionism's foundation on, and in, a future for all—in the good city (or country, or community).

In *Cities of Words*, Cavell sums up the perfectionist journey as existing on multiple temporal planes simultaneously, as an unwieldy struggle sourced in the past, present, and future:

> [W]e are already living a future life, reincarnating one past but open to one present. That we are the successors of ourselves ... and not necessarily succeeding in a given order or direction ... is a reasonable figure of the perfectionist life, seizing crises of revelation, good or bad, clear or confused, as chances of transformation.[88]

That the order and direction of one's life is not guaranteed is a given, but that it depends on other people is also inescapable—as Alan's friend Farran (Ritesh Rajan) tells him, 'No one can do anything by themselves' (s1:e4). For Nadia and Alan to finally move on from mourning the past to meeting the dawn of a (truly) new morning, they need each other. The fact that they aren't married, or remarried, like Cavell's couples, could evince a scepticism about political and social institutions, but not about people. If, as Nadia says, 'Being a person is a fucking nightmare'(s1:e8), that nightmare can turn into an exhilarating premonition of the future with the right partner, and the right point of view.

Notes

1 Stanley Cavell, *Cities of Words: Pedagogical Letters on a Register of the Moral Life* (Cambridge, MA: Harvard University Press, 2004), 141.
2 Cavell, *Cities of Words*, 84.
3 Ibid., 211, 215.
4 Ibid., 141.
5 Ibid., 2, 29.
6 This chapter discusses season 1 of *Russian Doll* only. Season 2, released in April 2022, takes a similar metaphysical, philosophical tack as season 1 through a different time-travel scenario. It also addresses themes of self-identity and intersubjectivity, inherited trauma, and Freudian maternal psychodrama. It does somewhat undercut the earlier season's focus on perfectionist aspiration through conversation and mutual acknowledgement, sending its two main characters on their own thematically related but largely individual quests for most of its running time. This, however, has little

bearing on the discrete time-loop world created in season 1 (which, in a clever flourish at the end of season 2, Nadia re-encounters through her travels across time and dimensions).

7   Cavell, *Cities of Words*, 110.
8   Ibid., 332.
9   Ibid., 367.
10 Ibid., 49.
11 Stanley Cavell, *Pursuits of Happiness: The Hollywood Comedy of Remarriage* (Cambridge, MA: Harvard University Press, 1979), 16, 84.
12 Cavell, *Cities of Words*, 390.
13 Cavell, *Pursuits of Happiness*, 17, 82.
14 Ibid., 57.
15 Stanley Cavell, *Contesting Tears: The Hollywood Melodrama of the Unknown Woman* (Cambridge, MA: Harvard University Press, 1998), 107.
16 Cavell, *Contesting Tears*, 47.
17 Ibid., 108.
18 Cavell, *Cities of Words*, 27, 31.
19 Ibid., 141.
20 Cavell, *Pursuits of Happiness*, 54.
21 Ibid., 55.
22 Cavell, *Cities of Words*, 16, 363.
23 Cavell, *Pursuits of Happiness*, 157.
24 Catherine Wheatley, *Stanley Cavell and Film: Scepticism and Self-Reliance at the Cinema* (London: Bloomsbury, 2019), 195–96.
25 Cavell, *Cities of Words*, 251.
26 Ibid., 422.
27 Ibid., 426.
28 Ibid., 424.
29 Ibid., 437.
30 Cavell, *Pursuits of Happiness*, 15.
31 Cavell, *Contesting Tears*, 157.
32 Other examples include *Physical* (Annie Weisman, 2021–), *Kevin Can F**k Himself* (Valerie Armstrong, 2021–22), *Back to Life* (Daisy Haggard, 2019–), *This Way Up* (Aisling Bea, 2019–), *Alma's Not Normal* (Sophie Willan, 2021–) and *Feel Good* (Joe Hampson and Mae Martin, 2020–21), the latter of which features a non-binary main character. The progenitor for this subgenre is *Fleabag* (Phoebe Waller-Bridge, 2016–19), which became a veritable cultural phenomenon after its BBC debut and spawned a rash of dark comedies about 'disruptive', often unlikeable women protagonists dealing with past trauma, mental illness, and/or current life crises. For more on female antiheroes in contemporary television, see Sarah Hagelin and Gillian Silverman, *The New Female Antihero: The Disruptive Women of Twenty-First-Century US Television* (Chicago: University of Chicago Press, 2022).
33 Cavell, *Cities of Words*, 33.
34 Ibid., 277.
35 Cavell, *Contesting Tears*, 88.
36 Alison Stone, *Feminism, Psychoanalysis, and Maternal Subjectivity* (London: Routledge, 2012), 90.

37 Cavell, *Contesting Tears*, 88.
38 As Mareike Jenner notes, '"quality" TV puts an emphasis on narrative complexity as a way to take full advantage of the serial form afforded by television'. *Russian Doll* can be seen as a continuation of the '"quality" sitcoms' Netflix produced from early in its run of original programming, which 'abandoned the three-camera setup, laugh-track or reliance on punchlines usually associated with the genre'. *Netflix and the Re-Invention of TV* (New York Palgrave Macmillan, 2018), 143, 145. For more on narrative complexity and serialized TV, see Catherine Wheatley's chapter in this volume.
39 Cavell, *Cities of Words*, 152.
40 Presupposing that Netflix *does* in fact constitute television in the 'TV IV' era, the 'binge-watching' model it popularized, in which all episodes of a TV season are released simultaneously (like *Russian Doll*'s), creates the option for a vastly different viewing experience than that of traditional television broadcasting. The near-uninterrupted flow from one episode to the next, or 'insulated flow', can facilitate an even more intimate engagement with a medium already noted for its intimacy, as viewers 'may already envision themselves as moving through that fictive world' of the series, finding it difficult, like Nadia, to 'escape'. Lisa Glebatis Perks, *Media Marathoning: Immersions in Morality* (Lanham: Lexington Books, 2015), quoted in Mareike Jenner, *Netflix and the Re-Invention of TV*, 126.
41 Another recent series, *The Good Place* (Michael Schur, 2016–20), also takes advantage of this 'reboot' scenario while expanding the perfectionist teacher/friend relationship further: instead of just a central couple, it features a small group of troubled misfits in the afterlife teaching and learning from each other at various turns. For more on *The Good Place* and 'reboot' film and television, see chapter 7 in this volume by Catherine Wheatley.
42 Cavell, *Cities of Words*, 140, his emphasis.
43 Ibid., 437.
44 Alan's speech to Beatrice, in which he concedes their relationship is over and tells her to 'be whoever you are' (s1:e7), demonstrates a Cavellian sense of acknowledgement and proposes Wittgenstein's rebuttal to the problem of other minds. Referring to Wittgenstein's notion that 'the human body is the best picture of the human soul', Cavell argues, 'The block to my vision of the other is not the other's body but my incapacity or unwillingness to interpret or to judge it accurately, to draw the right connections' (*The Claim of Reason: Wittgenstein, Skepticism, Morality, and Tragedy* [Oxford: Oxford University Press, 1999 (1979), 368]). In an echo of this idea, Alan describes the physical signs of his deteriorating union, which he previously chose to ignore or misinterpret. He tells Beatrice, 'No matter how much we think we're fooling people, our bodies, they can't keep lying the way that our minds can' (s1:e7).
45 Cavell, *Cities of Words*, 421.
46 Ruth is unquestionably a teacher figure for Nadia. Her status as a therapist also conjures comparisons to Dr Jaquith's psychological mentoring of Charlotte in *Now, Voyager*, and in many ways she represents a perfectionist exemplar of what Nadia could become, her next best self. But her close affiliation with Nadia's mother, and Nadia's childhood, makes her unable to offer a disinterested perspective—as a surrogate mother, she is too connected to Nadia's past trauma to play a role in perfectionist friendship.
47 Cavell, *Cities of Words*, 224.

48 Ibid., 154–55.
49 Ibid., 164.
50 Cavell, *Pursuits of Happiness*, 145.
51 Ibid., 145–46.
52 Ibid., 147, his emphasis.
53 Cavell, *Cities of Words*, 16.
54 André Breton, *Nadja*, trans. Richard Howard (London: Penguin Classics, 1999), 66.
55 Cavell, *Cities of Words*, 1.
56 Ibid., 2.
57 Ibid., 337.
58 Ibid., 307.
59 Stone, *Feminism, Psychoanalysis, and Maternal Subjectivity*, 93.
60 Ibid., 93
61 Cavell, *Cities of Words*, 206.
62 Cavell, *Pursuits of Happiness*, 13.
63 Ibid., 241; Cavell, *Cities of Words*, 215.
64 Cavell, *Cities of Words*, 424–25.
65 Cavell, *Pursuits of Happiness*, 149.
66 Ibid., 149.
67 Cavell, *Cities of Words*, 426.
68 Ibid., 427–28.
69 Cavell, *Pursuits of Happiness*, 163, my emphasis.
70 Cavell, *Cities of Words*, 218.
71 Ibid., 98.
72 In an allusion to continual perfectionist growth, Horse is obsessed with cutting off Nadia's voluminous hair, which he considers the 'old' her (s1:e3). A Puckish trickster figure, he recalls Shakespearian elements Cavell sees in remarriage comedy. If we consider the entirety of the world of *Russian Doll* as the Shakespearean 'green world', constituting 'a place beyond the normal world, where the normal laws of the world are interfered with; a place of perspective and education', Horse's domain of the city park is ironically more similar to what Cavell sees as the 'black world', one identified 'with the chaotic, dangerous state of nature'. In the series it is portrayed as a liminal shadow world caught between the human and animal. Cavell, *Pursuits of Happiness*, 172; Cavell, *Cities of Words*, 348.
73 Lauren Berlant, *Cruel Optimism* (Durham: Duke University Press, 2011), 3.
74 Ibid., 6.
75 Ibid., 195.
76 Cavell, *Pursuits of Happiness*, 152.
77 Berlant, *Cruel Optimism*, 199.
78 Ibid., 199.
79 Ibid., 4.
80 Ibid., 7.
81 Ibid., 8.
82 There are multiple references to the Greek myth of Ariadne, who aids Theseus' escape from the minotaur's labyrinth, throughout the series—one of the first video games Nadia designed is titled *The Legend Ariadne*. Alan hates the game, which functions as a microcosm of Nadia's predicament, because he says it's unwinnable and 'involves

a single character who has to do everything on her own' (s1:e6). Nadia plays her own game and can't beat it either, suggesting that escaping the time loop will only be possible if they work together.
83 Cavell, *Cities of Words*, 24, 263.
84 Jean-François Lyotard, 'The Sublime and the Avant-Garde', in *Postmodernism: A Reader*, ed. Thomas Docherty (New York: Columbia University Press, 1993), 246.
85 Cavell, *Cities of Words*, 32.
86 Berlant, *Cruel Optimism*, 201.
87 Cavell, *Cities of Words*, 84.
88 Ibid., 337.

6

'Nobody's Perfect':
Moral Imperfectionism in *Ozark*

Hent de Vries

'Did television give back as good as it took away?'
—Stanley Cavell, 'The Fact of Television'

If violation of legal and financial norms or statutes is the criterion for criminality, then few of the characters in *Ozark* (2017–22) are in any position to claim their innocence. In Barack Obama's neoliberal America—in the aftermath of the 'war on drugs' (which, on the face of it, seems strangely tangential in this TV series' storyline and, according to it, no longer even a priority for the government, whether at the state level or the FBI), in the wake also of the 'war on terror' (after all, while there is no small dose of terrorization and correlative damage throughout in *Ozark*, this is no *Homeland* [2011–20])—virtually no one we meet up close in this remarkable saga remains unscathed by, much less immune to, the perils of crime, the addiction to money, and the at times ruthless physical violence both cannot but impose. No single character we encounter seems able to live, let alone make a living, without becoming absorbed—or morally tainted, indeed, simply doomed—by the fatal power and trappings of capital and the criminality it cannot but invite. At the very least, all human relationships are submitted to the inviolable law of value that is less one of common use, according to one's needs, than one of exchange, such that all human exchanges we painstakingly follow are 'transactional'. In such a universe, gratuitous acts of kindness, never mind goodness or justice, are hard to come by. We see very few of them, indeed, but when they nonetheless happen, they touch us all the more.

In Karl Marx's definition, money is the universal equivalent. By contrast, in *Ozark*'s dystopian universe, it is anything but the emancipatory social or cultural equalizer with which not just Marx but especially so-called bourgeois ideology identifies it up to this day—on the presumption that money levels the historically, intimately connected playing fields that church and clergy, on the one hand, and castle and nobles, on the other, once fully dominated and exhausted, preparing their own demise and eventual overthrow along the way. And of the church and clergy, feudalism and nobility there remain in *Ozark* only shadows and caricatures: informal, evangelical revivalist movements, on one end, and local hillbillies, with ancient pedigree in the land (flooded out as it is by the incursion of modern technology and the need for electricity) and, we are told, not to be confused with groundless rednecks, on another. Between these polar opposites, the laws of tradition and of inheritance, of erstwhile authority and present brute power, are carefully registered and respected throughout. The story that Jacob Snell (Peter Mullan) recounts about church bells resounding from under the lake that drowned his family's land and property is a case in point. The way he and his spouse engage an unsuspecting yet unrelenting itinerant preacher and his expecting wife ruthlessly, as they interfere with the former's business distributing drugs over water and have accepted the offer to build an actual church on land, is yet another.

True, money 'makes the world go round', as Liza Minnelli famously sings in *Cabaret*, and indeed the capital and circular 'O' in *Ozark* is used as each episode's opening emblem for a reason—in the shape of a coin, it conjures also the grand yawning opening in which little vignettes or 'symbols' announce the subplots of each of the individual episodes. But then again, its circle of immanence is more and more closed off, just as its cycle of violence becomes more and more devastating with each turn and twist of the narrative, which ends up spiraling downwards, in a relentless descent into Dante Alighieri's no less than Marx's *Inferno*.[1] There is no emancipatory horizon in sight, as classical Marxism and liberalism once jointly claimed. Rather, we are witnessing the slow but steady descent into an inverted *Divina Comedia* in which, as Emmanuel Levinas once quipped, 'the laughter sticks in your throat.'[2]

Perhaps aside from *Succession* (2018–), no recent television series can lay greater claim to having spelled out in excruciating phenomenological and analytical detail what capitalism—itself always in the vicinity of crime (in *Ozark*, of drug lords, mobsters, bad cops, pharmaceutical industries, nativist locals, corrupt politicians, and no small dose of bad faith religious zealots, who, as said, unwittingly enable the sale of opioids from boats on the lake, much in the way Christ preached offshore, according to the Gospels, spreading a different "opium" under the people as vulgar Marxism would have it)—has manifested as the undeniable and increasingly painful truth of the last century and a half, namely this: '*Es gibt kein richtiges Leben im falschen.*' ('Wrong life cannot be lived rightly.' Or, rather: 'There is no right life within the false life.') This sentence, found in Theodor Adorno's *Minima Moralia*, aphorism 18, perhaps says it all, shedding light on the ways in which private lives are invaded, colonized, and turned inside out by the pursuit of money—and the property and freedom it promises but just as easily takes away. After all, as *Ozark* teaches us, freedom always and everywhere stands under the aegis and control of monopolies, cartels, clans, and corporations or even state apparatuses. Individual fates count for nothing in this historical and downright sociopathic logic where individual agency and small, often gratuitous acts of resistance and, perhaps, genuine freedom—without much reason, much less normative deliberation and justification, to back things up—are all we are left with and are all we must count on. No 'force of the better argument', to cite Jürgen Habermas' well-known mantra, can win us over here, only singular, even idiosyncratic *ways of doing* that *withstand full knowing* and are, for the rest, less than perfect by definition: unintended instances of some good in a world that experiences and acknowledges neither the Good nor a God, strictly speaking.

Adorno, who with Max Horkheimer devoted ample attention, during his American years, to developing a 'theory of the racket', just as he analysed the logic of monopoly (the psychological corollary of which was the character sketch of those on the gliding scale towards fascism, the F-scale, in *The Authoritarian Personality*), may have rightly seen that all things true, good, and beautiful, in contemporary America, have become increasingly refracted and distorted by the 'prism' of capital, whose kaleidoscopic effects are nothing short of catastrophic for individuals and society alike. In its distorted and distorting light, family and love relationships, like friendships, civic, and collegial bonds, all of which require trust and duration, are submitted to the invisible hand and, in fact, iron law—a quasi-Darwinian 'ecosystem', it is called at some point—of the economic, financial, and consumer market, whose unforgiving workings are amoral at best, cynical and violent at worst.

'Cause and effect', the 'survival of the fittest' (e.g., of hillbillies over rednecks, of those who have the sheer 'will' to assert themselves and rule and those who lack the stamina to do so and persist), or, in the main protagonist Martin (or Marty) Byrde's (Jason Bateman) more subtle analysis, the unavoidable, unintended consequences of individual, seemingly random decisions, which make sure that nothing happens for a reason—all these are among the philosophical and, largely, naturalist, if at times deep, metaphysical tropes invoked in *Ozark* by the characters in order to make sense where, to all appearances, there is simply none to be either found or made.

As a TV series, *Ozark* consists of four seasons. While the last season commences with an unsettling and misleading give-away in the first minutes of part one—namely with a car crash, involving the whole of the Byrde family, seemingly destined to finally meeting their Maker, perhaps fairly, if well before, at least, the children's time—the actual end and, indeed, *grand finale* of the series pans out very differently. Though all along we have been led to believe that, no matter what, this surely will all end very badly for the Byrdes, as much as we may have been rooting for one or the other and in this or that moment, as regular viewers or irresponsible binge watchers, the crime family in fact gets away with it all, which comes down to saying that the finale's ultimate reckoning is—morally and humanly speaking—hardly better than the fourth season's opening scene with its spectacular car crash falsely predicts. When a former, failed cop and private detective, Mel Sattem (Adam Rothenberg), who has been following the Byrdes' every move diligently and indefatigably, confronts them at last with the incriminating evidence of a murder in which they are, once again, the clear accomplices, he makes his point bravely, speaking for all of us, as much as we might not have liked his constant prying in their unflattering dealings with the drug world of the Ozarks and its regional as well as statewide politics: 'You don't get to win … the world doesn't work like that.' To which Wendy (Laura Linney) asks him a simple rhetorical question, which by now we all know how to answer: 'Since when?' After which Jonah (Skylar Gaertner) puts the dot on the proverbial 'i', agreeing for once with his mother on family matters, and with surprisingly little hesitation pulls the trigger (or so we are led to believe, as the screen fades to black and we, as viewers lose all residual hope we might still have invested in the youngest Byrde).

From the get-go, in episode 1 of season 1, *Ozark* already gives its *minimal moral* away, in a matter-of-fact way, without any apparent guilt or professed shame. Having been accused by his colleague and friend of leading a 'tragically subdued life' and just having found proof of his wife Wendy's infidelity, Marty, during the first family dinner we witness, lectures his daughter Charlotte (Sofia Hublitz) about the 'value of money', which she seems to either ignore or take for granted. Not so Marty. In his very first monologue, with which the series aptly opens and which, it seems, is his standard pitch, delivered in his still very much downscale Chicago office and addressed to baffled, overwhelmed client investors, he lays it all out:

> Scratch. Wampum. Dough. Sugar. Clams. Loot. Bills. Bones. Bread. Bucks. Money. That which separates the haves from the have-nots. But what is money? It's everything if you don't have it, right? Half of all American adults have more credit card debt than savings. Twenty-five percent have no savings at all. And only fifteen percent of the population is on track to fund even one year of retirement. Suggesting what? The middle class is evaporating? Or the American Dream is dead? You wouldn't be sitting there listening to me if the latter were true. You see, I think most people just have a fundamentally flawed view of money. Is it simply an agreed-upon unit of exchange for goods and services? $3.70 for a gallon of milk? Thirty bucks to cut your grass? Or, is it an intangible? Security or happiness—peace of mind. Let me propose a third option. Money as a measuring device. You see, the hard reality is how much money we accumulate in life is not a function of who's president or the economy or bubbles bursting or bad breaks or bosses. It's about the American work ethic. The one that made us the greatest country on earth. It's about

bucking the media's opinion as to what constitutes a good parent. Deciding to miss the ball game, the play, the concert, because you've resolved to work and invest in your family's future. And taking responsibility for the consequences of those actions. Patience. Frugality. Sacrifice. When you boil it down, what do those three things have in common? Those are choices. Money is not peace of mind. Money's not happiness. Money is, at its essence, that measure of a man's choices. (s1:e1)

Money, then, is the measure of Marty's choices, but it is also his unique 'gift', as is aptly pointed out by Del (Esai Morales), the drug cartel rep minding him (and one among several—three to be precise—who eventually suffer the fate they clearly deserve and that we, as viewers, come to firmly wish upon them as we witness their normless intelligence, ruthless efficiency, and unimaginable cruelty). And as the seasons progress, it becomes clear that perhaps only Jonah, Marty's son, comes closest to Marty's financial acumen, whose inner-worldly *askesis*—'I worked, came home, went to bed, got up, did it all over again'—defines the latter's outlook almost completely. Moreover, Marty's worldly acumen, not unlike that of the divine providential *oikonomia* of old, works wonders (of the more sinister kind) nonetheless, creating value out of nothing, or so it seems. Not exactly an angel ('In fact, the satisfying sound of your lover smacking the pavement is the only thing that gets me to sleep every night', he tells his wife, Wendy), Marty is a sort of angel nonetheless: an 'angel investor. I … I help turn around struggling businesses', as he aptly puts it. The clerk in the local Ozark regional office, who provides him with all the liens in the public records, shows her surprise in hearing this statement: 'You intend to make money out of businesses that aren't making any?' Marty gives an altogether accurate answer: 'In a roundabout way.' It is by this way—basically following the principles and logic of 'money laundering 101', as he calls it—that he is and, throughout the whole series, will keep 'trying to make everything right' (s1:e3). The *homo economicus* takes on quasi-godly salutary qualities, never mind the impure means to bring about the intended results about. Presumably, Marty's and, *a fortiori*, Wendy's working hypothesis is that there is nothing that money cannot fix, in principle, if not always in fact.

Ozark, then, is on one reading a brilliant visual adaptation of Max Weber's classic *The Protestant Ethic and the Spirit of Capitalism* with added touches of Marx, Nietzsche, and quite some Darwin to top things off—and with a passing reference to Melville's Bartleby who says 'I'd prefer not to.' But then, deep down, both Marty and Wendy go down the rabbit hole, all the way, by their own volition and with little hesitation, come to think of it: the playful 'shall we, shall we not' scene in Mexico, under drug lord Omar Navarro's (Felix Solis) roof, is, on close scrutiny, more of a conjugal, flirtatious dance than a serious or, for that matter, sincere process of moral adjudication of pros and cons.

As does *Succession*, *Ozark* portrays the family as a 'small business' and spouses as 'business partners', which need to adjust, adapt, and invest—to quite literally—survive. Even so, when asked, Wendy explains the flight or exile from Chicago to her friends with 'this is a family sabbatical. Return to simplicity' (s1:e7). Yet, for Marty, at least for most of the first season, up to its concluding episode, this togetherness is, as far as his alienated wife is concerned, based on 'necessity, not desire' (s1:e7). Marty and Wendy have no choice except cohabitating and cooperating. (Jacob Snell, about whom more in a moment, knows all about it: 'Tricky thing, combining work and marriage, but a blessing if it works.' [s2:e1])

In Wendy's first job in the Ozark region, showcasing and selling crappy houses on the lake, it comes down to this: 'I know to how sell [*sic*!] the idea of a happy family' (s1:e3), as if family were a commodity among others that can be sold or purchased as well. Later in the same season (e8), we learn that Wendy has had her share of tragedy (the loss of an unexpected and, so we discover, unwanted pregnancy after a car accident), but also that even well before she knew Marty she was 'an existential mess' with a penchant for breaking into people's houses, having a beer on their couch, only to come to the realization that she did 'not belong there', nor pretty much anywhere else. She has a deeper, darker side than Marty (unless dissociating, almost no matter what happens, which is his forte, is darker still). By the time we reach the final season's denouement, we find Wendy confessing that she's 'taking it one catastrophe at a time'. But even at that point such despair is paired with a frightening tenacity, kept up in the belief that 'we're *so* close' and epitomized in the invective thrown at Marty's ever more shaky resolve, namely to 'Have some fucking faith!' And, in fact, if one ignores the moral and human price paid at the end—the sacrifices made mostly by others, that is—one might conclude that she does, indeed, pull it all off. Indefatigable and unflinching in finding one manipulative scheme and way out of one predictable predicament after another, Wendy has indeed something monstrous about her. She is the ruse of reason incarnate. There is no price she is not willing to pay, no sacrifice she is not willing to make, as long as it is exacted primarily on others, that is, and furthers her ultimate game plan no matter what: to collect enough dirty money, found a philanthropic organization cum political action committee, and stretch all accrued power and its benefits out over the mid-Western states, to do some good in the world. No small amount of self-delusion and cynicism go hand in hand in all she undertakes with maximal fervor and minimal remorse.

But then, Wendy was once also into real politics—and very idealistic too—back in Chicago, working on 'Obama's second state legislature campaign' and being 'good at it. Goddamn it. I was really ... I was really good at it.' As she adds: 'I just loved everything he [Obama] stood for. What we are all trying to do together. I quit after Charlotte was born. Childcare was more than my paycheck, so ... And now, here I am. In Nowhere, Missouri. And Obama's Obama.' Buddy Dieker (Harris Yulin), her dying downstairs neighbour, who has sold his house to her under market price, under the condition that he can spend his last days in the basement, seems to agree and, having found reprieve from an endless, painful coughing attack, offers the following mixed praise for the then-President, whose overall Democratic agenda, it seems, he should in principle have supported: 'Well, he seems like a smart enough guy. Not that I'd ever vote for a Muslim' (s1:e6). A former labour union activist and retired Teamster with Kansas City mob connections, which the Byrdes get to use with some profit, his understanding and loyalties clearly go only that far. We meet Buddy nude, heading out for his morning's swim in the lake (and while Marty admonishes him, he doesn't care, having nothing left too lose in the little time he has still to live); we later see the Byrdes use his mausoleum after he dies from heart seizure as an unsuspected stashing place for cash.

Next to perhaps Jonah, Marty, and Wendy's son, who only in the final episode of the series reveals himself to be a true godson, ready to take over the family business if he really has to, it is the persona of Ruth Langmore (Julia Garner) who, literally and figuratively—again, up to the very end—survives much of the plot, if only barely, and then (like all the main and side characters who are young and still impressionable) deeply scarred and damaged. More precisely, she's the only one standing morally intact, however existentially devastated she may be. An unlikely and lonely hero. After all, while, as mentioned above, the series concludes by pulling a black screen politely over Jonah's presumed final, *Godfather*-worthy act, his role up until that revealing moment had seemed to prepare him for better things. There is a healthy curiosity and resourcefulness, next to a modicum of a moral compass, that makes Jonah stand out in many respects. The kid who would have had all the chances in the world (and still may, damaged goods as he is now, once the family returns 'home', which would be Chicago), resembles Ruth and especially her cousin, Wyatt Langmore (Charlie Tahan), even though the problematic upbringing and abject poverty that the latter two have suffered throughout would have condemned any other person to a life of sheer ignorance and, perhaps, justified resentment or at least resignation. And their fathers and uncles, respectively, haven't precisely offered a model to emulate but rather a dazzling display of everything one should surely avoid.

But even the most uncompromising moral compass, not to mention conscience, *Ozark* tells us, will end up distorted by the outside or inside pressures (here, mostly the instinctive urge to protect one's own very flawed family, from possible legal prosecution and worse). In the end, Jonah's moral universe aligns with that of his parents and sister: it is all right to kill to avoid running the risk of being captured or killed oneself. In the words of the actor who played his part, Skylar Gaertner, Jonah Byrde is at once 'an introvert' and 'entrepreneurial'. Although the killing of his uncle, Wendy's brother, and his parents' entanglement with the cartel and its crimes shock and appall him, Jonah, by his own initiative, quickly learns to handle guns and shoot (aided by his buddy, Buddy), just as he has his father's genius for grasping the mechanics of moving laundered money across accounts undetected.

Equalled only by her cousin, Wyatt—the only person in the series, aside from Charlotte, who seems to read books and does so even more avidly, irrespective of the tragic fact that with his growing up in trailers as a member of a dysfunctional family or tribe, college is not in the cards—Ruth, literally and figuratively also beaten down, in every situation seems to somehow get it. Not that she knows how to—she just does. Not surprisingly, she sets the ambition of getting Wyatt to consider and enter college as her most important goal in life. Damaged by an abusive father yet unwilling to betray her past ('I like my name', she says when offered a make-over identity by Marty), she remains at once a morally and politically disbelieving sceptic and a disillusioned if resolute pragmatist. Ruth's most citable and profound, deeply metaphysical mantra is, perhaps, this: 'I know shit about fuck.' But she is also the one who, in spite of all the epistemic impasses and normative morasses, acts always directly and decisively, wherever and whenever needed. Indeed, her sheer resilience, unmoored from any ethical principles, maxims and deliberations, practical wisdom and prudent considerations, is, for us viewers, hard to ignore and even harder to fathom. Ruth provides what is, perhaps, the series' best example of what moral *imperfectionism* might mean in post-Obama neoliberal America where, in the eyes of many, neither right- nor left-wing populism—with its extremes of nativist and nascent fascism, on the one hand, and, alas, much undervalued democratic socialist or even communist class- and mass-based (i.e., labor- and union-led) initiatives, on the other—proposes much of an appealing, much less successful, alternative thus far. When all is said and done (and much is said and done, too much on all scores, as polite conversation, next to polite company, are luxuries she cannot afford), it is hard not to admire, fear, and love her all at once. Ruth is fragile yet fierce, with a determination of will, inner strength, and, as it were, good ruthlessness that is an easy match for Wendy's similarly traumatized ego and attitude. The former presenting a rough but honest residual normative core—material for a minima moralia, in precisely Adorno's sense, in a time of economic and social downturn—whereas the latter offers a sad picture of an 'enlightened false consciousness [*aufgeklärtes falsches Bewusstsein*]' of which Peter Sloterdijk painted such a convincing portrait in his *Kritik der zynischen Vernunft* (*Critique of Cynical Reason*), arguably his most unsettling and compelling work, discovering the premises of *and* prelude to much of the cultural and political present in twentieth-century Germany in the interbellum Babylon of the Weimar Republic.

Although Ruth is relentlessly cold-blooded, when needed—as demonstrated by her willingness, on two occasions, to kill Marty and, on another, effectively killing her two uncles to prevent them from killing him—it is hard in the end not to empathize with her and cheer her on. We root for her to succeed, that is, to survive, because other moral options have discredited themselves in terms of their normative justification (and she, for her part, claims no pretense of having one). One comes to somehow 'love' Ruth, while it is hard to love Marty, a bit harder even to love Wendy—both of whom, it is true, unlike Ruth, respond to their challenges if not with rage and vehemence, then at least with near-stoic equanimity (in the case of Marty) and downright identification with the aggressor (in the case of Wendy), mimicking and at times outbidding the worst they are confronted with. It is only by way of this strange acquiescence found in going along with or outwitting the danger, becoming 'nobody' (*oudeis*) in order to survive, like the figure of *homo economicus* that Adorno, in *Dialectic of Enlightenment*, portrays in Homer's *Odyssey* and the character of Ulysses, that Marty and Wendy become a formidable match for the Mexican drug lords', FBI agents', mob bosses', bad cops', and corrupt politicians' maxims and impulses (all of whom pretend to put family, fatherland, or fortune and the common good first, in that order). In their doubling down on *anything goes*, it seems (including having one's bipolar brother killed, lest he might reveal too much in his unstoppable, uncontrollable rantings in the presence of whoever lends him an ear). Indeed, Marty and Wendy become veritable cartel leaders: directly, in the case of Marty, who steps in for Navarro while he is in FBI custody, and sets a bloody example when he needs to assert his authority among the 'lieutenants'; indirectly, in the case of Wendy, who handpicks Navarro's successor with a fatal consequence (i.e., Ruth's death).

Ruth, for her part, never abuses the trust of others, much less of those who deserve it or rely upon it (even Marty, when he asks her to save and protect his kids when he fears he might not make it back). In fact, foulmouthed Ruth trusts too much, even though there is no doubt she's the most desolate, betrayed, and lonely character in the series. As she faces her killer, in the final episode of season 4, it is hard to suppress the impression that Camila Elizondro (Veronica Falcón), who is willing to kill her own brother, Omar Navarro, on two occasions (one of them successfully)—and hence who has few scruples in asserting her newly gained power and avenging her son Javi's death—has some rare trepidation when facing Ruth, who, in her impeccably white dress, stands against the dark lake as a beacon of innocence, dignity, and utter strength. The victim needs to convince the perpetrator to commit her act and does so fearlessly, portrayed as a female Christlike figure, if ever there was one, expiating for all the innumerable sins committed in this long series, sins in which, as distant, comfortable spectators, we now feel somehow complicit, as we face the need to come to terms with a world that allowed all this 'shit' to happen in the first place and must see and set things aright, while realizing than one or two reforms or revolutions, much less merely the next election, will not be enough to heal the wounds and mend our ways. After all, a better normative, moral, or political theory, next to a more progressive legislative agenda and humane jurisprudence, while surely among the necessary conditions for bringing greater fairness and finite justice about, may not be sufficient to turn things around. An altogether different redemption of all things—a quasi-messianic *restitutio integrum*, as Walter Benjamin mused in his "Theologico-Political Fragment", echoing Origen of Alexandria's recalcitrant motif of the *apokatastasis* or resurrection of each and, perhaps, all things—will be in order to make things right again, if ever they were, until matters take a turn for the worse once more.

Paradoxically, Ruth is arguably the person whose moral vocabulary and normative self-justification is developed the least among the many dubious characters. The Byrdes, the Snells, the Navarros, and the local and federal law enforcement authorities, by contrast, excel in subtle rationalizations and casuistry. This remarkable difference, all by itself, contains important lessons: no morals result from moralism, nothing right comes from self-righteousness, one cannot straighten what was crooked at first.

At their best, though, what makes the Byrdes and some of the other protagonists also stand out is not so much cynicism—as we found, the 'enlightened false consciousness', i.e., the consciousness that *knows* what is false and wrong and persists in it anyway, knowingly and willingly—but rather a bogged-down, taciturn tenacity and resilience that sees through the perverse idea that not two but uncountable wrongs make a right. In such a universe, moral perfection—or, for that matter, moral perfectionism—cannot be the goal of one's philosophy or way of life, and some more or better imperfection is the next best option. As Marty tells another naive prospective client: 'It's not a perfect world' (s1:e7).

I borrow the term 'imperfectionism' from Leela Gandhi's formidable study *The Common Cause*. Gandhi defines its 'spiritual regimen' as that of a 'counter-askesis', of sorts. Found especially in anti-colonial and anti-fascist milieus, such ethical and political imperfectionism 'comprised aberrant practices of self-ruination, or anti-care of the self, aimed at making common cause both with the victims and abettors of unjust sociality (by defending the former and reforming the latter)'.[3]

While on the one hand it is tempting to understand *Ozark* as an indictment of the depravity of individual and social life under the conditions of neoliberalism, of money and capital, it might, on the other hand, be possible to discern in it also a multi-layered exploration of—often indirect—forms of resistance, however futile or indeed complicit. Using the best of the worst to arrive at some good, however provisional, however unsought.

It is certainly no accident that a central interest of the local drug-producing hillbilly family, led by Jacob and Darlene Snell (Lisa Emery), uses as its distribution system the many boats making up the floating church, mentioned earlier, while its courageous but all too naive minister preaches the way to overcome the devil (and whose baptism procedure, practised on his own baby, is hard to distinguish from waterboarding, come to think of it). It is through the latter that Marty and Wendy Byrde seek to launder more money by proposing to build a church on land (s1:e3), again, thereby unwittingly undermining the distribution of the Snell's heroin over water with the dire consequence that produces the—tactfully omitted, that is, visually censored—most brutal murder of the four seasons overall (there is some relief in the fact that some atrocities would even be too much for the TV series makers).

What we are left with are miniature portraits in moral fallibility. Jacob Snell's philosophy, shot through with biblical references, is deeply perverse: 'Man cannot tame what God wishes to be wild' (s1:e5). Yet, just before he is killed by his wife for being weak, he lectures the minister who naively believed that Marty Byrne was buying him an onshore church for the right reasons: 'Now, I don't know if Marty's a good man or a bad man. I think we're all good and bad' (s1:e7). A profound sense of finitude, of loss and vulnerability, animates these surroundings—with vultures, literally, circling the heavens—and Buddy, the dying housemate of the Byrdes, who takes his daily bath in the lake in Adam's costume, citing what is arguably Martin Heidegger's best line, itself a citation, in *Sein und Zeit*: 'we're all dying the minute we're born'—while adding: 'Goes fast. Don't waste it. *Don't* waste it' (s1:e3).[4]

What, then, is *Ozark*'s moral, its ethics and politics? It is, perhaps, that no matter how bleak—and false—our neoliberal world has turned out to be (*Bleak Liberalism* is the apt title of Amanda Anderson's brilliant book on related matters[5]), we always have *further choices* to make that, given the state of all present things or states to come, will be necessarily imperfect, yet without excuse. Moreover, whatever remnant of minimal truth, goodness, and beauty there is or will still be, our moral sense and experience, our justifications, cannot be based on mere deliberation, much less calculation, but require a sense of immediacy and urgency that no normative principles, axioms or rules, nor, for that matter, constitutional rights and jurisprudence, can clarify from the outset, thus imposing a responsibility that is nothing short of absolute as it cannot be relegated or delegated to some other instance or institution.

As Darlene objects to Marty's blunt appeal to the shared self-interests of the Snell clan and the 'second largest' Mexican drug cartel, led by Navarro, he (Marty) doesn't understand that for a 'people' with a 'history' and with 'pride', 'symbolism matters', as do 'gestures'. But Marty talks too much, Jacob and Del Rio (Nancy De Mayo) each seem to agree, especially when he lies. By contrast, 'It's just what you do' that counts in the end and speaks for itself. And if that means blowing off the head of a Mexican trafficker, here Del Rio, simply because he has been 'disrespectful', calling the Snells 'rednecks' (while they consider themselves 'hillbillies'), so be it. As we know as viewers, Jacob surely deserved it, having just pulled out two of Marty's toenails. And even if Darlene acknowledges she may have 'overreacted' a bit, Jacob, her husband, who surely does not approve, has her back (and kills Del Rio's lieutenant or associate, still standing). The cartel, after all, now in a profitable business deal with them, will just send another representative, another Mexican, since, as Jacob adds, calmly and laconically, piling more upon his wife's blatant xenophobia and racism: 'If there is something Mexico is full of, it is Mexicans.'

Moral imperfectionism may also mean this: people act on the basis of a 'principle of insufficient reason' (borrowing freely here from Quentin Meillassoux's helpful terminology, in *After Finitude*).[6] In Wendy's words: 'I don't believe that ... people actually need a reason to do the things they do. I mean, sometimes people just act. And then they come up with an explanation when they're looking back' (s1:e5). This conception lines up nicely with Marty's own, alluded to earlier. Responding to an insensitive remark from clumsy FBI informer Bruce (Josh Randall) in the hospital—in episode eight of the first season, after *Ozark*'s first car crash, which causes Wendy to lose the unborn child she has just said she didn't want to have—Marty says, 'Everything happens for a reason', further elaborating on the train of thought he had earlier, in the car, laid out to Wendy:

> You really believe that? You really think that there's some ... some preordained chart, floating around up in the ether, with our fate all figured out? ... Things happen because human beings make decisions, they commit acts ... and that makes things happen. And it creates a snowball effect with the ... you know, their world around them, causes other people to make decisions. Cycle continues, snowball keeps rolling. And even when that's not the case, when life's events are not connected to other people's decisions and actions, it's not some bullshit fucking test sent down from the universe—to check your resolve, you know ... I mean, what would the reason be for some healthy five-year old to get a brain tumor? Or why would a tsunami wipe out a village? You tell those families everything happens for a reason. No, sometimes people make decisions, shit happens, and we gotta act accordingly. Or you can ... crawl in a hole and die, you know? (s1:e8)

To act according to what has no reason, can have no reason. To perfect our lives and, *a fortiori*, those around us (family, clan, people, nation, humanity) means to work with and work through seemingly ineliminable imperfection, making the best of the least. In so doing, all bets are off; neither action nor inaction, theorizing nor flying blindly, impulsively, violence nor non-violence can be excluded per se. And when Marty responds to Jacob Snell that he doesn't operate like his (or Snell's) wife, who are 'always sitting on impulse', by claiming 'I am a businessman. I trust the numbers', (s1:e10) that is one lesson he hasn't yet learned. It is true that his genius—counting on numbers—buys him another day, like Prometheus, the ancient Titan and yet another trickster and master craftsman, with each day bringing another moment his heart (rather than liver) is eaten out, as if by punishment, for a debt that cannot be repaid.

Jacob Snell understands this better: 'All of life's a simple business arrangement. That's why you prepare for anything.' He himself, though, clearly does not suspect what is coming his way—alas, Darlene poisons him before he can kill her. But then, even if unprepared, Jacob might have forgiven her. As he tells Marty: 'Things happen. You apologize and you move on.' To which Marty objects: 'Am I supposed to believe that?' Jacob: 'The woman [i.e., Darlene] brought you fresh honey.' But Jacob's relationship with his wife is not so different from Marty's with Wendy. As he says: 'What do you do, Marty, when the bride that took your breath away becomes the wife that makes you hold your breath in terror?' (s2:e9) The answer seems to be: one watches it all play out and either dies as a result—as Jacob does—or survives, like Marty, precisely because facing the terror alone pulls one through in the end, as it strengthens the will and its resolve, come what may.

It has been recently suggested by Ryan Zickgraf in the socialist online journal *Jacobin* that *Ozark* 'was secretly a fictionalized version of the rise of the Democratic Party's royal family—the Clintons', who, according to the *Washington Post*'s reporting in 1992, had their own shady real-estate dealings in the Ozark Mountains, in the late 1970s.[7] As a television show, *Ozark* would thus join the ranks of the novel, more precisely *roman-à-clef*, by 'Anonymous' (in fact, columnist Joel Klein) published in 1996 and entitled *Primary Colors*, whose comedy-drama movie rendition in 1998 featured John Travolta and Emma Thompson as Bill and Hillary in their lead-up to the Democratic nomination in 1992. If this is the case, *Ozark* would be yet another addition to the relatively recent genre of television series described as 'Washington noirs', albeit at a distance in space and time, as the show, anticipating the affairs depicted by Klein's novel, explores what would have led up to the Clinton's presidential ambitions and eventual Washington years.

A more interesting question, in our context, however, would be: does *Ozark*, as a television series, make good upon Stanley Cavell's sceptical anticipations of TV as a modern art form, if not quite 'come of age'? If so, it would add a compelling chapter to the brilliant work done by Martin Shuster and others who explore the existential and, more broadly, ontological dimensions of so-called 'new television', without forgetting the aesthetic features and political connotations of the medium in question.[8]

In terms of our everyday naivety and tendency towards disappointment and avoidance, might we claim that, with this show, television—'the fact of television', as Cavell says—did 'give back as good as it took away'?[9] The answer should probably be that *Ozark*, along with some of the very best television series around, did and does all that exactly—provided we take its narrative and, as it were, 'moral', as a profound, if unsettling, extended, deeply metaphysical as well as down-to-earth pragmatic meditation of the imperfections underlying apparent ethical striving (to begin with protecting one's family) in an age in which the seemingly intractable imbrication of money and monopoly capital, property and class, crime and campaign finance, growing income and wealth inequality, including a presumed democratic politics, have doomed virtually every prospect of justice and fairness for all. Ozark holds up a quasi-dystopian mirror that shows that we viewers are not merely spectators, since we know and realize all too well what we see and are implicated by and complicit in, yet do not necessarily or immediately acknowledge, much less act upon. The dire situation and implications we see drawn up and out, with the series' relentless luminosity and darkness alike, may yet reflect back a different world to us though our reflex cannot be but to shy away from what we see, magnified by the series' miniature portraits of the *magna moralia* called for to fix this world (the only one, Cavell muses, in *The Claim of Reason*, we'll ever know or, at least, inherit). All this, then, in lieu or, perhaps, in view of a world that we might actually wish to live in and of which we might begin to become more worthy of, if only by unequivocally *negating* the present one.

Notes

1 Cf. William Clare Roberts, *Marx's Inferno: The Political Theory of Capital* (Princeton: Princeton University Press, 2017).

2 See my *Religion and Violence: Philosophical Perspectives from Kant to Derrida* (Baltimore and London: Johns Hopkins University Press, 2002) and, in this context, also my "On General and Divine Economy: Talal Asad's Genealogy of the Secular & Emmanuel Levinas's Critique of Capitalism, Colonialism, and Money," in *Powers of the Secular Modern: Talal Asad and His Interlocutors*, ed. David Scott and Charles Hirschkind, (Stanford: Stanford University Press, 2005), 113–33.

3 Leela Gandhi, *The Common Cause: Postcolonial Ethics and the Practice of Democracy* (Chicago: University of Chicago Press, 2014), 2.

4 Martin Heidegger, *Sein und Zeit* (Halle: Max Niemeyer, 1927), 245, translated as *Being and Time* by John Macquarrie and Edward Robinson, with a new Foreword by Taylor Carman (New York: Harper and Row, 1962, 2008), 289. Heidegger cites *Der Ackermann aus Böhmen*: "As soon as man comes to life, he is at once old enough to die."

5 Amanda Anderson, *Bleak Liberalism* (Chicago: University of Chicago Press, 2016).

6 Quentin Meillassoux, *Après la finitude. Essai sur la nécessité de la contingence* (Paris: Éditions du Seuil, 2006); *After Finitude: An Essay on the Necessity of Contingency*, trans. Ray Brassier (New York: Continuum, 2008).

7 Ryan Zickgraf, "Was *Ozark* Actually About the Clintons," *Jacobin*, March 17, 2022. Cf. Charles R. Backcock and Rachel LaFraniere, "Couple's 'Most Confusing' Deal Involved Real Estate in Ozarks", *Washington Post*, July 21, 1992.

8 Martin Shuster, *New Television: The Aesthetics and Politics of a Genre* (Chicago: University of Chicago Press, 2017).

9 Stanley Cavell, *Themes Out of School: Effects and Causes* (Chicago: University of Chicago Press, 1984), 238.

7

A Zigzag of a Hundred Tacks: Narrative Complexity in *The Good Place*

Catherine Wheatley

Eleanor Shellstrop is dead. She has been hit and run over by a mobile billboard truck advertising an erectile dysfunction pill after dropping a bottle of 'Lonely gal margarita mix for one' in a grocery store parking lot, and now her earthly life is over. But that is not the end of Eleanor's story, for she has now moved on to the next stage of her existence. Eleanor has lived a good life, and so she has entered heaven, or at least something like it. She is, she learns from a dapper gentleman introducing himself as Michael, in 'The Good Place': the final destination for those who have shown exemplary behaviour on earth. The Good Place is explicitly non-denominational, but it holds everything Eleanor could ever want, reserved for the best people who ever lived. Michael, a divine being, is the architect of the 'neighbourhood' in which Eleanor will spend her afterlife, and her unearthly host. He is here to welcome her and reassure her. Despite the ignominious ending to her time on earth, she is okay. Here, 'everything is fine'.

Or so it would seem. Some ten minutes into the first episode of NBC's *The Good Place* (2016–19), Eleanor realizes there's been a mistake. The system that sorts souls into the Good and Bad Places has confused her with another, different Eleanor Shellstrop ('the *real* Eleanor Shellstrop', according to the show's internal logic, acted by Tiya Sircar), a doctor and humanitarian whose sacrifices put her in a rather different league to *our* Eleanor (played with scrappy charm by Kristen Bell). A self-confessed 'Arizona dirtbag' who is, at best, 'a medium person', *our* Eleanor's job on earth was to defraud elderly people by selling them placebo tablets; she is selfish and amoral, not above shoplifting the odd handful of olives, or indeed swiping the cash from a dropped wallet. And her presence in The Good Place, it swiftly transpires, is destabilizing the entire neighbourhood: keeping the secret risks not only

Eleanor's safety but that of those around her, but confessing the error will almost certainly lead to eternal torture. Thankfully a third option presents itself in the form of Chidi Anagonye (William Jackson Harper), Eleanor's system-designated 'soulmate' and a former Professor of Moral Philosophy. Having conned Chidi into keeping her secret, Eleanor asks him to teach her how to be good, to let her be his 'ethical guinea pig'. The remainder of the series turns on Chidi's attempts to educate Eleanor, and Eleanor's attempts to be a better version of herself, and the consequences of these endeavours for both of them, for those around them, and ultimately for the entire human race.

As should be obvious from this brief synopsis, moral education is at the heart of *The Good Place*. As Chidi takes Eleanor through a customized Ethics 101, we encounter detailed explanations of Kantian deontology, Mill's utilitarianism, and Aristotelian virtue ethics. Chidi touches on Descartes, Nietzsche, Rawls and, in one tremendously entertaining *Hamilton*-inspired rap, Kierkegaard. One whole episode is dedicated to Philippa Foot's trolley problem,[1] while Chidi's own unwieldy doctoral thesis is based heavily on T.M. Scanlon's *What We Owe to Each Other*. Throughout the series, moreover, a moral education is presented as something that can only take place through conversation: initially between Chidi and Eleanor, and then between Eleanor and Michael (Ted Danson), and later between each of these three and the series' other principal characters: (deceased) British socialite and philanthropist Tahani Al-Jamil (Jameela Jamil), (deceased) failed DJ and sometime arsonist Jason Mendoza (Manny Jacinto), and Janet (D'Arcy Carden)—a kind of embodied operating system for the afterlife, the cosmic equivalent of Alexa or Google Home.[2] Add to this the fact that from season 2 onwards moral learning is configured as a process of repetition, both thematically and structurally—as the series comes to rely on the principle of the reboot—and *The Good Place* seems ripe for a reading through a Cavellian lens. After all, ethical improvement, friendship and education, conversation and repetition are all fundamental to the notion of moral perfectionism that Cavell explores within texts such as *Conditions Handsome and Unhandsome* (1990), 'The Good of Film' (2000), and *Cities of Words* (2004).

And yet while countless think pieces, several journal articles, and at least two edited collections have been devoted to *The Good Place*, covering topics such as theology, scepticism, and of course ethics, Cavell's name is nowhere to be found in this body of literature. This chapter aims to offer a first corrective to this oversight, looking at how moral perfectionism leads us to The Good Place (the place) and through *The Good Place* (the series) via what Cavell, after Emerson, calls a 'zigzag of discontinuous steps'.[3] I shall begin with an examination of what Cavellian perfectionism is, before turning to examine the thematic correspondences that *The Good Place* shares with the genre that Cavell sees as best exemplifying perfectionism in action: the remarriage comedy, asking how the latter transmutes, as it passes onto TV, into the sitcom. Finally, I will turn to the question of medium specificity to argue that the show's use of the sitcom format, coupled with what the scholar Jason Mittell has called the 'narrative complexity' prevalent within contemporary North American television, gestures towards perfectionism at the level of storytelling and poetics, taking it with us on a journey of a hundred tacks as it moves through various feints and misdirections and in so doing emphasizes the importance to the good life of repetition, seriality, the diurnal, and unending endeavour. If, as Cavell argues, 'good films [have] an affinity with a particular conception of the good', my argument here is that so does good television.[4]

'Where Do You Get That Ethics Stuff?'

As Chidi Anagonye explains at various points within *The Good Place*, ethical philosophy has historically been split into three schools of thought: deontology, utilitarianism, and virtue ethics. These theories are concerned with, respectively, doing one's duty, or maximizing the general happiness, or cultivating one's virtues. Each are proposed at various points within *The Good Place* as possible models for Eleanor, but each is ultimately found to be too restrictive to satisfactorily solve the complex ethical conundrums that present themselves to the inhabitants of The Good Place. Cavellian perfectionism, on the other hand, is both more and less than any existing philosophical theory and so circumvents the problems that sticking rigidly to one model of ethical thinking brings. Cavell describes it not as prescribing behaviours, but rather 'as emphasizing the dimension of the moral life *any theory of it might wish to accommodate*'.[5] It has to do with being true to oneself, with what Foucault refers to as the care of the self, and hence with a dissatisfaction with the self as it stands.[6] Romantics have spoken of the idea of becoming who you are. In the present day, we might say it has to do with self-improvement. For philosopher Stephen Mulhall, it is 'an understanding of the soul as on an onward or upward journey that begins by finding oneself lost to the world and requires a refusal of [current] society in the name of some further, more cultivated or cultured, state of society and the self'.[7]

Cavell identifies perfectionism less with canonical moral philosophers such as Kant and Mill than with figures who work between philosophy and literature, such as Ralph Waldo Emerson, whose work is a key touchpoint for Cavell, or with authors and playwrights such as Jane Austen, George Eliot, Matthew Arnold, Henrik Ibsen, George Bernard Shaw, and Henry James. Indeed, it is perhaps because perfectionism falls between philosophy proper and art that it is so often missing from overviews of ethical philosophy such as Chidi's. Rather than a set of arguments, perfectionism is articulated through a founding myth, which Cavell sets out as follows:

> Obvious candidate features are its ideas of a *mode of conversation* between (older and younger) friends, one of whom is intellectually authoritative because his life is somehow exemplary of a

representative of a life the other(s) are attracted to, and in the attraction of which the self recognizes itself as enchained, fixated, and feels itself removed from reality, whereupon the self finds that it can turn (convert, revolutionize itself) and *a process of education* is undertaken, *in part through a discussion of education*, in which each self is drawn on a journey of ascent to a further state of that self, where the higher is determined not by natural talent but by seeking to know what you are made of and cultivating the thing you are meant to do; it is a *transformation of the self* which finds expression in the imagination of a *transformation of society* into something like an aristocracy where what is best for society is a model for and is modeled on what is best for the individual soul, a *best arrived at in the view of a new reality, a realm beyond, the true world, that of the Good, sustainer of the good city, that of Utopia.*[8]

Put otherwise, perfectionism involves (at least) two individuals: one educator and one learner. Through conversation, the learner recognizes certain truths about themselves and as a result strives to be (and eventually becomes) better. But this self-transformation is not selfish: rather it is outward facing, and results in the creation of a better world: a *good place*. The conception of a doubled self and a doubled world provides a perspective of judgement upon the world as it is, measured against the world as it may be. We recognize that we can be better, if only we are willing to be. And we recognize too that the world can be better, if only we are willing to change it. This recognition is both 'inspiring and frustrating'.[9]

'I Was Dropped into a Cave, and You Were My Flashlight'

The central pairing within *The Good Place* is Eleanor and Chidi. He is introduced to us in the first episode as her soulmate, and while we swiftly learn that this is, at least on a superficial level, a mistake, the series in its entirety reveals that Eleanor and Chidi are indeed fated to fall in love. But before this they are student and teacher, and sometimes friends, and sometimes sparring partners.

Over the course of the four seasons, Chidi and Eleanor fall in and out of love, as Michael and other divine beings erase their memories for reasons both noble and nefarious. Their relationship plays out as a series of repetitions or returns, and the balance of power shifts from one version to the next. Throughout, Chidi encourages Eleanor to be less thoughtless, more mindful of the impact of her actions on others. At the same time, he learns from her to be less scared of the consequences of his actions, to act as well as think. This dynamic is played for laughs, as Eleanor's chaotic actions repeatedly place uptight, anxious Chidi into difficult situations. As they spar and bicker, they recall classic screwball couples of Hollywood's golden age, with, as the *New Yorker*'s Emily Nussbaum puts it, William Jackson Harper playing 'the bespectacled Cary Grant to Bell's bratty Katharine Hepburn. He makes her better; she makes him freer'.[10]

Nussbaum is alluding here to Howard Hawks' 1938 film *Bringing Up Baby*, which stars Grant as a repressed palaeontologist and Hepburn as a scatter-brained heiress and which is one in the genre of films that Cavell describes as the 'Hollywood Comedy of Remarriage'.[11] In these films, the central couple—who seem to have known one another forever—are forced apart by an internal dispute. The goal of the narrative is then to get them 'together *again, back* together'.[12] The only way they can achieve this goal is through a running conversation, even perhaps an argument, about what happiness is and whether one can change, and what one is willing to accept. Although each of the films that Cavell writes about charts a different course to the pair's ultimate reconciliation, they are united by seven common features:

1. The setting is domestic: the action takes place mainly in homes and occasionally offices.
2. The couple's relationship is childish, innocent, and often somewhat chaste-seeming.
3. Reconciliation comes about by way of conversation—a conversation that is witty, full of double entendres and concealed meanings.
4. These are conversations between equals, and yet the question of who is learning what is an important one.
5. The plot begins in a city but gets resolved in a move to a world of nature—in Shakespeare this is called the green world; in four of the seven remarriage comedies it is Connecticut.
6. The atmosphere of these films—as a result, often, of the witty dialogue—is comic, festive.
7. But the films do not close with a grand celebration—a festival—that marks the end of the story. Rather, they place emphasis on continuation and the ongoingness of the conversations that we have witnessed: stressing remarriage as repetition.

The Good Place adheres to almost all these conventions. The action starts and ends in the neighbourhood that Michael has constructed and which is apparently based on a small US town, replete with frozen yoghurt shops and general stores, and mostly takes place in the houses occupied by Eleanor and Chidi and Tahani and Jason. The characters take refuge and work out their differences in a number of different spaces, but notable is 'The Medium Place', a 'neutral zone' of sorts in which, Catherine M. Robb notes, a number of meaningful realizations take place.[13] Chidi and Eleanor kiss several times throughout the series, but only once are shown as having consummated their relationship, in The Medium Place (on a video tape of a version of their past that neither remembers). Being a sitcom, the atmosphere of the series is naturally festive (on which more below), but it does not close with a grand celebration; instead it finishes on an ambivalent note, as each of the characters embarks upon yet another new start (a point to which I shall return towards this chapter's close). And at the centre of all this is the matter of Eleanor's education by Chidi, what Cavell terms 'the new creation of a woman', and the question of whether Chidi will rise to the challenge.

For Cavell, the genre of the remarriage comedy is partly defined by the fact that it is the woman who comes to accept her sexual identity, acknowledge her desire. He writes: 'The man's lecturing indicates that an essential goal of the narrative is the education of the woman, where her education turns out to mean her acknowledgement of her desire, and this in turn will be conceived of as her creation, her emergence, at any rate as an autonomous human being.'[14] The women of these films listen to their lectures, 'because they know they need to learn something further, about themselves, or rather to undergo some change, or creation, even if no one knows how the knowledge and change are to arrive'.[15] So a woman wants to bring about a change in herself; she wants to be 'created'. And in order to do that she turns to a man, one who is able to educate her. Within these films it can only be a man who educates her: she has no mother, no female friends. All this is true of Eleanor, a woman who—at least during her time on earth—refuses friendship or obligations and who views all attempts at forging connection as cynical and self-interested. But this does not let the man off the hook: if the women choose these men to educate them, it is part of the film's (or, in this case, the TV show's) business to demonstrate what 'authorizes' this choice, and part of that has to do with the man's willingness to listen and learn in turn. Chidi first appears to us and Eleanor as a paragon of virtue, but it soon transpires that he is moralistic, and occasionally pompous: in the first season's stunning reveal we discover that all those hours studying ethics have not landed him in The Good Place, but The Bad Place—where Eleanor and Chidi have been all along. It turns out Chidi was so concerned with the theory of ethics that he failed to act, and ended up letting down friends, family, and lovers alike. Both Eleanor and Chidi are then flawed individuals, but together, over time, they learn to be better.

'Not Soul Mates … Just Soul Friends'

It doesn't require a great leap of imagination to see the modern sitcom as the natural legatee of the remarriage comedy.[16] The trope of the central pair who come together, fall apart, and come together again over the course of several seasons for no reason other than their own doubts and inconsistencies abounds in shows such as *Scrubs*, *How I Met Your Mother*, *New Girl*, *The Big Bang Theory* and—perhaps most famously—*Friends*, the TV show that teaches Michael everything he needs to know about human relationships.[17] Indeed, extending over multiple seasons and episodes, the television series arguably allows the remarriage comedy to emphasize questions of repetition even more effectively than the feature film, hence perhaps the migration of romcom from large to small screens. With the temporally enlarged format though also comes a shift of emphasis, from the couple in (more or less) isolation to their embeddedness within a larger network of relations. The romantic couple, that is, is placed within a group, usually of friends, rather than a family set-up. These friends tend to rotate around the couple, who encapsulate a kind of heightened or extreme version of the various interweaving friendships that appear within the show (it's worth noting that many of these sitcoms also feature a central 'bromance' between male characters, which echoes the heterosexual pairing but drains it of its sexual connotations). The extended group members support the central relationship and are also visibly and narratively affected by its ups and downs. As such they come to embody the wider society or community within which the perfectionist relationship operates. In *The Good Place*, this role is played by Michael, Janet, Jason, and Tahani—the self-elected members of 'Team Cockroach'—whose journeys towards the attainable but unattained self are shaped by and shape Eleanor and Chidi's central journey. As the series progresses it becomes clear that they are not merely supporting players; they are also on a journey of moral education.

According to Cavell, to live a moral life, to endlessly become our best selves, we need the 'friendly and credible words of others'.[18] We need to see ourselves through the eyes of another. And we need to decide whose view of us is most valuable to us. This need not however only be a romantic partner. The version of moral perfectionism that Cavell describes in *Cities of Words* is contingent on the presence of inspiring examples: figures who are able to hold themselves open to self-overcoming, whose orientation towards their own better selves is realized and displayed to us in such a way as to reveal our present state as dissatisfying and hence to encourage us to turn away from it. This is Emerson's 'friend' or 'true man'—'a figure that may occur as the goal of the journey but also its instigation and accompaniment'.[19] Cavell also refers to this figure as the 'exemplar' (a term developed from Nietzsche) or 'the advanced figure who sets those who approach him on a path of education'.[20] The exemplar is usually older and is essentially impersonal, interested in helping the younger friend to realize their own self-overcoming, not in satisfying any of their own personal desires (in particular, not any romantic ones), but this is not always the case.

In the finale of season 1 of *The Good Place*, we learn that Eleanor is not the only human who belongs in The Bad Place. In fact, Eleanor, Chidi, Jason, and Tahani are already *in* The Bad Place: they are participants in a fake reality, built by Michael (in fact a demon) with the purpose of torturing them psychologically for thousands of years.[21] Eleanor is selfish, Chidi indecisive, Tahani narcissistic, and Jason perhaps just stupid. All of them are doomed. When Eleanor realizes the ruse, Michael simply clicks his fingers, erasing their memories and the experiment with the intention of taking it from the top. In season 2, however, we discover that the attempt at a do-over has failed: it transpires in the episode 'Dance Dance Resolution' that Michael has rebooted the experiment 802 times, and in all those attempts Eleanor has found Chidi, he has agreed to help her, and Eleanor (and on one occasion,

Jason) has foiled the experiment. Now, the series pivots: Michael—on the verge of being fired by his superiors for his failure to successfully pull off the experiment—proposes that the humans join forces with him to escape to the *real* Good Place. They agree—on the condition that Michael join the ethics classes being delivered now to the entire group by Chidi.

In this new configuration, Chidi remains the teacher, and indeed the exemplar: Eleanor only assents to trusting Michael 'because that's what Chidi would do' (Season 2, Episode 4, 'Team Cockroach'). But now the emphasis has shifted from the pair to the group, and the conversation at the heart of perfectionism becomes diffuse, as the members of the group learn to learn from one another. As the series continues, the pairings shift and each member of the group assumes at various moments the role of mentor and mentee. Eleanor, for example, is able to teach Michael what it is to live with grief, and Chidi how to overcome despondency; Tahani encourages the others to be bold; Jason models self-acceptance. Here is how Cavellian perfectionism differs from Aristotelian virtue ethics: while the latter suggests that we should internalize the behaviours of the exemplar so as to change and eventually become like them, Cavell suggests that through conversation with the exemplar we learn to think things through and become the best version of ourselves. Hence the group members repeatedly ask Chidi not to teach them to be good, or even to be a better person, but to be 'a better Tahani/Eleanor/Michael', and Chidi, for his part, is able to see the best in each one of them, and encourage them to embrace what makes them good. Their task, meanwhile, is 'not to find the thing [they] have always cared about', (which for Eleanor would be shrimp scampi, margaritas, and a good time; Chidi the ultimate answer to his philosophical questions; Tahani her parents' approval; Jason—well, who knows?!) but to discover 'whether [they] have it in [them] to care about something'.[22]

This is the trajectory that the series demonstrates. Over the course of season 1, we see Eleanor become a better person, coming clean to Michael in 'The Eternal Shriek' about being the source of the problems in the neighbourhood, and returning from The Medium Place to save Chidi and Tahani in 'Mindy St. Claire'. During season 2, Michael, Tahani, Jason, and Chidi all also make substantial progress (although the latter three ultimately fail a test of moral fortitude, the sacrifices they are willing to make for one another offer evidence of their improvement). In that season's finale, Michael argues that their posthumous self-improvement is testament to the afterlife's flawed system: if humans can get better after they're dead, why judge them at the end of life? In response, they are offered a second chance at life, with the aim of seeing whether they can improve if encouraged.

As it turns out, they each return to their old habits. It is only when they rediscover one another that they begin once again to be better people: moral education, *The Good Place* reaffirms, cannot happen in isolation. On numerous occasions, we see one or another member of the group consider abandoning the others—as a result of selfishness, despondency, or competing desires

(Chidi, for example, falls in love with an outsider, Simone, who reflects back to him the person he believes he is, rather than the person that the others see). But repeatedly, the members of Team Cockroach return to the others, not out of duty or self-interest, but because these individuals are the people whose opinions each most values, in whose company each is able to become a better version of themselves: the people who can help them reach the unattained yet attainable self that lies just beyond. As C. Scott Sevier notes, the show reiterates in a number of ways that moral development is only possible because of friendship: 'by the title of Episode 7, "Help is Other People"; by Chidi's discovery that the "answer" (to the ultimate questions) "is Eleanor"; in the series' penultimate episode, "Patty", when the ancient philosopher Hypatia asserts that what ultimately "saved" our four protagonists (as well as everyone else in The Good Place) was their friendships', and in Eleanor's advice to Mindy St. Claire, near the end of the final episode, that 'There is greater happiness waiting for you if you form bonds with other people.'[23]

Everyone Needs a Teacher

Mindy lives in The Medium Place, and she declares herself to be 'fine' there. But when a person says she's fine, as the old joke has it, she is usually anything but. *The Good Place* even makes this same joke in its season finale, when one of the characters, John, posthumously 'hooks up' with Alexander the Great: 'more like Alexander the Fine', he tells Tahani, 'if you know what I mean' (s4:e13, 'Whenever You're Ready'). Perhaps Eleanor should have known something wasn't right when she was first assured that in The Good Place 'Everything is fine'. We might say that Mindy's fine-ness represents a kind of Emersonian conformity, an acceptance of a world that is substandard, an unwillingness for things—not just ourselves, but the world that surrounds us—to be transformed.

For Cavell, it is not enough that in perfectionism we strive towards becoming better versions of ourselves, or even that we help our friends to become better versions of themselves: the transformation of the self must also lead to the transformation of society. Hence the couples of remarriage comedies must return from the Green Place, just as neither Eleanor, Mindy, nor humanity as a whole can take refuge forever in the moral neutral zone that is The Medium Place. Cavell explains:

> The lives of remarriage couples ... arrive at a moment in which they have to reaffirm their marriages by taking them intact back into participation in the ordinary world, and attest their faith, or perception, that they consent to their society as one in which a moral life of mutual care is pursuable, and worth the show of happiness sufficient to encourage others to take care of their lives further, as if happiness in a democracy is a political emotion.[24]

He continues: 'a society is worth our loyalty if it maintains good enough justice to allow criticism of itself, and reform'.[25]

In *The Good Place*'s third and fourth seasons Eleanor, Chidi, Tahani, and Jason face the question of whether the world is worth their loyalty, and how the lessons that they have learned might benefit not only themselves, but society at large. Up until this point, the characters have taken the rationale for acceptance into The Good Place at face value. The system, as explained by Michael in the pilot episode, is as follows: every human action performed during a lifetime is scored, and on their death the final total is used to determine whether they have earned enough points to reach The Good Place. Planting a tree, for example, earns +7.83 points, while stiffing a waitress deducts -6.83. In the season 3 episode 'The Book of Dougs', though, Eleanor and the gang realize that the increasing complexity of modern life has introduced unintended consequences to all actions and decisions, resulting in net point losses for ostensibly good acts. As a result, no human has been admitted to The Good Place for over 500 years. At this juncture, the challenge becomes one of overhauling the system, so as to ensure that *others* can reach The Good Place. After a series of experiments, the gang settles on a solution based on their own afterlife experiences: in 'You've Changed Man' they suggest that each dead human should be subjected to personalized tests of moral development, and will be rebooted as many times as they need until they pass the test (possibly never passing it); in each successive try, they will retain some of what they have learned in the form of a 'little voice in your head' (s4:e13, 'Whenever You're Ready').

There is yet a further twist in the tale. In helping each other to become good, Team Cockroach make the world—and the afterlife—a better place. And so they are admitted, finally, to the *real* Good Place, where they discover that heaven isn't all they hoped it would be. An eternity of perfection, it turns out, is boring. This tracks with what Cavell has to say about perfectionism, which crucially does not imply perfectibility—the attainment of some state of perfection. Instead, each attained state of the self (or society) always projects or opens up another state, the realization of which we must commit ourselves to anew. As Cavell writes in 'The Good of Film', in perfectionism (unlike in virtue ethics) 'the soul's journey to itself is not pictured as a continuous path directed upward to a known point of completion but rather as a zigzag of discontinuous steps following the lead of [my] "unattained but attainable self".'[26] The Cavellian perfectionist is constantly striving for what Cavell calls 'the unattained yet attainable self'.[27] Hence every attained state is effectively perfect just as it is—and yet it could still be *more* perfect.

The version of The Good Place that the gang encounter is that envisaged by Aristotelian virtue ethics: the very best of people exist here in a fixed state of perfection. But with nothing left to strive for, they atrophy. As a solution, the gang install an exit door, which offers each individual an end to their time in utopia. No one knows where this door leads, but what is crucial is that it offers a next step, a beyond. Knowing that there is an end to their time in The Good Place helps the residents to appreciate their setting.[28] Knowing that their journeys will continue inspires them to keep striving to be the best version of themselves, while never achieving it. The gang—people—can always be better (and better is better than fine). But no one should ever be best, because this suggests an end point. In the series finale, 'Whenever You're Ready', Eleanor cites the final line of T.M. Scanlon's book *What We Owe to Each Other*: 'Working out the terms of moral justification is an unending task.'[29]

Moral education in *The Good Place* is thus ultimately proposed to be an ongoing process of repetition, aided by the friendly and credible words of others. The real moral learning takes place not in Chidi's classroom, but in the interactions between these friends, as they exchange witty dialogue and share laughs and ask, time and again, what binds them together, what they owe to one another. Since these individuals are studying ethics, their conversations often turn on what Cavell might call 'standard moral problems' ('matters of equality or of the conflict of inclination with duty, or of duty with duty, or means with ends'), and in this respect they depart from the remarriage comedies.[30] Yet the representation of ethical philosophy within *The Good Place*, I would hazard, is something of a McGuffin. Indeed, the discussions of philosophy that the group share often end in disappointment with existing models, which are often manipulated by the all-too-flawed characters to suit their own desires and versions of morality. Such sophistry is most comically demonstrated when Eleanor uses a clever bit of rhetoric to shift blame for their problems from herself to Michael, emphasizing how graceless the gambit is by finishing: 'How do you like them ethics? I just ethics'd you in the face, Chidi!' (s1:e7, 'The Eternal Shriek'). As Eleanor comes to learn, and as she explains to Janet in the series' closing moments, moral education does not take place in the classroom but in the world. It involves 'messing up and trying again and messing up again and getting things wrong and trying to make them right'. Vitally, she says, it involves self-transformation through friendship; learning things all by ourselves *and* learning to ask for help. As the series closes on Michael, having finally become human and thus subject to the same moral complexities as the rest of mankind, the message is redoubled: having spent an eternity trying and failing to play the guitar, he finally picks out a tune, and thanks his tutor profusely. 'Everyone needs a teacher', she tells him (that teacher is, in a neat bit of casting, played by Danson's own wife Mary Steenburgen, a veiled suggestion, perhaps, that the couple is yet at the heart of perfectionism).

'A Warped Version of Nietzsche's Eternal Recurrence'

So far I have discussed *The Good Place*'s thematic and narrative exemplification of perfectionism. Before drawing to a close, however, I want to argue that the show also demonstrates its commitment to perfectionism through repetition at a structural level.

Since moral progress is not linear, it makes sense that the show's structure also rejects linearity in favour of what Jason Mittell terms 'narrative complexity': 'the redefinition of episodic forms under the influence of serial narration'.[31]

> Rejecting the need for plot closure within every episode that typifies conventional episodic form, narrative complexity foregrounds ongoing stories across a range of genres. Complex television employs a range of serial techniques, with the underlying assumption that a series is a cumulative narrative that builds over time, rather than resetting back to a steady state equilibrium at the end of every episode.[32]

Narrative complexity is not simply what we might call episodic seriality—series of limited duration whose episodes tell a continuous story. Rather, it indicates a willingness to play with the conventions of storytelling by putting the relationship between discrete episodes and seasons, and the series overall, into play. As a result, Sarah Hatchuel and Claire Cornillon argue, the narratively complex (or 'semi-serial') TV show lends itself naturally to considerations of ethics, since it invokes an ethics of care through its narrative structure, which resists linearity, playing on 'rewriting, repetition, variation, instability, revival'.[33]

This seems an apposite description of *The Good Place*, which begins after all with a dead woman waking up. The show comprises four seasons of thirteen episodes each (season 4 technically comprises fourteen, since the season finale is a double-length episode) and draws on a number of established patterns for interweaving long-term story arcs within episodic parameters, such as individual flashbacks (familiar to many audiences from shows such as *Lost*, a primary influence on the show) or topic-of-the-week structures (particularly prominent in season 1, when Eleanor embarks on her ethics lessons). The trope that it leans most heavily on, however, is the reboot, a device more commonly associated with feature films (such as, for example, *Palm Springs*, *50 First Dates*, *Eternal Sunshine of the Spotless Mind*, or *Groundhog Day*—a film of which Cavell was particularly fond).[34] The reboot—which takes the form of a memory wipe—comes to play an increasingly important role over the course of the four seasons, both at the level of story and structure. Season 1 turns around Eleanor's mistaken assignment to The Good Place and her efforts to be a better person, and closes with a click. Season 2 swiftly dispatches with the season 1 premise, and turns instead—after 802 reboots (compressed into a three-minute montage)—to Michael's failure and his decision to join Team Cockroach. Season 3 sees the humans' memories erased once more, as they are returned to earth, and then back to the afterlife, where they discover that the point system is fundamentally flawed, before closing with a reprise of the original experiment and the wiping of Chidi's memory alone. At the centre of season 4 is the overhaul of the whole system, and the introduction of Team Cockroach's new plan for the afterlife, in which humans are rebooted over and again until such a point as they are finally able to show significant moral development.

As Ariane Hudelet points out, the universe of the show is therefore radically reoriented with each season.[35] Michael moves from being an angel to a demon, a good demon, a resident of The Good Place, and finally human. Eleanor transforms from a dirtbag to an architect. The fake Good Place turns out to be the Bad Place, and the real Good Place turns out to be not so good after all. The points system that the first three seasons depended on doesn't, after all, add up. There is little solid ground on which to plant our feet. If Mittell explains that seriality is often articulated at the level of characters, and of memory in particular—'people reference previous occurrences such as romantic connection or personal discovery, expressing continuity through dialogue and character action'—then we cannot count on this, for the characters have no memories.[36] If time, too, is an essential element of seriality, then it is almost impossible to grasp what *The Good Place*'s storytime is, since time is measured differently on earth and in the afterlife, which is of course infinite and which is counted in 'Jeremy Bearimys', looping circuits referred to by the name they seem to inscribe. Janet and her fellow artificial intelligences can meanwhile perceive all time and no time. Even space provides no reliable bearings, since the various settings that the characters inhabit can be wiped and reset at will, erasing all trace of the events that have previously taken place there.

All that remains is the characters themselves and their relationships: the one constant in the show's ever-shifting framework. In this sense, the show departs from what Hatchuel and Cornillon claim is the tendency of such semi-serial shows to decentre the 'main' characters by using the format to bring in peripheral characters and heterogeneous perspectives,[37] as much as Hudelet's argument that it is the progress of the individual that underpins the semi-episodic format.[38] As the humans are repeatedly reconfigured in order to yield different—better—results, so the show twists and changes shape, reinventing itself anew each season in order to show a different aspect of the ethical conundrum at its centre-point. Ultimately *The Good Place* reveals that alongside friendship, the reboot is the key moral improvement: it is only through trying, failing, and trying again, that humans—all humans—can learn to be better, to strive towards the unattained yet attainable self. Following Emerson's voyage of a hundred tacks, the show thus takes to a logical conclusion Hatchuel and Cornillon's claims that

> Semi-serialized television shows, through the way they bring value to each episode, embed an ethical vision within their own narrative structures. [In them], the formulaic and episodic aspects seem to invite viewers to consider repetitions as fruitful instead of static, as

empathetic instead of emotionally dry. [The] formulaic/procedural aspects encourage us to see individual lives as precious and worth fighting for, whether they be the lives of anonymous people or loved ones.[39]

The Good Place's semi-serial narration and reboot structure work, as many narratively complex TV shows do, at least according to Hatchuel and Cornillon, to emphasize the fact that ethical choices are not made once, but are an ongoing series of decisions.

Conclusion: 'Help Is Other People'

The comedies of remarriage conclude not in an ever after but in a present continuity of before and after; they transform festival into festivity; they correct not error but experience. These three features lead Cavell to describe the remarriage comedies as 'diurnal comedies', or comedies of dailyness. Within them, marriage is conceived of as the decision to wake up every morning and decide to remain married, as 'a willingness for repetition'. There is no happy ending; there is only the beginning of a new day.

The Good Place opens with a woman who has achieved her happy ending. Eleanor Shellstrop is literally (at least as far as she knows) in heaven. But this supposed ending is only the beginning, an opening onto 'the next phase' of her existence. In the very first shot of *The Good Place* we see her opening her eyes, waking (to a new morning?). This motif will be repeated throughout the subsequent four seasons, as Eleanor is rebooted and starts her day anew. Chidi, too, will open his eyes to a new day. So, metaphorically, will every one of The Good Place's central six. In the series finale each of these characters, now installed in the *real* Good Place, will come to feel a sense of calm, of having settled debts and come, as it were, to a spiritual standstill. And this would seem a perfect place to leave them. Living their best lives. But the ship tacks once more, and Chidi, Eleanor, and Jason each opt to pass through a door to another dimension. They don't know what is through it. But they know that a new beginning—a beginning, again—promises more than a happy ending. *The Good Place* is then by Cavell's standards, a 'good' show, 'one that bears up under criticism of the sort that is invited and expected by serious works within the classical arts ... works in which an audience's passionate interest, or disinterest, is rewarded with an articulation of the conditions of the interest that illuminates it and expands self-awareness'.[40] Embedding repetition and perfectionism at its heart, what the series teaches us over the course of its four seasons is that happiness is—to borrow a cheesy self-help phrase, but one that is appropriate here—not the destination but the journey; that self-improvement cannot be achieved alone, but only with the help of others; that self-improvement is an unending task, and that ethical choices are not made once, but must be made over and again, at every minute of lives—and even, perhaps, our deaths.

Notes

1. It's worth noting that an episode of another 'nicecore' TV show, *Unbreakable Kimmy Schmidt*, is also dedicated to the trolley problem.
2. In his foreword to Kimberly S. Engels's *The Good Place and Philosophy*, the show's creator, Michael Schur, describes the history of ethical philosophy precisely as a conversation. 'Scanlon was talking to Rawls, who'd been talking to Kant, who'd been sniffing at Aristotle. Philippa Foot was talking to Mill, and then John Taurek snapped at the people who'd talked to her. The ideas were fascinating, but the *conversation* was the fun part. And as long as humans walk the planet, it occurred to me, it would never end' (Michael Schur, 'Foreword', in *The Good Place and Philosophy*, ed. Kimberly S. Engels [Hoboken: Wiley Blackwell, 2021], xx).
3. Stanley Cavell, 'The Good of Film', in *Cavell on Film*, ed. William Rothman (New York: State University of New York Press, 2015), 337. Kristin Boudreau observes that Cavell develops the idea of the zigzag journey through inconsistency from Emerson who writes that 'the voyage of the best ship is a zigzag line of a hundred tacks. See the line from a sufficient distance, and it straightens itself to the average tendency. Your genuine action will explain itself, and will explain your other genuine actions' (Ralph Waldo Emerson, *Essays and Lectures* [New York: Library of America Press, 1983], 266) of as well as Henry James, who in *The Portrait of a Lady* describes his erratic heroine thus: 'In matters of opinion she had her own way, and it led her into a thousand ridiculous zigzags' (Henry James, 'The Portrait of a Lady', *The Atlantic*, December 1880. Available www.theatlantic.com/magazine/archive/1880/12/the-portrait-of-a-lady/632369/). See Kristin Boudreau, 'The Haunting of History: Emerson, James, and the Ghosts of Human Suffering', in *Stanley Cavell, Literature, and Film: The Idea of America*, ed. Áine Kelly and Andrew Taylor (London: Routledge, 2013), 82.
4. Cavell, 'The Good of Film', 334.
5. Stanley Cavell, *Conditions Handsome and Unhandsome: The Constitution of Emersonian Perfectionism* (Chicago: University of Chicago Press, 1990), xxxi. My emphasis.
6. Michel Foucault, *The Care of the Self* (History of Sexuality vol. 3) (London: Penguin, 1990).
7. Stephen Mulhall, *Stanley Cavell: Philosophy's Recounting of the Ordinary* (Oxford: Oxford University Press, 1998), 265.
8. Cavell, *Conditions Handsome and Unhandsome*, 6–7. My emphasis.
9. Stephen Mulhall, 'Film and Philosophy: Digital Cinema and Moral Philosophy', Karlsruhe ZKM Lecture, [unpublished], 27.
10. Emily Nussbaum, 'Dystopia in *The Good Place*', *New Yorker*, February 6, 2017.
11. Stanley Cavell, *Pursuits of Happiness: The Hollywood Comedy of Remarriage* (Cambridge, MA: Harvard University Press, 1981).
12. Stanley Cavell, *Cities of Words: Pedagogical Letters on a Register of the Moral Life* (Cambridge, MA: Harvard University Press, 2004), 10.
13. It is here, Robb points out, that Eleanor first finds out she has told Chidi she loves him, where Janet and Jason figure out how to have sex for the first time, and where Michael and the humans build and test out their new experimental Good Place neighbourhood for the first time in season 4. This is all possible because The Medium Place exists apart from society, 'allowing the characters to creatively experiment with

who they are, what they believe in, and how they interact with each other'. Catherine M. Robb, 'The Medium Place: Third Space, Morality, and Being In Between', in *The Good Place and Philosophy*, 76.
14 Cavell, *Pursuits of Happiness*, 84.
15 Ibid., 56.
16 For an extended discussion of this topic, see the conversation between Shahidha Bari, Sarah Churchwell, Robert Hanks, and Catherine Wheatley, 'The Philosophy of Love (Actually)', available at the London Forum: www.lse.ac.uk/cpnss/events/Oldevents/Spring2020/3-Philosophy-of-Love-Actually/The-Philosophy-of-Love-Actually.
17 'So, to prepare to meet all of you, I studied the human concept of friends. I even watched all ten seasons of the show *Friends*. Boy, those *Friends* really were friends, weren't they? Although, and I realize this is the kind of observation that would only occur to the mind of an eternal being: how did they afford that apartment? A waitress and a chef with those Manhattan real estate prices' (Season 1, Episode 6, 'What We Owe to Each Other').
18 Cavell, *Cities of Words*, 16.
19 Cavell, *Cities of Words*, 27.
20 Cavell, 'The Good of Film', 337.
21 This set-up is, as various critics have pointed out, a version of Sartre's *Huis Clos*. See for example C. Scott Sevier, 'The Good Place and The Good Life', in *The Good Place and Philosophy*.
22 Stanley Cavell, *Must We Mean What We Say?: A Book of Essays* (New York: Charles Scriber's Sons, 1969; Cambridge: Cambridge University Press, 1976; updated version, 2002), 350.
23 C. Scott Sevier, 'The Good Place and The Good Life', 55.
24 Cavell, 'The Good of Film', 348.
25 Ibid.
26 Cavell, 'The Good of Film', 348.
27 Cavell, *Conditions Handsome and Unhandsome*, 12.
28 That finitude restores the meaning to life that an endless life filled with endless possibilities makes impossible is the key argument of Todd May's *Death: The Art of Living* (London: Routledge, 2009). May was one of two philosophy professors who acted as consultants to the series (the other being Pamela Hieronymi).
29 T.M. Scanlon, *What We Owe to Each Other* (Cambridge, MA: Harvard University Press, 1998), p.361.
30 Cavell, 'The Good of Film', 347.
31 Jason Mittell, *Complex TV: The Poetics of Contemporary Television Storytelling* (New York: New York University Press, 2015), 18.
32 Ibid.
33 Sarah Hatchuel and Claire Cornillon, 'The Ethics of Serial Narrative Structure', *SERIES*, vol. 6, no. 1 (2020), https://series.unibo.it/article/view/10393. Hatchuel and Cornillon are building here on the work of Sandra Laugier in 'L'éthique comme attention à ce qui compte', in *L' économie de l'attention*, ed. Yves Citton (Paris: Le découverte, 2014), and *Nos vies en séries* (Paris: Climats, 2019).
34 There are exceptions, notably the Netflix series *Russian Doll* (2019), beautifully written about in this volume by Michelle Devereaux (see chapter 5).

35 Hudelet links the narrative complexity of the reboot to a certain unease around contemporary politics, claiming that the point system is neoliberalist and arguing: 'This play on the discrepancy between different levels of diegetic consciousness and memory characterises several series of the last decade, which thus thematise the difficult of contructing knowledge in a world that is increasingly complex and fragmented.' Ariane Hudelet, 'The Good Place: Il faut cultiver notre voisin', in *Les Séries: Laboratoires d'éveil politique*, ed. by Sandra Laugier, (Paris: CNRS Editions, 2023), 173–188 (175).
36 Mittell, *Complex TV*, 23.
37 Hatchuel and Cornillon, 'The Ethics of Serial Narrative Structure', 59–60.
38 Hudelet, 'The Good Place', 3.
39 Hatchuel and Cornillon, 'The Ethics of Serial Narrative Structure', 63.
40 Cavell, 'The Good of Film', 335.

8

Im/Moral Perfectionism: On TV's Two Worlds

Jeroen Gerrits

Introduction: On Living in Two Worlds

The opening pages of Stanley Cavell's *Cities of Words*, his 2004 book based on a course on moral perfectionism, contain no less than twenty epigraphs. Each of these 'guardians or guides at the entrance of this book', Cavell comments, forms a variation of a shared theme, namely the 'insight of a split in the human self, of human nature as divided or double'.[1] He later adds Kant's formulation of this insight: 'Man lives in two worlds.'[2]

This insight apparently runs through the history of Western philosophy: epigraphs range from Plato and Aristotle to Emerson and Thoreau; from Kant, Mill, and Rawls to Freud, Marx, and Nietzsche. It pervades literature, too: quotations from Milton, Ibsen, and Whitman are listed, as is a comment from G.B. Shaw's Professor Higgins. The variations on the theme include distinctions between a world of sense (bondage) and a world of reason (freedom); a world in which we live ('converse') and a world we think; an intelligible world and one that transcends human powers of knowing. It encompasses private and public worlds, inner and outer ones, as well as a distinction (in *A Doll's House*) between 'an incomprehensibly unjust present world and a world of freedom and reciprocity which is almost unthinkable'.[3] Each one of them, Cavell sums up, 'provides a position from which the present state of human existence can be judged and a future state achieved, or else the present to be judged to be better than the cost of changing it'.[4] What emerges here, in this 'pattern of disappointment and desire' on which Cavell bestows the name of moral perfectionism, is a distinction between what we could call an actual (inevitably disappointing) world of the everyday and an eventual (say virtual), more desirable, even if as yet unapproachable world to come.

The promising (or less unacceptable) eventual world is not necessarily an imaginary one, as opposed to the real one in which we live. Rather, as Cavell elaborated in an earlier essay ('Declining Decline', published in 1989), it is a world that responds to or emerges from the very disappointment we experience in the everyday, 'as if the actual is the womb, contains the terms, of the eventual'.[5] The eventual corresponds to our longing for the overcoming of daily life's lack in 'certainty or fastidiousness or accuracy or immediacy or comprehensiveness'.[6] In our desire to overcome this lack, we run the risk of demanding metaphysical absolutes, of violating the limitations of our human ways of knowing and doing things in ways that inflict violence on others or ourselves. Hence Cavell warns that 'the ordinary has, and alone has, the power to move the ordinary'.[7] Thus a moral perfectionist, far from adhering to a moral doctrine that would equally apply to all, remains committed to their specific place in the actual without resigning to it, without confining themselves to conformity, without numbing any desire they could call their own, without resorting to two of the most 'politically devastating passions' according to Cavell: cynicism and disillusion.[8]

As Cavell conceives it, then, moral perfectionism does not seek to mend the split in the human self. A perfectionist refuses to live their life in a way that forecloses all paths to the eventual, no matter how slim the chances of its realization. Nor will they commit to an ideal or principle if that requires disregarding their actual situatedness.[9] Perfectionism further emphasizes the opacity or non-transparency of the present state of our interactions, and it assumes that gaining a perspective on our lives, on our conflicting desires, and on our place in society cannot be achieved alone. It depends, on the contrary, on a mirroring confrontation with a friend, or on what Nietzsche calls my most worthy enemy: one who does not simply accept my present stance, who does not necessarily agree with me, but who helps in eliciting my position and my desires by keeping the conversation open.[10] A perfectionist, in short, aspires to a further self, without however positing that a final state of the soul be reached; they keep insisting on a more just or less intolerable world, on keeping alive the power to demand the change of the world as a whole, even while positing that the eventual remains—and always remains—to be realized into the actual. So a basic assumption of a perfectionist moral outlook is that, unable to rest peacefully in either of the two worlds, humans are conditioned by an openness that is also a restlessness.

Cavell not only finds that the idea of two worlds, or of split selves, pervades philosophy and literature: it is a prominent theme in (and beyond) golden age Hollywood cinema as well. *Cities of Words* pairs philosophical-literary texts with movies in combinations that may initially seem brow-raising: Emerson—*The Philadelphia Story*; Locke—*Adam's Rib*; Mill—*Gaslight*; Kant—*It Happened One Night*; Ibsen—*Stella Dallas*. Cavell warns in the introduction that he wants to avoid the impression that 'philosophy left to itself requires compensation by revelations within the medium of film', affirming instead 'that film, the latest of the great arts, shows philosophy to be the often invisible accompaniment of the ordinary lives that film is so apt to capture (even, perhaps particularly, when the lives depicted are historical or elevated or comic or hunted or haunted)'.[11]

To get to the point, I will postpone the question as to how moral perfectionism accompanies the films Cavell discusses in *Cities of Words* until the end of this essay, turning instead to the medium of TV by asking a double question. First: does Cavell's claim that film is not merely a form of art (a claim I will take here for granted), but indeed (as he put it in the quoted passage) 'the *latest* of the great arts' further imply that television (being a later medium than film) does *not* rank among the great arts? And, second, is television, an audiovisual medium arguably even better equipped at capturing the ordinary than film is,[12] likewise accompanied by an invisible philosophy? Or more specifically, does television engage moral perfectionism in the same way as Hollywood does? This latter question seems all the more pertinent to me considering that so many contemporary shows are precisely premised on the existence of two worlds. In what follows, I will elaborate on the two-world premise of contemporary drama shows and argue that it indeed differs from moral perfectionism's accompaniment of Hollywood cinema. Before doing so, I will first address the initial part of the question, about TV's status as a form of art.

... But First, 'The Fact': Art TV?

It is commonplace by now to say that, since the later 1990s or perhaps the millennial turn, TV has entered a new golden age, if not a succession of such ages.[13] The often-implied claim is that television has (finally) matured and achieved the status of art. The relevant contemporary TV shows are grouped by a variety of names, such as Art Television,[14] Quality TV,[15] New Television,[16] or Complex TV.[17] I am not now going to repeat or summarize the various reasons behind this historical turn, nor indeed do I intend to challenge this widely perceived change itself. I do find significance, however, in Cavell's willingness, expressed more than a decade before the first of the 'mature' shows were even broadcast, to 'accept ... that television has come of age, that this, these programs, more or less as they stand, in what can appear to be their poverty, is what there is to understand'.[18] What had yet to be accepted back in 1982 (when the relevant essay 'The Fact of Television' was published) was not only the fact of television having become an intrinsic part of the daily lives of so many, but also that its sheer existence, which ranks 'at once among the most obvious and the most mysterious facts of contemporary life', did not occur *despite* a supposed triviality of its programs.[19] To be sure, Cavell does not argue that the sitcoms and soap operas of those days were in fact more complex than was generally understood. Instead, he insists on an intuition that informed so many of his writings, namely that the most ordinary can often be the hardest to understand, not because of its supposed complexity, but because its deep familiarity hides it in plain sight. What Cavell proposes, in short, is that TV needs to be taken seriously in its apparent poverty rather than await a richer future (or rely on video artists) to deserve our critical (or philosophical) attention. None of this is to deny that TV programs since the publication of 'The Fact of Television' have indeed become more complex, as Jason Mittell convincingly argues. But before turning our attention to the narrative complexity of contemporary TV shows, let us see what Cavell is willing (or asking us) to accept with this 'acceptance of television as a mature medium of art'.[20]

To take TV seriously in its apparent poverty, Cavell finds that we first need to acknowledge that 'the poverty lies not in the medium's discoveries, but rather in our understanding of these discoveries'.[21] As a preliminary observation it is worth noting that this formulation resonates with Cavell's earlier writings on film (especially in *The World Viewed*, originally published in 1972), in which he sides with Michael Fried's take on modernist art (contra Greenberg), according to which a true masterpiece engages not the discovery of *the* essence of its medium but the various *ways* of discovering (or 'acknowledging') its medium, or of discovering new media within it. With his choice of terminology ('the medium's discoveries'), then, Cavell unfolds his discussion of TV within discourse of modernist art.

Among the discoveries made by TV, an 'immediate difference' from film impresses itself on Cavell that helps explain why the former medium had so persistently been perceived as immature (at the time of his writing at least). Whereas in cinema, as indeed in more traditional forms of art such as painting, it is the business of individual masterpieces (movies, or even scenes) to perform the task of discovery or revelation (Cavell brilliantly discusses, for example, how Capra's *It Happened One Night* acknowledges the medium's intrinsic aspect of the focal point),[22] individual works in television do not primarily bear significance in and of themselves. The relevant aspect of television is rather its 'rule or format'. What matters, Cavell writes, is 'not this or that day of "I Love Lucy" but the program as such'. In other words, the significance of any episode lies foremost in its being an instantiation of its format. To some (Cavell specifically mentions Leslie Fiedler) this 'evanescence of the instance', this predominance of 'formulas', refutes TV's claim to art.[23] Yet in Cavell's view, the expectation that individual works carry the burden of discovery accounts for our lack of understanding of TV's discoveries. What this prevents us from seeing is that, as Cavell argues, TV's status as a mature medium is grounded in the idea of *seriality*. In seriality TV finds what we could call its intrinsic play of difference and repetition, which we can distill from Cavell's explanation of two of TV's basic formats, the sitcom and the soap opera. The soap opera, with its 'more or less endless narration across episodes, linked by crises', nevertheless produces 'repetitions and recurrences [that] bear a significant relation with those of series in which the narrative comes to a classical ending each time'. In case of the sitcom, by contrast, the 'substitution of the unknown new element to initiate the generation, the element of difference, can be any event that alters the situation comically'.²⁴

Let us linger on this for just a bit. Cavell claims here that the sitcom and the soap opera approach the play of difference and repetition from opposite ends. The sitcom's episodic form (which Cavell calls a *series*—a term conventionally distinguished from the continuous form of the *serial*) is repetitive because each instantiation keeps resetting to the same situation and rarely acknowledges events that happened in previous instances. The variables introduced in each episode trigger developments that change this initial situation, thus producing a difference between the current episode and all previous ones. By contrast, the continuity of the soap opera's narrative form can more readily be associated with an ongoing self-differing process, yet the recurrence over time of similar events and relational dynamics tends to produce repetitive, fractal structures. So 'the aesthetics of serial-episode construction' suggests to Cavell that 'what is under construction is an argument between time as repetition and time as transience'.²⁵

I will leave an exposition of the ontological implications of this difference between film and TV (a difference captured verbally in the transition from the phrase 'a succession of automatic world projections' to 'a current of simultaneous event reception') for another occasion.²⁶ Suffice it for now to say that, by countering arguments against TV's maturity and analyzing the medium's discoveries, Cavell is at the very least willing to leave open the question as to whether TV ranks among 'the greatest of the arts' regardless of its future developments.²⁷ At the same time, I find it striking just how aptly Cavell's assessment of the televisual, serial-episodic aesthetic—this 'argument between time as repetition and time as transience'—anticipates major developments in TV *avant la lettre*. This is perhaps nowhere more evident than in his passing comment on *Hill Street Blues* (which at the time of his writing had only just begun airing). This show, Cavell writes, 'seems to be questioning the feature of a series that demands a classical ending for each instance, hence questioning the distinction between soap opera and series'.²⁸

Complex TV

The significance of *Hill Street Blues* (NBC, 1981–87) on subsequent developments in TV has often been pointed out. Kristin Thompson, for instance, writes in hindsight that it pioneered the 'trend in hour-long dramas toward a more dense weave of multiple storylines developing simultaneously'.²⁹ Indeed, she points out that the show initially struck viewers as too complex: to improve the show's ratings, NBC felt forced to simplify its narrative structure by completing at least one plotline per episode while continuing others—a pattern, Thompson writes, that was soon to become the norm.

Jason Mittell elaborates on these innovative narrative structures underlying the 'changing landscape of American Television' in his 2015 book

Complex TV.³⁰ Ever since the turn of the millennium, Mittell writes, television has been marked by a narrative complexity that '*redefines episodic forms under the influence of serial narration*'.³¹ Echoing Cavell's distinctions discussed above, Mittell explains that in the conventional episodic form (best exemplified by the sitcom), each episode resets back to a 'steady-state equilibrium',³² regardless of previous plot developments and introduces a variable element to generate a new instantiation of the show, requiring a strong sense of plot closure all its own. The serial form, by contrast, typically presents a 'cumulative narrative that builds over time'³³—a time that may well go on forever without reaching a sense of closure or final resolution (as in soap operas). With the idea that complex narrative 'redefines episodic forms under the influence of serial narration', Mittell claims that the TV series of the past two decades have tended to proceed by way of episodes, each with its own sense of consistency, which nevertheless accumulate over time. Some isolated events can be critical in the way they hold an episode together, just as some plot developments mark a specific season, while others carry across.

Although characteristic of it, however, this criterion of 'episodic seriality' does not as yet sufficiently explain complex TV narrative, Mittell warns. What makes narrative complex, rather, is its simultaneous development of multiple plotlines that diverge and intersect across variable spans of time. 'In conventional television', Mittell writes,

> episodes feature two or more plotlines that complement each other: a main A plot that dominates screen time and secondary B plots that may offer thematic parallels or provide counterpoint to the A plot but rarely interacts with it at the level of action. Complexity ... works against these norms by altering the relationship between multiple plotlines, creating interweaving stories that often collide and coincide.³⁴

A basic example of his concept of narrative complexity, then, is the relatively marginal event that serves as a backstory or a counterpoint to a more dominant plotline in one episode that returns later on to become a more dominant plotline when it intersects with a different development. Alternately, a major plotline (say 'Who Killed Laura Palmer?') may break down into a multitude of minor developments vying for dominance and reorienting the major plot drive at each new intersection or twist (as in the notorious case of *Twin Peaks*). Narrative complexity can thus take on various forms in contemporary TV. Mittell distinguishes, for instance, between centrifugal and centripetal variations. The former tend to push the narrative outward, away from a narrative center or main character towards a complex web of interconnectivity (*The Wire* being a prime example). Centripetal shows (such as *Breaking Bad*), by contrast, fold inward by delving into a central character's psychological complexity.

Buffy, Tony, and TV's Two Worlds

Cutting across these variations of complex narration, the idea of living in two worlds, or of split selves, appears to me a remarkably persistent feature of so many TV shows that make up this changing landscape of American television. As in the case of the epigraphs (and chapters) in Cavell's *Cities of Words*, this theme can itself take on a variety of shapes, as I shall demonstrate later on. Taken collectively, however, they seem to me to form a pattern that differs from the one Cavell traced throughout the histories of philosophy, literature, and Hollywood cinema. Surely, no TV show would do without patterns of disappointment and desire—nothing on earth would. But this pattern does not seem to take on the form of, or extend into, a distinction between an actual and eventual world. Instead, the protagonists of contemporary TV dramas appear to be living in two worlds *simultaneously*, each being as actual as the other. What fuels the drama and causes the self to split, then, is the field of tension between partially overlapping but oftentimes incommensurable worlds.

I will illustrate this based on two trendsetting examples as diverse as *Buffy the Vampire Slayer* (WB, 1997–2003) and *The Sopranos* (HBO, 1999–2007). Both shows meet complex TV's basic criterion of 'episodic seriality'. *Buffy* provides episodic consistency and resolution by borrowing *The X-Files'* conception of the 'monster of the week'—usually a metaphor for some actual teenage anxiety. At the same time, each episode contributes to long-term storylines, including but also exceeding seasonal arcs (the 'monster of the season' is generally referred to as 'Big Bad' and successively incarnated in 'The Master', Drusilla, Mayor Wilkins, Adam, Gloria, Warren, and 'The First Evil').

Initially, the episodes of *The Sopranos* followed a dense structure, with multiple plotlines running through episodes that were not clearly divided in acts. Kristin Thompson discusses how the show basically followed the formula pioneered by *Hill Street Blues*, and points out that the weave of ongoing plotlines was apparently still too dense. As happened to its predecessor, then, *The Sopranos* settled for fewer separate plotlines after its first four episodes, typically sticking to one rather than two closure lines per episode and two (instead of five or six) ongoing arcs.[35] Mittell on his part emphasizes that *The Sopranos* ended up being 'far more episodic than it is typically remembered to have been'.[36] He points out that the show's most celebrated episodes (starting with the fifth) were highly self-contained. He also finds that the show's longer story arcs were less sweeping than on *Buffy*. Despite the fact that *The Sopranos*' 'seasonal unity is far more tied to theme or character than to plotting or the rise and fall of a specific "big bad" as on *Buffy*', Mittell nevertheless concludes that '*The Sopranos* exemplified the model of serially infused episodic television that typifies most complex television'.[37]

While the formula that determines the number of ongoing plotlines, the duration of story arcs, the complexity of interweaving nodes, and the balance between episodic consistency and serial continuity varies between these shows, and indeed within each, both *Buffy* and *The Sopranos* are groundbreaking examples of complex TV. As for their content, it is obvious that the shows belong to different genres—*Buffy* being a horror/fantasy/vampire show while *The Sopranos* falls squarely under the mobster genre. In terms of style, tone, and mood, too, these shows are as far apart as the antipodal characters of Tony Soprano (a depressed, middle-aged, Italian-American mafioso, played by James Gandolfini) and Buffy Summers (the high school cheerleader-cum-slayer incarnated by Sarah Michelle Gellar). Yet a shared premise is no less obvious than these differences. Just as Buffy desperately longs to be your typical high school girl with some success in class and in love, in being a good friend and cheerleader, in belonging to her 'Sunnydale' world, so Tony thinks of himself as a family man who raises his teenage children in his suburban New Jersey home in hopes that they will 'enjoy the little moments that were good' (s1:e13) as they grow up to live meaningful lives outside of the mob. If Buffy's everyday longings, however modest, continue to be frustrated by fate—she has been selected as the latest in a long line of young female monster-fighters—Tony struggles to provide for one family (his relatives by blood) by leading another (the DiMeo crime family to which his father already belonged). In other words, Tony and Buffy equally aspire to *the low*—a term Emerson mentioned in his essay 'Self-Reliance' in the same breath as *the near* and *the common*, as opposed to *the sublime* and *the beautiful*. But just as the Big Bad creatures from the Hellmouth force wannabe-average-girl Buffy to play the role of the heroine, alienating her from 'her own' world and dragging her into the *lower-yet*, Tony finds himself facing his own kind of big bad creatures that keep pulling him back into the underworld of crime.

There are, no doubt, important differences in the way these protagonists relate to the situations into which they are thrown. Unlike Buffy, for instance, who only agrees to take on her fated slayer role in an attempt to be over and done with whatever demons happen to be around, Tony does not seek to denounce, much less give up, his mobster existence, although he tries hard to keep it separate from his life as family man. Yet such differences in attitude, which persist despite being challenged on both ends as the seasons unfold, only underscore the shared condition of Buffy's and Tony's split lives: they live in two partially overlapping but incongruent worlds simultaneously.

Where these two worlds meet, punctuate the membrane, seep through or spill over, it is as though a coupling between heterogeneous systems generates an internal resonance with an amplitude that exceeds the force of events in each world taken separately. A multitude of storylines tends to cluster at such events, which are often initiated by anomalous figures or objects that move across the divisions between worlds and trigger this resonance. In *The Sopranos*, the strong female types—Tony's mother Livia Soprano (Nancy Marchand) and his therapist Dr. Jennifer Melfi (Lorraine Bracco) first and foremost—function as such *transversals* (to draw from a Deleuzian vocabulary); in *Buffy*, boyfriend/vampire Angel (David Boreanaz) and sister Dawn (Michelle Trachtenberg) perform similar roles.[38] I will briefly recapitulate an instance of the latter, on which I elaborated previously, namely Dawn's pivotal role in the critical episode entitled 'Normal Again' (s6:e17).[39] I will then look more closely into an example from *The Sopranos*, taken from 'The Happy Wanderer' (s2:e6).

The Dawn of Incompossible Worlds

In the *Buffy* episode 'Normal Again', which comes late in the series' penultimate season, the relation between Buffy's two worlds becomes incompossible, to borrow yet another Deleuzian term (which he himself borrowed from Leibniz): two alternative worlds are equally possible yet mutually exclusive.[40] It is premised on a condition specific to this episode alone, which as such is a limit case, but its implications reverberate through the series as a whole. Buffy either has a dream of being in an asylum (a dream caused by a poisonous demon), or her slayer existence has been a product of her schizophrenic mind (a condition for which she has been hospitalized for six years—the full duration of the show being on air). In one world, Buffy's doctor and parents try to convince her that she can only be cured by detaching herself from her illusionary world, her slayer existence, and her circle of imaginary friends. When Dawn in the other world seeks to convince her sister that the asylum is a hallucination whereas their mutual feelings are real, Buffy responds: 'Sure it is. 'Cause what's more real: a sick girl in an institution or a kind of super-girl, chosen to fight demons and save the world?' Despite the ironic force of that argument, the tables can be turned here as well: in the asylum world, Buffy may not have a sister, but her parents are both there to support her. In the slayer world, by contrast, Buffy's parents had been divorced, and when her mother passed away, her father failed to show up to take on the role of the parent, which contributed to Buffy's increasing sense in which that world appears dead to her. Both worlds, then, contain elements that may seem fantastic wish-fulfillments from the perspective of the other.

Either way, becoming 'normal again' requires a detachment from the other world. As I have said, this premise is a limit case, but the point it thus pushes to the limit should be well taken: the actuality of the one world denies the *actuality* of the other: there is no question of either being virtual or eventual. And this is the case for all 'normal' situations in the series too. That is, when the coupling of the two actual worlds does not lead to incompossible situations, it produces an interstitial, commingled space in which Buffy's most intense encounters take place. So much so that, as Angel keeps reminding her, there may not be a normal for Buffy to return to: her 'natural place' is now located in this space between the low and the lower limits of the human.

Tony's Moral Ambiguity

If Buffy thus pushes the distinction between two worlds to the point of mutual exclusion, Tony Soprano generally has a hard time keeping his two worlds apart. Indeed, *The Sopranos'* celebrated sense of irony owes much to the one bursting through in the other. Just think of Tony's son AJ on his way to a school dance chaperoned by the Mafiosi 'uncles' Paulie and Silvio for want of an available parent. Traveling in a limousine (AJ: 'Do you think this is a stretch?') and accompanied by a dressed-up girl two heads taller than him, the teenager would clearly be living his gangster fantasy ('Can we have some of that whiskey?') were it not for those two stubborn, unglamorous men sitting right across from him (s1:e12, 'Isabella').

An interesting variation of this theme occurs in the second season episode 'The Happy Wanderer' (s2:e6). Here Tony's two worlds commingle when a Nissan Pathfinder finds its way from the one into the other. Tony tells his therapist, Dr. Melfi, about a friend of the family named David 'Davey' Scatino (Robert Patrick), who has an outstanding gambling debt. Tony had tried to talk Davey out of his high-stakes poker game, but Davey insisted on sitting at the table and now owes Tony a sum (\$45,000) larger than he can afford. It so happens that Davey's son Eric (John C. Hensley) is a close friend of Tony's daughter Meadow (Jamie-Lynn Sigler). To pay off part of his debt, Davey offers Tony the Nissan Pathfinder he had bought for his son (and which he now takes back under the pretense that Eric violated the off-roading prohibition). Despite knowing about his daughter's friendship with Eric, Tony gifts the car to Meadow. Unsurprisingly, she angrily refuses to accept it once she recognizes the SUV as her friend's, slamming various doors as she runs off to her bedroom.

Offended in turn by Meadow's refusal, Tony storms into her room, pointing fingers at her as he rubs it in how he got the car, and claiming that he is justified in demanding whatever payment Davey Scatino could offer. When Meadow defends her friend by saying that he has nothing to do 'with his asshole father' and that Eric 'didn't do anything to you', Tony counters by pointing out that not just the car, but indeed all Meadow has ever received is tied to his work: if she wants to take 'the moral highway' by declining a dirty gift, he continues, she 'can go sleep in a f*ing bus station'. The camera lingers on a speechless Meadow as Tony exits her room (00:45:30–00:46:30).

Tony's tirade sorts an immediate effect. When Meadow subsequently discusses the issue with Eric, who had asked her to force her father's hand to return the car, she insists that he acknowledge his own father's responsibility for the loss of his vehicle. Eric angrily refuses and breaks up their friendship, calling her father a 'f*ing lowlife'. As he runs off with slamming doors, the camera once again lingers on a speechless Meadow until the scene breaks off (00:47:30–00:48:33).

While the Scatinos play but a marginal role in *The Sopranos* and drop out of the series shortly after this specific episode (Davey recurs briefly in two other episodes this season), the scenes under consideration form a complex narrative node with reverberations throughout the series as a whole.[41] In that sense, the episode mirrors the one I discussed from *Buffy the Vampire Slayer*. But it indeed forms a reverse image of it: whereas the *Buffy* episode postulates the coexistence of mutually exclusive worlds, forcing the heroine to make a choice between them, this *Sopranos* episode centers on the uneasy mutual implication of two hardly compatible worlds. Tony is often desperate to keep these worlds separate, but now that Meadow is about to go to college and—so he hopes—escape his world of crime, he wants her to acknowledge the base of his support. To be sure, he does want Meadow to choose one world over the other, yet by telling her that she can go sleep in a bus station if she wishes to take the moral highway, he also suggests that her moral position is not to be determined in abstraction. If she refuses the car as a gift, he tells her, he will sell it and use the money to buy her all the ordinary things she never failed to accept—'clothes and food and shoes and CD players and all the rest of that shit' (00:46:00). The episode further implies that a world of lowlifes may not be that neatly distinguished from a world of respected citizens in the first place, and that obligations and consequences, disappointments and desires are to be reckoned with on either side.

The moral significance of this encounter, however, appears to escape Tony himself, and perhaps to an extent Melfi as well. In so doing, *The Sopranos* pushes the question of moral perfectionism in a way *Buffy* rarely does. Two episodes after the event (s2:e8, 'Full Leather Jacket') Tony brings up the fight with Meadow over the SUV with his therapist. He is still resistant to the idea of psychotherapy and likes to downplay any idea that he may have any psychological or moral issues, so he brings up the encounter with Meadow as some random issue they could discuss to kill the time while in session: 'Okay, spin the wheel: here's something that's been bothering me' (00:37:21). Moving to the edge of his seat, he asks Melfi why he had to drag his daughter through the mud by explaining to her how he got the car. The question is meant as an amusing riddle, but he loses his temper when Melfi replies that he may have wanted to teach his daughter a lesson about 'moral ambiguity' now that she is getting ready to leave the nest. 'You people are something', Tony snaps. 'I give my daughter a car to rub her face in shit and you're telling me I did something noble?' (00:39:24). Whereupon he insists they end the session.

Tony may not be transparent to himself, then, but that did not stop him from wanting to explain himself, first to Meadow and then again to Melfi. In that sense, he gets as close to being a moral perfectionist as he ever will. His moral lesson takes on the form of an ordinary conversation (in Soprano style, of course, hence shot through with expletives) rather than of a philosophical argument or a theoretical discussion. He aspires to an eventual world for Meadow, but not by allowing her to disavow her actual situatedness.

On the other hand, Tony hardly seems interested in learning the moral of his own lesson or his motivations behind the education of his daughter, even when Melfi considers them noble. As his response to Melfi indicates, Tony does not think highly of himself as a moral character and lacks the conviction to transform either himself or his world. As he rails at once against his own therapy and against a sense of general moral decline, Tony tends to resort to cynicism and disillusion—precisely those political passions Cavell warned against.

Tony may indeed be 'complex', as Kevin L. Stoehr argues, 'in the sense that his moral character appears at times to be saturated by an attitude of passive nihilism while, at other times, he struggles actively to overcome such a life-negating stance'.[42] In Stoehr's reading, however, the former attitude gains the upper hand. Especially relevant considering the scene under consideration is the fact that a passive nihilist is someone, Stoehr explains, 'who flounders in his moral ambiguities and who eventually refuses to rise above the negativity in his own life'.[43] While this refusal becomes more evident in the fourth season, in which Tony rejects Melfi's offer of an alternative form of life that would allow him to escape his life of crime (s4:e1), terminates his therapy (s4:e11), and separates from his wife Carmela (s4:e13), it is already clear in the episode under discussion that Tony acts at least as much from a sense of self-serving defensiveness as from an interest in his daughter's moral education. Tony does not merely refuse to return the car so as to teach Meadow a lesson in moral ambiguity; it is an expression of his own moral ambiguity as well. 'I'll eat it before I give it back. What am I, a sucker?' he barks at Meadow—meaning, I take it, that he cares at least as much about saving face as about doing the right thing (00:45:50). He may in the end be just as concerned about his power play with a Mafia rival like Richie Aprile, or act more from resentment for 'Happy Wanderers' like Davey Scatino (as the episode's title suggests) than with the more 'noble' motivations Melfi ascribes to him. In a word, even as he is subconsciously teaching his daughter a lesson in moral ambiguity, Tony himself gets entangled in a complex node spun across his two worlds.

Moral Perfectionism and Moral Devolution

While moral ambiguity is not a condition unknown to moral perfectionism, a perfectionist does aspire to a further self, not perhaps by seeking enlightenment, but by trying to make themselves less dark. If a perfectionist finds it irrational not to act on one's desires, this obviously implies that one needs (and wants) to know one's desires, work one's way through conflicting desires; hence one needs to obey the demand of making oneself intelligible. Without the desire, indeed without the demand for a trans- or reformation of self and world, perfectionism would fail to be a moral outlook at all. Again, this transformation neither implies an overcoming or rejection of the actual, nor a recourse to an altogether different world; the actual, ordinary world is rather thought of as the womb of the eventual. As Corcuff and Laugier put it, 'the ordinary is both one of the main sources of our problems and the place where tentative solutions can be formulated',[44] to which we may add that formulating, expressing, and aspiring to solutions may be more critical than their realization.

Even with these qualifications in mind, one would be hard pressed to call Tony Soprano a moral perfectionist. If his character undergoes any changes at all, Stoehr, for one, would formulate them in devolutionary terms:

> Even though he is undergoing analysis, [Tony] is not successful in trying to overcome [his moral weaknesses and inner emptiness]. The 'development' of Tony's character could be viewed as increasingly similar to the typical devolution of those dislocated and demoralized protagonists in film noir and neonoir. As he finds no hope of renewed faith in traditional and conventional values, Tony clings more than ever to the past, fears the future.[45]

It is not a new idea that, like Tony Soprano, many (male) characters of contemporary TV are subject to a moral devolution, or masters of moral ambiguity at least. Mittell, for instance, elaborates on the case of Walter White (Bryan Cranston), protagonist of *Breaking Bad* (AMC, 2008–13). Unlike Tony, Walter was not born into crime, and while the show offers a rationale for how this most ordinary of men manages to break bad (to cover his medical bills), Mittell argues that viewers are challenged to keep rooting for Walt as he continues to fall deeper into the criminal world, and to determine the point at which he reaches the point of his 'moral dissolution'. All the while, Mittell writes, '*Breaking Bad* presents Walt as a master rationalizer for his increasingly hideous actions'.[46] The idea of characters 'rationalizing the obscene' could be applied with equal force to shows like *House of Cards* (from which I take this specific expression), *Dexter*, *24*, or *The Handmaid's Tale*, to name but a few examples.[47]

Mittell points out that our fascination with the hideousness of television's master rationalizers stems in part from their 'Machiavellian intelligence', a concept he borrows from Blakey Vermeule to explain how 'success in socially complex environments depends on the ability to understand and manipulate other people'.[48] While I certainly underscore the significance of this type of intelligence (I spoke elsewhere of a pervasive 'digital will' in contemporary media to manipulate other minds),[49] I find that, in and of itself, it neither explains our fascination for these 'difficult men' (to borrow Brett Martin's expression[50]) nor does sufficient justice to the complexity of the moral issues at stake in each of these cases, which strike me as variations of the *Sopranos* scene analyzed above. While Melfi too may be rationalizing the obscene when she makes Tony's 'shit' look 'noble', her shift of perspective is not without ground or merit. Her reassessment of Tony's fight with Meadow shows us how messy our moral problems often are, how the assessment of a problem is part of the problem, and how context dependent each case can be. As I have argued, Melfi's own account of Tony's lesson in moral ambiguity may have its limitations too. As viewers we are thus to educate ourselves, as Sandra Laugier points out in *Nos vies en séries*, not by evaluating characters, but by the way they put problems into words and by determining just how much context is relevant to assess it. In that sense, Machiavellian masterminds and complex narrative can be seen as important contributors to our own moral education, not by showing us the way out of problems necessarily, but by offering up the challenge of finding our way into them. Dismissing Tony as an 'outright amoral villain', as Mittell likes to do,[51] appears to me to avoid rather than to address the moral stakes of contemporary TV.

To be sure, not all contemporary TV shows center on such masterminds. Buffy surely belongs to a different strand of genius, and Laugier demonstrated just how many women of all varieties have come to prominence in contemporary drama shows.[52] Yet what I already argued in the case of Buffy applies to many other female protagonists as well: from the double lives of Laura Palmer (*Twin Peaks*, ABC, 1990–91) and Veronica Mars (*Veronica Mars*, UPN/The CW, 2004–07) to June Osborne/Offred's split existence as a Handmaid in Gilead (*The Handmaid's Tale*, Hulu, 2017–) or Cora's literal underground attempts to escape the long arms of slavery (*The Underground Railroad*, Amazon, 2021), they too tend to live in two worlds. As in the case study of Tony, it is on the crossroads of (or in the gaps between) these two worlds that many of the problems we encounter in contemporary TV occur, though the nature of the relations that exist between these worlds varies both between and within shows.[53]

Conclusion

I draw a twofold conclusion from this account of contemporary TV's two-world premise by relating it, respectively, to film and to ourselves as viewers.

I argued that this premise does not primarily function as a way of mapping frustration (with the actual) and desire (for the eventual), or, more generally, to imply a temporal succession of worlds, or an emergence of one world from another, as it does in Cavell's account of moral perfectionism. Rather than emphasizing their succession, TV shows rather center on the simultaneity of two worlds. In so doing—we can call this the first fold of this conclusion—they live up to what has long been considered a strength of the medium. In 'The Fact of Television', Cavell himself defines the basis of TV in terms of simultaneity (of currents of event reception), over and against the definition of film in terms of succession (of automatic world projections). The serial-episodic construction of more contemporary complex TV shows, as conceived by Mittell, likewise relies on the simultaneous development of multiple storylines. These parallel storylines still intersect and diverge across variable spans of time, of course—one of the most obvious differences between films and TV shows precisely resides in the latter's extensive duration—and it would neither be very accurate nor very informative to deny TV characters any development over time (as Roberta Pearson does).[54] Still, the two-world premise, while not incompatible with a moral perfectionist outlook, changes the odds precisely insofar as the former implies a re- or transformation of the self and/or the world. Indeed, many of the Hollywood films Cavell discusses in *Cities of Words* (and elsewhere) are premised on a change in the situation of the actual, usually instigated by a change undergone by the protagonist. Think of Peter who finally acknowledges the reality of his dream after having sent Ellie back behind the blanket/screen (*It Happened One Night*, Frank Capra, 1934), or of Tracy blowing off her marriage to George to reunite with Dexter after dropping her high moral standards (*The Philadelphia Story*, George Cukor, 1940). Paula escapes Gregory's gaslighting after her revelatory conversations with Brian (*Gaslight*, George Cukor, 1944) and, beyond Hollywood, we can see how Félicie follows her whims back to Paris after an epiphany in church, not because she prefers Loïc over Maxence but so as not to foreclose a chance encounter with Charles—which indeed takes place (*A Tale of Winter*, Éric Rohmer, 1992). The takeaway point from these examples is not that moral perfectionism presupposes happy endings, but that its protagonists are likely to end up undergoing a transformation, or at least that their conversations with friends lead to enough insight in themselves that they want to open up the possibility of such a change. By contrast, many of the characters in contemporary TV shows are, if not subject to a moral devolution per se, then at least forgoing the question of reformation that would suggest a perfectionist aspiration. Even when Tony occasionally appears to harbor such aspirations below his own moral radar, as in the 'Happy Wanderer' episode discussed above, he still dismisses the mere suggestion of attaining a further self. At the same time, I argued that we would miss much of the show's force if we simply deem him immoral.

Contemporary TV shows, in short, do not primarily ask us to judge their protagonists and characters based on pregiven moral standards. Indeed, it quite misses the mark to either deny or affirm the idea that Tony Soprano (or Walter White, Dexter Morgan, Frank Underwood, Marty Byrde, among so many others) is a moral perfectionist. What matters, rather, is that TV shows, as Laugier has argued, are even better at capturing the ordinary than films are, and are more interwoven into the very fabric of the daily lives of us viewers, who spend extensive periods of time following their characters, anticipating new episodes and reflecting on past ones with friends or online fan communities.[55] The second point of this conclusion, then, is that moral perfectionism, as the outlook that asks us to take our own positioning in the very fabric of our everyday lives into account when determining or evaluating our actions and inclinations, also asks us how we assess the problems and conflicts we encounter on the shows we are watching, and to what extent we can relate to the lives of its characters, or translate theirs to ours. In this latter relation, or translation, we may find another expression of the premise of two coexisting worlds, which we may at times find hardly compatible and at other times hard to keep apart.

Notes

1   Stanley Cavell, *Cities of Words: Pedagogical Letters on a Register of the Moral Life* (Cambridge, MA: Belknap Press of Harvard University Press, 2004), 1.
2   Cavell, *Cities of Words*, 129.
3   Ibid., 1.
4   Ibid., 2.
5   Stanley Cavell, 'Declining Decline', in *This New Yet Unapproachable America: Lectures after Emerson after Wittgenstein* (Albuquerque: Living Batch Press, 1989), 46.
6   Cavell, *Cities of Words*, 4.
7   Cavell, 'Declining Decline', 47.
8   Ibid., 113.
9   In this sense, moral perfectionism distinguishes itself not only from deontology and consequentialism, but also from moral theories that center on the concept of justice. In *Cities of Words*, Cavell singles out John Rawls in this regard, since he indeed posits that one should disregard one's actual position in society in determining the principles of justice. For an elaboration on Cavell and Rawls within the context of prominent moral outlooks, see Jeroen Gerrits, 'La pertinence politique du perfectionnisme moral', in *La voix et la vertu: variétés du perfectionnisme moral*, ed. Sandra Laugier (Paris: Presses Universitaires de France, 2010).
10 On the importance of disagreement in moral perfectionism, see Jeroen Gerrits, 'Disagreement as Duty: On the Importance of the Self and Friendship in Cavell's Moral Philosophy', *European Journal of Pragmatism and American Philosophy*, vol. 2, no. 1 (2010), https://journals.openedition.org/ejpap/937.
11 Cavell, *Cities of Words*, 5–6.
12 See Sandra Laugier, *Nos vies en séries: Les séries, une nouvelle école de philosophie* (Paris: Climats, 2019).
13 This is often considered TV's third golden age, following Robert J. Thompson's designation of a second golden age in the preceding decennium and a first in the 1950s. See Robert J. Thompson, *Television's Second Golden Age: From Hill Street Blues to ER* (New York: Continuum, 1996); and Kim Akass and Janet McCabe, *Quality TV: Contemporary American Television and Beyond* (London: I.B.Tauris, 2007).
14 Kristin Thompson, *Storytelling in Film and Television* (Cambridge, MA: Harvard University Press, 2003).
15 Thompson, *Television's Second Golden Age*; Akass and McCabe, *Quality TV*.
16 Martin Shuster, *New Television: The Aesthetics and Politics of a Genre* (Chicago: University of Chicago Press, 2017).
17 Jason Mittell, *Complex TV: The Poetics of Contemporary Television Storytelling* (London: New York University Press, 2015).
18 Stanley Cavell, 'The Fact of Television', in *Cavell on Film*, ed. William Rothman (Albany: State University of New York Press, 2005), 61. (Originally published in *Daedalus*, vol. 111, no. 4 [1982], 75–96.)

19 Cavell, 'The Fact of Television', 59–60.
20 Ibid., 62.
21 Ibid., 61.
22 Cavell discusses *It Happened One Night* in *Cities of Words*, but he published a more comprehensive account of the film (which includes the discussion of the shift from soft to 'hard' focus) in *Pursuits of Happiness*. See Stanley Cavell, *Pursuits of Happiness: The Hollywood Comedy of Remarriage* (Cambridge, MA: Harvard University Press, 1981).
23 Cavell, 'The Fact of Television', 63.
24 Ibid., 66, 68.
25 Ibid., 82.
26 Ibid., 72.
27 Cavell made a similar move in 'More of *The World Viewed*', the 1979 essay in which he responds to criticism of his discussion in his 'little book on film' as to whether film has moved from being the last of the traditional arts to a state of modernism. He interestingly does so by considering that film itself exists in two states (or worlds) simultaneously: 'I am prepared to modify my claims about film's modernism by saying either that movies from their beginning have existed in a state of modernism, from the beginning have had to achieve their power by deliberate investigations of the powers of their medium; or else that movies from their beginning have existed in two states, one modern, one traditional, sometimes running parallel, sometimes crossing, sometimes interweaving; or else that the concept of modernism has no clear application to the art of film.' Stanley Cavell, *The World Viewed: Reflections on the Ontology of Film* (Cambridge, MA: Harvard University Press, 1979), 219.
28 Cavell, 'The Fact of Television', 66.
29 Thompson, *Storytelling in Film and Television*, 55.
30 Mittell, *Complex TV*, 2. An earlier version of this discussion of Mittell's work was included in my essay on *The Handmaid's Tale*; see Jeroen Gerrits, 'From Episodic Novel to Serial TV: *The Handmaid's Tale*, Adaptation and Politics', *Open Philosophy*, December 12, 2021.
31 Mittell, *Complex TV*, 18; italics in the original.
32 Ibid.
33 Ibid.
34 Ibid., 42.
35 See Thompson, *Storytelling in Film and Television*, 53–55.
36 Mittell, *Complex TV*, 29.
37 Ibid.
38 As Ronald Bogue succinctly put it in 'The Transverse Way', 'what is striking about these transversals is not simply that they interconnect [but that] they interconnect entities that are closed in upon themselves, seemingly without communication'. In so doing, he further elaborates, transversals 'assemble multiplicities, yet in such a way that the differences among entities are not effaced but intensified' (Ronald Bogue, *Deleuze's Way: Essays in Transverse Ethics and Aesthetics* [Aldershot: Ashgate, 2007], 1–2). Deleuze draws the idea of transversals in part from the early writings of his collaborator Félix Guattari, but develops it with particular relevance for my purposes in *Proust and Signs*. The related idea of coupled systems generating an internal resonance derives from Deleuze's conception of series. See, for example, *Difference and Repetition*, trans. Paul Patton (New York: Columbia University Press, 1994), 117.

39 See Jeroen Gerrits, 'When Horror Becomes Human: Living Conditions in *Buffy the Vampire Slayer*', *Modern Language Notes*, vol. 127 (December 2012), 1059–70, esp. 1067–69; and Jeroen Gerrits, 'Ici-bas et encore plus bas: la projection empathique en «Buffy the Vampire Slayer»', in *Philoséries: Buffy, tueuse de vampires*, ed. Sylvie Allouche and Sandra Laugier (Paris: Bragelonne, 2014).

40 On the concept of the incompossible in its relation to film, see, for instance, Deleuze's analysis of *Last Year at Marienbad* in *Cinema 2: The Time Image* (Minneapolis: University of Minnesota Press, 1989), esp. 103–05.

41 Beyond the chiasmic interactions between Tony–Davey–Meadow–Eric, several plotlines interweave in this scene to form a complex node spun across Tony's two worlds, with the Pathfinder functioning as traversal. Since the Scatinos are connected to Georgetown University, for example, the exchange feeds into the long story arc of Meadow's transition to college. A duet Meadow and Eric were about to perform at a singing contest with a scholarship award, and which, as an unexpected lucky consequence of the sudden breakup with Eric, Meadow now gets to perform solo, further contributes to this arc. At the same time, because Davey already had outstanding gambling debts to Richie Aprile (David Proval)—a ruthless capo in the DiMeo crime family who resents his subordination to Tony and will eventually rival him with Uncle Junior's backing—the implications of the SUV gift exchange reverberate through the realm of the underworld as well. (Since Richie violated Mafia code for debt collection and broke up Tony's poker game by attacking Davey at the table, Tony imposes that Davey pay him off first before Richie will be allowed to collect another dollar from him.) The complexity of the node runs deeper still—for example because Richie dates Tony's sister, or because Tony's resurrection of the high-level poker game is a consequence of Uncle Junior's house arrest—and the amplifying effect of coupled worlds inspires new developments as well. An example of the latter is the parallel plotline that culminates two episodes later, when Tony again gives a gift away, a leather jacket this time, offered to his housemaid's Polish husband to the offense of its original donor—Richie Aprile (s2:e8, 'Full Leather Jacket').

42 Kevin L. Stoehr, 'It's All a Big Nothing: The Nihilistic Vision of *The Sopranos*', in *The Sopranos and Philosophy: I Kill Therefore I Am*, ed. Richard Greene and Peter Vernezze (Chicago: Open Court, 2004), 44. Drawing here on Nietzsche's *The Will to Power*, Kevin Stoehr distinguishes between active and passive nihilism: 'Nietzsche … tells us that passive or negative ("incomplete") nihilism is a rejection of seemingly fixed values and institutions without the spiritedness that allows one to become an individualistic self-creator … On the other hand, active or positive ("complete") nihilism is the process of becoming a creative individual while rising above mere resentment and life-negation' (Stoehr, 'It's All a Big Nothing', 39). His point being that Tony remains stuck in passive nihilism.

43 Ibid.

44 Philippe Corcuff and Sandra Laugier, 'Introduction: Pour un programme d'inspiration cavellienne d'analyse des séries TV', *TV/Series*, vol. 19 (2021): §12, my translation, http://journals.openedition.org/tvseries/5014.

45 Stoehr, 'It's All a Big Nothing', 44.

46 Mittell, *Complex TV*, 154–55.

47 In *House of Cards* (Netflix, 2013–18), a political rival (Heather Dunbar) uses the expression to qualify Frank Underwood's political cunning (s3:e4, 'Chapter 30').

In *24* (Fox, 2001–10), the 'obscene suggestion' to 'take [Jack] Bauer out' unfolds a complex node of ambiguous positions bouncing back and forth between deontological and consequentialist arguments (s4:e24, 'Day 4: 6:00 a.m.–7:00 a.m.'). And in *The Handmaid's Tale* (Hulu, 2017–), Commander Waterford justifies the subjection of women to sexual servitude in the theocratic state of Gilead by putting his finger on actual flaws of democratic societies in the process. Perhaps the most complex rationalization occurs in *Dexter* (Showtime, 2006–13), with each season offering new twists to the blanket 'justification' for serial-killing tendencies.

48 Mittell, *Complex TV*, 143, 145; see Blakey Vermeule, *Why Do We Care About Literary Characters?* (Baltimore: Johns Hopkins University Press, 2011).

49 See Jeroen Gerrits, *Cinematic Skepticism: Across Digital and Global Turns* (Albany: State University of New York Press, 2019).

50 Brett Martin, *Difficult Men: Behind the Scenes of a Creative Revolution: From the Sopranos and the Wire to Mad Men and Breaking Bad* (New York: Penguin Press, 2013).

51 Mittell, *Complex TV*, 143.

52 See Laugier, *Nos vies en séries*, esp. the section '18 femmes et demie', 231ff.

53 For examples of such variations, consider how Tony adheres to traditional values like loyalty and respect in both worlds, even while he becomes more likely to fail to live up to them in the one world the more he sticks to them in the other. Or think of Buffy, to take another example, who starts treating a 'sucky roomie' as though she were a demon, which primarily reveals the waning of her own humanity. That her suspicion turns out to be correct when she rips off the girl's face only goes to show how awkward things can start to look when one world enters into the other. (I have argued elsewhere how this moment initiates Buffy's growing detachment from both worlds, culminating in the incompossibility discussed above.)

54 Roberta Pearson, 'Anatomising Gilbert Grissom: The Structure and Function of the Televisual Character', in *Reading CSI: Crime TV Under the Microscope*, ed. Michael Allen (London: I.B.Tauris, 2007).

55 See Laugier, *Nos vies en séries*, 45ff.

PART III
EVERYDAY EDUCATION

9

The Sublime and the American Dream in *Fargo*

Hugo Clémot

Synopses

Fargo (the film: Ethan and Joel Coen, 1996)

It is winter in Minneapolis, Minnesota. Jerry Lundegaard is an inept used-car salesman who thinks he can get out of financial trouble by getting a ransom from his wealthy father-in-law, Wade Gustafson: he therefore has his wife, Jean, kidnapped by two thugs. But things are going to turn out badly because of the stupidity and violence of the two criminals he hires. The case is assigned to policewoman Marge Gunderson, who, in the course of her investigation, will come to question her beliefs about the goodness of the world and of human beings.

Fargo (the series: Ethan and Joel Coen, Noah Hawley, FX, 4 seasons, 41 episodes, 2014–)

It is winter in Bemidji, Minnesota. Lester Nygaard is an inept insurance salesman who has been bullied by his wife and harassed since high school by a man named Sam Hess. In a hospital waiting room, he meets Lorne Malvo, a hitman on the run, who offers to kill Hess, an offer Nygaard does not refuse. This is the beginning of a vicious circle of lies and murders that will change the lives and relationships of police officers Molly Solverson, Bill Oswalt, and Gus Grimly.

Introduction

When one presents philosophy to novices, it is common to start by differentiating between two types of questions that one may spontaneously have to answer. Some questions can be answered by seeking out the facts: in a direct way, by discovering the facts for oneself or by experiencing them oneself; or, in an indirect way, by asking advice from specialists or witnesses. These questions are often referred to as 'factual' or 'empirical'. There are, however, other types of questions that cannot be answered in this way. With these 'philosophical' questions, we already see and know everything needed to answer. In other words, we have all the experience necessary to answer, but we can fail to see what is in front of us, to recognize what we already know without realizing it.

In finding an answer to philosophical questions, the difficulty lies in one's state of mind: when a philosophical question arises, one is a bit like Dr Watson when he realizes that he has seen, has heard, and knows the same things as Sherlock Holmes, but that he has nevertheless 'passed by' the event, to use Stanley Cavell's term.[1] The difference lies in the fact that, for Watson, the observed facts were nothing but ordinary and banal—that is to say, without interest—whereas Holmes knew how to be attentive to what makes them strange. One could say that philosophical work aims at making us similar to Sherlock Holmes: it seeks to make us change our way of seeing, to modify the perception of our experiences by giving back to the ordinary its strangeness.

This work will often be preceded by an experience that raises a suspicion that there might be more going on than appearances suggest. This philosophical encountering of wonder is quite frequently felt at the cinema or when watching television series. Films or television series can therefore be the occasion for a philosophical experience that opens the way to a philosophical work. Richard A. Gilmore, in his fascinating work on the film *Fargo*, argues:

> Perhaps *the* philosophical intuition is that there is more going on than mere appearances suggest. It is the sense that a more complicated dynamic may be at work in a situation than at first appears. You may have the sense that there is more going on, but not be at all clear what that more is; philosophy is all about tracking down what that more might be. There is a point in watching movies at which this idea inevitably begins to dawn on you. You begin to register signs, clues, that there may be a larger narrative at work simultaneously to the explicit narrative of the primary plot of the movie. This might be called the meta-narrative of a movie.[2]

By looking back at the Coen brothers' film, I am going to try to find out if there is a philosophical meta-narrative at work in the first season of the *Fargo* TV series—the film's adaptation.

Fargo: When Ordinary People Are Confronted with Evil

Originally, *Fargo* was a ten-episode television miniseries, adapted from Ethan and Joel Coen's 1996 film of the same name.[3] As noted by Marc Cerisuelo and Claire Debru in their book *Oh Brothers!*,[4] the film represented the vogue for thrillers and serial-killer stories,[5] a trend that has yet to subside more than twenty years later—as evidenced, for example, by the success of such series as *Dexter* (James Manos, Jr., Showtime, 2006–13), *Hannibal* (Bryan Fuller, NBC, 2013–15), and *Mindhunter* (Joe Penhall and David Fincher, Netflix, 2017–19). In the film, the serial killer is named Gaear Grimsrud. The series is focused on his counterpart, the character of Lorne Malvo, but it is less concerned with the psychological strangeness of the psychopath, unlike *Silence of the Lambs*, or with the complexity of the plot, as in *Dexter*, than with how the ordinary people who will cross his path will be affected by the encounter. This is evident from the first episode, where Malvo's toxicity successively infects Lester Nygaard, the boy in the motel, and Sam Hess' oldest son.

In one of the bonus features, writer and executive producer Noah Hawley talks about his desire to show that Malvo has infected Lester with his evil, a phenomenon that finds literal illustration in the fact that his hand does indeed suffer from an infection, caused by one of the pellets from Malvo's rifle used to shoot at police chief Thurman.

The authors of *Oh Brothers!* tell us that the Coen brothers' works intentionally reflect what makes James M. Cain's novels[6]—such as *Double Indemnity*, *Mildred Pierce*, and *The Postman Always Rings Twice*—so interesting and powerful when compared to the books of Dashiell Hammett or Raymond Chandler: namely 'the abandonment of criminal folklore; Cain's stories are about "real people", ordinary individuals shown in their mundane everyday lives—and who are as if sucked into crime'.[7]

In his psychological particularity, the character of Malvo is part of a long line of horrible Coenian villains, succeeding 'the monstrous biker in *Raising Arizona*, Charlie Meadows in *Barton Fink*, ... Big Dan in *O Brother* and especially Anton Chigurh in *No Country for Old Men*',[8] whose function is not so much to embody an authentic possibility of human immanence, but to ensure the role of representing the absolute evil, a representation that confers on them a form of transcendence.[9] Very clearly identified with the wolf on several occasions starting from the first episode, Malvo also takes up Chigurh's critical discourse against moral rules and ordinary social institutions.[10]

Cerisuelo and Debru note that the Coens' formal innovation is most radical when it aims to represent the powers of evil, as in the horrific thirteen-minute sequence in which a character is buried alive in *Blood Simple* (1984),[11] or in the scene in *Raising Arizona* (1987) in which Gale Snoats emerges from the mud, in defiance of any realism.[12] The supernatural, even surreal nature of Malvo's strength is also affirmed very early in the series, since, from the first episode, he manages to escape from Nygaard's home by mysteriously disappearing into a dead-end basement.

As for the other characters, it is undeniable that we find in the series, as well as in the film, the 'loving attention' that Cerisuelo and Debru identify in the Coens' work as early as *Raising Arizona*,[13] and which, in the end, is a love of the Good, embodied by the character of Marge. Like Marge in the film, Molly is indeed 'structured, ordered, solid ... in opposition to the chaos of Evil in the film, the objective eye of the camera imposing on us at a regular rhythm symmetry as a visual value of reference'.[14]

Fargo and the Sublime

This general interpretation of the film's purpose is solidified by a close analysis of the scene of Marge's reunion with Mike Yanagita, a former high school classmate who wakes her up by calling her on the phone in the middle of the night. Sitting next to her on the bench and putting his arm around her shoulders, Mike quickly seeks physical contact with Marge, but gets a firm and clear refusal from her, then lies to her about the death of a wife he never had and breaks down in tears while feeling sorry for himself. Cerisuelo and Debru see this scene as

> a strange digression ... as the umpteenth way of trampling on the rules of the detective story; a process intended to bring us back to the verisimilitude of life's vagaries. Nevertheless, the episode is bizarre, starting from nowhere and leading nowhere, except as a reintroduction of the Coen-style love triangle where, in this instance, the lover is doomed to failure before he even appears. But taking into account the deductive faculties of the young woman ... one can notice that as soon as she finds her friend in the Minneapolis restaurant, she understands that he is beating around the bush. And that out of tact, she *plays* the fool.[15]

This interpretation is credible and reasonable. Because it seems rather fruitful for understanding the series, we can also evoke the interpretation proposed by Gilmore in the chapter of his book *Doing Philosophy at the Movies* entitled 'The American Sublime in *Fargo*'. Gilmore sees this part, in addition to the following scene with the phone call, as the essential moment of the film.[16]

During that phone conversation with a friend, Marge learns that Mike has lied to her about his marriage and his job situation, and has kept his psychological problems from her. In the moments that follow, while she is driving her car, Marge is confronted with the moral abyss of her former classmate. She is so 'surprised' that it seems to make her question her overly ordered view of the world. She then appears to realize that she is not as satisfied with her life as she has tended to believe until now. Indeed, the fact that she did not tell Norm, her husband, about Mike's phone call, nor about her restaurant date with him, says something about the state of her marriage. She tests her own abyss and emerges stronger.

This experience is philosophical insofar as it allows Marge an opportunity to realize that her first encounter with Jerry Lundegaard passed her by in the same way as did her encounter with Mike. In other words, she realizes that she failed to pay attention to certain dimensions of the moment she was experiencing. Yet, while Marge is undoubtedly amazed, Gilmore argues that her experience also creates the feeling of the sublime. Indeed, Marge's emotion here is similar to what we feel when we realize the inability of our imagination to offer us a definitive idea of what we are experiencing, as well as the power of our mind when we manage to apply it rationally.

To understand this definition requires a return to the notion of the sublime, insofar as this situation does not seem typical of the examples given by Immanuel Kant, the philosopher to whom we generally turn when we think about the sublime experience.

Kant and the Sublime

First, let us note that Kant can, on occasion, bring astonishment closer to the sublime:

> *The astonishment*, very close to fright, the horror, and the sacred thrill that seize the spectator at the sight of mountains rising to the sky, of deep gorges where the waters run wild, of isolated places filled with shadows and a melancholy that invites reflection, etc., do not really arouse fear, because the spectator knows he is safe, but they simply try to make us surrender to the imagination so that we can feel the capacity of this power to combine the movement of the soul thus aroused with its relaxation and thereby to dominate nature in ourselves, but also outside ourselves, insofar as it can influence the feeling of our well-being.[17]

In *Fargo*, both in the film and in the series, there are 'isolated places filled with shadow and a melancholy that invites reflection'. This leads Cerisuelo and Debru to describe the film as a 'veritable outdoor *huis clos*, with its fixed shots of deserted roads and vast frozen expanses under an opaque sky [which] visually focuses on the flatness of the country, its horizontal dimension'.[18] It is not absurd to find in this description something similar to what Kant poetically characterizes as the way in which one must look at the ocean to experience the feeling of the sublime, namely as 'a transparent mirror of water that is limited only by the sky'.[19] In one of the extras that accompany the DVD, Hawley describes Minnesota as the last outpost of civilization in a vast wilderness where the cold is a genuine challenge to human survival, evoking the two conditions—grandeur and power—for an experience of the sublime in the Kantian sense.

We know that, for Kant, the feeling of the sublime is in fact a complex pleasure, composed of two moments: for something to be sublime, it is necessary that there was, first, 'the feeling of a momentary stop of the vital forces' caused by a representation of the form of an object that does 'violence to the imagination',[20] which is accompanied then 'by an effusion that is that much stronger' thanks to the 'feeling of a suprasensible power within ourselves'.²¹ For example, the visitor to the pyramids of Egypt or to the St Peter's Basilica in Rome experiences at first the 'impotence of their imagination to present the idea of a whole',²² but, quickly following, the power of the reason which was able to conceive and build such structures. Similar to Descartes's famous example of the chiliagon,²³ which serves to illustrate the superiority of understanding over imagination, since we cannot summon in our mind the image of a thousand-sided polygon, whereas we can easily think its definition, the experience of the sublime is relative to the grandeur that Kant qualifies, for this reason, as 'mathematical'. Born, for example, from the spectacle of the pyramids of ice or the dark raging sea,²⁴ it reminds us of 'the Idea of the humanity in us as subjects'—that is to say, 'the rational destination of our powers of knowledge'.²⁵ The sublime is thus a mixed feeling of displeasure, linked to the experience of the finitude of imagination, and of pleasure in thus seizing the superiority of reason over imagination and the sensitivity on which it depends.

This superiority of reason over nature in ourselves, which would remind us of our 'destination', our 'vocation' as free and moral subjects, can also be experienced in front of spectacles that are likely to arouse fear—in other words, the feeling that arises in front of a power that we try to resist, or an evil, 'when we do not find our power to be equal to such an evil',²⁶ such as threatening rocks, storm clouds, volcanoes, hurricanes, the ocean, etc. Indeed, as long as we find ourselves safe, we are able to experience the feeling of the 'dynamic sublime' which consists in simultaneously finding a moral power in ourselves that allows us to resist 'nature in ourselves',²⁷ i.e., to sacrifice our sensible interests (goods, health, life) out of respect for 'the Idea of humanity in us as subjects'.²⁸

The characters in the series have several opportunities to experience this dynamic sublime. Indeed, they are all confronted with an evil that seems to have an irresistible power. One thinks of the first meeting between Malvo and Gus at the end of the first episode, or the first time Molly sees Malvo's picture,²⁹ but also of the 'miraculous' events of which Stavros Milos, the 'king of supermarkets', is victim.³⁰ Milos illustrates the difference between superstition and religion according to Kant,³¹ insofar as he is too afraid of God's power to make it the occasion to feel a sense of respect for Him and for the destination, superior to nature, which is our own. Similarly, few characters manage to convert the negative emotion of their physical inability to fight against evil into a positive pleasure linked to the conviction of the invincibility of their moral superiority over it. Indeed, it takes Molly's courage to go after colossi during a storm, as in episode 6, and Gus's courage to dare to enter the wolf's den, as in the last episode.

Fargo and the 'American Sublime'

In his writings on the film *Fargo*, Gilmore argues that there is a specifically American experience of the sublime that depends on what constitutes a specifically American abyss. Gilmore justifies this reduction of the experience of the sublime to an experience of the abyss, which is at the same time self-revealing—something that has to do with the subjectivity of the subject of the sublime—with reference to a phrase by the American transcendentalist philosopher Emerson: 'There may be two or three or four steps, according to the genius of each, but for every seeing soul there are two absorbing facts,—I and the Abyss.'[32]

Gilmore then determines what the specifically American character of the abyss may consist of by referring to what he calls the 'American myth': a complex myth, composed of other myths such as:

> the myth of newness, of being traditionless; the myth of moral purity or innocence; the myth of the wild West which is a myth of open spaces, of closeness to nature, of a certain comfort with violence. Another aspect of the American myth, which is also part of the American Abyss, is the myth of the American dream. I take the idea of the American dream to be based on the idea of self-creation, including the idea of the self-made person—one who pulls him- or herself up by their own bootstraps, to be a self-made millionaire before turning thirty, to transcend, by his or her own powers, the limitations of class, prejudice, tradition, and his own past.[33]

Lester, or the Abyss of the American Dream

It is obvious that the characters of Jerry Lundegaard, in the film, or Lester Nygaard, in the series, are caught up in this American dream and confronted with the abyss of their inability to sell (cars or insurance policies, correspondingly). The dialogue between Lester and a young couple expecting a child is hilarious in this regard: while the parents-to-be have only come to attach the mother to the father's insurance policy in joyful anticipation of the baby's birth, Lester seeks to scare them into buying his comprehensive life insurance 'plus' by mentioning several common types of accidents in which the father could suddenly die. As Gilmore writes, the American dream also contains the dream of being able to buy everything and being able to consume everything, which makes Jerry and Lester doubly unsuccessful in being such bad salesmen.[34] As they fail to achieve the American dream by respecting the rules, they both decide to not follow them any more, violating the social contract, something that, in the case of Lester, will be suggested to him by Malvo. For Lester, the encounter with Malvo is a return to the state of nature insofar as it constitutes an encounter with the Hobbesian man, who 'is a wolf to man' and who is driven by the passions of competition, defiance, and glory.[35] It is also sublime, in the Kantian sense, insofar as it is an encounter with an evil force, which Lester cannot understand and which he does not believe himself able to oppose, at least in the beginning, but which attracts him because it seems to reveal the existence of a power within himself that he has never been able to exercise. This experience confirms in him the conviction about his own selfhood that is expressed by the sentence 'What if you're right and they're wrong?', which appears on the famous poster of a red fish swimming against the current of yellow fish that he has hung in his cellar.

Lester's problem is that the strength he discovers in himself through his encounter with the abyss that is Malvo—which is what Emerson calls 'self-reliance',[36] or the power to be true to one's desire—is a strength that is misdirected. He does not use this experience as an opportunity to become aware of the vulnerability and uncertainty of his beliefs, in particular his belief that, in order to be happy, he must be able to do what his brother does, starting with buying a washing machine. There is something very Girardian in the way that his first victims will also be his first models, whether it is the character of the awful school bully, Sam Hess, or that of his brother. Indeed, we know that, for René Girard, desire is mimetic—that is to say, modelled, imitated on that of a mediator-model—and can give rise to jealousy, hatred, and finally violence if the mediator comes to constitute the main obstacle to obtaining an object of desire too scarce to be shared.[37] In short, instead of having a properly philosophical experience that starts with destabilizing his convictions in order to reach a more lucid understanding of his desires and to faithfully commit to them, Lester finds in Malvo a new model to imitate, a big fish that swims against the current by feeding on others, thus confirming his erroneous conception of the American dream and inciting him to finally dare to assert himself at the expense of others. Remarkably, Gilmore wrote of Jerry that he exemplifies the concept of the *serious man*, as found in Simone de Beauvoir—that is, a man who conceives the world and moral values as fixed and certain—in 2005, four years before the release of the Coen brothers' film *A Serious Man*. In Emerson's terms, Lester clings to the American dream that is in fact a nightmare, preferring to master and manipulate the world and others through cunning and force rather than by acknowledging their independent existence. Unable to relate properly to the experience of the abyss, Lester cannot help but fall into it, literally.

Bill Oswalt, Stupidity, and the Two Laughs

The feeling of the sublime can also fail to be experienced properly when the evil seems too great to be resisted, including morally. This is the case with Bill Oswalt, the officer who has been appointed chief to replace Thurman, when he announces to Molly that he is leaving the police force. The affection that we can feel for this character, despite his stupidity, allows us to enjoy one of the frequent springs of comedy in the Coens' films, and thus in this television transposition—in fact, several critics of the Coen brothers notice this 'tenderness'.[38] In a text on *Raising Arizona* (1987), Gilmore gives an account of this in reference to what he calls the Platonic theory of humour. In the allegory of the Cave,[39] he sees a distinction between two types of laughter: the laughter of the prisoners who laugh at the philosopher who has come down into the cave to educate them, but is unable to be the best at recognizing the various shadows passing by; and the laughter; and the laughter of the philosophers, on the outside, who see the man who has just been freed, blinded by the light of the sun and stumbling. The first laughter is a laughter that ridicules and expresses the feeling that the one who laughs is superior to the one who makes them laugh, while the second is a laughter similar to that of parents who see their child taking its first steps, a laughter full of joy and love. The former excludes, while the latter includes the one laughed at in the community of men—because the latter laughter is also directed at those who laugh, insofar as they recognize, in the efforts of those who stumble, their own past and present efforts to stand up, to hold on, and even to rise in existence. In the work of the Coens, laughter is more often of the second type than the first. It refers to the perfectionist requirement that Cavell first spotted in the remarriage comedies of the 1930s and 1940s, and then in the writings of American transcendentalists such as Thoreau and Emerson, who spoke of an 'optative mood' to refer to the—very American—sense of being free and responsible for determining who one wants to be.[40]

If the character of Bill Oswalt, the officer who becomes chief even though he is less competent than Molly, remains endearing to us in spite of his authoritarianism and his mistakes, it is because little by little we understand that his stupidity results less from a closed mind linked to a too-high self-esteem and to the certainty of being right, than from a partially voluntary blindness to a truth about the human soul, which he intuits, but refuses to face because he does not feel able to bear it. If laughter can finally be born from observing him, it is because we recognize in his efforts to preserve his idealistic conception of existence our own efforts not to lose sight of the fact that there is good in the world, in spite of the force of evil, which often seems irresistible. This laughter thus fulfils a double function of distancing us, of freeing us from a fear that can sometimes assail us to the point of making us give up certain projects, while at the same time revealing to us the humanity that we share with this character.[41]

Marge and the Comedy of Remarriage

In his chapter on the film *Fargo*, Gilmore argues that it is an experience of the sublime that leads Marge, the police chief, to become aware of what she missed during her previous interview with Jerry Lundegaard, the sleazy car salesman who had his wife kidnapped by dangerous criminals. The sublime is understood here in the 'dynamic' sense of an experience of encountering an evil—that is, a power that we judge to be superior to our own, but to which we nonetheless believe we can offer resistance out of respect for 'the Idea of humanity in us as subjects'.[42] This experience comes after Marge's meeting with her former high school classmate and the telephone revelation of his lies and propensity for sexual harassment: it is indeed a moment in which Marge has the opportunity to 'look into the infinite, which constitutes for [her sensibility] an abyss' where she can experience the necessity of 'moral feeling'. Consequently, the experience of the sublime is the opportunity to live a sceptical experience, to question the foundations of our beliefs and our actions. It could even be an experience of the discovery of the absence of such foundations. In place of this non-existent foundation is an abyss of infinite depth, which can be opened at any moment by our doubts and our daily mistrust when we refuse to recognize others and to show ourselves by accepting to be defined by our uncertain choices. At the edge of the abyss that is the life of her former high school classmate, Marge becomes aware of her own abyss, but also of the fact that, despite all the imperfections of her life—her provincial 'hick' side, the very slow pace of her life, as if she were already retired, etc.—she and Norm, her husband, are 'doing really well',[43] considering the dangers that threaten and the doubts that might paralyse them.

Similar to Joyce's *Ulysses*, where Leopold Bloom seeks to find a way to return to the marriage bed, i.e., to reaffirm his marriage to his wife Molly, the film *Fargo* thus ultimately becomes the story of a woman who has left the marriage bed and seeks to return to it by overcoming a number of obstacles. If Cavell is correct in thinking that the *Odyssey* is the first story to be structured as a remarriage comedy, which would account for many of the multiple references to Homer's epic in the Coens' 2000 film *O Brother, Where Art Thou?*, which is also a comedy of remarriage,[44] then we can conclude that there is indeed a continuity.

Molly, or Raising America

My idea is that Fargo, the series has slightly shifted the issue of remarriage by refocusing it around the question of whether it is still possible to make babies. I point to the first episode, the title of which, 'The Crocodile Dilemma', refers to a parent's crucial and impossible choice of saving their child's life.[45] The episode repeatedly features pregnant women and the concerns that pregnancy can inspire in expectant parents, whether it's the wife of Thurman, the police chief soon to be murdered by Malvo, or the young couple to whom Lester Nygaard awkwardly tries to sell an insurance policy.

As a reprise of a dialogue from *Raising Arizona*,[46] the exchange between the couple and Lester is triply instructive. It reveals, on the one hand, the extent of Lester's professional incompetence and inability to sell anything because he is incapable of putting himself in other people's shoes. But it also constitutes a sceptical commentary on the world: one can never be sure of what will happen, of being able to take care of the baby, a scepticism reinforced by Malvo's speech on social rules later in the episode, and on the impossibility of preventing danger, except by living in a very close-knit community—a speech given to Gus's Jewish neighbour at the end of episode 5. The exchange also makes us wonder if Lester's inability to put himself in the couple's shoes might not be because he has a problem with the idea of having a baby, a problem that may have to do with his erroneous and dogmatic conception of happiness, modelled on his brother's material and professional success.

This scepticism about the possibility of having children in such a cruel world is brought up again in great detail by Lou, Molly's father, in the second episode:

> Lou: There's the kind of things a schoolteacher gets exposed to, truancy and the like, and then there's the stuff a cop sees, murder and violence, and general scofflawery, and then there's the kind of deal you're looking at now.
> Molly: Which is?
> Lou: Which is, if I'm right … savagery, pure and simple. Slaughter, hatred, devils with dead eyes and shark smiles. One day, you're gonna get married and have kids … and when you look at them, their faces, you need to see what's good in the world. 'Cause if you don't, how you gonna live?

In fact, like Marge in the movie, Molly will be pregnant at the end of the series. The reference to the baby is also present in the strange transposition of Marge and Mike Yanagita's reunion scene suggested in the series. In episode 3, Molly meets up with a long-lost friend at a restaurant. This friend asks her if she's dating anyone, before explaining that she's recently divorced. This scene is pretty much the same as in the film, with the major difference that the young woman is not a sick man with a tendency to harass women. On the contrary, from the point of view of her sexuality, this woman seems rather fulfilled, since she does not hesitate to meet people through dating websites, even if she is sometimes made to regret it. It is on the mention of one of these meetings that the scene closes, the young woman explaining how she saw baby spiders coming out of the neck of her lover, while they were having sex.

Thus we find a digressive character in this scene, similar to the film, and its absurdity could serve as a reference to the human propensity—admittedly more or less marked depending on the person and the moment—to utter nonsense. However, this scene finds a strange echo later in the episode, during Molly's first meeting with Gus Grimly and his daughter, Greta. While sitting at Lou's, her father's restaurant, Molly has just asked Greta, to break the ice while waiting for the order, if she has a boyfriend. She asks then if they have ever heard of a spider laying eggs in the neck of a human being and relates her friend's story using the expression 'baby spiders', before concluding: 'Not sure if I want to live in a world where something like that can happen to a person.'

The issue for Molly in the series will therefore be whether it is still possible to have children—that is, to continue to 'see the good in the world', despite its horrors. In a sense, Molly has the answer to this question right in front of her: what is essentially good in the world is the goodwill of the single father who, out of fear for his daughter, did not do his duty as a policeman but had the courage to confess his fault to Molly and will do anything to make amends. To see the good in the world would thus be to experience the Kantian sublime, in the 'dynamic' sense—in other words, as an experience of the irresistible character of the forces that threaten us and, at the same time, as a revelation of the moral, supernatural destination of the human being.

This leads me to agree with Noah Hawley's notion that the series has two endings: the first one in episode 8, when Molly tells Gus, 'We're doing good', showing that she has accepted her place despite the injustice of the universe; and the second one when Gus kills Malvo in his lair.

The first ending comes a year after the decisive scene in which Molly sees Bill Oswalt acknowledge that he was wrong, while refusing to hear that he continues to be wrong when he doesn't want to believe in Lester's guilt and his brother Chaz's innocence. Even though it is difficult for her, because of the affection she feels for Bill, Molly will gradually learn to detach herself from things that do not depend on her, to recognize that she cannot control the world and others, starting with Bill, and therefore to let things go ('let it go') despite what she thinks she knows. She will learn, thanks to Bill, to stop behaving like Lester—to question her desire to see him behind bars in order to prove that she is right. Through the intimacy of her ordinary professional and friendly relationship with Bill, Molly discovers that she must let go, that she must stop clinging to fixed ideas and that she has a life to lead, a life that can be happy as long as she accepts that the world and others can escape her. Molly's experience of the sublime is thus an opportunity to rediscover Cavell's 'truth of skepticism',[47] meaning that it is futile to seek to know the world and others in order to master them, even if scepticism rests on the fallacy that it should be possible. The wisdom that Molly achieves, and that Cavell recommends, is that we must recognize the world and others, admitting that they are separate from us and accepting this separation. From the moment Molly recognizes the otherness of Bill and the world, she opens herself to the good in the world in general, and to the good in her ordinary marital relationship with Gus in particular. The bedroom scene depicts Molly's wisdom, in contrast to the behaviour of the fast-talking policewoman in the screwball comedy we see on the television screen.[48]

It is precisely this wisdom that neither Lester Nygaard nor Jerry Lundegaard have, since it is his sense of invincibility (after all, he has escaped the consequences of two murders by getting rid of his two lifelong 'enemies', Sam Hess and his brother) and omnipotence that will lead Lester to want to take on Malvo and, in a sense, to have the upper hand. Lester thus has the hubris that Gilmore believes he detects in the character of Llewelyn Moss in *No Country for Old Men*, the hunter who will attack his prey, Anton Chigurh, without realizing that the latter will prove to be a far more formidable predator. In clutching the $2 million briefcase found at the crime scene,

Moss resembles Jerry Lundegaard's character when he clings to the idea of getting a million-dollar suitcase, which for him is the American dream. As Emerson wrote in 'The American Scholar', 'All things have two handles: beware of the wrong one.'[49] Lester does not know how to grasp the right handle of the American sublime, and thus becomes a sample of the worst in America, while Molly, because she knows precisely how not to cling to the American dream but instead how to convert her gaze to see what good the world and others, including Bill Oswalt, can have, she does know how to hold the right handle.

This brings us back to the question of remarriage and what Cavell might have said about it when he made it the question of American community. In the last scene of the show, after receiving a phone call telling her that Lester has fallen into an ice hole in a lake on the Canadian border, Molly returns to her couch with Gus and Greta, to watch a TV show. To Gus, who tells her that he will soon be awarded a medal for his courage, Molly replies that she is proud of him and that the medal is his, even though she will become the chief of police. This scene echoes not only the atrocious exchanges between Lester and his wife in the first episode, where she tells him she is ashamed of him, but also the first words heard in the series: a recording playing in Malvo's car. They are the words of a man, whom we do not yet know to be Malvo's former victim, whom he had to convince to have his wife murdered: 'She won't stop, you know? Day after day ... I was a maker ... I hope they do it tonight ... When she's sleeping. But I'm scared.'[50]

We can see this return as a way of recalling the political stakes of the question of a possible future for the couple in America or elsewhere: if America is a universal dream rather than a real country, will we know, once the myths of moral purity and the self-made man have been exhausted, how to find a new way of dreaming, of living together? Will we be able to reinvent the American myth, or will we have to resign ourselves to the nightmare of a world populated by men whose only reason and desire are like those of Malvo and Lester—that is to say, a world where man is a wolf to man?

Conclusion

I began this chapter by asking myself the following questions: Can season 1 of *Fargo*, the series, cause a feeling of philosophical wonder? In other words, can it raise a suspicion that there is more going on in the world than suggested by appearances? And are these things, which are really happening behind appearances, likely to feed a philosophical 'meta-narrative' that the series would hold for us—a narrative beyond the story we are told? Finally, despite the many differences between the two works, how faithful is the series to the Coen brothers' film from which it is adapted?

To answer these questions, I began by turning to Marc Cerisuelo and Claire Debru's general interpretation of the film: that what the Coens would say about James M. Cain, namely that 'Cain's stories are about "real people", ordinary individuals shown in their mundane daily lives—and who are as if sucked into crime', would be true of their own films, and in particular *Fargo*. Cerisuelo and Debru's book allowed me to situate the character of Lorne Malvo in the lineage of the horrible Coenian villains whose function is not so much to embody an authentic immanent human possibility as to ensure the role of representative of absolute evil, whose representation confers upon them a form of transcendence.

However, from Cerisuelo and Debru's perspective, the meeting between Marge and Mike in the restaurant is conceived as 'a process intended to bring us back to the verisimilitude of life's ups and downs', but it is nonetheless a 'strange digression', a 'bizarre' episode. By contrast, Richard Gilmore's interpretation of this scene seemed more fruitful to me: according to him, the meaning of the meeting is indeed linked to the following scene, that of the telephone revelations about Mike's past. Confronted with the moral abyss of her former comrade, Marge is led to question her too ordered conception of the world and of others. She might then realize that she is not as satisfied with her life as she has tended to believe. Just as she failed to see what Mike's behaviour and her own conduct meant, she realizes that she failed to see the abyss that Lundegaard's behaviour during his interrogation sought to hide. This interpretation therefore seems relevant to understanding what appears to be a key moment in the film. According to Gilmore, this epiphanic experience of the abyss has to do with the emotion of the sublime.

I thus sought, in the third part, to recall the most famous conception of the sublime, that of the German philosopher Immanuel Kant, for whom this emotion, which occurs in particular in the subject confronted with an evil whose force is such that resisting it does not seem possible, is complex. First, it is indeed composed of the negative emotion of the physical impotence of the subject to fight against an evil which exceeds them, but also of the positive pleasure linked to the conviction of the invincibility of their moral superiority over the evil. It seemed to me, then, that when Molly dares to go after colossi in a snowstorm, or when Gus dares to enter Malvo's lair, these ordinary individuals must have had something like an experience of the sublime.

If the question of what it means to inherit in philosophy is central to the thought of the philosopher Emerson as a pioneer of the discipline in America,[51] it is not surprising to find in him a conception of the sublime as a self-revealing experience of the abyss. Insofar as this experience is linked to what Gilmore calls the 'American myth'—a complex myth, one dimension of which is linked to the famous American dream—it made sense for me to consider *Fargo*, the series, from the point of view of how the main characters react to the sublime experience of the abyss provoked by the encounter with absolute evil, as Gilmore does in relation to the film.

I then found that, while Lester does discover in himself, through his encounter with the abyss represented by Malvo, a strength that Emerson calls 'self-reliance' and which is, for the philosopher, the power to be true to one's desire,[52] this strength is misdirected by Lester who uses it only to control and manipulate in order to imitate his brother and Malvo. Rather than using the encounter with the abyss as an opportunity for moral uplift, Lester mistakenly believes that he can become stronger if he frees himself from all moral principles.

I then noted that the feeling of the sublime can also fail to be experienced correctly when the evil seems too great to be resisted, including morally. This is what happens to the character of Bill Oswalt, whose apparent stupidity is in fact linked to a voluntary blindness in order not to have to face the truth about the human soul that he intuits but is unable to bear.

Unlike Jerry, Marge makes the experience of the abyss an opportunity for moral uplift. Rather than deepening the doubts about her marital life that her secret behaviour expressed, she reaffirms her fidelity to her desire for him and the life they have together. As in Joyce's *Ulysses*, where Leopold Bloom seeks to find a way to return to the marriage bed—that is, to reaffirm his marriage to his wife Molly—the film *Fargo* thus also becomes the story of a woman who has left the marriage bed and seeks to return to it by overcoming a number of obstacles: what Stanley Cavell has called a comedy of remarriage.

In the end, it is not surprising that Marge's alter ego in the series is named Molly, although I tried to show that Noah Hawley had shifted the issue of remarriage by refocusing it around the question of whether it was still possible to have children in a world where people like Malvo or Lester committed such atrocities. The crucial issue for this main character, but also for us, the viewers, is therefore how to continue to 'see the good in the world', despite its horrors. The solution, which seems to correspond to the first ending envisaged by Hawley, is to let go: this is what Molly does when she realizes that she must learn to relinquish things that are not in her control, to recognize that she cannot control the world and others, and thus to let things go despite what she thinks she knows about them, in order to open herself up to what is good in the world in general, and what is good in her ordinary marital relationship with Gus in particular.

To recognize that one may not be able to master the world and others without losing sight of what is good in the world is finally to recognize that one can be confronted with a force that one cannot physically or socially resist, and yet not lose control of one's intention and fidelity to one's desire. To do so is to be ready to look into the social abyss without fearing that one is no longer a person of sufficiently goodwill to be able to build a community.

Notes

1 Stanley Cavell, 'Something Out of the Ordinary', in *Philosophy the Day after Tomorrow*, trans. N. Ferron (Paris: Fayard, 2011), 16.
2 Richard A. Gilmore, *Doing Philosophy at the Movies* (Albany: State University of New York Press, 2005), viii.

3 An anthology series, with seasons that are independent of each other, it has since had three other seasons. The 'anthological' character must however be qualified: not only does season 2 present events to which season 1 frequently alludes (which makes it a sort of *prequel*, i.e., a season that recounts the events that preceded a season that was released earlier), but one of the 'games' of the scriptwriters consists of creating more and more links between events and characters of the different seasons as new seasons follow.
4 M. Cerisuelo and C. Debru, *Oh Brothers! Sur la piste des frères Coen* (Paris: Capricci, 2013).
5 *Fargo* was released following the triumph of Jonathan Demme's *Silence of the Lambs* (1991), Quentin Tarentino's *Reservoir Dogs* (1992), and David Fincher's *Seven* (1995). Cerisuelo and Debru, *Oh Brothers!*, 87.
6 'We always thought that at Columbia University's Low Library, where the names of Aristotle, Herodotus, and Virgil are carved into the top of the columns, the fourth name must be Cain.' *The Coen Brothers: Interviews*, ed. William Rodney Allen (Jackson: University Press of Mississippi, 2006), *passim*; quoted in Cerisuelo and Debru, *O Brothers!*, 136.
7 Cerisuelo and Debru, *O Brothers!*, 138–39. The authors are more explicit in the chapter devoted to the film *Fargo*: 'The Coens make no secret of the fact that they consider that a criminal plot must be set among ordinary, awkward people without panache ("this is a true story"). From this perspective, violence is contagious and spreads as if under a one-way influence: evil corrupts good, never the other way around.' Ibid., 91.
8 Ibid., 92.
9 'Transcendent' is that which belongs to an order of reality different from and superior to the one under consideration. 'Immanent' is that which belongs to the same order of reality as the considered order.
10 Anton Chigurh's speech in *No Country for Old Men*: 'If the rule you follow brought you to this, of what use was the rule?' In episode 6 of the series, Malvo continues to blackmail Stavros Milos through Chumph, who reads to him over the phone, with a device that makes his voice unrecognizable, a text of his own invention. The text is a parable that tells the story of a little boy, 'born in the woods and raised in the fields' who, never having been able to reach the protection of a home and envying those who lived there, sees the wolves appear and whisper.
11 Cerisuelo and Debru, *O Brothers!*, 29–30.
12 Ibid., 43–44.
13 Ibid., 34.
14 Ibid., 95.
15 Ibid., 94–95.
16 I return below to the content of this appeal and its importance. See 'Marge and the Comedy of Remarriage'.
17 Immanuel Kant, *Critique of the Faculty of Judgment*, trans. A. Renaut (Paris: GF Flammarion, 1995), 252.
18 Cerisuelo and Debru, *O Brothers!*, 84–85.
19 Kant, *Critique of the Faculty of Judgment*, 254.
20 Ibid., 226.
21 Ibid., 232.

22 Ibid., 234.
23 René Descartes, 'Meditation Six', in *Metaphysical Meditations* (Paris: GF Flammarion, 2021), 318.
24 Kant, *Critique of the Faculty of Judgment*, 238.
25 Ibid., 239.
26 Ibid., 243.
27 Ibid., 247.
28 Ibid., 244.
29 Following a question from a St Paul policewoman in s1:e3, Molly replies that Malvo may well be the culprit in the three Bemidji murders because 'It's a nasty enough fella' to have done it.
30 Stavros Milos is the 'heir' of Nathan Arizona, the king of raw, ready-to-paint furniture in *Raising Arizona*.
31 Kant, *Critique of the Faculty of Judgment*, 246–47.
32 Ralph Waldo Emerson, *Journals* (1866), quoted in Gilmore, *Doing Philosophy at the Movies*, 60.
33 Gilmore, *Doing Philosophy at the Movies*, 60.
34 Gilmore, *Doing Philosophy at the Movies*, 61.
35 Thomas Hobbes, *Léviathan*, I, Chapter XIII, trans. R. Anthony (Paris: Giard, 1921), 203–04.
36 Ralph Waldo Emerson, 'Self-Reliance' (1841).
37 See René Girard, *Mensonge romantique et vérité romanesque* (Paris: Grasset, 1961).
38 Georg Seesslen, 'Looking for a Trail in Coen County', in *Joel and Ethan Coen*, ed. Peter Körte and Georg Seesslen, 230, 277. See also the idea of loving attention discussed above in Cerisuelo and Debru.
39 Plato, *Republic*, VII.
40 Ralph Waldo Emerson, 'The Transcendentalist' (1841).
41 In his book *Jokes: Philosophical Thoughts on Joking Matters*, Ted Cohen defines the dual function of laughter as allowing us to 'liberate ourselves from certain oppressions, and to achieve an intimacy of a very specific kind'. See Ted Cohen, *Jokes* (Chicago: The University of Chicago Press, 1999), 10, quoted in Gilmore, '*Raising Arizona* as an American Comedy', in *The Philosophy of the Coen Brothers*, ed. Mark T. Conard (Lexington: University Press of Kentucky, 2009), 15–16.
42 See what Marge says to the *serial killer* she has just arrested, as she leads him to prison: 'There are other things in life than money. Don't you know that? And you're here now. And it's a beautiful day. I really don't understand.'
43 'Heck, Norm, you know, we're doing pretty good.' A phrase repeated in the series by Molly (who says 'We're doing good') in s1:e8 in a very slow scene, which Noah Hawley holds as crucial, since it might as well be the end.
44 Stanley Cavell, 'L'odyssée des frères Coen', trans. Élise Domenach, *Libération*, 8 November 2007.
45 See the version given by Lucien de Samosate in *Les Sectes à l'encan*, trans. E. Talbot, in *Œuvres complètes de Lucien de Samosate*, Tome 1, XIV (Paris: Hachette, 1866), 210: 'Let us suppose that a crocodile has kidnapped [your child], when he was wandering on the bank of a river, and that he has then promised to give him back to you, on condition that you would tell him exactly whether he intends to give him back to you or not; what do you think the crocodile's resolution is?'

46 Summary dialogue from *Raising Arizona*: 'Dot: You probably got the life insurance all squared away. Ed: Have we done that yet, honey? Dot: Got to do that, Hi ... What would Ed and little angel do if a truck splattered your brains all over the interstate? Ed: Yeah, honey. What if you get run over? Dot: Or you got carried off by a twister?'
47 Stanley Cavell, *The Senses of Walden*, trans. B. Rival and O. Berrada (Courbevoie: Théâtre Typographique, 2007 [1972]), 113.
48 The title of the film is *The Adventures of Kitty O'Day* (William Beaudine, 1945).
49 Ralph Waldo Emerson, 'The American Scholar' (1837), trans. Christian Fournier, *Critique*, no. 491–92 (June–July 1992), 550.
50 Pilot pre-credits.
51 See Christiane Chauviré, 'De la difficulté d'hériter en philosophie. Emerson, Cavell et la philosophie en Amérique', *Critique*, no. 491–92 (June–July 1992), 428–34.
52 Emerson, 'Self-Reliance'.

10

TV Time, Recurrence, and the Situation of the Spectator: An Approach via Stanley Cavell, Raúl Ruiz, and Ruiz's Late Chilean Series *Litoral*

Byron Davies

Tracing out the concerns about audiovisual media shared by the US philosopher Stanley Cavell (1926–2018) and the internationally renowned Chilean filmmaker Raúl Ruiz (1941–2011) would seem to provide a study of significant philosophical commonalities that are nevertheless occasionally refracted by differences in tastes, sensibilities, politics, and frames of reference. What Cavell and Ruiz shared was a sense that the 'poetry' afforded to the cinematic image in its automatically produced character—the singular audiovisual moment or involuntary gesture caught on film—meant that film escaped certain notions of hierarchy that have been thought to govern the other arts. Cavell and Ruiz also articulated their understandings of film's natural poetry via an overlapping set of philosophical concepts, including Walter Benjamin's *optical unconscious* and Nietzsche's *eternal recurrence of the same.*

Where they differed, however, was in the forms of films that attracted their attention, and in which they located the most powerful expressions of the medium's poetry. Early in his writing, Cavell's receptions of modernism and auteurism informed his focus on complete, autonomous films, with identifiable makers.[1] His concern with the situation of the spectator rather than producer, and the film spectator's supposed relief from the responsibilities of agency, likewise informed his attention to films in their aspects as 'finished'.[2] Though Cavell's attention was not at all exclusively occupied by classical Hollywood narratives, when he came to write his famous studies of Hollywood genres, there remained a thread between his earlier emphasis on 'complete'

Byron Davies, 'TV Time, Recurrence, and the Situation of the Spectator: An Approach via Stanley Cavell, Raúl Ruiz, and Ruiz's Late Chilean Series *Litoral*' in: *Television with Stanley Cavell in Mind*. University of Exeter Press (2023). © Byron Davies. DOI: 10.47788/UUOB5662 films and the notions of narrative completeness marking those Hollywood films (most obviously in the resolution of conflicts marking remarriage comedies). Throughout these stages of his film writing, Cavell framed the spectator as a reader—or 'performer' of interpretations—of complete works rather than as a co-producer of something incomplete.[3]

In contrast, Ruiz's writing on film is perhaps most famous for the criticisms of classical Hollywood narrative—what Ruiz calls 'central conflict theory'—in the first volume of his book *Poetics of Cinema*.[4] For Ruiz, classical narrative and its stress on conflict resolution served to occupy our attention at the expense of the poetry of the cinematic image. This critique of dominant Hollywood modes was the most vital expression of his opposition to US cultural imperialism. (He was nevertheless attracted to watching Hollywood films *against the grain*, particularly in appreciating the poetic qualities in the imperfections of Hollywood B movies and serials from his youth.)[5] This critique was also bound up with his non-modernist, 'baroque' emphasis on the poetic and imaginative possibilities of filmic fragments, particularly individual shots, as well as his later criticisms of auteurism as 'a regular claim of Western *doxa*'.[6] With these ideas, Ruiz communicated his sense of the spectator as anything but relieved of agency and in fact as something like a co-producer, at least of those films that opened up imaginative possibilities in their imperfections and incompleteness (and especially in their resistance to narrative completeness).

I want to explore a little further the idea that Cavell found the cinematic image's poetry within classical narratives while Ruiz found that very same thing outside those narratives (or despite them), as well as how the views of each came together with differing conceptions of the spectator. But I also contend that the crux of any encounter between Cavell and Ruiz must lie in their conceptions of *television*, since it was this medium that brought out their strongest points of connection in thinking about seriality, the temporality of an audiovisual medium, and the situation of the viewer. Of prime importance here are Cavell's brief remarks on soap operas in his 1982 essay 'The Fact of Television',[7] since it was precisely what Cavell found bemusing about soap operas from the perspective of his conception of film—their operating according to the principle of 'series' rather than autonomous works, their resisting classical narrative resolutions—that allowed, in Ruiz's case, for soap operas and especially Latin American *telenovelas* to stand as exemplars of the audiovisual poetics that fascinated him.

These possibilities, I will claim, lie in how serial-episode construction facilitates an 'argument' between, on the one hand, our repetitive needs and drives and, on the other, the transient stories we tell 'out of' those needs and drives. This is the development of an idea that Cavell himself sketches in 'The Fact of Television',[8] though I will insist that, in appreciating its consequences, we should pay close attention to Ruiz's late work for Chilean TV, and especially how Ruiz used televisual formats as ways of examining the nature of storytelling and the recurrent needs at play in our being spectators of stories. Therefore, this chapter will build up to a reading of Ruiz's late miniseries *Litoral, cuentos del mar* (*Littoral: Tales of the Sea*, 2008), consisting of fantastic, complexly nested tales told by sailors aboard a Chilean ghost ship. Some of these tales are arguably assimilable to classical narratives, including even a story of remarriage. But by using the series' episodic format to uncover the recurrent needs underlying those same stories, Ruiz aims to lay bare the limits of pictures of spectators as 'outside' narratives (a kind of picture that Cavell's own writing on filmic narratives could, again, be understood as exemplary of). At least, this will be my reading of *Litoral*'s poignant conclusion, when a sailor-storyteller finds himself at once the spectator of a scene taken from classical narrative and also having to recognize, with great pain and difficulty, the role of his own recurrent fantasies and needs in its construction.

Filmic Poetry and the Situation of the Spectator

Some Commonalities and Differences between Cavell and Ruiz

Though Cavell and Ruiz were colleagues at Harvard in 1989–90, the year that Ruiz was Visiting Lecturer in the very department—Visual and Environmental Studies—that Cavell had earlier helped to found, it is difficult to determine whether they had any substantial interaction.[9] Nevertheless, we can be tempted by thinking they would have had something important to say to each other, since in the period following his stay at Harvard, Ruiz would go on to produce perhaps the most philosophically informed reflection on film ever written by a major international filmmaker: his two-volume (with extant notes for a planned third volume) *Poetics of Cinema*.[10] This is a book striking in its knowledgeable references ranging from strands of contemporary analytic philosophy with which Cavell might have considered himself in 'conflict',[11] to earlier figures like Russell, Moore, and Whitehead,[12] to figures of great significance to Cavell like Benjamin, Kuhn, Nietzsche, and Wittgenstein.[13] The references to Benjamin and Nietzsche are particularly notable for their roles in Ruiz articulating the sense he appeared to share with Cavell of cinema's natural poetry—a notion that in the cases of both Cavell and Ruiz grounded their senses of the possibilities of film escaping hierarchies found in other arts, as well as the necessities of a certain indiscriminateness in film taste.[14]

The line connecting these concerns is the camera's ability to capture the involuntary, accidental, and unnoticed—the sort of phenomena broached in Benjamin's references to the camera's access to the 'optical unconscious'[15]—and the natural weight or interest that these phenomena can bear for us. Though it took some time for Cavell to relate these concerns explicitly to Benjamin and the optical unconscious,[16] they are for him major organizing themes beginning with his 1971 book *The World Viewed: Reflections on the Ontology of Film*. These include his observations in that book that 'in any film, however unpromising, some moment of interest, even beauty, is likely to appear',[17] as well as his later expression of a 'natural vision of film' as one in which 'every motion and gesture, however glancing, has its poetry, or you may say its lucidity'.[18]

For these reasons, we can be struck that, for all Cavell's comparative attention to classical Hollywood narratives, he especially emphasizes singular, otherwise 'incommunicable' moments or gestures that could just as well supply the fundamentals of avant-garde films (such as what P. Adams Sitney called 'lyrical' films[19]) that have refused those same structures: 'the curve of fingers that day, a mouth … spools of history that have unwound only for me now, and if not now, never'.[20] These concerns remain central in his studies of classical Hollywood genres like comedies of remarriage. For example, we find it in his observation that 'The poetry of the final appeals for forgiveness in *The Lady Eve* [Preston Sturges, 1941] is accordingly a function of the way just this man and this woman half walk, half run down a path of gangways … and how just these voices mingle their breaths together.'[21] We should not neglect the mutual inflection for Cavell of these singular moments and their context within a classical narrative resolution; but neither should we neglect the way in which the latter context typically sends Cavell's fascination straight to those singular, poetic moments.

There are echoes of all these ideas in Ruiz's writing, though often carried by Ruiz's blunter style. In the second volume of *Poetics of Cinema* he asserts that 'cinema is condemned to be poetic'.[22] He also paraphrases with approval the Chilean poet Jorge Teillier's remark that 'any film no matter how terrible … would have at least five minutes of good poetry'. And he suggests that for these reasons 'cinema breaks out or it seeks to break out from quality criteria which … can be applied to all the other arts'.[23] In the book's first volume he explicitly relates these phenomena to Benjamin's optical unconscious (to which he devotes an entire chapter): in other words, that 'mass of details which remain invisible to the naked eye and which the lens renders eloquent'.[24]

Finally, we should note how much of Ruiz's concerns about film's capacity to capture involuntary human gestures, and its consequent poetry, is informed by his peculiar reception of Nietzsche's notion of the *eternal recurrence of the same*. (Two of Ruiz's major French films of the 1970s, *L'Hypothèse du tableau volé* [*The Hypothesis of the Stolen Painting*, 1978] and *La vocation suspendue* [*The Suspended Vocation*, 1978], were collaborations with Pierre Klossowski, author of the classic 1969 study of the eternal recurrence, *Nietzsche and the Vicious Circle*.[25]) For Cavell and Ruiz alike, Nietzsche's proposal of seeing one's life as a repeatable cycle played a variety of roles in articulating their visions of film: including, for Cavell, a way of figuring both film's automatic reproducibility and the forms of 'diurnal repetitiveness' and 'festivity' communicated in remarriage comedies.[26] In Ruiz's case, Nietzschean notions of recurrence allowed him to express his attraction to ouroboros- or Möbius-strip-like narratives that refused closure,[27] as well as the distinctive kinds of repetitiveness and circularity manifested by 'immortal stories' and folkloric legends.[28]

In fact, these notions of recurrence are at least doubly related to Ruiz's thinking about the optical unconscious and film's ability to capture the involuntary and accidental. On the one hand, the singular moments caught on film can constitute the concrete particularization of an immortal story or transtemporal legend. On the other hand, a wide collection of such singular moments (which Ruiz connected to Aby Warburg's 'museum of reproductions', or Bilderatlas Mnemosyne[29]) would 'point out the continuity of the same gestures, the same human attitudes, and the same intensity of feeling throughout history'.[30] In other words, for Ruiz, filmic poetry not only consisted of capturing singular moments, but also of situating them within the wider context of, as Cavell happened to put it, 'the repetitive needs of the body and the soul'.[31] The possibilities of an audiovisual medium communicating those repetitive needs will become especially important when we turn, in the following part, to both Cavell's and Ruiz's thinking about television.

An Overly Simple Reconciliation between Cavell and Ruiz

But before coming to television, I have to address what already suggests itself as an easy reconciliation between Cavell's and Ruiz's thinking about film. The proposed reconciliation would go as follows. Ruiz memorably criticized classical Hollywood narrative via his objections to 'central conflict theory', which he associated with certain applications of Aristotle's *Poetics*, with Ibsen and Shaw, and with the contemporary film scholar David Bordwell.[32] For Ruiz, whose anti-imperialism characterized his earlier documentary work in Chile in support of Salvador Allende's Popular Unity government and continued in his exile following the 1973 US-backed coup, this critique was political as well as aesthetic. (In *Poetics of Cinema* he says of 'the globalization of central conflict theory' and US imperialism: 'Such synchronicity between the artistic theory and political system of a dominant nation is rare in history; rarer still is its acceptance by most of the countries in the world.'[33]) Thus, what attracted Ruiz to Hollywood B movies and films like Edgar Ulmer's *The Black Cat* (1934) were not the 'claims' made by their narratives upon him, but rather the non-narrative poetic qualities lying in the imperfections (including continuity errors) that escaped classical narrative impositions.[34]

In contrast, Cavell did not share Ruiz's specific political commitments, and his defense of Hollywood's intellectual importance did not take into account those critiques of US dominance, like Latin American Third Cinema, that were integral to the context of Ruiz's early working years.[35] Cavell's filmic frames of reference were much wider than his reputation sometimes suggests, but we cannot deny that even his writing on filmic 'modernism' and 'neo-Hollywood' is mostly framed by works abiding by classical narrative structures of the sort Ruiz criticized.[36] Nevertheless, the proposed reconciliation would remind us of Cavell's comparative focus on singular poetic moments within classical narrative structures. Therefore, once we factor out the differences in politics and tastes, as well as somewhat differing senses of significant 'accidents' on film—continuity errors never seemed to have the poetic significance for Cavell that they had for Ruiz[37]—there is no impediment to understanding Cavell as primarily a reader of Ruizian moments in classical narrative cinema: of those singular poetic moments spilling out of those structures.

What makes this reconciliation overly simple is that it discounts even larger differences between Cavell and Ruiz regarding their conceptions of the forms of bearers of filmic significance, of film's hold on our attention, and perhaps most importantly of the model spectator. Sketching out some of these differences will be the concern of the rest of this part of the chapter, allowing us to understand better the importance of a possible encounter between Cavell and Ruiz via television.

I have already noted how Cavell's receptions of modernism and auteurism informed his sense in *The World Viewed*, as well as in some later writing, of films as 'complete', 'finished', 'autonomous' works by identifiable makers.[38] In contrast, commentators have frequently noted Ruiz's 'baroque' or 'postmodernist' emphasis on the filmic fragment as both a bearer of significance and of awaiting significance to be added by the spectator.[39] Thus, in Ruiz's memorable formulation, 'when we see a film of 500 shots, we also see 500 films',[40] the 500 films are meant to be products of the viewers' creative imaginations: Ruiz is adamant in refusing the former, *official* film any ontological priority other than as a springboard for the latter imaginings. Cavell instead associates the filmic spectator with the viewing of a kind of work that does not lack completeness—or rather, if it did, it would raise doubts about the auteur's commitments and responsibilities to the viewer. Moreover, in *The World Viewed* the model spectator viewing a complete work is understood to be 'absent' from the world screened, as well as relieved from the responsibilities of agency that Cavell thinks characterize, say, the procedures of theatre, such as the audience's participation in the conventions sustaining the performance of a play.[41] Thus, for Cavell it needs to be emphasized that this spectator is absent from a film that is fixed across projections, a relation that contrasts with the variability across performances (including varying relations between spectators and actors) that characterizes live theatre.[42]

While Ruiz hardly denies that something like Cavell's model might characterize the typical film spectator of classical or well-formed 'complete' narratives, he prizes the spectator who operates as an 'experimental delinquent'.[43] For this kind of spectator, who playfully shirks the claims that a well-formed narrative might make on them, film viewing is neither associated with relief from agency nor with, as Cavell once put it, a 'moving image of skepticism',[44] but rather with something approaching an equal encounter between two agencies. According to Ruiz, a film 'is aesthetically valid insofar as the film views the spectator [eliciting these forms of creative delinquency] as much as the spectator views the film'.[45] Ruiz's dialogic conception of the relation between film and spectator likewise plays a role in his discomfort with strong emphases on differences in variability between film projection and theatre performance.⁴⁶ Similarly, it appears that Ruiz's attraction to interactive video-discs and arborescent narratives—in 1996 he produced with students an interactive CD-ROM adaptation of Robert Louis Stevenson's *Suicide Club*—had to do with their making explicit a way in which there had always been space for the imaginative, 'delinquent' spectator even within older film formats.⁴⁷ Also, it is especially in those moments in which we spectators are near-asleep or bored, having lost the story's thread, that, thanks to the resulting oneiric expanse, 'we can finally say that we are *in* the film'.⁴⁸ Thus, for Ruiz, who contrasted these oneiric moments with how our attention was seized by well-constructed classical narratives, there was much at stake in opposing models of spectatorship that combined narrative completeness with an image of the spectator as *outside* the film.

Consequences of Creative Reading versus Creative Making of Films

These are some seemingly harsh contrasts—and the present unavoidability of interactivity in digital audiovisual media might anachronistically bias us towards Ruiz's side—so we need to recognize the extreme subtlety and provocation with which Cavell expresses his perspective. The last chapter of *The World Viewed*, in particular, presents a beautiful, finely drawn account of film's hold on our attention as well as an important challenge to easy invocations of the spectator's imagination. But it is also the expression of a very particular sensibility about film. There Cavell notes that, 'Those who miss serious radio will say that, unlike television, it left room for the imagination. That seems to me a wrong praise of imagination, which is ordinarily the laziest, if potentially the most precious, of human faculties.'⁴⁹ He then says of the 'world of sounds' projected by radio and the 'world of sights' projected by silent film that '[i]n neither is imagination called upon'.⁵⁰ A few pages later, in discussing connections between film and Wittgenstein on aspect-seeing, Cavell does in fact call upon imagination, but with some notable restraints: 'unlike the triangle and the duck-rabbit and all other optical illusions, I must surround the [photographed] face with a reality—as though the seeing of a reality is the imagining of it'.⁵¹ That is, we cannot surround the filmed face with just any imagining: it must be grounded in 'a reality', or one of the many 'incompatible' realities that film presents and that 'vie for my imagination'.⁵²

In the same chapter Cavell can even begin to sound like Ruiz in saying that film 'escapes Aristotelian limits according to which the possible has to be made probable'.⁵³ But following a wonderful list of accepted improbabilities in classic Hollywood stories, he explains our acceptance of, say, filmic 'werewolves and vampires' as grounded in 'the knowledge which makes acceptable film's absolute control of our attention'.⁵⁴ Ruiz was no less fascinated by these narrative improbabilities, but—as a champion of the creative possibilities of distracted, oneiric spectatorship—he found little to cherish in our acceptance of them in contexts of absolute attention. Rather, these improbabilities were important because they allowed our minds to wander, rendering these films' images parts of our very own films.

Cavell is rightly remembered as a philosopher who made the case for wide creative possibilities in reading, and even wide creative possibilities in the attribution of an author's intentions.[55] If he did not allow for the same relative limitlessness in a work's constitution that Ruiz did, this also had to do with his sense of the responsibilities of defining works that would allow for meaningful disagreements in readings.[56] Therefore, some of these differences between Cavell and Ruiz can be attributed to the differences in perspective between a creative reader of films and a creative maker of films. (Cavell might sometimes take the perspective of a film director, but this is always in the course of a reading of a given film, not in the course of appropriating fragments that would yield new films.[57]) It is part of the convenience in contrasting Cavell and Ruiz that they conscientiously articulated these different perspectives through a difference between, respectively, the picture of a spectator being on the *outside* and that of being on the *inside* of a film.

What happens to these perspectives when they are confronted by television?

Time and Recurrence on Television

Ruiz and Television

Ruiz's filmmaking life was a life of deep involvement with television. Following his earliest filmmaking efforts as well as a period of travel in the US, in 1964–65 Ruiz spent six to eight months in Mexico, where he linked up with Chilean producer of Mexican *telenovelas* Valentín Pimstein, one of the architects of what would eventually become the Televisa *telenovela* empire.[58] By Ruiz's account he was hired to write dialogue for the endings of episodes, into which he would surreptitiously insert lines of poetry by Eliot and Pound.[59] One Pimstein-produced *telenovela* for which he wrote complete episodes was *María Isabel* (1966), a classic of the format, and one to which Ruiz would later make extended reference in his Chilean feature *Palomita blanca* (*Little White Dove*, 1973, released 1992).[60] Ruiz would later also draw on *telenovelas* in his US production *The Golden Boat* (1990) and most conspicuously in *La telenovela errante* (*The Wandering Soap Opera*, 1990, finished and released in 2017).

Beyond his stay in Mexico, Ruiz's formative period in the 1960s also included his involvement in a variety of television programming, including editing sports coverage for Chilean TV.[61] Following his exile in 1973, television was integral to his production. The West German channel ZDF funded the filming in Honduras of *Utopía o el cuerpo repartido y el mundo al revés* (*Utopia or the Scattered Body and the World Upside Down*, 1975).[62] After that, much of Ruiz's work in France in the late 1970s and early 1980s was supported by efforts from L'Institut national de l'audiovisuel (INA) to bring non-mainstream film to French television (though only a portion of Ruiz's work in fact made it to the air).⁶³ One of Ruiz's major works of the 1980s, *Manuel na Isla Das Maravilhas/Manoel dans l'île des merveilles* (*Manuel on the Island of Wonders* or *Manoel's Destinies*, 1984), was presented in distinct miniseries formats for Portuguese and French television.⁶⁴ Also, incorporating elements of television was central to Ruiz's feature films: in *Treasure Island* (1985, which also happened to feature Mexican *telenovela* star Pedro Armendáriz Jr.) the film's plot becomes fantastically melded with the production of a TV action-adventure series.

It seems that the period around 1989–90 (that is, of Ruiz's stay at Harvard, and the time when he was beginning to think through the ideas that would constitute the first volume of *Poetics of Cinema*) was of special importance for his thinking about television. He originally wanted his fall 1989 filmmaking course to allow students to 'create a simulation of a television schedule', including 'talk shows, news, serial dramas, games', although apparently he did not follow through on this plan.⁶⁵ Nevertheless, the feature he directed while at Harvard, *The Golden Boat*, a collaboration in New York with the performance group The Kitchen, incorporated elements of not only Mexican *telenovelas*, but also sitcom laugh tracks and TV crime dramas. Since March 1990 marked the end of Pinochet's military dictatorship, later that year Ruiz returned to Chile to test the new freedom of expression available in his native country.⁶⁶ The resulting unfinished experiment, *La telenovela errante* (finished posthumously by Ruiz's wife and collaborator, the accomplished filmmaker Valeria Sarmiento), drew from Ruiz's impression of postdictatorship Chile as a kind of *telenovela*.⁶⁷ Some elements of the unfinished film made their way into the Chilean setting of Ruiz's 1991 contribution to *A TV Dante*, a series for the UK's Channel 4 that originated with Tom Phillips and Peter Greenaway.

Importantly, the last decade of Ruiz's life was often characterized by projects that brought together questions about TV formats, Chilean national identity, 'immortal stories', and folkloric legends. These included his 2002 experimental documentary series for Chile's Ministry of Education, *Cofralandes*, as well as his two late series for TVN (Chile's national public television channel), *La recta provincia* (2007) and *Litoral* (2008).⁶⁸ (We might also include here Ruiz's internationally successful 2010 series *Mistérios de Lisboa* [*Mysteries of Lisbon*], in which Portugal arguably functions as a displaced Chile.⁶⁹) In the following part of the chapter I will discuss the special importance that I think *Litoral* has in relation to the issues already raised in the previous part about narrative and spectatorship. For the rest of this part I want to say a little more about Ruiz's thinking on television, seriality, and *telenovelas*, in light of those previous issues, and how it allows for a striking possible encounter with Cavell's writing on television.

Delinquent Spectatorship and 'The Fact of Television'

A large factor in Ruiz's attraction to televisual formats was that, unsurprisingly, they facilitated kinds of delinquent spectatorship. The medium's reliance on what Cavell called 'switching' between currents or modes of programming allows for a special amorphousness in the constitution of works that would have been attractive to Ruiz's 'baroque' emphasis on the aesthetic potential of the fragmentary and of what spectators can make out of the fragments they encounter in audiovisual media. This is the kind of amorphousness sometimes at play in concerns among TV scholars about where a broadcast work begins or ends, and thanks to which we can find an almost Ruizian style of TV viewing pursued with deliberate seriousness in, for example, a representative 1983 article by Mike Budd, Steve Craig, and Clay Steinman that analyzed a single 1981 broadcast of *Fantasy Island* as though the commercials were inseparable from the episode itself.[70] We of course find this amorphousness, and the attendant opportunities for delinquent spectatorship, even further facilitated when we switch between TV channels. This was of particular interest to Ruiz, who in *Poetics of Cinema* sketches a 'theoretical fiction', in which he imagines switching between channels, finding the same 'little man' in each program, as though he were being followed by this person across the switching.[71] It is important in noting Ruiz's sense of the continuity between channel-switching and delinquent filmic spectatorship—particularly if we recall Ruiz wanting to figure the latter as our being *inside* films—that his vignette ends with the realization that the little man on TV is himself: 'our own image'.[72]

Some of the foregoing might risk overstating the audiovisual anarchism that Ruiz located in television, since in his notes towards the third volume of *Poetics of Cinema* he also associates TV programming with a certain regularity and timelessness that he likens to the popular legends and recipes pervading eighteenth-century almanacs.[73] The idea that TV consists of an 'argument' between 'time as repetition' and 'time as transience' (we might add, between regularity and delinquency) is itself central to Cavell's essay 'The Fact of Television'.[74] But in order to appreciate that idea's importance we have to understand that when Cavell was invited to write that essay in 1982 he was not prepared to display anything like the comfort with televisual formats that Ruiz consistently showed.

There are several reasons for this, including Cavell's avowed familiarity with film and early radio rather than TV, as well as of course the then-widespread distrust of TV among intellectuals that he interrogates in that essay. But another major factor is that TV's aesthetic principles can present problems for Cavell insofar as he views them through what we have already seen as his perspective on the 'autonomy' of films. In other words, Cavell's approach is the exact converse of what makes TV unproblematic from the perspective of Ruiz's views on cinema: they both see the medium's constituent parts as heteronomous. Thus, again, for Cavell the medium is characterized by forms of 'switching' between modes and currents rather than by the forms of narrative 'succession' that he tends to associate with autonomous films.[75] Even when it comes to narrative formats on TV, he understands them to be related to each other not as autonomous works (in the way that autonomous films might be related to each other through the relation that Cavell calls 'genre-as-medium'), or as parts of an autonomous work (like the stages of a classical narrative), but rather as members of a series, a relation that he calls 'undialectical'.[76]

Despite or because of Cavell's bemusement with some of these features of television, his account of the medium contains great insights, some of which are prepared for by his remarks on soap operas. Early on Cavell notes a relation between soap operas and resistance to classical endings.[77] He later takes an interest in another non-classical feature of soap operas, namely their exceptionally long running spans. (This is in effect Cavell's approach to Dennis Porter's much-quoted observation that, unlike classical Aristotelian narrative's beginning, middle, and end, the soap opera 'belongs to a separate genus that is entirely composed of an indefinitely expandable middle'.[78]) Then, remarkably comparing these long running spans to the ambitions of the French *Annales* historians (their 'getting beyond the events and the dramas of history to the permanencies, or anyway to the longer spans, of common life'), Cavell reconsiders the importance of his earlier remark that 'serial procedure is undialectical'. He says, 'the span of soap operas can allow them to escape history, or rather to require the modification of the concept of history, of history as drama'.[79] What Cavell soon arrives at is the important insight that serial procedure allows for a peculiar relation between 'dramatic, transient' episodes and exactly those 'undialectical', *undramatic* permanencies: 'what is under construction [in serial procedure] is an argument between time as repetition and time as transience'.[80] (Cavell here links this insight to Nietzsche's *Zarathustra*, presumably thinking of its formulations of the eternal recurrence.) Thus, extraordinarily, having begun with some uncertainty about what to make of TV serialization's heteronomous parts, Cavell arrives at the suggestion that long-running soap operas might have the power to place transient narratives within the wider context of what he elsewhere calls 'the repetitive needs of the body and the soul'.[81]

The Fact of Telenovelas

I have emphasized Ruiz's lifelong relation to *telenovelas*, and much of what Cavell says about soap operas could certainly help to account for this abiding relation in Ruiz's work. The daily serial procedures that Latin American *telenovelas* share with US daytime soap operas relieve expectations about classical endings within individual episodes. (Here we should recall Ruiz's personal relation with writing episode endings for Mexican *telenovelas*.) Also, daily serial-episode procedure can resist the easy application of 'central conflict theory' insofar as the format allows for the proliferation of conflicts, without any single conflict occupying our attention. (It must be admitted that, in the case of *telenovelas*, the fuller possibilities of such proliferation, which Argentine scholar Oscar Steimberg has called the format's late 'postmodern' or 'neo-baroque' style, were not explored in the format until well after Ruiz's work for Pimstein in Mexico.[82])

In fact, while Cavell locates soap operas' capacity to escape 'history as drama' in their long running spans, this points to a major difference between US soaps and Latin American *telenovelas*. Despite their shared daily serial procedures, while soaps resist closure in their open running spans, *telenovelas* typically have contained running spans (usually about a year) and determinate story arcs and central characters (out of which the proliferation of conflict might still result).[83] Nevertheless, the *telenovela* format allows for its own distinctive relation to recurrence and 'immortal stories'—its own way of constructing an 'argument' between transient dramas and repetition—that we can imagine would have particularly fascinated Ruiz. I am referring to the forms of resurrection that take place *between* series.

On the one hand, as Ana M. López puts it, 'Whereas the US soap's lack of closure implies a spectator that is knowledgable of the history of a specific community, the telenovela spectator recognizes actors and stars and awaits their appearance and fictional reincarnation in each new telenovela.'[84] This form of resurrection is already familiar from film, indeed from Cavell's writing on stardom, though there are likely unique dialectical possibilities arising between it and daily serial procedures.[85] On the other hand, the stories themselves can be resurrected: *telenovelas* have historically relied on both synchronic 'remakes' (production of preexisting scripts for specific national markets) and diachronic remakes (the retelling of established stories). Beyond the many remakes of televisual classics like the Peruvian *Simplemente María* (which shared some basic plot elements with *María Isabel*, itself remade by Televisa in 1997),[86] remakes are regularly produced of stories that stretch back to the *telenovela*'s origins in Cuban *radionovelas* of the 1940s.[87] In 2001 Televisa produced its third televisual version of the Cuban radio classic *El derecho de nacer* (1948). In 2010 it was estimated that sixty percent of Televisa's *telenovela* productions were remakes.[88] Thus, whereas Cavell sees in soap operas an argument between transient daily episodes and the recurrences offered by long durations, in *telenovelas* we can often see an argument between transient daily episodes and recurrent, 'immortal' stories.

The late Spanish-Colombian communications theorist Jesús Martín-Barbero is especially known for linking some of these features of *telenovelas* to oral storytelling traditions.[89] For him, the *telenovela* preserved from those traditions the predominance of a 'telling to' relation between program and spectator.[90] I have already presented the differences between Cavell and Ruiz on film spectatorship as differences between a perspective in which it is natural to talk about a spectator's being *outside* a film and one in which it is natural to talk about their being *inside* a film. For all Cavell's willingness in 'The Fact of Television' to note differences between film and television, including the differences in perception that he calls 'viewing' a film versus 'monitoring' TV, he does not explicitly consider the possible inapplicability in television of his earlier picture of our *absence* from a world screened.[91] Nevertheless, in closing this part of the chapter, I want to note two features of *telenovelas* and soap operas that raise the question of this earlier picture's inapplicability.

Telenovelas, *Soap Operas, and the Limits of 'Absence'*

The first of these features could be understood as alluded to by Martín-Barbero's treatment of the 'telling to' relation in *telenovelas*. When a transtemporal and trans-geographic story is understood as rendered for one's particular historical moment, one's particular demographic,[92] or one's nation or community, that concrete particularization will not seem like an autonomous work available to just any audience, but specifically as *told to* 'us'. These formats can thus stand in for a wider phenomenon of targeted audiovisual material that, when we are made conscious of this relation, can be unsettling in the frank presentation of what is specifically designed to speak to our desires, needs, and fantasies (or authors' interpretations of those fantasies). At the extreme, once we have uncovered something of the recurrent desires that Cavell suggested these serial formats can open up to us, we can find ourselves presented with fictionalized reflections of those aspects of ourselves (our naked fantasies and desires) that, if we were to encounter them in reality—as Freud proposed—might lead us to flee the scene.[93] (As consummate corporate products, both *telenovelas* and soap operas were early adopters of focus-group strategies and of viewer feedback in determining story arcs.[94] Data-collection by digital streaming platforms can now pursue these strategies with alarming precision.)

The second respect in which *telenovelas* and soap operas can be understood as putting pressure on the idea of a spectator's *absence* also connects with Martín-Barbero's 'telling to' relation, but more specifically with the spectator's role in filling in gaps between the series' discrete episodic parts. Discussing Proust's idea that an author ideally gives a reader an optical instrument with which to understand themselves, Gérard Genette says that 'the real author of the narrative is not only he who tells it, but also, and at times even more, he who hears it'.[95] In a similar vein, and drawing on ideas from reader-response theory, the soap opera scholar Robert C. Allen discusses the 'structuring gaps of the text', which 'mark the point of intersection between the horizon represented within the text and the horizon brought to the text by the reader'.[96] For Allen, the soap opera (and here we can include the *telenovela* as well) is a format much of whose interest rests with its extreme dependence on regular structuring gaps—daily gaps between weekday screenings, followed by a weekend gap—within which 'the viewpoint of the reader is free to wander'.[97] Noël Carroll also discusses the special way in which soap operas allow for viewers to take over the storytelling function, facilitating 'gossip' between broadcasts.[98] (These practices continue with broadcasts of *telenovelas* and soap operas to this day, thanks to which they can constitute an interesting contrast to gapless 'binge'-watching on streaming platforms.)

Thus, even though we had earlier understood Ruiz's talk of delinquent spectatorship and the viewer's presence in films as coming from his perspective as a filmmaker looking to make new films out of audiovisual fragments, we also have reason to think that something in those ideas (which contrast with Cavell's treatment of the film spectator's *absence*) characterizes the typical condition of the spectator of certain gap-based serial formats. Having brought together these elements of serial television (Cavell's 'argument' between repetition and dramatic transience, the spectator's self-recognition via both the presentation of their fantasies and their creative involvement in continuing a story with gaps), we are now prepared to examine the reflections on storytelling presented in Ruiz's late series *Litoral*.

Litoral, Storytelling, and Spectatorship

Introducing Ruiz's Litoral

In 2006 Ruiz signed a contract to write and direct three series with TVN that would mark the beginning of the channel's celebrations of Chile's bicentennial.[99] Ultimately Ruiz only produced two of these series, both concerned with folkloric and storytelling traditions in Chile: *La recta provincia* (2007), which focused on rural storytelling traditions, and *Litoral* (2008), which focused on, as its subtitle put it, 'tales of the sea', as well as some urban folklore, set in and around the port city of Valparaíso.[100] (Both are period series with fantastic contemporary interventions; *Litoral* appears to be set in the 1930s to 1940s but also allows for modern cars, cell phones, and email.) The four episodes of *Litoral*, which will be my concern for the rest of this chapter, aired on Saturdays at 10pm in September 2008, garnering, as Alejandra Rodríguez-Remedi tells us, 'higher-than-feared (though admittedly unexceptional) ratings'.[101] The two series for TVN not only reflected Ruiz's lifelong attachment to fantasy and folklore but also, it seems, formed his response to what he saw as that era's interest in 'folkloric films', among which he mentioned the film versions of *The Lord of the Rings* (Peter Jackson, 2001–03) and *The Golden Compass* (Chris Weitz, 2007).[102] It also seems that in this period Ruiz was continuing to think about *telenovelas* and their connections to older narrative formats.[103]

According to Ruiz, the stories composing *Litoral* were inspired by those he would hear from his father, a merchant marine captain.[104] Also, for him what set *Litoral* apart from *La recta provincia* was its introduction of a 'formal experiment', in that the later series did not just present stories or their narration by characters but also the process of their 'production':[105] the process of inventing or retelling stories *to others*, thus incorporating the possibilities of others' interruption, collaboration, and revision. Despite these interesting ambitions, *Litoral* has not received as much attention as other late work for TV by Ruiz (like *Cofralandes* and *Mysteries of Lisbon*), and even somewhat less attention than *La recta provincia*. A major reason for this, I believe, is that it is easy to treat *Litoral* as simply a late rehashing of the elements of one of Ruiz's earlier international successes, his 1983 French film *Les trois couronnes du matelot* (*Three Crowns of the Sailor*). Both the series and the film concentrate on ghost ships—the *Lucerna* in *Litoral*, the *Funchalense* in *Three Crowns*—based on the legend from Chiloé (the region of Ruiz's birthplace in southern Chile) of the *Caleuche*, a wandering ship occupied by the souls of disappeared sailors.[106] Also, both works employ metanarratives involving storytelling sailors, just as they both develop the notion of the maritime 'immortal story', with allusions to the short story of that name by Karen Blixen (Isak Dinesen) and its 1968 film adaptation by Orson Welles.[107]

Nevertheless, according to Michael Goddard, Ruiz was unsatisfied with *Three Crowns of the Sailor*, particularly its overly rigid script, and in a 2004 interview Ruiz said that he found that film's success 'grating'.[108] Thus, the question of *Litoral*'s narrative innovations partly turns on Ruiz's reasons for returning decades later to a work he had somewhat disavowed. My contention is that Ruiz found in episodic, televisual formats possibilities for exploring the narrative open-endedness and repetition that he thought was natural for *Litoral*'s themes (and that, presumably, he regretted not being able to explore fully in *Three Crowns of the Sailor*). From what we know of Ruiz's ambitions for the series—of showing the 'production' of stories—and what we have seen of Cavell's views on the philosophical possibilities of repetition on serial TV, this would indeed seem like a natural fit: a series that could link different stories to our recurrent needs and desires might also capture our recurrent motivations in telling, receiving, and revising stories. Ruiz was of course limited in a four-episode miniseries as far as the kinds of repetition and openness he could explore. But therein also lies *Litoral*'s inventiveness. The series is one of Ruiz's most radical experiments in ouroboros- or Möbius-strip-like narratives, so that while the *storytelling* ends after four episodes the *story* itself is revealed never to end, or even to have a determinate beginning. (The series also has a way of suggesting that storytelling can partake in its own atemporality, which I will address further below.) It does this through a proliferation of forms of temporal loops, *mise en abyme* (narratives containing themselves), metalepsis (interactions between characters across narrative levels), and the undoing of any supposedly privileged metanarrative level, so that each storytelling level contains all the others.[109]

Litoral is clearly not a *telenovela*, though one of its component stories is a kind of *radionovela*, and its DigiBeta shooting format gives it the distinctive look of inexpensive TV productions of the era, including many *telenovelas* and soap operas.[110] It must be admitted that Ruiz employed variations on the just-mentioned narrative devices throughout his filmic work, and he was obviously inspired by similar devices in films he admired, like the stories-within-stories and *mise en abyme* structure of the Polish director Wojciech Has's *Rękopis znaleziony w Saragossie* (*The Saragossa Manuscript*, 1965).[111] My claim, though, is that *Litoral* represents a special convergence of those narrative devices and episodic televisual formats. This convergence allows, in a Cavellian vein, for the series' 'argument' between transient narratives and the recurrent needs lying behind those narratives. It also allows, as we will see, for a poignant representation of a spectator as 'inside' a story of their own making.

Litoral *and Fantasy*

I am developing the idea that *Litoral* explores the role of fantasy in the construction of stories, and specifically how fantasy mediates a relation between transient, 'classical' narratives and recurrent, 'undialectical' needs. Therefore, before discussing some of the individual stories composing *Litoral*, I want to mention the prominence the series gives to homosocial, heterosexual male fantasy, and specifically its display of how stories about women are constructed by men and for men. On the one hand, the women in *Litoral*'s stories are very frequently represented as supplicating to heterosexual male fantasies in their roles as sex workers, wives, and lovers, and these stories frequently turn on questions of their 'faithfulness' to certain men. On the other hand, we know from the beginning that these stories ultimately originate among the male storytelling sailors aboard the *Lucerna* (even if the series also complicates the notion of a privileged metanarrative level).

A reading of *Litoral* as implicitly feminist would rightly strain credibility: the series shares its world and sensibility with the male world of the *Lucerna*.[112] Still, we know that *Litoral* is in constant conversation not only with *Three Crowns of the Sailor* (for which similar worries arise), but also with a film that gives prominent place to issues of women's subordination, 'unknownness', and unrecognition: the 1990 film *Amelia Lopes O'Neill* by Valeria Sarmiento, Ruiz's wife and editor of *Litoral*, with a screenplay by Sarmiento and Ruiz. Sarmiento's film is consciously a melodrama of a woman's unknownness and unrecognition leading to her death: according to the feminist film critic Françoise Aude, the film 'spells out the consequences of machismo'.[113] (Much more needs to be said about *Amelia Lopes O'Neill*'s connection to Cavell's concept of the 'melodrama of the unknown woman' and its feminist critics.[114]) The film shares *Litoral*'s setting of 1930s–1940s Valparaíso, the same recurring bolero by Sarmiento and Ruiz's frequent collaborator Jorge Arriagada, and a male storyteller–male audience framing device. Most importantly, it shares a protagonist ('Amelia López' in *Litoral*) with several of *Litoral*'s stories, one of which (to be discussed below) is a clear remixing of elements from *Amelia Lopes O'Neill*.[115] Obviously, Ruiz's remixing of elements from his wife's film will raise for many its own questions of unrecognition. My present claim is that *Litoral*'s deliberate remixing of elements of a melodrama of unknownness like *Amelia Lopes O'Neill* makes these questions inescapable for the series' conception of itself: a conception that was itself the product of a remarkable decades-long collaboration between Sarmiento and Ruiz. This claim will be in the background of my discussion of the series' exploration of the role of fantasy in story construction.

Recounting Litoral

I will now present the major events of *Litoral*'s four 45-minute episodes. 'Episode I' opens with words superimposed over a seascape: supposedly found on a hanged sailor who sailed on the *Lucerna*, they describe the ship as occupied by crew members who were neither living nor dead. We then hear the voice-over narration of Ariel Cortínez (Santiago Meneguello), a new crew member on the *Lucerna* who has passed a week on the ship without seeing anyone; he spends his time reading comics that appear to show him passing time on that same ship, reading those same comics. (*Mise en abyme* self-looping characterizes the series' very first moments.) Finally Ariel is called to a ship's assembly where he meets the other crew members and learns that they spend their time telling stories. Lots are drawn: some members must jump the ship, while another who could very well be Ariel's physical double, Segundo Arrávida (Daniel Kiblisky), finds himself the night's appointed storyteller.

Segundo proceeds to tell the story, which we see played out, of his romance in San Felipe, near Valparaíso, with a woman called Amanda la Triste ('Amanda the Sad', Francisca Walker), three of whose boyfriends have died in accidents. As the story proceeds Segundo learns that Amanda has a 'brother', Ruperto (Juan Pablo Miranda), whose spirit and voice sometimes take over Amanda's body. Outside his wedding with Amanda, Segundo is warned against marrying her by a man (Hugo Medina) who says he is Amanda's father and a former crew member of the *Lucerna*. We see that at night the voices of Amanda and Ruperto have switched bodies, until Amanda's father arrives, shooting the body of Ruperto and causing both to collapse. As we return to the metanarrative on the *Lucerna*, Cabizbajo ('Crestfallen', Julio Silva Montes) expresses his disappointment with Segundo's story since it is no different from the Jewish tale of a *dybbuk* that he used to hear from his grandmother. After Segundo concedes that the story never happened to him, Ariel says that he is ready to continue the tale, and we now see the story of Ariel's romance with Amanda: including some of the same scenes as before, with Ariel in place of Segundo, though with Segundo still present, looking on as jealous witness. Newly married to Amanda in the story, Ariel goes to work with the arrogant Policarpo Parada (Pedro Vicuña), whom we have already seen as a crew member on the *Lucerna*. As Segundo yet again takes over as narrator, closing out the episode, we witness his bonding with Policarpo over the latter's stories, told in a bar for retired sailors.

'Episode II' opens with one of Policarpo's stories, beginning with his arrival on the *Lucerna*. (Though Cabizbajo says this was a different *Lucerna*, it is indistinguishable from the one in the metanarrative.) This story centers on a series of mysterious blank letters that arrived on the ship. Once it is deciphered that they in fact describe the captain's wife's affairs with the entire crew, it is decided to keep their contents a secret from the captain (Marcial Edwards), who nevertheless locks himself in his quarters, reciting poetry and growing literal horns. Though these are Policarpo's stories as told to Segundo, the latter is interrogated about them in the metanarrative on the *Lucerna*, even with Policarpo present. (That metanarrative was itself—we must remember—originally introduced by Ariel's voice-over narration.)

The narrative levels then become even more complicated. As Policarpo describes to Segundo his practice of illicitly reading the ship's mail, the narration is taken over by the sailor Esparta (Roberto Cobían) in a letter describing his mysterious encounter in the port of Caldera with the ghost Amelia López (Chamila Rodríguez), who took him back to 1934 to ask him to father her child. In this first story of Amelia López, Esparta refuses the offer because there would be no novelty in the story he could tell about it afterward. (It is indeed a version of the maritime 'immortal story' that appears in Karen Blixen's short story and Orson Welles' film.) On finishing the letter and disembarking in Valparaíso, Policarpo decides to follow the address marked in the several photos of Amelia López that he has found in the ship's mail, though what he in fact finds is a different haunted house occupied by triplets (Ana Laura Racz). When afterward a retired thief (Dióscoro Rojas) tells Policarpo that this house has been uninhabited for some time, he returns there, only this time to find Esparta and several other sailors gathering around Amelia López. Esparta answers equivocally to Policarpo's question about whether they are living or dead.

'Episode III' opens by reminding us that the previous stories have been relayed by Policarpo to Segundo, who has been relaying them to the 'contemporary' *Lucerna*. Policarpo and Segundo together walk to a teahouse/brothel, where Segundo interrogates Policarpo about the plausibility of his stories. (Ariel is shown following them, now playing the role of outside witness.) Policarpo then tells another story involving Amelia López, this time supposedly dictated by her in a letter to her husband, the ship's Third Officer (Nicolás Poblete)—which Policarpo had again illicitly read—describing her affair in Valparaíso with a man in a blue suit (Nicolás Eyzaguirre). Once word gets out on the ship about this, the Third Officer commits suicide. Again shown disembarking in Valparaíso, Policarpo is hailed from a slow-moving train by Amelia, who confesses that she had invented the story in the letter to make her husband jealous, and as a result of his suicide is now 'selling' her body. After they pass a 'night of love' together, Policarpo goes searching for Amelia, only to be told by a man on the train (Ignacio Agüero) that he had in fact been alone there the day of his supposed encounter with Amelia, and to be shown a newspaper headline of her murder several days earlier. Ultimately Policarpo encounters the ghosts of the Third Officer and Amelia, the latter dressed in a bridal gown, both waving to him from the slow-moving train, reconciled after death: their remarriage accompanied by Jorge Arriagada's bolero.

Policarpo finally parts from Segundo, saying that despite his story Amelia is still alive, and indeed right away Segundo finds her in the teahouse/brothel, with Amelia remarking on Policarpo's practice of incorporating those in his surroundings into his stories. Suddenly Segundo hears a radio program called *The Voice of Chile*, which turns out to be emanating from a real man squeezed inside the teahouse/brothel's radio, Antuco (Arturo Rossel), who also claims that Amanda la Triste works there and that he inherited the blue suit of one of her dead boyfriends. Antuco then launches into the story of how he, like many others, had received the gift of a perfectly fitting blue suit from Inquilino ('Tenant', Francisco Medina), and after asking about the origins of these suits had found that they were delivered to Inquilino in a cemetery by a dead man, Finado ('Deceased', Eugenio Morales), in exchange for hot dogs. We then hear Finado's own account to Antuco of how this bizarre situation came about, beginning with his having worked with Inquilino as grave robbers when they were offered a large sum of money by Don Nadie ('Nobody', Hernán Vallejos) for the clothes they stole from the dead. But when Inquilino used this money to buy a produce shop, he found that his customers' purchases would spoil before they returned home.

'Episode IV' opens by repeating the scene of Inquilino's interactions with his customers and Don Nadie's explanation that his money is for squandering, not investing—hence cursed. Inquilino decides to accompany his customers to their homes, all while telling jokes (accompanied by laugh tracks). This moment leads to a remarkable exchange among narrative levels, as following his joke to a woman (Valentina Muhr), they both register their extradiegetic interruption by the voice of a customer in the teahouse/brothel (Daniel Isler), who insists that he knows the rest of their story, and whose story is in turn interrupted by Antuco's voice in the radio, and again by the extradiegetic voice of Cabizbajo on the *Lucerna*, who objects to the bewildered customer that they are telling stories, not giving classes on telling stories. As we return to Finado's story as told to Antuco, we learn that Finado's new taxi business had no more luck than Inquilino's produce business, again because the money from Don Nadie was cursed. Don Nadie then explains to Finado and Inquilino how he started buying up the clothes of the dead: it was work offered him by the demonic 'angel of tailors' Otto Carisma (Héctor Aguilar), whom he met at a magic show when he was financially ruined and near suicide, and who hinted to him that suits can contain souls. Following Finado's account of his own random murder, we now have the full story of how he began magically yielding blue suits from his grave. And with the story of his blue suit finally complete, Antuco leaves the radio, 'cramped' from his time inside there.

As we finally return to the metanarrative on the *Lucerna*, Segundo and Ariel are uncertain about which of them should continue the 'story'—we soon understand that they are referring to the story of Amanda la Triste that began in the first episode—and so it is suggested that they continue it together. We then see both Segundo and Ariel in the teahouse/brothel, witnesses to an exchange between Amanda and Amelia, uncertain whether this 'theatre scene' is meant 'for you or for me'. Ariel's voice-over narration gives way to Segundo's, describing his following Amanda and Amelia outside only to be hailed from a house by a man (Álvaro Rojas) who introduces himself as Ortega Calera, Amanda's dead first boyfriend. As Amanda's two other dead boyfriends enter the room (Maximiliano Golberg and an uncredited actor), they are introduced to a very perturbed Segundo ('Amanda's current boyfriend') and examine petitions on the wall: this peculiar space includes not only photos of scenes from previous stories in the series, but also letters asking for miracles to be performed by the boyfriends, as if they were Catholic saints. Most importantly, the lights suddenly dim and behind a screen the boyfriends watch a scene acted out for them by Amanda and her father ('Father and daughter: the never-ending story', as Ortega puts it), set to sweeping dramatic music. As Amanda asks for her father's advice about a secret she is keeping from her husband, he pulls out a miniature model of the *Lucerna* that he bought from a supplier of items robbed from graves. This was, of course, Don Nadie, and in a scene of the sale we learn that it had belonged to a sailor of the shipwrecked *Lucerna* (on which Amanda's father had also sailed).

In a demonstration of the model's powers, Don Nadie blows on it, initiating a slow whispered version of the voice-over narration by Ariel with which the series began.[116] This model is the very same *Lucerna* as that in the metanarrative that has 'contained' the story of the model. Both living and dead, the crew members are also revealed to be both inside and outside this story, both miniature and large. Amanda's father has in fact been listening at night to the stories emitting from the model, and he now uses a magnifying glass to show Amanda the ship's crew members gathering to take a group photo (from which Segundo is strikingly excluded). Over close-ups of Segundo and Ariel, her father mysteriously says, 'There I am, and there is your current husband.' Following a deceptive 'The End' title (in English, hence Ruiz's mischievous nod to a Hollywood ending) and the music's swelling, the scene ends to the applause of the boyfriends, who talk about seeing other plays together ('a romance, a swashbuckler'), but also to Segundo's continued confusion and disturbance: he is now faced with being at once the spectator of a scene and stranded in a story of his own telling. Finally, over close-ups of the wall's photos and letters, we hear the voice of Policarpo reading a poem about the life and death of yet another sailor on the *Lucerna*, with Arriagada's bolero taking us out of the series one last time.

Litoral *as an Argument between Different Temporalities*

This synopsis should make clear that *Litoral* is no ordinary series, though I am also arguing that its extraordinariness lies in its attention to the wider contexts for the telling of individual stories ('the repetitive needs of the body and the soul') that commonly arise for serial televisual formats. I am again referring to the way that soap operas can move beyond dramatic history towards undialectical 'permanencies', as Cavell suggests, as well as how *telenovelas* can constitute their own 'argument' between transtemporal, trans-geographic 'immortal stories' and their concrete particularizations for specific audiences. *Litoral* achieves this effect not only through its forms of temporal looping and its attention to the construction and revision of stories, which I have already mentioned, but also through its presentation of storytelling as something that takes place in realms located outside of time.

Thus, the series begins and ends with stories told in atemporal spaces occupied by the living dead: the *Lucerna* and the room shared by Amanda's 'sainted' boyfriends. The suggestion that storytelling originates in such realms could mean several things. For example, the generation of these atemporal spaces, especially the *Lucerna*, could be Ruiz's attempt to create audiovisual equivalents to the paradox formulated by Gérard Genette that, while we know that telling takes time, fictional narrators typically occupy nothing but the 'atemporal space of the narrative as text': a 'miraculous syncope' freed from time.[117] While there is strong reason to take this proposal seriously as a reading of *Litoral*, it still does not make contact with the series' specific character as a televisual series. Thus, I think there is even more promise in emphasizing the series' atemporal spaces as ways of figuring the first half of the 'argument' between 'time as repetition' and 'time as transience' that Cavell thinks characterizes serial formats like soap operas.

The other half of that 'argument' would, of course, be captured in the series' individual stories, many of which constitute a contrast with the above-mentioned atemporal spaces in their allowing for classical narrative structures. Some of these even participate in the classical narrative structures important to Cavell, most obviously in the story of remarriage between Amelia López and the Third Officer (which also happens to be the story that draws most heavily on elements from the melodrama *Amelia Lopes O'Neill*). The latter story also shows that the effects of Ruiz putting a classical, transient narrative in a wider, 'atemporal' context need not be ironizing or dismissive. On the contrary, even within the context of Policarpo's inventions and revisions, I find that story's final image of Amelia and the Third Officer on the slow-moving train, newly remarried after their deaths, accompanied by Arriagada's bolero, to be one of the most genuinely poetic and haunting images of remarriage, and its own distinctive way of 'inhabiting time', in either film or television.[118]

As that last point brings out, Cavell also associated those classical genres with their own distinctive temporalities: 'the melodramas [sketch] a past frozen and compulsively active in the present, the comedies [propose] an openness to the future'.[119] For Cavell these genres even displayed their own distinctive forms of recurrence, like the compulsion to repeat supposedly characteristic of the melodramas (and here we might connect that feature to Esparta's refusal, in *Litoral*'s first Amelia López story, to be drawn into the compulsive repetitions of an 'immortal story'); or like the sense of 'diurnal repetitiveness' and 'festivity' characteristic of the remarriage comedies.[120] (The image that occasions Cavell connecting remarriage comedy to Nietzsche's eternal recurrence, the human figurines skipping into the clock at the end of *The Awful Truth* [Leo McCarey, 1937], is a natural companion to the image of Amelia López's posthumous remarriage.[121]) This observation fits well with the earlier proposal that Cavell locates moments of Ruizian poetry inside classical narratives: Ruiz was clear in his expectation that filmic poetry communicate temporal recurrences. Nevertheless, in 'The Fact of Television'

Cavell himself had to make the distinction between dramatic transiences and the more radical, 'undialectical' permanencies communicated by long-running serial formats. These are the recurrences that are more difficult to grasp without moving outside classical notions of dramatic progression, including those structuring Hollywood genre films.[122] *Litoral* is remarkable in how it puts certain classical structures (including their respective notions of recurrence) in explicit conversation with the more radical permanencies underlying the impulse to tell stories, which the series communicates via its forms of temporal looping and its generation of atemporal spaces.

A Sideways-on View of Fantasy

It is important to clarify the role of fantasy in the notion of an 'argument' between 'time as repetition' (or even atemporality) and 'time as transience' that I am claiming *Litoral* makes explicit. An interesting formulation of this role is provided by Slavoj Žižek when he says, 'Fantasy is the primordial form of narrative ... [and] narrative as such emerges in order to resolve some fundamental antagonism by rearranging its terms into a temporal succession.'[123] In a commentary on this passage given in the course of a compelling Lacanian reading of the work of David Lynch (whose temporal loops have sometimes been compared with Ruiz's), Todd McGowan says, 'we do not employ fantasy to escape from the horrors of time, [but rather] we employ fantasy to construct time as a respite from the horrors of repetition ... By providing a narrative and temporal structure through which we can have experiences, fantasy delivers us from the timeless repetition of the drive.'[124] In other words, it would be too horrible for us to face what Cavell calls 'the repetitive needs of the body and the soul' without some mediation by fantasy and the temporal, narrative categories that fantasy makes out of those needs.

The previous considerations are friendlier to Cavell's style of thinking (the existential seriousness he assigned to psychoanalysis, his own writing on fantasy in film) than they are to what was apparently Ruiz's habit of wanting to puncture certain psychoanalytic pretensions.[125] Nevertheless, in closing, I want to suggest how naturally these considerations fit with the very Ruizian idea of a spectator being *inside* an audiovisual story—or at least fit with how Ruiz expressed that idea at the end of *Litoral*. I should note that ideas of mediation can also seem to inform Ruiz's visual style, such as in his conspicuous uses of distorting, stretching anamorphic lenses, which in *Litoral* happen to be combined with shots mediated by liquids like water and even (at the beginning of the Amanda la Triste story) the traditional Chilean summer drink of wine with peaches.[126] These effects typically raise the question of from which fantasy-mediated perspective a given moment is being seen. Likewise, the notion of the spectator, thus drawing the viewer's attention to their own condition as such, is raised not only by the various recipients of the stories in *Litoral*, but also by the series' representations of Segundo and Ariel as witnesses *within* each other's stories.[127]

As I have repeatedly mentioned, the series ends with the poignant image of Segundo stuck within a story of his own creation (or a story somehow created between himself and Ariel). His perturbation throughout this moment only partially has to do with his realization that he has entered the ranks of Amanda's dead boyfriends and is now stuck within their shared atemporal space. Even more important is that, having passed through the various forms of story construction and atemporal spaces composing *Litoral*, he is now prepared to look sideways-on at the role of his own fantasies in his relation to the scene (again, presented behind a screen) between Amanda and her father. Segundo recognizes that the only thing standing between this 'transient' story and the more difficult questions about our permanent, 'undialectical' needs (represented by the *Lucerna*) is the rather frail—because revealed to be created by him—impositions of his own fantasies.

This is why Segundo is visibly troubled by the other boyfriends' easy acceptance of this scene, their treating it as no different from any of the other entertainments that, it is suggested, they regularly enjoy together. Knowing his role in the construction of the surrounding story, Segundo recognizes that the present entertainment could not exist without him: it is *for* him. Furthermore, if we are to understand the other boyfriends to have arrived at that same space via a learning process similar to Segundo's, then what is disturbing for him is not just their easy acceptance of the scene as entertainment, but their doing so knowing full well the role of their own fantasies in its making. Likened to saints, the boyfriends' cool acceptance of these clashing perspectives might be exactly what takes them outside of ordinary troubles and sensibilities. And then, the ordinary troubles and sensibilities represented by Segundo would be those that can lead to philosophical questioning.

For Ruiz, a philosophical-filmmaker, there was always a special impetus to give us an *image* of what it meant for a spectator to dream themselves inside a story. Cavell's own writing on film and television gives us a further sense of what that could mean, and what it could contrast with. The fact that *Litoral* relies steadily but idiosyncratically on recognizable televisual formats is a large part of why we can open ourselves up to its concluding image of Segundo placed permanently as a spectator within a narrative of his own creation, just as those same formats allow us to see ourselves in his situation, leaving us as haunted in this recognition as he is.[128]

Notes

1   Stanley Cavell, *The World Viewed: Reflections on the Ontology of Film, Enlarged Edition* (Cambridge, MA: Harvard University Press, 1979), xiv, 7, 9, 108, 231n2.
2   Cavell, *The World Viewed*, 118, 160, 229.
3   Stanley Cavell, *Pursuits of Happiness: The Hollywood Comedy of Remarriage* (Cambridge, MA: Harvard University Press, 1981), 34–38.
4   Raúl Ruiz, *Poetics of Cinema*, vol. 1, trans. Brian Holmes (Paris: Éditions Dis Voir, 1995), 9–23.

5   Ibid., 9–10, 60, 84–86. See also Michael Goddard, *The Cinema of Raúl Ruiz: Impossible Cartographies* (New York: Wallflower Press), 17, 90, 109, 119. Also Raúl Ruiz, *Entrevistas escogidas—filmografía comentada*, ed. Bruno Cuneo (Santiago: Diego Portales, 2013), 123–25, 140.
6   Raúl Ruiz, *Poetics of Cinema*, vol. 2, trans. Carlos Morreo (Paris: Éditions Dis Voir, 2007), 61.
7   Stanley Cavell, 'The Fact of Television', in *Themes Out of School: Effects and Causes* (San Francisco: North Point Press, 1984).
8   Cavell, 'The Fact of Television, 265.
9   Personal correspondence on this question with Alfred Guzzetti, Robb Moss, Richard Peña, and William Rothman.
10 The two volumes and the material for the third volume are collected in Raúl Ruiz, *Poéticas del cine* (Santiago: Ediciones Diego Portales: 2013).
11 See Ruiz's applications of Donald Davidson's and Judith Jarvis Thomson's theories of action in elaborating his opposition to 'central conflict theory': *Poetics of Cinema*, vol. 1, 13, 15, 18. See also Ruiz's application of Jaakko Hintikka's distinction between 'recursive' and 'strategic' linguistic paradigms to filmic narratives: ibid., 85. We also know that Ruiz read a variety of contemporary Anglophone philosophers that included David Lewis (*Poéticas del Cine*, 367), Joshua Knobe (ibid.), Michael Dummett, Richard Rorty, and Alva Noë, among others: Ruiz, *Diario*, ed. Bruno Cuneo (Santiago: Ediciones Diego Portales, 2017), vol. 1, 127, 183; vol. 2, 569, 586. On Cavell and 'conflict', see Toril Moi, *Revolution of the Ordinary: Literary Studies after Wittgenstein, Austin, and Cavell* (Chicago: University of Chicago Press, 2017), 9–12.
12 Ruiz, *Poetics of Cinema*, vol. 1, 7, 21, 22, 27, 70, 90, 114; vol. 2, 49, 58; *Poéticas del cine*, 408.
13 Ruiz, *Poetics of Cinema*, vol. 1, 32, 48, 50, 51, 57–71; vol. 2, 77, 39, 87.
14 For Cavell on indiscriminateness, see *The World Viewed*, 3–15.
15 Walter Benjamin, *The Work of Art in the Age of Its Technological Reproducibility and Other Writings on Media*, ed. Michael W. Jennings, Brigid Doherty, and Thomas Y. Levin (Cambridge, MA: Harvard University Press, 2008), 37, 278.
16 Stanley Cavell, 'What Photography Calls Thinking', in *Cavell on Film*, ed. William Rothman (Albany: State University of New York Press, 2005), 126.
17 Cavell, *The World Viewed*, 104, cf. 7.
18 Stanley Cavell, 'The Thought of Movies', in *Themes Out of School*, 14.
19 P. Adams Sitney, *Visionary Film: The American Avant-Garde 1943–2000* (Oxford: Oxford University Press, 2002). See also Rebecca Sheehan's use of Cavell in approaching Stan Brakhage's lyrical films: *American Avant-Garde Cinema's Philosophy of the In-Between* (Oxford: Oxford University Press, 2020), 112–67.
20 Cavell, *The World Viewed*, 148.
21 Cavell, *Pursuits of Happiness*, 52.
22 Ruiz, *Poetics of Cinema*, vol. 2, 22.
23 Ibid., 11.
24 Ruiz, *Poetics of Cinema*, vol. 1, 32.
25 Pierre Klossowski, *Nietzsche and the Vicious Circle*, trans. Daniel W. Smith (Chicago: University of Chicago Press, 1997).

26   Cavell, *Pursuits of Happiness*, 263. The eternal recurrence is also a point of connection between Cavell and Deleuze that D.N. Rodowick emphasizes throughout *Philosophy's Artful Conversation* (Cambridge, MA: Harvard University Press, 2015).
27   For example, forms of temporal looping characterize all the episodes of *The Twilight Zone* that, according to Alejandra Rodríguez-Remedi, Ruiz would show in his classes at the University of Aberdeen (2007–08): 'Walking Distance' (Robert Stevens, 1959), 'Young Man's Fancy' (John Brahm, 1962), and notably two different versions of 'Shadow Play' (John Brahm, 1961; Paul Lynch, 1986). See Rodríguez-Remedi, 'Raúl Ruiz, Speculative Bricoleur: Pedagogical and Televisual Ruptures', in *Raúl Ruiz's Cinema of Inquiry*, ed. Ignacio López-Vicuña and Andreea Marinescu (Detroit: Wayne State University Press, 2017), 92. Another film that Ruiz would show, *Dead of Night* (Alberto Cavalcanti, Basil Dearden, Robert Hamer, Charles Crichton, 1945), in part fascinated him for having a looping structure that supposedly inspired Bondi, Gold, and Hoyle's cosmological hypothesis of a universe without beginning or end: *Poetics of Cinema*, vol. 2, 108.
28   Ruiz, *Poetics of Cinema*, vol. 1, 82, 120; *Poéticas del cine*, 417–35.
29   Ruiz, *Poetics of Cinema*, vol. 1, 50–51. A Warburg-inspired Mnemosyne also makes an appearance in Ruiz's film *Généalogies d'un crime* (*Genealogies of a Crime*, 1997).
30   Ruiz, *Poetics of Cinema*, vol. 1, 50–51.
31   Cavell, *Pursuits of Happiness*, 262.
32   Ruiz, *Poetics of Cinema*, vol. 1, 14; *Entrevistas escogidas*, 144. For Bordwell's response to one of Ruiz's characterizations of his work, see 'Ruiz, Realism, and … Me?', *Observations on Film Art*, August 7, 2011, www.davidbordwell.net/blog/2011/08/07/ruiz-realism-and-me/ (accessed August 27, 2022).
33   Ruiz, *Poetics of Cinema*, vol. 1, 21.
34   Ibid., 84–86. See also Goddard, *The Cinema of Raúl Ruiz*, 109. For Ruiz on continuity errors, see also *Poetics of Cinema*, vol. 1, 23, 60, 109.
35   See Fernando Solanas and Octavio Getino, 'Towards a Third Cinema', in *Film Manifestos and Global Cinema Cultures*, ed. Scott MacKenzie (Berkeley: University of California Press); Jorge Sanjinés, 'Problems of Form and Content in Revolutionary Cinema', in ibid. Ruiz's own relation to Third Cinema was extremely complicated: see Goddard, *The Cinema of Raúl Ruiz*, 13, 23, 25, 106–07. For Ruiz's descriptions of his relation to Third Cinema, see *Entrevistas escogidas*, 29–35, 146–47, 184–85, 248, 301.
36   Cavell, *The World Viewed*, 76, 82.
37   See Cavell on shifts in continuity across reverse shots, and his question about whether anything could be meant by them: *The World Viewed*, 143.
38   See for example Stanley Cavell, 'On Makavejev on Bergman', in *Themes Out of School*. On this aspect of Cavell in relation to filmic fragments, see my 'Found Footage at the Receding of the World', *Screen*, vol. 63, no. 1 (Spring 2022), 123–29.
39   Ruiz, *Poetics of Cinema*, vol. 1, 116–18; vol. 2, 72. One widely cited essay on Ruiz and the baroque is Christine Buci-Glucksmann, 'The Baroque Eye of the Camera (Part 1)', in *Raúl Ruiz: Images of Passage*, ed. Helen Bandis, Adrian Martin, and Grant McDonald (Melbourne: Rouge Press, 2004). See also Valeria de los Ríos, *Metamorfosis: Aproximaciones al cine y la poética de Raúl Ruiz* (Santiago: Ediciones Metales Pesados, 2019), 44–58.

40. Ruiz, *Poetics of Cinema*, vol. 2, 10.
41. Cavell, *The World Viewed*, 23, 26, 102.
42. Ibid., 228–30. On this theme in Cavell, see my 'Accidents Made Permanent: Theater and Automatism in Stanley Cavell, Michael Fried, and Matías Piñeiro', *MLN*, vol. 135, no. 5 (2020), 1283–314.
43. Ruiz, *Poetics of Cinema*, vol. 1, 60. See also Goddard, *The Cinema of Raúl Ruiz*, 91, 109.
44. Cavell, *The World Viewed*, 188.
45. Ruiz, *Poetics of Cinema*, vol. 2, 10. A similar idea of a co-emergent and bilateral seer–seen relation between viewer and film is also central to Vivian Sobchack, *The Address of the Eye* (Princeton: Princeton University Press, 1992).
46. Ruiz, *Poetics of Cinema*, vol. 2, 110.
47. Ruiz, *Poéticas del cine*, 322–23. Ruiz's *Suicide Club* CD-ROM was a collaboration with students from Duke University, Piedmont Community College, and the North Carolina School of the Arts. Patricia Yeh, 'Epworth Becomes Stage for New Video Disk', *Duke Chronicle*, November 25, 1996, https://dukelibraries.contentdm.oclc.org/digital/collection/p15957coll13/id/107701/rec/13 (accessed August 27, 2022).
48. Ruiz, *Poetics of Cinema*, vol. 1, 119, my emphasis. This is also one of the major structuring ideas of Ruiz's film *Mémoire des apparences* (*Life Is a Dream*, 1986).
49. Cavell, *The World Viewed*, 150. Here Cavell appears to be speaking from views on the imagination represented by Pascal: *Pensées and Other Writings*, trans. Honor Levi (Oxford: Oxford University Press, 1995), 16–20.
50. Cavell, *The World Viewed*, 150. For discussion of these passages in connection with Cavell's views on sound in film, see Kyle Stevens, 'The World Heard', *Discourse*, vol. 42, nos. 1–2 (2020), 32–33.
51. Cavell, *The World Viewed*, 158.
52. Ibid.
53. Ibid., 156.
54. Ibid., 157.
55. See Cavell, 'A Matter of Meaning It', in *Must We Mean What We Say?: A Book of Essays* (Cambridge: Cambridge University Press, 2002), 225–37.
56. This idea is related to Cavell's concerns with the grounds for pointing out what a divergent reading may be missing. See Cavell, 'The Avoidance of Love', in ibid.. Thanks to Joshua Kortbein for his suggestions on this question.
57. Cavell is often interested in characters serving as surrogates for the film director, though he usually emphasizes the director's ability to stand back from a finished work. See *Pursuits of Happiness*, 66, 107–08, 218, 221.
58. Personal correspondence with Bruno Cuneo. Ruiz's accounts of this period's timeline would sometimes differ: see *Entrevistas escogidas*, 68–69, 125–26.
59. Ibid., 126.
60. On *María Isabel*, see Luis Reyes de la Maza, *Crónica de la telenovela: México sentimental* (Mexico City: Clío, 1999), 54–58.
61. According to Bruno Cuneo in personal correspondence, Ruiz worked for the program *Goles y marcas* (*Goals and Scores*), hosted by Sergio Brotfeld on the University of Chile's Channel 9. On Ruiz's other work for Chilean TV at this time, see *Entrevistas escogidas*, 125–26.

62 Goddard, *The Cinema of Raúl Ruiz*, 32.
63 Ibid., 37–58.
64 Ibid., 82.
65 Personal correspondence with Ruiz's former student, the filmmaker Laura Colella. The above quotations come from the official description of Ruiz's course: Harvard Faculty of Arts and Sciences, *Courses of Instruction 1989–1990*, vol. 11, no. 5, August 21, 1989, https://nrs.harvard.edu/URN-3:HUL.ARCH:100359777 (accessed August 27, 2022).
66 Goddard, *The Cinema of Raúl Ruiz*, 94. On a previous visit to Chile during Pinochet's dictatorship Ruiz did manage to make a short film for French television, *Lettre d'un cinéaste ou le retour d'un amateur de bibliothèques* (*Letter from a Filmmaker, or The Return of a Library Lover*, 1983).
67 Ruiz, *Entrevistas escogidas*, 250. Despite the reference to *telenovelas* in the film's title, here Ruiz uses the more typically Chilean term '*teleserie*'.
68 Rodríguez-Remedi, 'Raúl Ruiz, Speculative Bricoleur', 86.
69 Compare with Adrian Martin, 'Displacements', in *Raúl Ruiz: Images of Passage*, 48, 49.
70 Mike Budd, Steve Craig, and Clay Steinman, '"Fantasy Island": Marketplace of Desire', *Journal of Communication*, vol. 33, no. 1 (1983), 67–77. These scholars' analysis focused on the televisual unities that Raymond Williams called 'flow': ibid, 73. This article's approach has been criticized by one of the major defenders of the applicability of classical narrative models in television, Kristin Thompson. See her *Storytelling in Film and Television* (Cambridge, MA: Harvard University Press, 2003), 15–16, 147–48.
71 Ruiz, *Poetics of Cinema*, vol. 1, 70–71.
72 Ibid., 70.
73 Ruiz, *Poéticas del cine*, 417–18, 421.
74 Cavell, 'The Fact of Television', 265.
75 Ibid., 257–58.
76 Ibid., 258.
77 Ibid., 244–45.
78 Dennis Porter, 'Soap Time: Thoughts on a Commodity Art Form', *College English*, vol. 38, no. 8 (1977), 783.
79 Cavell, 'The Fact of Television', 263. The perspective offered here might be contrasted with Cavell's sketch in *The World Viewed* of how it became natural to think of history as dramatic: 90–94.
80 Cavell, 'The Fact of Television', 265.
81 Cavell, *Pursuits of Happiness*, 262.
82 Oscar Steimberg, 'Estilo contemporáneo y desarticulación narrativa. Nuevos presentes, nuevos pasados de la telenovela', in *Telenovela: Ficción Popular y Mutaciones Culturales* (Barcelona: Gedisa, 1997), 17–28, 22. Steimberg's model for the 'neo-baroque' *telenovela* is the Argentine series *Antonella* (1992). See also André Dorcé, 'Latin American Telenovelas: Affect, Citizenship and Interculturality', in *The SAGE Handbook of Television Studies*, ed. Manuel Alvarado, Milly Buonanno, Herman Gray, and Toby Miller (London: SAGE, 2014), 257, 264.
83 Ana M. López, 'Our Welcomed Guests: Telenovelas in Latin America', in *To Be Continued ...: Soap Operas Around the World*, ed. Robert C. Allen (London: Routledge,

1994), 258. Ruiz did remark on his fascination with long-running *telenovelas* like those of 300 or 600 episodes produced by Brazil's Rede Globo: *Entrevistas escogidas*, 125. But Cavell likely had in mind US soaps like *Guiding Light* (1952–2009) and *Days of Our Lives* (1965–present) that would go on to run for tens of thousands of episodes.

84 López, 'Our Welcomed Guests', 258.

85 Cavell, *The World Viewed*, 25–29. On Ruiz's childhood fascination with this kind of 'resurrection' on film, see *Entrevistas escogidas*, 140; Goddard, *The Cinema of Raúl Ruiz*, 17, 90.

86 The extremely popular 1969–71 Peruvian version of *Simplemente María* was in fact a remake of the much less popular 1967–68 Argentine version. See Arvind Singhal, Rafael Obregon, and Everett M. Rogers, 'Reconstructing the Story of *Simplemente María*, the Most Popular *Telenovela* in Latin America of All Time', *Gazette*, vol. 54 (1994), 1–15.

87 López, 'Our Welcomed Guests', 270–71. Jesús Martín-Barbero, 'Memory and Form in the Latin American Soap Opera', in *To Be Continued*, 277–78.

88 Mercedes Medina and Leticia Barrón, 'La telenovela en el mundo', *Palabra Clave*, vol. 13, no. 1 (2010), 86. See also Dorcé, 'Latin American Telenovelas', 255.

89 Jesús Martín-Barbero, 'Introducción', in *Televisión y melodrama: Géneros y lecturas de la televisión en Colombia*, ed. Jesús Martín-Barbero and Sonia Muñoz (Bogotá: Tercer Mundo, 1992).

90 Martín-Barbero, 'Introducción', 30.

91 Cavell does implicitly consider this possibility at the end of 'The Fact of Television', when he notes that 'the medium of television makes intuitive the failure of nature's survival of me', which is the opposite of the sense of the world's being 'complete without me' that, in *The World Viewed*, he had claimed that film communicates. 'Fact of Television', 267–68; *The World Viewed*, 160.

92 Dorcé, 'Latin American Telenovelas', 257–62. As López points out, *telenovelas* are explicitly class-based in a way that contrasts with the more typical gendering of US soaps: 'Our Welcomed Guests', 260.

93 Sigmund Freud, *Dora: An Analysis of a Case of Hysteria*, trans. James Strachey (New York: Macmillan, 1963), 101.

94 Dorcé, 'Latin American Telenovelas', 256. Robert C. Allen, *Speaking of Soap Operas* (Chapel Hill: University of North Carolina Press), 50–51.

95 Gérard Genette, *Narrative Discourse*, trans. Jane E. Lewin (Ithaca: Cornell University Press, 1980), 262.

96 Allen, *Speaking of Soap Operas*, 78.

97 Ibid., 80.

98 Noël Carroll, 'As the Dial Turns: Notes on Soap Operas', in *Theorizing the Moving Image* (Cambridge, MA: Cambridge University Press, 1996).

99 Rodríguez-Remedi, 'Raúl Ruiz, Speculative Bricoleur', 71, 86. Felipe Larrea Melgajero, 'El narrador Raúl Ruiz y la *invención* de Chile', *Hybris*, vol. 8, no. 2 (2017), 94.

100 According to Rodríguez-Remedi, the series was shot 'over two months in and around Santiago (Melipilla), Valparaíso (Quilpué), and Chiloé Island with the support of the Chilean Navy' ('Raúl Ruiz, Speculative Bricoleur', 88).

101 Ibid., 87. The entirety of the series is currently available on YouTube, though unfortunately without subtitles. Episode I: www.youtube.com/watch?v=XrXZDYEzmGw; Episode II: www.youtube.com/watch?v=2ck7oesY0xQ; Episode III: www.youtube.com/watch?v=pxjT41DlZ6k; Episode IV: www.youtube.com/watch?v=cmNWaNXrNZY (accessed August 27, 2022).
102 Ruiz, *Poéticas del cine*, 417. Larrea Melgajero, 'El narrador Raúl Ruiz', 93.
103 Goddard, *The Cinema of Raúl Ruiz*, 172.
104 Ibid.
105 Interview with Diego Brodersen, '¿Por qué no jugar con el cuento infantil?', *Página/12*, April 3, 2009, www.pagina12.com.ar/diario/suplementos/espectaculos/5-13403-2009-04-03.html (accessed August 27, 2022).
106 See Zuzana M. Pick, 'The Dialectical Wanderings of Exile', *Screen*, vol. 30, no. 4 (1989), 56. The *Caleuche* also plays a role in Ruiz's short film about Chile for the UK's Channel 4, *Las soledades* (1992).
107 For a comparison between *Three Crowns of the Sailor* and Welles' *Immortal Story*, see Catherine L. Benamou, 'Inter-*auteurial* Itineraries and the Rekindling of Transnational Art Cinema: Raúl Ruiz and Orson Welles', in *Raúl Ruiz's Cinema of Inquiry*, 109–12.
108 Goddard, *The Cinema of Raúl Ruiz*, 71. Ruiz and Benoît Peeters, 'Annihilating the Script', in *Raúl Ruiz: Images of Passage*, 24.
109 On 'metalepsis', see Genette, *Narrative Discourse*, 234–36.
110 Rodríguez-Remedi, 'Raúl Ruiz, Speculative Bricoleur', 88.
111 On the significance of Has's film to Ruiz, see Goddard, *The Cinema of Raúl Ruiz*, 97, 99, 128, 131, 169; Rodríguez-Remedi, 'Raúl Ruiz, Speculative Bricoleur', 92.
112 This also constitutes part of the series' difference from *La recta provincia*, in which several female storytellers are shown to occupy the same metanarrative level as the male storytellers.
113 Françoise Aude, *Cinéma d'elles, 1981–2001* (Lausanne: L'âge d'homme, 2002), 105. Quoted in Adrian Martin, 'Amelia Lópes O'Neill', *Film Critic: Adrian Martin*, www.filmcritic.com.au/reviews/a/amelia_lopes_oneill.html (accessed August 27, 2022).
114 Cavell, *Contesting Tears: The Hollywood Melodrama of the Unknown Woman* (Chicago: University of Chicago Press, 1997). Tania Modleski, *Feminism without Women* (London: Routledge, 1991), 8–11.
115 In Sarmiento's film, Amelia Lopes is played by Laura del Sol. 'Amelia Lopes' is also the name of the *telenovela* actress played by Kate Valk in *The Golden Boat*. It appears that Ruiz and Sarmiento used several variations on the name's spelling: see also Ruiz, *Diario*, vol. 2, 513.
116 Ruiz also noted the influence on *Litoral* of the stories of Hans Christian Andersen: *Entrevistas escogidas*, 216. This moment in the series recalls Andersen's miniature toy characters, as in 'The Shepherdess and the Chimney Sweep' and 'The Steadfast Tin Soldier'.
117 Genette, *Narrative Discourse*, 223. Genette's principal formulations of this idea come from Proust. According to Ruiz, one of whose most popular films is an adaptation of *Le temps retrouvé* (*Time Regained*, 1999), part of what attracted him to filming Proust was the possibility of capturing kinds of atemporality on film: *Entrevistas escogidas*, 236.
118 See Cavell, 'The Thought of Movies', 7.

119 Stanley Cavell, *Cities of Words: Pedagogical Letters on a Register of the Moral Life* (Cambridge, MA: Harvard University Press, 2004), 109. See also Rodowick, *Philosophy's Artful Conversation*, 274–75ff.
120 Cavell, *Pursuits of Happiness*, 263.
121 Ibid., 256–63; Cavell, 'The Thought of Movies', 7. Within the category of atemporal or transtemporal remarriages, we might also add the reconciliation between Genjūrō (Masayuki Mori) and the spirit of his dead wife Miyagi (Kinuyo Tanaka) at the end of Mizoguchi's *Ugetsu* (1953), which Cavell discusses in 'What Becomes of Things on Film?', in *Themes Out of School*, 180–81, and 'The Fantastic of Philosophy', in *In Quest of the Ordinary* (Chicago: University of Chicago Press, 1988), 188. Within Ruiz's filmography, we can also add the remarriage between William (Jean-Marc Barr) and the spirit of Anne-Marie (Elsa Zylberstein) that concludes *La maison Nucingen* (*Nucingen House*, 2008), which Ruiz filmed in Chile some months prior to filming *Litoral*.
122 Cavell could also be understood as approaching this point when he contrasts the film *Dead of Night*, based on temporal looping (and, as I noted above, significant to Ruiz for that reason) with those horror films like *Night of the Living Dead* (George Romero, 1968) that, based on human transformations across classical narrative progressions, 'form a shadow genre of remarriage comedies' (*Pursuits of Happiness*, 222–23). In other words, on this reconstruction of Cavell's contrast, temporal looping ends up being closer than classical narratives to the undialectical permanencies proper to long-running serial TV, a proposal that I am arguing Ruiz also develops in *Litoral*. James McFarland has helpfully raised the question of whether Cavell is referring to the 1945 film or the 1974 Bob Clark film also called *Dead of Night*, but this proposed focus on temporality might help us to see what would be at stake in his referring to the former. See James McFarland, 'When There's No More Room in Hell, Should We Read Stanley Cavell?', *Discourse*, vol. 42, nos. 1–2 (2020), 140–72, 170n21.
123 Slavoj Žižek, *The Plague of Fantasies* (New York: Verso, 1997): 10–11.
124 Todd McGowan, *The Impossible David Lynch* (New York: Columbia University Press, 2007), 202. McGowan also quotes in a similar connection the statement by Freud on fantasy that I paraphrased at the end of the previous part of this essay (218). On Ruiz's impressions of Lynch, see *Entrevistas Escogidas*, 166–67; Goddard, *The Cinema of Raúl Ruiz*, 172–73.
125 See Goddard, *The Cinema of Raúl Ruiz*, 135. For Cavell on fantasy in film, see *The World Viewed*, 80–97; 'What Becomes of Things on Film?', 177–83; and 'The Fantastic of Philosophy', 181–88. McGowan also cites Cavell's views on fantasy in film: *The Impossible David Lynch*, 252n3.
126 On Ruiz's use of anamorphic lenses, see Goddard, *The Cinema of Raúl Ruiz*, 161–64.
127 This device can be compared with the placing of witnesses and eavesdroppers in windows and doorways throughout *Mysteries of Lisbon*.
128 I am grateful to the audience for my online presentation of this paper at the 'Art and Knowledge' lecture series at the Martin Luther University of Halle-Wittenburg in June 2022, and I thank Anke Breunig for the invitation to give that talk. I want to acknowledge Bruno Cuneo, director of the Archivo Ruiz-Sarmiento in Valparaíso, Chile, for addressing my many questions about Ruiz. Others who helped me with my questions about Ruiz included Laura Colella, Alfred Guzzetti, Adrian Martin, Robb Moss, Richard Peña, Jonathan Rosenbaum, and Daniela Salazar. Thanks also

to William Rothman for correspondence about Cavell and eternal recurrence. This essay also benefited from a conversation with Gordon C.F. Bearn about Cavell and the baroque. Other friends who helped in my research and in the development of these ideas included Antonia Alarcón, Ignacio Azuceta, Marcela Cuevas Ríos, Joshua Kortbein, John McCurley, Javiera Núñez Álvarez, and Laura Núñez Álvarez. I also want to acknowledge a discussion group in Mexico City in 2020 that took up Ruiz and *Poetics of Cinema*; members of that group with whom I have stayed in touch about Ruiz include Jorge Negrete, Mariana Dianela Torres, and Abraham Villa.

11

Homeland: An Education in Trust

Thibaut de Saint Maurice

One of the consequences of Islamic terrorism since the end of the 1990s is a crisis of trust, with the attacks deepening the lack of trust in the capacity of modern democracies to ensure the security of their population. This chapter shows how the television series *Homeland* (Showtime, 2011–20) could act as a resource to educate viewers about democratic life: not through reassurances about the power of intelligence agencies, but by allowing viewers to regain or restore trust in the democratic experience itself.

Such a hypothesis may seem at best surprising and at worst naive. To establish this hypothesis, we must confront at least four problems. The first problem lies in considering a television series as a resource for the political and moral formation of its audience when it is also a product of the culture industry. As Theodor Adorno points out, the culture industry produces consumer goods—not works that are capable of any kind of formation or transformation in consumers: 'The culture industry fuses the old and familiar into a new quality. In all its branches, products which are tailored for consumption by masses, and which to a great extent determine the nature of that consumption, are manufactured more or less according to plan.'[1] Consumers of this industry, which include viewers of television series, would be dominated by the logic of technological capitalism. The latter is constantly extending its logic by subjecting leisure time to standardized entertainment: 'the repetitiveness, the selfsameness, and the ubiquity of modern mass culture tend to make for automatized reactions and to weaken the forces of individual resistance'.[2] So, there would be a power of television—one that lies in training individuals in order to subject them to societal control. This power would not seek to educate the audience or even invite them to express their own voice.

The second problem arises when trying to understand the scope and uses of a television series that depicts intelligence agencies and deals with international relations. As Jutta Weldes and Christina Rowley show, these elements of popular culture should not be underestimated because 'popular culture not only reflects but also constitutes world politics'.[3] When it comes to describing a vision of world politics that it then develops, *Homeland* is a controversial series. Despite its efforts to depict an alternative narrative for the foundations of the so-called 'war on terror', the series was perceived as legitimizing the discourse and reasons put forward to justify it.[4] It was also seen as maintaining fear of 'the other'[5] and reproducing racist and Islamophobic stereotypes.[6]

The third problem lies in the conditions of production of the series, and the collaboration between the writers, actors, and the Central Intelligence Agency (CIA) in particular. As Tricia Jenkins notes, 'the Agency extended its hand to the series' writers, producers and actors'.[7] How, then, can we not doubt the independence of the series? If the CIA did indeed support the series, is it not propaganda? This is what Weldes calls the first mode of the relationship between popular culture and international politics, or 'state uses of popular culture'.[8]

The fourth problem, a philosophical one this time, involves asking what kind of 'education' and what kind of 'democracy' we are talking about when we talk about the education of democratic life made possible by a television series that originates in popular culture. *Homeland* is not exactly a show for children. So what meaning does the word education have for adults? Is it not paternalistic to suppose that grown-ups can be educated by fiction? Finally, what does democracy mean in the series if we need to be educated about it? If we agree that democracy is based on recognition of the individual freedom of each person, is it not contradictory to demand an education in this freedom?

To address these problems and support the hypothesis put forward above, I will situate my remarks in a double framework. The first framework is that of television studies, which examines the series as an *object*. This approach relies on a renewed understanding of television offered by Jason Mittell in what he calls 'complex TV'.[9] The second framework is one provided by Stanley Cavell's philosophy of film, which approaches the series as an *experience*. Continuity between film and television is possible today thanks to the work of Sandra Laugier[10] and Martin Shuster,[11] who insist on the educational power of a series in the sense of an education for adults that aims to develop their capacity for change (or to transform themselves). Because of their presence in everyday conversation, films and series provide an excellent opportunity for this. From these two frameworks, the analysis that follows in this article is a 'reading' of the series—in the sense that Cavell produces 'readings' of films[12]—based on the experience of watching eight seasons of *Homeland* between 2011 and 2020.

This essay is organized in two sections. The first section presents *Homeland* as a multilayered object, whose narrative and aesthetic variety expresses a moral and political complexity that is properly democratic. The second section shows how watching *Homeland* provides the spectator with a singular experience about trust as a condition for the democratic way of life.

Breaks in the Framework for *Homeland*: Analysis of a Complex Object

Homeland is a television series that was originally broadcast on the cable channel Showtime between 2011 and 2020. It includes eight twelve-episode seasons through which we follow the work of CIA agent Carrie Mathison and several of her colleagues in their fight against terrorism (and more broadly, against anything that threatens American democracy). For the first five seasons, *Homeland* tells a story about the war against Islamist terrorism. Season 6 marks a turning point by introducing another subject: the production of fake news and Russian attempts to destabilize American democracy. Seasons 7 and 8 show the tensions between the United States and Russia; while the war on terrorism remains present, it becomes a secondary issue in relation to geopolitical rebalancing between political forces. Throughout the series, Mathison has a troubled relationship with the CIA. She is suspended, then reinstated, then permanently disbarred. At her side is Saul Berenson, deputy director, who is also sidelined several times. Other characters such as Dar Adal, CIA black operations director, and Peter Quinn, a former CIA paramilitary officer, complete the picture and present a much darker side of the Agency.

In more than one way, the *Homeland* series fits perfectly with Mittell's description of complex TV. The serial dynamics of this fiction give the work a strong narrative complexity. The viewer who watches this series at length, episode after episode and season after season, can follow it effectively only by participating in the construction of the narrative unity. Construction involves relaying the various narrative frames. Contrary to what Adorno claims, the viewer of this series does not occupy the univocal role of a consumer. Moreover, the extent of the offer in terms of television series, as well as the diversification of channels and platforms, suggests that the choice to watch one series over another, or to continue to watch it over abandoning it for another, draws on multiple personal motivations that cannot therefore be reduced to the simple logic of consumption. Due to its seriality, the object lends itself to a different relation with the viewer—one of interaction and construction. As Umberto Eco reveals, seriality requires an 'encyclopedic capacity' and the practice of an 'enlarged intertextuality' from the spectator.[13]

These terms are useful for articulating the differences between various moments of the series. But they are also useful in positioning the series in relation to various points of reference, whether fictional or real. Seriality, in this specific poetic context of complexity, does not create a standardized work. Instead, it gives place to distinctive and singular practices on the part of authors, producers, and even channels that take advantage of seriality to create new relations with viewers. Complex TV is thus a condition for 'quality TV' from HBO, which has inspired channels such as FX and Showtime. Such series are products of the culture industry that avoids dumbing down for their audiences. From these poetic foundations, a TV series can be understood as a new form of art that cannot be reduced to just content for viewers' consumption.[14]

Homeland was not the first television series to focus on the war on terror. The series *24* also did so from 2001 through 2010 and again in 2014, but from a different perspective. In *24*, the challenge is to thwart the occurrence of an imminent attack in the upcoming twenty-four hours. The whole story adopts the ticking time bomb scenario, making the ability to provide security contingent on the effectiveness of the action. In *Homeland*, the 9/11 attacks have already taken place; if there is indeed a question of preventing other attacks, the challenge is not so much to act but to act with full knowledge of the facts. It is therefore an understanding of terrorism that is required. This understanding relies on both the quality of information and the quality of information analysis that we are able to produce. As the issue moves from the effectiveness of action to the quality of understanding, it is essential for the series to account for the complexity of the interactions that are being analysed. And this is what *Homeland* does, through a skilful narrative construction that reveals complexity through ruptures in the initial framework of its narrative.

The main difference between *Homeland* and other series or fiction about terrorism lies in the way that *Homeland* integrates into its narrative a set of breaks in the original framework of representation, as French sociologist Eric Macé explains in his heuristic analysis.[15] Starting with a framed representation of the war on terror, the series considers the off screen and the reverse angle (or *contrechamp*). In the end, it even discusses the evolution of this original framework to reveal fluidity and complexity.

Homeland begins by presenting an expected framework. The framework of the war on terror emerges in the opening credits of the first season, which mixes television archives with the symbolic evocation of characters. There are references to several attacks against the United States, from the 1988 Pan Am plane attack in Lockerbie and the attack on the World Trade Center to American interventions in Iraq and Afghanistan. Although the credits mix several different kinds of terrorist threats, the idea of the original framework is simple: since the end of the Cold War, the Arab and Muslim world have constituted the primary threat to the security of the United States.

This framework of the war on terror is a familiar starting point for the viewer, as evidenced by the television archives and, in particular, by *24* (the earlier series by the producers of *Homeland*, Alex Gansa and Howard Gordon). From there, *Homeland* puts forward three challenges that introduce complexity into what would otherwise have remained a simplified and Manichean framework of a 'crusade against terrorism'.

The first intervention occurs through references to what we could call off-screen effects. Several times throughout the series, *Homeland* describes harmful effects, collateral damage, blunders, or the brutality of the war on terror along with its human and moral consequences. The transformation of American soldier Nicholas Brody into a terrorist is not explained by the trauma of his captivity, for example, but by the trauma of an American drone strike on a school in Iraq that killed eighty-two children—including one, Issa, the son of his jailer, to whom he had become attached (s1:e9, 31:18–41:50). The video that Brody then recorded to claim responsibility for his future attack was an opportunity to denounce what appeared at the time to be a war crime. Later, in season 4, a new drone strike (this time ordered by Carrie) is subject to the same treatment. And later again, in season 8, when she finds herself on the field of this strike, Carrie remembers the event and we see her doubt.

The continuity of this narrative throughout the eight seasons introduces reflexivity about both the series and the CIA's drone programme. It is another way to show the complexity of choosing rightful means to defend a just end. According to Macé, this rupture in the framework can be interpreted in the language of sociology as a 'counter-hegemonic rupture' against the closing effect of an ideological framework.[16] This first intervention sets up a critical questioning of the primary framework for the actions of a democratic government in its fight against terrorism.

The second intervention in the framework is produced by reverse-angle effects. Here again, on several occasions during the series, various characters are used to restore a balance of point of view. Some characters have the opportunity to explain the 'good reasons' for their terrorist or populist commitment, to the point of presenting them as acts of 'resistance' in the new asymmetrical war regime that is terrorism. Examples include Brody, an American soldier who is committed to the cause of Abu Nazir (season 1) and Haqqani, the Taliban leader (season 4) or, more unexpectedly, Brett O'Keefe, a populist podcast host and propagator of destabilizing fake news (season 7), and Yevgeny Gromov, a controversial officer of the Russian GRU, the foreign military intelligence agency (season 8).

Throughout the series, there is some attempt to feature conversations between characters who do not share the same vision of the world. Even if these conversations do not lead to a shared consensus, they expose a plurality in point of view and extend an opportunity for the viewer to think about the issue. The conversation between National Security Advisor Saul Berenson and trolling podcast host O'Keefe (s7:e3, 21:30–24:07) is an opportunity to explicitly articulate the reasons that motivate O'Keefe and to begin to acknowledge the relevance of his position—even if his position is inconvenient for democratic life. Far from propaganda about a sweet and perfect democracy, *Homeland* succeeds in showing the opposite through off-screen and reverse-angle effects that allow the viewer to hear a plurality of voices and confront competing points of view.

The third rupture involves the evolution of the original framework of the war on terror towards one of the game of international relations and the balance of oppositions. This reframing impulse is embodied in particular by the character of Berenson who, at every opportunity (especially in seasons 3 and 5, but also in season 8), tries to abandon military options in favour of diplomatic ones. The movement of the series, from its first to its eighth season, takes part in this reframing: the series begins by focusing on the war against terrorism, but ends with new faces of opposition between the United States and Russia.

Thus, if one focuses on the first seasons, especially the first three seasons based on the narrative arc of Brody's return and the terrorist threat he represents, *Homeland* is indeed less complex than it seems. The expression of Brody's motivations, the questioning of the use of drones, and the staging of the CIA's vulnerability are not enough to deconstruct and completely delegitimize the framework of the war on terror, as Jack Holland notes.[17] But such analysis is only based on a partial reading of the series, which gives rise to an important point about analytical method: *Homeland* has eight seasons that are not independent of each other. Instead, they answer to and reflect on each other. Just as one cannot judge a book by its cover, one cannot judge a complex TV series by one or several seasons alone, as Holland and Louise Pears do. Surprisingly, so does the 2014 book *Homeland and Philosophy*, which focuses on the situations, scenes, or characters of the first season while discussing them as examples of classical philosophical issues, such as the personal identity issue or the influence of traumas on the moral life, etc.[18]

This does not mean one cannot say anything about a series before it is over. But it does mean that one cannot claim that part of a series expresses the whole series, or that the end of a series was contained in the beginning. Since this does not correspond to the way that these series are actually written, it does not account for the experience that the series creates in the viewer who follows it. Taken as a whole, the series changes its face over time: the main characters of *Homeland* are not Carrie and Brody, but Carrie and Saul. The main narrative arc is not the terrorist threat of a returned prisoner of war, but the difficulties—internal and external—that the CIA must face to ensure the security of the United States. As *New Yorker* journalist Emily Nussbaum says, series are works about time.[19] So, they must be considered in light of the entire length of the time they embrace.

Taken as a whole, from beginning to end (and especially in terms of its serial dimension wherein each new season introduces reflexivity about the preceding ones), *Homeland* is a fiction that progresses from a certain vision of the war on terror (seasons 1 to 3) to eventually show its failure (seasons 4 to 6). This then leads into questioning the role of the CIA in the political and democratic game unfolding at national and international levels (seasons 7 and 8). Thanks to its seriality, or evolution through time and continuity, *Homeland* gradually weaves an aesthetic and political alternative to the confrontation of war. It does so by bringing complexity, plurality, and regulation into the geopolitical game.

The evolution of this story is compatible with the education of the spectator on the complexity of the contemporary world. It expresses a certain vision of democratic values and a certain democratic conception of international relations. The interventions mentioned above stage an important question about the possibility of a democracy being as democratic in its ends as in its means. A question of means is also a question of the legitimacy of an intelligence agency, such as the CIA, in addition to its methods.

Is *Homeland* a propaganda series? In her work on how the CIA collaborates with film and television productions, Jenkins gives a balanced answer to this question. For her, *Homeland* presents a break in the representation of the CIA in popular culture and therefore in the manner of collaboration for a production:

> On many levels, the CIA's decision to assist these cultural producers, who engage with some of the most morally complicated aspects of the Agency's war on terror, including the use of torture and the drone program, constitutes a much-needed move away from propaganda that traditionally comes out of the PAO[20] and towards a newfound capacity to admit both nuance and mistakes in the Agency's efforts even while trumpeting its successes.[21]

We are thus witnessing a new way for the CIA to defend its image. Even as it accepts fiction that questions its practices, the Agency still manages to defend its role and its contribution to safeguarding national interest and security. There is indeed a game of influence, but it is no longer propaganda. The CIA now enters a game of communication and lobbying usually practised by associations and professional unions. For this reason, we do not agree with Deepa Kumar and Arun Kundnani's analysis of how *Homeland* continues to justify national security policies as *24* does.[22] Once again, this analysis is based on only three seasons of the show. And when it comes to considering the whole series, the CIA is portrayed, time and again, as unable to identify an imminent terrorist threat (season 1), as vulnerable (season 3), as resorting to illegitimate drone strikes (seasons 4 and 7), and finally as more concerned with its own power than with the public interest (seasons 7 and 8). A reading of the series as a whole, through its eight seasons, therefore leads one to believe that the collaboration between the CIA and the creative team of the series brings out a much more nuanced representation of the CIA. There is certainly still a question of influence, but it is posed within the new public space now constituted by popular content that recounts and questions the strategies and role of an intelligence agency in a democratic country.

An analysis of the poetic, aesthetic, moral, and political complexity of *Homeland* allows us to answer the first three problems noted at the beginning of this chapter. *Homeland* is not merely a standardized consumer product of the culture industry. The development of its narrative goes beyond the initial framework of the war on terror. The moral complexity of the characters and described situations even goes so far as transforming the way that the CIA thinks about its own image and the defence of its interests in the public space. As such, the series can be a resource for democratic debate. In the following section, I show how *Homeland* provides an original moral experience by restoring trust as the foundation for the democratic way of life.

Homeland: Restoring Trust in Light of New Complexity in the Modern World

Homeland was born from the trauma of the 9/11 attacks. These attacks are the event that made it possible to reveal the vulnerability of American power. Many years of war against terrorism, both in Afghanistan and Iraq, have failed to erase doubts about this vulnerability. This is because the deployment of traditional military power on the ground, with its compromises in violence and lies, has emerged as an undemocratic means of defending democracy. Terrorism in the early twenty-first century therefore addresses a new moral and political complexity: how can the public continue to trust a democratic government that has so little capacity to defend itself and provide security for its citizens?

The crisis of trust expressed through terrorism reveals a deeper crisis of trust in democracy under the complex conditions of the modern world, according to sociologist Anthony Giddens.[23] Today, Islamic terrorism is a new facet of this complexity. In a more structural way, we can think of this crisis of trust as rendering it impossible for us to give an account of our certainty as it relates to the experience of democracy. The vulnerability exposed by Islamic terrorism, the fear that it entails, and the seeming irreconcilability between different worldviews that it reveals can also be thought of as an expression of the scepticism that haunts the ordinary of our condition, in Cavellian thought.[24]

So, how do we remedy this crisis of trust? What outcome can we hope for from this scepticism? Here, a series such as *Homeland* becomes a resource for restoring trust. Because it is a series that develops over a lengthy period of time, the spectator is led to *follow* it. A series is a fictional narrative that the viewer is compelled to follow regardless of its complexity. It teaches the viewer to be patient, to not judge too quickly, and to not give up on characters. Following a series over a lengthy period of months or years is itself a matter of trust.

But trust is involved at another level as well: by watching season after season of *Homeland*, the audience follows a narrative, characters, and plots that stage something to which the viewer usually does not have access. The world of intelligence normally escapes the public gaze. This means that the series familiarizes the spectator with a closed professional universe. It creates a kind of democratic inventory for a dimension of reality where power is forged.

Throughout each episode, the spectator rediscovers the double principle (identified by Niklas Luhmann) wherein familiarity is the condition for trust and trust is 'a mechanism for reducing the social complexity of the modern world'.[25] Yet the continuity of democratic life needs this trust. Trust is its very foundation, as John Dewey says:

> we have had the habit of thinking of democracy as a kind of political mechanism that will work as long as citizens were reasonably faithful in performing political duties. Of late years we have heard more and more frequently that this is not enough; that democracy is a way of life.[26]

At the same time, this reasonable trust is not a definitive fact. It needs to be maintained by a shared experience and nourished by the possibility of ordinary conversations:

> Democracy as a personal, individual way of life involves nothing fundamentally new. But when applied, it puts a new practical meaning in old ideas. Put into effect, it signifies that current enemies of democracy can be successfully countered only through the creation of personal attitudes in individual human beings. It means we must get over our tendency to think that democracy's defence can be found in any external means, whether military or civil, considered as separate from individual attitudes so deep-seated as to constitute personal character.[27]

In its own way, *Homeland* is a fiction that tells us about the continuity of this democratic conversation—about situations, choices, and issues that are traditionally excluded from it. The whole point of the series is to present the conflict between characters as conflicts of 'personal attitudes' and not the justification of the use of intelligence, paramilitary, or military means. This explains why, for example, Carrie continues to work in the defence of democratic values (whether through a foundation, a law firm, or the advice she can give to presidential candidate Keane) even when she is no longer employed by the CIA.

As the production of *Homeland* progressed, it actually imposed itself as an element of the debate about democracy in the United States. This debate appeared, for example, in Michael Cornfield's article 'The Political Education of "Homeland's" Carrie Mathison' in the *Washington Post*.[28] However, the debate was also relevant in each democratic country where the series was broadcast.[29] Conversation about the series thus became a common democratic experience. This experience occurred in all three senses, as Dewey put it in *Democracy and Education*: it allowed for the existence of a plurality of points of view; it constituted an alternative to or critical experience of resisting the seizure of power by experts and politicians; and it animated a conversation about the legitimate interests and goals of the community that needed to be protected. In this way, *Homeland* confirms Dewey's thoughts about democracy. It is not merely a form of government, but a 'conjoint communicated experience'.[30]

Homeland's singular contribution to this question lies in the way that it makes trust the foundation of the democratic way of life. This narrative is constructed by interweaving levels of what could be called 'games of mistrust and trust' that amount to an education in trust. Across eight seasons, the series establishes a certain dialectic of trust and mistrust wherein the challenge is to learn how to build self-reliance and trust in others as a response to the threats posed to democratic life. This dialectic of trust is present at four different levels.

On an initial level, the dialectic unfolds in Carrie's relationship with herself: can she rely on herself? She is a brilliant agent who is suffering from mental illness. She must learn to live with her illness and use it as an advantage. Throughout the series, we witness her progress. Her character clearly stages the possibility of becoming better, both as an agent and as a person. She transforms herself in a perfectionist manner, becoming more comprehensible to the viewer over time, like the heroines whose transformations Cavell describes in the 'remarriage comedies' and melodramas he studies.[31]

The second level involves the relationship between Carrie and Saul (and the Agency, more broadly). Here, the question is: how can we trust ourselves despite the many good reasons we may have to mistrust each other? The series shows not just the fragility of trust, but also how successful intelligence work is impossible without trust. Even the CIA cannot know everything. Trust is required precisely when information is incomplete. Recurrent conversations or negotiations between Carrie and Saul represent the mechanism of trust-building, which is never simple or predetermined.

The third level lies in the relationship between the CIA and the presidency. This narrative arc runs throughout the whole series, but especially in the final two seasons. The question is: how can trust be maintained without giving in to the temptation of conspiracy? Trust is required between human beings, citizens, colleagues, but also institutions. Democracy is real not when it has the right institutions, but when these institutions function in a democratic way.

The fourth level exists in the relationship between the presidency and the people. The question here is: how can we avoid giving in to illiberal temptations and maintain mutual trust? The finale of the seventh season stages this issue (s7:e12). President Elizabeth Keane resigns in the face of growing public distrust, but her resignation creates an opportunity for her to reflect on trust as a condition for maintaining a democratic form of life. She shows how doubt and mistrust lead to division, which then becomes a weapon for the enemies of democracy. Thus, the issue is how to trust each other while also acknowledging self-reliance. The series presents several versions of characters who manage to overcome the fear of 'the other' and the temptation to deny this fear, such as Carrie Mathison, Nicholas Brody, Saul Berenson, and Peter Quinn. When the character of President Keane decides to resign (s7:e12), she makes the choice after uncovering the possibility of self-expression free from the fear that made her give in to illiberal temptation.

So, what measure of trust can we experience in *Homeland*? *Homeland* provides the possibility to explain trust, to explain the reasons for it, in an open conversation. Trust is not a single decision. It is given to and received from another in the moment that each expresses their own voice.

Homeland offers more to viewers than the realism of the work of CIA agents. It is distinguished by the realism of the moral experience in terms of what constitutes the main moral resource in the fight against terrorism. We can have all the security services and carry out all the military actions we want. But without self-reliance or trust in others (and especially trust in others' self-reliance), without the conversation that makes it possible to share a common conscience, we will not be able to fight effectively against the fear of 'the other', fear of an attack, and internal or external threats to democracy.

Through such games of trust and mistrust, we come to think of trust as the spectacle of characters with the capacity for change. They are able to trust each other where they were once distrustful, or able to distrust what once seemed unquestionable. Eventually, they are able to question, clarify, and express their own *experience*. This is the key to the relationship between Carrie and Saul; all the other relationships in the series are serial variations of this process. Cavell defines adult education specifically as the ability to change: 'in this light, philosophy becomes the education of grownups ... The anxiety in teaching, in serious communication, is that I myself require education. And for grownups, this is not natural growth, but change.'[32]

If Cavell is interested in cinema and in the popular comedies and melodramas of the 1940s, it is precisely because they represent characters who change, who try to express their own experience more precisely, who are looking for their own voice, underneath the voice of their functions. They thus constitute for us experiences of education as self-transformation. In their own ways, both Laugier[33] and Shuster[34] show how this philosophy of education through or with cinema is, today, made relevant through or with the television series, especially due to their length.

From the first to the final episode of *Homeland*, this game of different forms of trust constitutes the moral field for the series itself—as well as the basis of a moral experience for its viewer. The problem of this moral experience can be formulated as follows: on the one hand, lack of trust makes living together impossible and leaves room for fear of 'the other'; on the other hand, overconfidence makes it impossible to see danger and represents a new kind of threat. So, democracy needs us to clarify, day after day, the reasons for our trust in our way of life, and more precisely, in our democratic and ordinary way of life. Watching *Homeland*, watching Carrie and Saul's own questions and clarifications, can help us interrogate the way a democracy has chosen to face new kinds of threats.

Conclusion

Due to its subject matter, the power of its characters, and the effectiveness of its narrative, *Homeland* established itself as a 'good series' for critics and viewers alike. What seems important for us to underline in conclusion is how a series—one that stages the work of CIA agents, written in collaboration with the CIA, born within the framework of the war on terror and which could therefore be suspected of being a propaganda work—actually can constitute an authentic democratic resource.

How the series was received and fed into ordinary conversations, made visible in journalistic criticism, is an example of democratic conversation. When *Homeland* was released, it was immediately positioned in relation to *24*. It was contrasted with a series that also started from the framework of the war on terror, but which had been strongly criticized for its legitimization of undemocratic means (such as torture) and for its ideological hegemony. As *New Yorker* critic Emily Nussbaum wrote after seeing the first few episodes, '"Homeland" [is] the antidote for "24".'[35]

For the viewers of *Homeland*, following its characters over ninety-six episodes is an act of learning to trust them—yet a form of trust with eyes wide open to the issues and the complexity of what is represented on screen. An experience is important not because it conforms to reality, but because it can change what is called reality. And that is the specific power of fiction—especially popular fiction, including a complex, temporally extended example such as a television series.

Notes

1 Theodor Adorno, 'Culture Industry Reconsidered', in *The Culture Industry*, ed. J.M. Bernstein (London and New York: Routledge, 2001), 98.
2 Theodor Adorno, 'How to Look at Television', in *The Culture Industry*, 160.
3 Jutta Weldes and Christina Rowley, 'So, How Does Popular Culture Relate to World Politics?', in *Popular Culture and World Politics: Theories, Methods, Pedagogies*, ed. Federica Caso and Caitlin Hamilton (Bristol: E-International Relations Publishing, 2015), 19.
4 Jack Holland, 'Constructing Counter-Terrorism (in *Homeland*, *24* and *The West Wing*)', in *Fictional Television and American Politics: From 9/11 to Donald Trump* (Manchester: Manchester University Press, 2019).
5 Yvonne Bezrucka, 'Digital Media, Fears, and Their Ontological Demagogic Power: Utopia, Homeland, Occupied', *Pólemos*, vol. 14, no. 1 (2020), 147–61. https://doi.org/10.1515/pol-2020-2009.
6 Louise Pears, 'Telling Terrorism Tales: Narrative Identity and *Homeland*', in *The Politics of Identity*, ed. Christine Agius and Dean Keep (Manchester: Manchester University Press, 2018).

7   Tricia Jenkins, *The CIA in Hollywood: How the Agency Shapes Film and Television* (Austin: University of Texas Press, 2016), 169.
8   Weldes and Rowley, 'How Does Popular Culture Relate?', 19.
9   Jason Mittell, *Complex TV: The Poetics of Contemporary Television Storytelling* (New York: New York University Press, 2015).
10 Sandra Laugier, 'Popular Cultures, Ordinary Criticism: A Philosophy of Minor Genres', *Modern Language Notes*, vol. 127, no. 5 (2012), 997–1012.
11 Martin Shuster, *New Television: The Aesthetics and Politics of a Genre* (Chicago: University of Chicago Press, 2017).
12 Stanley Cavell, *Pursuits of Happiness: The Hollywood Comedy of Remarriage* (Cambridge, MA: Harvard University Press, 1981).
13 Umberto Eco, 'Innovation & Repetition: Between Modern & Postmodern Aesthetics', *Daedalus*, vol. 114, no. 4 (1985), 161–84.
14 Shuster, *New Television*. See also *De l'artification: Enquête sur le passage à l'art*, ed. Roberta Shapiro and Nathalie Heinich (Paris: EHESS, 2012).
15 Éric Macé, 'Des cadres de guerre vulnérables? La série *Homeland*, une heuristique critique de la «guerre au terrorisme»', *Réseaux*, vol. 199, no. 5 (2016), 71–97.
16 Macé, 'Des cadres de guerre vulnérables?'.
17 Holland, 'Constructing Counter-Terrorism'.
18 *Homeland and Philosophy*, ed. Robert Arp (Chicago: Open Court Publishing, 2014).
19 Emily Nussbaum, *I Like to Watch: Arguing My Way Through the TV Revolution* (New York: Random House Trade Paperbacks, 2020).
20 The PAO is the Public Affairs Office of the United States Department of Defense, whose purpose is to deal with the media.
21 Jenkins, *The CIA in Hollywood*, 166.
22 Deepa Kumar and Arun Kundnani, 'Imagining National Security: The CIA, Hollywood, and the War on Terror', *Democratic Communiqué*, vol. 26, no. 2 (2014), 72–83.
23 Anthony Giddens, *The Consequences of Modernity* (Cambridge: Polity Press, 1991).
24 Stanley Cavell, *The Claim of Reason: Wittgenstein, Skepticism, Morality, and Tragedy* (Oxford: Oxford University Press, 1979).
25 Niklas Luhmann, *Vertrauen: Ein Mechanismus der Reduktion sozialer Komplexität* (UTB/UVK/Lucius, 2014).
26 John Dewey, 'Creative Democracy—The Task Before Us', in *The Later Works*, vol. 14 (Carbondale: Southern Illinois University Press, 2008), 240–45.
27 Dewey, 'Creative Democracy'.
28 Michael Cornfield, 'The Political Education of "Homeland's" Carrie Mathison', *Washington Post*, December 26, 2014.
29 See James Donaghy's reviews of *Homeland* in *The Guardian* at www.theguardian.com/tv-and-radio/2020/may/03/homeland-finale-review-claire-danes-thriller-goes-out-with-a-bang. For French reviews, see Pierre Langlais's article '*Homeland* saison 7: entre démocratie sacrifiée et sacrifices pour la démocratie' at www.telerama.fr/series-tv/homeland,-saison-7-entre-democratie-sacrifiee-et-sacrifices-pour-la-democratie,n5628701.php. For German reviews, see Doris Akrap's article 'Freispruch für Carrie' in *Zeit Online*. www.zeit.de/kultur/film/2014-12/homeland-vierte-staffel-carrie-mathison-kritik?utm_referrer=https%3A%2F%2Fwww.google.com%2F.

30 John Dewey, *Democracy and Education: An Introduction to the Philosophy of Education* (Sterling: Stylus Publishing, 2018), chapter 7.
31 Stanley Cavell, *Pursuits of Happiness*, op.cit.
32 Cavell, *The Claim of Reason*, 1–2.
33 See Laugier, 'Popular Cultures, Ordinary Criticism.
34 See Shuster, *New Television*.
35 Emily Nussbaum, "Homeland": The Antidote For "24"', *New Yorker*, November 29, 2011.

12

Small Acts
Paul Standish

Closing Time

Topic and theme, of so much that is to follow, are established in the opening sequence of *Mangrove*, this opening episode of Steve McQueen's *Small Axe* TV series.[1]

In a semi-dark basement room, against the background music of Versailles' 'Long Long Time', we hear the clatter of dominoes or dice, laughter, jibes, and friendly banter amongst Black men huddled around tables. The camera moves close behind their backs. A middle-aged man gets up from the table, slips money into his pocket, exchanges friendly words, and leaves. From below, we see and hear him walking up stone steps, into the daylight outside. Wrought-iron railings spike the pale sky. As he crosses the road, the camera, now above, zooms out to reveal the urban landscape, streets coming to life. The camera tracks him as he crosses waste land, past children skipping through waist-high weeds, children balancing as they walk a plank, children jumping onto an abandoned mattress, past towering concrete arches of a flyover under construction, past graffiti that reads 'Wogs Out' (in black) and 'Powell for P.M.' (in white) … Bob Marley sings 'Try Me'.

The man—Frank Crichlow (Shaun Parkes)—crosses another street, greets and is ignored by a woman he passes, heads for a shop front, a café, a restaurant perhaps, where three or four young men are gathered. 'Try Me' gives way to a voice-over, whose unmissable clarity intercuts with language of the street:

> Voice-over: *These are new men, new types of human beings. It is in them that are to be found all the traditional virtues of the English nation, not in decay, not in decay as they are in official society but in full flower …*
> Crichlow: Rita!

Voice-over: ... *because these men have perspective* ...
Crichlow: Is where you been? (Rita walks past, ignoring him)
Voice-over: Note particularly that they glory in the struggle. They are not demoralized, or defeated, or despairing persons. They are leaders, but are rooted among those they lead.
Crichlow: Linton, I tell you enough times, you're catching your tail in front of here boy.
Linton: Just liming with the limers, man.
Crichlow: Get your backside somewhere else.
(Linton sucks his teeth and exchanges glances with his friends. Catching Crichlow's eye, he breaks into a smile and laughs openly. Laughing, the young men walk away.)
Linton: Oh man.
Crichlow: Respect bright, man.
(Crichlow enters the shop and puts a large sign in the window: 'BLACK OWNERSHIP'.)

Who are these people? In 1968 Frank Crichlow opened the Mangrove, a restaurant in Notting Hill serving West Indian food and providing a meeting place for the local community. Notting Hill, then a run-down part of London, had gathered a sizeable West Indian population, early arrivals, the 'Windrush generation'—that is, those who had sailed to England on the Windrush in 1948, and then those, like Crichlow himself, who had arrived some five years later. Crichlow had earlier established a bar called El Rio, which had a somewhat seedy reputation. This new venture was to be a respectable restaurant, and it was a great success—a focal point for the local community but also, against the odds, a symbol of radical chic. The police were suspicious and tried six times in its first year to shut it down. It was also in 1968 that Enoch Powell, sometime Health Minister and then Shadow Defence Secretary, delivered his notorious 'rivers of blood' speech, opposing the Labour Government's 1968 Race Relations Act. Quoting Virgil's *Aeneid*, he expressed fears of rising levels of immigration: 'as I look ahead, I am filled with foreboding; like the Roman, I seem to see "the River Tiber foaming with much blood".' The voice-over of this opening scene, unmissable in its high-pitched florid elegance, is that of Darcus Howe (Malachi Kirby). Howe had come to London from Trinidad in the early 1960s and quickly made his way to this part of London. He worked for a time at the Mangrove restaurant. A leading member of the Black Panther movement in the UK, he was to become a respected journalist and writer, an important, highly articulate spokesman for his generation.

Mangrove depicts the escalating interference of the police and the demonstration this eventually provoked. A peaceful protest march was violently suppressed by the police, and arrests were made. Nine people were indicted under the newly constituted offence of 'violence and affray', which potentially carried a long-term prison sentence. In a clearly ostentatious move that aggravated the seriousness of the situation, the court case was transferred to the Old Bailey, the highest court and an icon of British justice. The film depicts the anxiety and fear of the accused in the course of the legal preparations. The court case lasted twelve weeks, and it made legal history: the accused were acquitted of all the major charges. The defendants emerged with considerable dignity, especially Altheia Jones-LeCointe (Letitia Wright) and Howe himself, who had defended themselves; the nefarious behavior and tactics of the police were exposed. The verdict remains a significant landmark in the improvement of race relations. Yet it did not prevent the police from raiding the restaurant again, repeatedly, and pressing charges against Crichlow. Not only was he acquitted, he was awarded £50,000 in damages, an unprecedented payment from the police.

The radical chic image the Mangrove acquired is less surprising than might initially be thought, especially given Crichlow's earlier career. In the 1950s he had had success as a member of a band, and with the proceeds he had opened El Rio Café. The West Indian style of El Rio appealed partly because of its contrast with the rather stiff, more inhibited patterns of English culture, and in Crichlow's own words it became a 'school or university' for hustlers, attracting the rebellious and street-smart.[2] It figured in the scandal that, in the early 1960s, was to rock the British establishment. As a young woman, Christine Keeler went there often, as did John Profumo, the Conservative Minister for Defence with whom she had an affair; she was at the time seeing the Russian military attaché. Profumo lied about the affair in the House of Commons and was forced to resign; the Prime Minister, Harold Macmillan, resigned as a matter of honor. The scandal brought about a major cultural change in the ways those in power were seen, in the behavior of the press, and in openness about sex.[3] El Rio and subsequently the Mangrove restaurant played significant roles, actual and symbolic, in wider cultural and political change.

McQueen's dramatization of these events largely leaves out this political backstory. The avoidance of any glamorization draws attention instead to the Mangrove's place in the ordinary lives of local, especially Black, people. The Mangrove is certainly not presented as, and was not, a smart restaurant; more an informal café. And the lives of those central to these events are shown to be relatively impoverished, weighed down by everyday tiredness and work, and by insidious smoldering injustice. The dramatization draws from the style and preoccupations of the *World in Action* documentary series and of 'Armchair Theatre' and 'Play for Today', groundbreaking developments in British television in the 1960s. These plays were often characterized by a social realism that examined the fabric of ordinary lives, exposing barriers of class, race, and gender, as well as more surreptitious social repression. In some respects McQueen's filming and dialogue emulates features of that social realism, though the camerawork is more fluid—for example, the camera amongst the domino-players, the long tracking shot of Crichlow crossing the waste land—than 1960s technology and studio settings would have achieved. Just occasionally, the dialogue seems pointedly expository in function, even slightly artificial, perhaps an artful gesture towards the television drama of the time.

Mangrove's opening scene draws attention, then, to threats to the ordinary lives of West Indian people living in London at the time. It exposes problems not only of race but of its intersection with social class and gender, language and education, art and expression, institution and authority. These themes reverberate through the series.

But we must digress. What is it to open a TV series? What constitutes *Small Axe* as a series?

It was a coup for McQueen that the BBC agreed to broadcast the series over five weeks at 9pm on a Sunday night. This is a 'prime time' slot—when peak viewing figures are achieved and TV companies showcase their best programs. It is after the 'watershed' of 9pm, when more challenging content can be shown. 'These are national stories', McQueen has said, 'so I wanted the stories to go through the bloodstream of the country.' Scheduling at this time on BBC One would give the series a legitimacy that would persuade his mum to watch too.[4] But this 'coup' is also bracketed with an irony, a joke that McQueen partly exploits. 'Prime-time television' harks back to an earlier time. The issues of scheduling that used to preoccupy program controllers have partly been dispelled by the increasing availability of programs, any place, any time. McQueen's achievement with this scheduling is more symbolic than actual. But the symbolic is no less a part of our real world.

The consequences of this new accessibility are, however, more far-reaching. While the actual screening of the series on the BBC followed the specified sequencing of the five films, a viewer might well access and view them differently—perhaps in an extended binge session, perhaps out of sequence, perhaps viewing some episodes more than once, perhaps watching an episode in fragments between other activities, perhaps, and in the case of *Small Axe* quite commonly, viewing an episode on its own (and so obviously losing something of what constitutes it within the series). My own initial impression, having first viewed the series over five weeks as scheduled, was to find in their sequence a spiraling of effect, each story circling around overlapping themes, each drawing out aspects of earlier episodes with intensifying effect, all this in the absence of any unifying narrative or common cast of characters. For although there are sometimes cryptic references or allusions that connect the episodes, there is no direct link from one episode to the next. For all that they cohere, thematically, topically, these are separate stories; one closes, and another opens; and this spacing, separation in space and time, close to one another, closed off from one another, seems important in determining the manner of their reception—that is, the experience of viewing the series. The films might be shuffled and viewed in a different order, and then perhaps a different coherence would be achieved.

So, *is* this set of films a series? The concept of genre is not of great service here, not least because it is crucial that the five films have been presented together by their creator and curator as—at least for now—a closed set. The parenthesis is prompted not by any indication from McQueen but by the technology: *Small Axe* appears by default on a variety of platforms as '*Small Axe*, Series 1'. The series is sometimes referred to as an anthology, and this prompts questions regarding how and with what effect its items are collected. Stanley Cavell's remarks on the 'philosophy of collecting' are made in the last chapter of a collection entitled *Philosophy the Day after Tomorrow*. In the opening remarks of the book's introduction, he writes: 'The interaction of the themes, and perhaps disciplines, of the opening pair of the ten texts to follow are developed variously, in scope and concentration, in succeeding chapters.'[5] This pair comprises 'Something Out of the Ordinary', one of Cavell's most explicit treatments of the theme of race, and 'The Interminable Shakespearean Text'.

The chapter on collecting, 'The World as Things', invites the consideration of a point of departure in Wittgenstein's preface to the *Philosophical Investigations*,[6] a work that brings together the 'precipitate' of investigations into meaning, consciousness, understanding, and much more. It does this in 693 short numbered paragraphs,[7] sometimes in sequences around a particular topic, sometimes with overlaps as the text moves from one topic to another, and sometimes with sudden jumps. The sketches of landscapes that are produced are the products of the 'natural inclination' of thought,[8] the topics approached again and again, each time from a different angle. The book, Wittgenstein writes, is 'really just an album',[9] a collection of remarks. But it is not a collection like, say, the collection of butterfly specimens in the Natural History Museum. Whereas that collection is arranged hierarchically by genus and species, according to a taxonomy, the connections in the *Investigations* are not systematic: the impression is given that thought is allowed to flow, from one topic to another, by way of overlaps and contiguities. This is closer to the way we normally think. Its method is the laying of examples alongside one another, not examples as instances of common types but examples that constitute different cases, where thought is guided by analogy. Cavell's own discussion in 'The World as Things' might itself be seen as an anthology of remarks, its 18 numbered sections proceeding not in a linear fashion so much as by association and connection. But these numbers, 693 and 18, are still very different from 5, and this thought has a bearing on how—once again, in the absence of continuity of storyline or of character and setting—what constitutes *Small Axe* as a series might be clarified. Here are two ideas.

Small Axe is a pentaptych. To say this is not to eradicate but to weaken the pull of assumptions of linear narrative. The five 'episodes'—the very term, the default of recorded TV, reinforces the idea of a single road—are panels in a composite painting. Perhaps they are all of equal import; perhaps one can be given greater prominence, perhaps be made physically bigger than the others, as when clicking to select or highlight an item in an array online. Click on *Mangrove*, and it becomes the keynote for the series. Click on another episode, and the items arrange themselves differently around it.

Highlight one film, and the others become its ramifications or steps on the way. Then again the handiness of five, of four fingers and an opposable thumb, prompts the thought that we can pick up different threads of the fabric, have different starting points, which itself seems like a democratizing move, defying any tidy synopsis or global overview. The religious connotations of the pentaptych are, moreover, not to be denied.

But consider also another possibility. *Small Axe* is a mangrove. The branches extend, setting down roots in different locations and contexts, and growth from each makes possible further interconnections. Mangrove growth can stabilize riverbanks, strengthen foundations afforded by shifting sandy earth, and spreading canopies of branch and foliage create a darkened, protective space beneath, a space that can nurture commensal life. The invocation of this tropical tree should, in a sense, be no surprise, because it figures in the founding formulations of negritude, explicitly in Aimé Césaire's 'La condition-mangrove', and then later, more recessively, in the celebration of the rhizophoric in Édouard Glissant, and later still, by extension, in the crossings of Paul Gilroy's *Black Atlantic*;[10] it is a fitting name for a Caribbean restaurant. '*Noire la mangrove reste un miroir*', Césaire writes. '*Aussi une mangeoire.*'[11] ('The black mangrove remains a mirror. / Also a feeder.'). And he speaks of surviving the allure of the forest in the rocking chair of a tidal balancing ('*La dodine / Celle du balancement des marées.*'). This is not just to appeal to a now familiar theme of hybridity but to realize something of the dynamics of this series. The narratives of the films are plainly there, but their grouping as a series, the relationship between them, invites not just a comparison of stories—an intertextuality extending beyond this series—but some sense of each of the others as pictorially present or parallel, pictorially and perhaps audibly too, given McQueen's advertising of the 'great soundtrack' that runs through them.

Do we not see this tidal balancing in the tensioned lives of the people in these films? Immediately following the opening sequence ('Try Me' is still playing), we see Crichlow in the restaurant, issuing instructions to the kitchen staff: 'OK, we gonna do fish curry, goat curry, mutton curry … my mother's crab and dumplin. But, first, we will start with the roots.' He takes a large knife and slices clean through a yam. Then this cuts abruptly to a television screen, where Darcus Howe is being interviewed. He is seen in a close-up cameo-like image, the camera peering, as it were, through a more or less oval window in a black screen:

> Interviewer: Trinidadian barrister, Darcus Howe, thinks things could build up dangerous social tensions.
> Howe: The policeman who frames a black man is doing so with a confidence that the system is going to give him a conviction. And a section of the community, who one must call the most alienated, either are going to turn to crime in that they are going to be arrested anyway, or seek their revenge against society in another form. Now, at this point in time, that form

has not been expressed, and I hope it wouldn't be, but one must be very direct here and say that the police must either stop it or the black community will have to stop them doing it.

The camera retreats to reveal the television set and, gathered around in this ordinary suburban sitting room, Darcus's partner Barbara Beese (Rochenda Sandall) and other friends:

> Ah …
> Fantastic!
> Barbara Beese: Excellent work.
> C.L.R. James (Derek Griffiths): A toast! A toast to my beautiful wife Selma, who brought this vitally important program together.
> Selma James (Jodhi May): And to my husband, the great C.L.R. James, whom I thank for his great love and support.
> C.L.R. James: And Darcus, he's a leader! He'll make a great lawyer one day.
> Barbara Beese: Yeah, he done all right, didn't he? But let's get one thing straight. Darcus isn't interested in being a barrister. He's interested in change. To change! (They toast.)

Near the end of the film, in his closing remarks at the court case, Howe begins:

> The time is out of joint. Oh cursed spite, that ever a Black people were born to set it right. We say it's closing time. But in a certain sense the matter has just begun, for I believe that this case has opened issues which are likely to decide the shape and future of British society, I believe, and Europe. I believe that this case has opened issues, it has seared the consciousness of the Black community to the extent that a history of Britain cannot be written without it … You have heard a lot about the Mangrove restaurant. It has been portrayed as an ordinary restaurant with licensing problems. How ignorant can you be? How superficial and surface-like can people be? 'It's not his fault, his masters' fault.' … 'Black people are criminals, ponces, and prostitutes.' That is a myth that has been created about us … It has something that was located somewhere in the stench of British colonialism—his masters again. In defending itself against attack, a community is born, and wherever a community is born, it creates institutions that it needs. Frank Crichlow, he wasn't conscious of the fact that he was forming a community restaurant … We created the Mangrove. We formed it, we shaped it to our needs … And so, when the Mangrove came under attack from the police—not once, not twice, but three times, members of

the jury, three times—we said 'No more!' I have been forced to take a stand and to take a stand I will. It's closing time, it's closing time. History will take its course, so frequently a brutal one, and we will continue to resist, intelligently and reasonably. That is what the demonstration was about—an intelligent and reasonable resistance to certain concrete facts.

It's closing time. People are closing for a fight. This court case is coming to a close. It is happening here in the Old Bailey, this intimidating neoclassical emblem of British Empire and British justice. This is the place in which these people have been tried, a place—as Ian Macdonald (Jack Lowden), the defense barrister, wryly tells some of the defendants—that has its own witchcraftery. Things are closing in on the British Empire.

'History is on my side.' With the verdict, Howe's avowed confidence that this is so is heroic and redemptive. McQueen's restraint, in some respects, in the recounting of the events subtly intensifies this but also sets these events against the backdrop of scenes of ordinary life. The wide blade falls, and the yam splits in two. This small act, 'starting with the roots', opens the Mangrove restaurant. These everyday acts of preparing, serving, and eating food are equally important in the possibilities of community McQueen depicts.

What is at issue in this film and much of what follows in the series, however, is not what justice consists in—this is not in doubt—but how it is to be achieved. Will the oppressed parties overcome formidable odds? What resources of character and culture are revealed or generated in this struggle? The matters that are brought to a head in the court case are literally what Cavell has referred to as headline issues, and there is no questioning their moral significance. But when philosophical theorizing about morality gravitates towards headline issues, it risks losing sight of the permeation of morality in the fabric of ordinary lives with language. Consider Sandra Laugier's words here:

> My project is to show the relevance of ordinary language philosophy for ethical and political issues by developing an ordinary conception of politics for thinking about civil disobedience and radical democracy, and an ordinary conception of ethics for thinking about care and gender inequality. This systematic exploration of the (theoretical and practical) question of the ordinary is anchored in ordinary language philosophy, the 'rough ground' of the uses and practices of language; it leads to further investigating the denial or undervaluation of the ordinary as a general phenomenon in contemporary thinking.[12]

The paralleling of Howe's rhetorical brilliance in articulating his case with the establishment and running of what became a community restaurant, which is realized—pictorially, musically, dramatically—in more specifically filmic ways, provides powerful expression of this.

Voice and representation must be conceived beyond this rhetorical brilliance, to take in everyday conversation. Considering how people commonly speak and interact in circumstances less severe or differently charged than the courtroom opens themes of gender and care, and these coalesce in the films' concern with the finding of voice. *Mangrove* plainly illustrates success at the court case, spearheaded by Howe's and Jones-Lecointe's brave and brilliant self-defense: these exemplary individuals speak for themselves and their community. But the 'rough ground' of language must extend into everyday interactions, with their successes and failures, their sharings of sentiment, intimacies, misunderstandings. Television brings these matters—the high drama and the everyday—into our living rooms, the very circumstances of which, unlike the cinema, invite conversation, and so a new kind of scrutiny. This can be done in ways that present fantasies of these things, redoubling the shadows on our walls, tranquilizing us as docile subjects and better consumers; here too there is space for criticism, but its edge is easily dulled. A series such as *Small Axe*, however, realizes something of the hopes expressed nearly fifty years ago by Raymond Williams, roughly at the time the series is set. Referring to the 'inexpensive, locally based yet internationally extended television systems, making possible communication and information-sharing on a scale that not long ago would have seemed utopian', he writes: 'These are the contemporary tools of the long revolution towards an educated and participatory democracy, and of the recovery of effective communication in complex urban and industrial societies.'[13]

In Cavell's view, these are matters, extending through our lives in language, of consequence for the individual and the community. People try to say what they mean and mean what they say, but there are also ways in which they shy away from this, sheltering in conformity, avoiding recognition. 'I do not know in advance', he writes,

> how deep my agreement with myself is, how far responsibility for the language may run. But if I am to have my own voice in it, I must be speaking for others and allow others to speak for me. The alternative to speaking for myself representatively (for *someone's* consent) is not speaking for myself privately. The alternative is having nothing to say, being wordless, or even mute.[14]

How far is this conception of voice at issue in the films? How far are series significant in these matters?

Silly Games

Strong narrative drive and social realist styling give way in *Lovers Rock* to something more expressionistic.[15] This is one of the two films that present fictional stories, while the others vary in how, and how far, they seek documentary verisimilitude. *Lovers Rock*'s realism lies in its evoking of a familiar scene. In the 1970s young Black people were often refused entry to clubs or bars, and their solution was to organize their own parties. A room in a large house would be cleared of furniture, a sound system would be installed and, with these makeshift arrangements, the party would begin, often running through the night.

Set in 1980, *Lovers Rock* refers to a romantic reggae form which combines the heavy Jamaican base with a more melodious top line. The ambiguity of the phrase points to the film's mood and theme. Fragments of narrative and character give way to music and dancing: the camera, through most of the film, longer than one might expect, stays with the music and the dance, as if absorbing the atmosphere, alcohol, weed. As at the start of *Mangrove*, it moves close amongst the bodies, moving amongst the silhouettes of shoulders and heads and hairstyles, bodies close in each other's arms, with the reds and purples and silver-threaded mauves of the girls' dresses luminous in this darkened space. Before this we see the preparations: the furniture removed and the sound system tested, women preparing food in the kitchen, and this cross-cuts with the figure of Martha (Amarah-Jae St. Aubyn), sneaking out of her house at a late hour to go to the party. At the party she meets Franklyn (Micheal Ward), and at the end of the night they will leave together. But these little stories are thin threads running through the atmosphere and mood of the film.

Music dominates. The interactions and conversations that take place are strongly gendered and often competitive but burdened by a kind of indirectness and avoidance. Martha is upset because her friend, Patty (Shaniqua Okwok), has left without telling her. It seems she is about to go, when Franklyn calls to her:

> Franklyn: Martha. Yo, star! Wait now. Just to say you drop somethin. Me turn me back for a sccond now. An where you ah run go? What'm, me spite you? So where you ah go? Heh?
> Martha: My friend left.
> Franklyn: Who?
> Martha: Patty. She gone.
> Franklyn: Oh. Beef patty? (She turns away, sneering.) All right! All right, no bother get irate. It's a joke me ah made.
> Martha: Don't even know no one.
> Franklyn: So what, you nah know me?
> Martha: I don't know you.
> Franklyn: Ah, wha'da you? Ay? What, the dance nah sweet? My breath nah fresh?
> Martha: Yeah, but you pile on the aftershave, innit? Come like Pepe Le Pew. What's that? Brut tirty-tree?
> Franklyn: You're right now blaadclaat. Give I ah next dance. Ah, easy now. Come on, come on.

The sparring is given added edge by the interplay of different registers of speech, with her artful mixing of her London lingo with phrases from his patois. The brief conversation is followed by a sequence in which just one song is sustained. 'Silly Games' had been a hit in 1979, and it became a feature of the parties, even an anthem where the women would sing along. The sequence here is extended for over ten minutes, towards the end of which they sing *a capella*, their singing punctuated by the calls of Samson (Kadeem Ramsay) and Parker B (Alexander James-Blake) at the turntables:

> I'm just wanting you
> *(How long?)*
> For so long it's a shame
> *(Whoa! I want dat ting)*
> Every time I hear your name
> *(Singalong yo!)*
> Oh! The pain!
> Boy, how it hurts me inside
> *(That's what I'm talkin bout)*
> Cos every time we meet
> We play hide-and-seek
> I'm wonderin what I should do
> Should I dare come up to you?
> And say 'How do you do?'
> Would you turn me away?
> You're as much to blame
> Cos I know you feel the same
> I can see it in your eyes
> *(Whoop, whoop, whoop!)*
> But I've got no time
> To live this lie.
> Yet in my mind I'll say
> I'll just play it shy
> It's a tragedy
> That you and me
> We don't even try
> You're as much to blame
> Cos I know you feel the same
> I can see it in your eyes.
> But I've got no time
> *(Samson and Parker B ...)*
> To live this lie
> I've got no time
> To play your silly games.
> Silly games.

At the end of the song, 'silly games' is repeated, and the word 'games' then reaches a very high note, supposedly inspired in its composer by an advertisement for Memorex that showed Ella Fitzgerald hitting such a note and breaking a glass. Here the women strain and just succeed in singing this note, and then extemporize in a humming and harmonization, gospel-style, rhythm provided by the shuffling of their feet and the quiet clicking of heels on the wooden floor.

When Martha and Franklyn go home from the party, now in the early morning daylight, he takes her to the small garage where he works as a mechanic.

> Franklyn: Sorry for de mess.
> Martha: I'm glad we leave. I see it in your eyes.
> Franklyn: An am them sweet you?

They embrace and kiss. But the door opens, and Franklyn's boss, who is about their age, comes in and says, cheerily: 'Oi, oi! What's goin on ere then? Could hardly ... Well, it's well dark in here, innit? Didn't recognize ya.' Franklyn is flustered but switches effortlessly and unselfconsciously into London speech.

> Franklyn: Sorry about that, boss. It's, it's the big light, innit? You know how it's usually too bright.
> Boss: Right. Too bright. Gave me a fuckin seizure you lot did, for fuck's sake. Look at you, eh! Hello, love.
> Franklyn: Listen, boss, we ... we're not stoppin, yeah? We just popped in on our way home.
> Boss: Right, well, glad you're here. Couple of things ...

Martha and Franklyn walk to a bus stop and stand there kissing. The bus arrives, and behind them we see a man stepping off the bus, carrying a big cross. The conductor of the bus seems to wait for a moment while they kiss. 'Seats up top', he says, as Martha steps onto the bus, and then from the upper floor we can look down with her, over her shoulder, to see Franklyn waving from the street below, and behind him, on the grass verge, the man unfolding his cross. The cross is jointed so that it can be transported more easily. Now he is carefully bolting the vertical parts together. He walks away down the road, carrying it on his shoulder.

We see a cross also in Martha's room and below it we see her shadow as she climbs back in through the window. Quietly, she puts her coat and bag under the bed and, with her mauve party dress still on, slips into bed, a smile on her face. Within minutes, it seems, there is banging on the door. 'Get up! Get up! Time for church! Time for church!'

The crossing of registers in language and dress—is she perhaps already dressed for church?—suggests not so much the problems of 'code-switching' but something else. It is a field of discursive play and exuberance through which possibilities of expression are extended. What in any case is this London speech? Is it Cockney (always contested) or Multicultural London English (MLE) (so academic) or Jafaican (not so much fake-Jamaican as a new product muddling Turkish, Arabic, Punjabi fragments)? Martha and Franklyn's conversation is born of fragments and possibilities.

My Day in Court

In the course of the trial of the Mangrove nine, Frank Crichlow is tempted by his barrister to break away from the other defendants: to plead guilty to lesser charges and deflect the brunt of the prosecution onto them. The barrister is persuasive, and it seems briefly that Crichlow is persuadable, were it not for the interventions of Altheia Jones-LeCointe and others, who help him to realize the effects of this divisive strategy. There is, then, a complexity around his character and its development. He is trying to run a restaurant, not to be a champion of civil rights, as Howe's closing remarks acknowledge. The camera records moments of self-realization on his face at various stages and especially as the court case proceeds. This development stands out because the issues the film raises are of flagrant injustice, and the positions and roles of the agents are relatively clear-cut. With the third of the films, *Red, White and Blue*,[16] however, the depth of self-doubt and personal struggle in the face of moral conflict come more to the fore, in a manner suggestive of the Black *Bildungsroman*. The film falls within the genre of the television police series, which had acquired a new realism in British broadcasting with *Z Cars*, which ran from 1962 to 1978, written initially by Allan Prior. The familiar living-room presence of the central characters in the series and its unglamorized stories of ordinary crime would very likely have played a part in the lives and education of the people depicted in *Red, White and Blue*.

The film dramatizes the experience of Leroy Logan (John Boyega), a young West Indian man working as a research chemist. He has been successful academically and is good at his job. But he is restless with the desire to do something to contribute more directly to his community. Logan exercises at the local athletics track, and the friend he trains with, who is a policeman, asks him why he does not consider joining the force. The idea lingers in Logan's mind, and eventually he takes steps towards this. At about the same time, however, his father, Kenneth (Steve Toussaint), a truck-driver, is involved in an incident with the police. He has parked his large lorry in a relatively narrow suburban street while he is buying some food from a kiosk. As he turns round, he sees two policemen standing by his vehicle. When they tell him he is parked illegally, he insists that he is not and, quoting the regulations, proceeds to fetch a tape measure from his cab and to measure its distance from the white line in the middle of the road. While he is doing this, one of them rushes him from behind and pins him against the cab.

They proceed to beat him up badly, and he ends up in hospital. When, in real life, though this is not obvious in the film, Leroy went to visit him, he was unable to recognize him amongst the other patients because his father had been so badly injured.

The conflict of loyalties is painful. Leroy's white friends continue to encourage him to join the force, as does his wife, Gretl (Antonia Thomas), tentatively, and his aunt (Nadine Marshall), more vociferously—she has long been an important influence. When his father learns his son's intentions, he is horrified.

At his interview for the police, Leroy acquits himself confidently, even flaunting his ability to switch register and switch back: 'there are divisions and misunderstandings, and I think I could change that ... I think we need to look each other in the eye, man to man. Given the chance, we'll soon realize we're not different. I've tried jellied eels, so if the boys are up for it, I'll have em eatin rice'n'peas in no time, I promise you that.' This cuts to Leroy's father, Kenneth, speaking to a lawyer, Mr. Purling, whom he is just showing to the door of their house. 'If you were white, these charges wouldn't stand. Do try to hold onto the fact that you have a tentative case for unlawful arrest.' Kenneth shuts the door and moves to the living room, where the family are sitting at the table, Leroy standing to the side, leaving the remaining chair for his father.

> Leroy: So? What do you think?
> Kenneth: Me not know. Him beat on bout how me case tentative.
> Daughter: Imagine. And he's supposed to be on our side.
> Leroy: There's a whole heap of charges, Dad. Obstructing the highway, assaulting an officer, resisting arrest ...
> Kenneth: So what you sayin?
> Leroy: No I'm ...
> Daughter: D'you ... Do you think it would help to get in touch with the Commission for Racial Equality, see if they can ... ?
> Leroy: No, Dad, she's right. It would help to get the backing of an organization like that.
> Kenneth: Just make the solicitor gwaan an do im job. I want my day in court! I wanna see that dutty police officer in the dock! I want to look in em eye!

Mr. Logan finds out that his son is going ahead with his application to the police when two police officers come to the house to verify the address. Horrified, he shuts the door in their face. Immediately after, he is banging on the door of his sister's house:

> Kenneth: Is you put that raas foolishness in my son head! (shouting) You see what them done to me, but you still fill up him head with nonsense! Leroy is MY son! Not yours ...

> Aunt: Firs ting, Leroy is not a boy! Second, how the hell you come to my front door?!
> Kenneth: Who else cosy up with the police like she an them side? … What idiot sense em make fe stoop an join ah police? Man av PhD!
> Aunt: Oh! So you feel it's my fault!
> Kenneth: Is you make em gwaan so. Is only you want work with em police and friend them up and God knows what else, because yuh nah have nah man fe sweet yuh.
> Aunt: Talk about me? Look at your stubborn self. Don't watch me! Yuh take air from your wife's mout so she can't breathe. Treat your daughter-in-law like dirt. Make your son pack up and leave. Now step from my door! (She shuts the door in his face.) Damn raas!

When Leroy is leaving home to go to the residential police college for his initial training, his father says, at the final moment, that he will drive him there. They drive, in silence, and we hear the Bee Gees' 'How can you mend this broken man? / How can a loser ever win? Please help me mend my broken heart and let me live again.' When they arrive, we see Leroy getting out of the car, his brief gesture of affection to his father apparently refused, and walking towards the steps ahead. His father gets out of the car and calls: 'Leroy!' Leroy looks back, and his father walks up to him. Still from inside the car, through the windscreen, we see them talking briefly and embracing. Then his father stands and watches as Leroy walks up the steps.

When the day of his father's court case arrives, and the family are waiting to enter the court, they receive surprising news.

> Kenneth: Are they ready for us?
> Mr. Purling: Not quite, Kenneth. The police have officially capitulated. We will not be going to court.
> Leroy: Wait, how?
> Hyacinth (sister): Just like that?
> Gretl: What's going on?
> Mr. Purling: Well, you've a fair judge, and a substantial number of witnesses, plus the fact that the police have dropped all charges against you. If I'm perfectly honest, I think they knew they'd lose.
> Gretl: Dropped all charge? But he's innocent.
> Mother: So that's it? We won?
> Mr. Purling: It's not so much a win as a recognition of their chances of victory, Daphne. They'll settle out of court. You'll probably get a substantial payout, Kenneth. I'll warrant they'll want to avoid the publicity … given your son.

Leroy: What do you say, Dad. They're playing a long game ... It's not ideal, but it's better than nothing.

Kenneth: I want my day in court. I want look in dem eye. That's what them promise, right? In this country? Your day.

Gretl: Yes, they do.

Mr. Logan walks off to the toilets. After a few moments, Leroy goes to find him. He looks through the door, and we see the double-image of his father—his back and his face in the mirror—with Leroy, diminutive in reflection, like a child between two images, looking at him but unable to say anything, his father approaching, his father receding.

In his early days in the force, Leroy finds himself treated by other police officers with contempt and provocation, subjected to malicious pranks and exposed to real danger, and he agonizes over whether he has done the right thing. In the last scene of the film, Leroy seems exhausted. He comes in at night and finds his father sitting in a darkened room, drinking white rum. He sits and pours himself a glass.

Kenneth: My mudda. Let me tell you what my mudda used to say to me. She said: 'Son, if I walk past a cemetery, and I see you did grave, an that's all you can do cos you av no learnin,' ... she says 'I will be upset. But if I pass by there, an you digging graves ... with an education ... then that is what you choose to do ... an I must support that.' My mudda, boy. You know how I find. The world, it just ... move forward. Always do. Big change! That is a ... slow-turning wheel.

Leroy: Sometimes, I think, the earth needs to be scorched, replanted, so something good will come of it. Something good.

He holds his glass out to his father, and they touch glasses and drink. As the credits run through, we hear Kris Kristofferson's 'For the Good Times'. This is mutual acknowledgement and redemption of a kind. When the credits end, we see the monochrome photograph of a boy, perhaps twelve years old, holding a bike, fixed to the handlebars of which is a Union Jack. The monochrome photograph stands in counterpoint to the title of the film, which names the colors of empire. The photograph puts some black in the Union Jack.[17]

The film does not show the illustrious though far from untroubled career in the police that Logan went on to lead. Once again this is an important holding back on McQueen's part.

Care

When Alex Wheatle (Sheyi Cole), as a young man, walks through the prison and enters—or rather is abruptly pushed into—his prison cell, he finds that his cellmate is a Rastafarian, Simeon (Robbie Gee).[18] The man welcomes him but explains, apologizing, that he, Simeon, must have the lower bunk on account of 'the proximity to the shitter', the open toilet in the cell. He has bad diarrhea as he is on hunger strike. He is welcoming nevertheless: 'Anything you want, just … just help yourself.'

Alex, at the age of about ten, walks into the care home where he lives. He is surprised by the care worker—'Auntie', a middle-aged English woman—who comes towards him purposefully and slaps him violently around the face. 'Do you want to end up in hell? Is that what you want? Cos that's precisely what's going to happen if you carry on playing up! Now I know you've been fighting.' She twists his ear. 'You get up them stairs and wash them dirty little hands before dinner! And you go straight to bed. I don't wanna hear a word from you tonight. You understand?' 'Yes, Auntie', the boy replies tearfully.

As we watch Alex in the dormitory in the night, when he realizes he has wet his bed, we hear a report being read. We have already had an intimation of this in the opening titles of the film, which are in a tired, typewritten, Courier-like font, the main title underlined, on white paper.

> Alex Alphonso Wheatle, born 3rd January 1963. Alphonso, an illegitimate child, was received into care under Section 1 of the Children's Act 1948 on the 17th April 1964, as the private foster mother by whom he was placed by his putative father, was unable to continue caring for him. His mother, Mrs G, a married woman, deserted him at birth. He was placed in a council nursery initially and transferred in February 1966 to the children's home where he is now living.

'Wheatle's wet his bed again. Auntie!' 'You dirty little bastard', says Auntie, slapping him again around the face. 'As if I don't do enough for you. I'm sick to death of your disgusting behavior.' She forces a soiled cloth into his mouth. 'What have I done to deserve you? You are a horrible, nasty little boy.'

In the prison cell, Alex is sitting on the top bunk in the semidarkness, and there is the sound of diarrhea. Finding the stench unbearable, Alex curses and threatens Simeon and, in the end, physically attacks him. The Rastafari calmly overpowers him and holds him firmly in his arms, eventually stilling his frenzy.

> Simeon: Listen, man. I want to hear. What is your story?
> Alex: My story?
> Simeon: What?
> Alex: I ain't got no frickin story.

> Simeon: All right. All right. All right. All right. All right. All right. Listen. All night me have, and my ears is fully open. Huh? So just start at the beginning.

These are Simeon's words—'Simeon', as the Bible tells us, the one who listens to the word of God, and now the one who cannot, or *will* not, digest the food he is given, the one who knows that education lies elsewhere.

The scene cuts to a close-up of a cassette player. The boys are now about fourteen, and there are just a few of them in the class and no teacher. The two boys at the cassette player are listening. 'What is this music?' asks Alex. 'Reggae music.' 'What, the song?' 'Nah, not the song. Why, do you like it?' 'I love it!' Alex answers. The song is in fact 'Satta Massagana' by The Abyssinians; the Amharic '*Satta Massagana*' translates as 'He Gave Praise'. A white boy at the other side of the room, almost frantic with agitation, shouts out at them: 'Turn that coon wog crap off! We ain't in Africa now.' 'What are you gonna do, fool?' says Alex, and there is a fight. Two teachers rush in and overpower Alex and take him out of the room. They put him in a straitjacket, leaving him lying on the floor.

The telling of Alex's story is achieved in a kind of stream of consciousness, through the intercutting of scenes from childhood with where he is now.

> Alex: Why are you even here, dread?
> Simeon: I was arrested at the gates of Westminster Abbey with a pickaxe, big so. Me tell their judge me intent on destroying the tomb of Edward the Confessor in retaliation for the desecration of all the Egyptian king by the European man. Me gonna bruk it up. He give me six months.
> Alex: So you're serious about your stuff then, innit?
> Simeon: Rasta is not … is not a religion. Is my life.
> Alex: What are you writing?
> Simeon: Why you ask me that?
> Alex: No reason.
> Simeon: Me write some. Just notes, man. I don't really have the talent. What me blessed with is for the love of reading. Readin's what shaped my life.
> Alex: Is that your family?
> Simeon: Yeah. The woman in the white dress are me mother. The minister's sister.
> Alex: Keep in touch?
> Simeon: Not for a long while now, no. Cha! Nuff bout me now. Me never suffer like you, you know. You know me end up in a prison, right? So come on, youth, man, what happened to you?
> Alex: I took a wrong turn.

> Simeon: No, man. Listen up now. Not one man, woman or a child ever learned anything in life without making a mistake.
> Alex: For me, it was always about the music. That was it, dread.
> Simeon (sings): 'One good thing about the music / When it hits you, you feel no pain.'[19]

We need some history. 'If yuh don't know yuh paass, how can yuh know yuh fewtcha?' During his reign (1042–1066), Edward the Confessor initiated the building of Westminster Abbey, the first Romanesque building in England, the place where his remains still lie. He was recognized supposedly for his piety, but also for his zeal in suppressing the Welsh and the Scots. It was a still relatively local colonialism that, almost a thousand years later, precipitated the Troubles in Northern Ireland and the hunger strike of IRA prisoners at the Maze Prison. *Hunger* (2007), McQueen's first feature film, addressed this topic.[20] Those who were held had asked to be treated as political prisoners, but this was refused. Had this been granted, they would, amongst other things, have been allowed to wear their own clothes. Refusing to wear the prison uniform, they wore nothing but the blankets from their beds, and they smeared excrement on the walls of their cells. So, in *Hunger* and in *Small Axe* the 'stench' of colonialism extends from metaphor to this literal expression of oppression. Simeon knows this history.

But why is Alex even here? In the early hours of Sunday, 18 January 1981, fire broke out at a house party in New Cross, south-east London. The blaze killed thirteen Black people, aged between fourteen and twenty-two, and two years later one survivor took his own life. It was described, thirty years later, by Darcus Howe as 'the blaze we cannot forget'.[21] There was outrage at the handling of the incident by the police and the media, which rejected allegations of arson and concluded that the fire had started by accident in the home. The New Cross Massacre Action Committee, which Howe had been called upon to organize, held a demonstration, during which many people were arrested. Alex was one of them.

The film presents these events through a series of black-and-white still images, accompanied by a reading by Linton Kwesi Johnson of his poem 'New Crass Massahkah'. Here is an excerpt:

> But wait
> You not remember how the whole of
> Black Britain did wrack with grief?
> How the whole of Black Britain
> Did turn a melancholy blue?
> Not the passable blue
> Of the murderer's eyes
> But like the smoke of gloom
> On that cold Sunday morning.
> But stop

> You no remember how the whole of
> Black Britain did turn a fiery red?
> Not the callous red
> Of the killer's eyes
> But red with rage
> like the flames of the fire.

With the contemplation of the photographs and the poem, there is a progression in the film from introspective stream of consciousness to more public forms of recollection and recovery of the past. There is also the symbolism of digestion. Simeon's refusal to eat is not only a tactic designed to force recognition of political oppression; it is also a more visceral recoil at the education he has been given—an education manifest in the very buildings and memorialization he sought to attack, with their ceremonial inscription of power. He cannot stomach this. He hungers for something different.

'What me blessed with is for the love of readin', says Simeon. 'Readin's what shaped my life.' Witnessing Alex's cynicism about his prospects, Simeon urges him not to be overwhelmed by tribulation. 'Free yourself from the negativity, man ... There's enough talk of ism an schism an racism. Me no defend nobody against the charge of racism ... But the main thing you have to worry about in dis here country is the system of class and classism.' He explains the economy of exploitation and suffering of Black people, from slavery to the limited prospects for some children in inner-city schools today. 'You have to supplement what em teach you by teaching yourself ... You have to unlearn what you have learn.' He offers Alex all the books he has in the cell and hands him the one he thinks he should start with: *The Black Jacobins* by C.L.R. James.

'It was always about the music', Alex says, and this leads to a more sustained narrative of his years living in Brixton as a young man. He fancies he might write a song, and comes up with some lines and a dirge-like refrain, repeating the words 'the uprising'. In the closing scene however, he meets a friend he has not seen for some time, who quickly persuades him to buy a typewriter. In fact, Alex Wheatle was to become a writer of teenage fiction, and one of his novels has the title *The Uprising*.[22] Plain type on white paper returns at the end of the film to reveal not the conditions of Alex's birth, the problems he presents, the care he has received, but rather that

```
Alex Wheatle has written over 15 novels for young
   adults.
He has received many awards including an MBE for
   services to literature.
```

Reading

In the opening pair of chapters in *Philosophy the Day after Tomorrow*, Cavell's attention is turned to terms of criticism and praise. In 'Something out of the Ordinary', Cavell examines an early sequence from the 1953 Vincente Minnelli film *The Band Wagon*. The sequence depicts the return to Broadway of an aging song-and-dance man, Tony Hunter (Fred Astaire), whose career has faded and who is hoping to make a comeback. As the train approaches New York, some fellow passengers, unaware that Hunter is in the carriage, are talking about him and saying he is a has-been. When the train arrives at the station, reporters are gathered, a red carpet laid out. He preens himself imagining this is for him, only to find himself upstaged by Ava Gardner, who is also on the train. Occasions of the withholding and expression of praise raise questions throughout the film concerning what constitutes genuine praise, which Cavell elaborates elsewhere in a variety of contexts. What is accuracy in critical appraisal? What is the place within criticism of affirmation and celebration? What connection, if any, with religious praise?[23]

Affirmation and celebration find their opposites in cynicism, negativity, and debunking. In 'The Interminable Shakespearean Text', Cavell turns to a literary critic he admires, Kenneth Burke, whose 'theory of the criticism of books' contrasts with the 'almost total pedagogical successes, for periods over the twentieth century, of logical positivism, and critical close reading, and deconstruction'.[24] Burke's theorizing has a homespun air, which rarely relates itself to prevailing philosophies of literature or language. Cavell aligns this approvingly with the dismantling of doctrines found in J.L. Austin. My—I think, parallel—unease is with a similar pedagogical dominance of thinking about race. Critical Race Theory is to be acknowledged and valued, but its praise slips quickly into pedagogically convenient orthodoxy: we know in advance what all this is about, we are authorized to decry, debunk, and explain away, and we do this with the 'elations of indictment'.[25] This dulls critical reception of history, politics, and works of art. Simeon has doubts about the 'isms', emphasizes attention to class, and recommends history and C.L.R. James.

Pedagogical dominance is evident also in preoccupations of a certain kind with authenticity, arising, as Cavell shows, in textual controversies attaching to different versions of Shakespeare's plays. Expert critics direct their energy towards determining the authentic and authoritative version; Cavell explores possibilities opened by bringing different sources together, and hence, the expert complains, he is guilty of conflation. Criticism of conflation depends, however, upon a false view of what language is—that is, that the primary function of words is to name things. This loses sight of what we do with words. Cavell defends conflation in broader terms too, linking it with Emerson's remarks in 'Experience' (paraphrased here): experience makes impressions on us, and these impressions are a product of mood, tone, and occasion. Meaning is made in different cases. It depends upon actions and actors.[26]

Cavell's appreciation of actors is surely matched by McQueen's eulogy to the actors in *Small Axe*. The cast list includes actors who may be familiar from other films or TV shows, connecting the series through developing constellations. Once again, meaning is generated through dynamic crossings between the films. There are crossings of peculiar pertinence, moreover, between the actors' roles and performances, and their actions in real life. 'Every Black person understands and realizes the first time you were reminded you were black.' These words come from an impromptu speech made by John Boyega on 3 June, 2020 at the Hyde Park protest rally over the killing of George Floyd. Impassioned and emotional, he urged the protesters to remain peaceful; and he went on that same day to shoot scenes depicting the contempt and provocation from his fellow police officers suffered by Leroy Logan.[27]

Religion is neither prominent nor thematized in the films, but it is part of the fabric of the communities we see. Sometimes it is there in a gently comedic way. When Kenneth Logan's sister says grace at the family meal, she prays for Leroy, about to leave for his police training, but does not miss the opportunity to add: 'and grant us the wisdom to accept his decision, even as we struggle in our ignorance to understand it'. At the barb of 'ignorance', Kenneth opens his eyes. And then, in *Lovers Rock*, in more visual terms, there is the man who gets off the bus. The cross carried by the West Indian community can be folded and carried on a London bus.

Small Axe, then, foils formulaic responses and invites something more than orthodoxy of thinking. The series arises from McQueen's reflection on his own life and circumstances: these five acts in a discontinuous whole depict episodes in the lives of West Indians in England during the decades spanning the late 1960s and early 1980s, ending around the time of the Brixton Riots, just two years into Margaret Thatcher's eleven-year reign. The conception and production of the films took place during a decade when the UK, a country divided, voted to leave the EU, when the Windrush scandal exposed hypocrisy in the administration of British citizenship, when it became necessary again to affirm that Black lives matter, and when monuments were destroyed. McQueen turns away from the big screen and to the domestic medium of television. The last and most autobiographical of the episodes depicts something like his own experience of growing up in the outer, nondescript western suburbs of London, and of education stymied by dyslexia.

This final episode, called *Education*,[28] focuses on Kingsley (Kenyah Sandy), a twelve-year old boy who, because he cannot read, is removed from normal school and sent to a school for the 'educationally sub-normal'. From his family life it is clear that Kingsley is intelligent and thoughtful. His older sister and, increasingly, his mother recognize this, while his more taciturn father's response is that the boy needs to learn a trade. The film's opening suggests a yearning in the child: Kingsley, in rapt attention, is looking up at the stars on the ceiling of the Planetarium in London. This aspiration hints at a Nietzschean aristocracy of the self, and his name perhaps intimates something of this, recalling also the suggestion of kingliness in the name Leroy Logan. Early in *Red, White and Blue*, the camera looks, with Leroy, down a microscope. There are wonders above and below.[29]

His mother is politicized by what has happened. At her initiative, he escapes into education through a voluntary Saturday morning school, which begins with breakfast and where, in *Kings and Queens of Africa for Children*, he discovers that Black people also have a history. McQueen himself went to the first such Saturday school, in Hammersmith in the early 1970s. Kingsley quickly learns to read, and the closing scene shows him avidly reading this book, over breakfast, at home. He reads out loud. His parents watch, his big sister helps when he falters over a word, his parents catch one another's eye.

As he reads and the scene closes, as the credits come up, the music comes in, extraordinarily: it is Bach's *St John Passion*, the sublime final chorus, before the closing chorale. And—as we see again the starry heavens—it brings with it a kind of redemption...

> Ruht wohl, ihr heiligen Gebeine,
> Die ich nun weiter nicht beweine,
> Ruht wohl
> und bringt auch mich zur Ruh!
> Das Grab, so euch bestimmet ist
> Und ferner keine Not umschließt,
> Macht mir den Himmel auf
> Und schließt die Hölle zu.
>
> Rest well, sacred bones,
> for which I no longer weep—
> rest well,
> and bring me also to my rest.
> The grave that is yours,
> that holds no further suffering,
> for me opens heaven
> and closes hell.

But if—in the film—you listen carefully, you hear something else. Is it interference? A faulty connection? ... You hear a quiet, rhythmic tapping or clapping, in a barely obtrusive syncopation with the music. Anyway, you are hearing something new. And you realize ... you wonder, is this Kingsley listening too, listening and tapping in his ignorance of the protocols of this sacred piece, but noticing the beat, hearing the falling cadences, the strong bass line, and moving with the sound? This closing is praise, and the film ends in praise. Catharsis in our living rooms and a cross carried on a bus.

Reflecting on the films, McQueen has said that these are not local but national heroes: the films show these 'British subjects—how they fought and won against adversity'.[30] But, as I have suggested at various points, the films hold back from any full statement of achievement: they hold back to make way for a different kind of praise.

The testimony, the trial, are over (... that testimony, that trial), but *Small Axe* continues as a testament. Like the history it depicts, it plays its part, here on this screen in front of me. It tries its audience, just as continuing injustice puts us continually all on trial. Is this too high-minded, too pious? 'Try me.' Try ME. Thoreau tries his neighbors with his questions—irritates, bores, tires them, puts them on trial.[31] Reality, he tells us, may cleave us in two: 'If you can stand right fronting and face to face to a fact, you will see the sun glimmer on both its surfaces, as if it were a cimeter, and feel its sweet edge dividing you through the heart and marrow, and so you will happily conclude your mortal career.'[32]

'If you are the big tree, we are the small axe.' Originating in an African proverb, this expression became familiar through the 1973 Bob Marley song, 'Small Axe', from the 1973 album *Burnin'*. We see and hear the fall of the blade as Frank Crichlow cuts through the yam. We picture Simeon, pickaxe raised at the doors of Westminster Abbey. But the axe can also be 'acts', given the silencing of the T in the patois. The wielded axe cuts and divides, laying bare both blatant and subtle forms of exclusion and demoralization inflicted on Black people by British society. To make a film, a film in five acts, with this critical edge, you must begin by borrowing an axe, but you can return the axe sharper than when you borrowed it. McQueen borrows the best practices of television documentary and drama, melding these with his skills as filmmaker and artist. The montage of the sequence works with spiraling effect, culminating with *Education*, which demonstrates painfully the failures of education but leads from them to a possible catharsis.

During the Harlem Renaissance, Alain Locke claimed that culture is appropriation. McQueen's appropriation is not only stylistic and methodological but found in the substance of the experiences he recounts. There is an uneasiness in this that should be felt in the reception of the films—an uneasiness often covered over in the familiar strident voices raised in discourses of antiracism, and in the powerful responses they too easily evoke, in art, the academy, and political life. Yet how far can the series avoid the appropriation of antiracist expression by a sympathetic, right-minded liberal culture, which, in the administration and structures of its art and presentation, is inclined to neutralize the political point of the works that are its ostensible concerns? This is a risk that the series must run. But if you can sit right fronting and face a fact …

Sit in front of your television screen, and perhaps you will find the sweet edge of *Small Axe* dividing you to expose something different. This is a turning of response, turning you over, turning you in, towards possibilities of thinking something new. These small acts provide the glimmer of new ways of living with race. Hence, of democracy too.

Notes

1 Screenplay: Alastair Siddons and Steve McQueen. Director for the series: Steve McQueen.
2 See Margaret Busby, 'Frank Crichlow Obituary', *The Guardian*, September 26, 2010, www.theguardian.com/world/2010/sep/26/frank-crichlow-obituary-civil-rights-activist.

3   The Profumo Affair is itself the subject of a TV series, *The Trial of Christine Keeler*, created by Amanda Coe and first aired on the BBC in 2019 (Ecosse Films), and an earlier film, *Scandal*, directed by Michael Caton-Jones (1989).
4   'What You Need to Know about Small Axe on BBC One', interview with Sarah Hutton, *Good Housekeeping*, November 10, 2020, www.goodhousekeeping.com/uk/lifestyle/a34093859/small-axe-cast-plot-air-date-spoilers/.
5   Stanley Cavell, *Philosophy the Day after Tomorrow* (Cambridge, MA: The Belknap Press of Harvard University Press), 1.
6   Ludwig Wittgenstein, *Philosophical Investigations*, trans. Elizabeth Anscombe, P.M.S. Hacker, and Joachim Schulte, revised 4th edition by Hacker and Schulte (Oxford: Blackwell, 2009).
7   These sections comprise Part I of the *Investigations*. Part II, compiled by his literary executors, has a different form.
8   Wittgenstein, *Philosophical Investigations*, P3.
9   Wittgenstein, *Philosophical Investigations*, P4.
10 Paul Gilroy, *Black Atlantic* (Cambridge, MA: Harvard University Press, 1995).
11 Aimé Césaire, *Moi, laminaire* (Paris: Seuil, 1982), 30.
12 Sandra Laugier, 'The Ethics of Care as a Politics of the Ordinary', *New Literary History*, vol. 46 (2015), 217–40, 217.
13 Raymond Williams, *Television: Technology and Cultural Form* (London: Routledge, 1974), 151.
14 Stanley Cavell, *The Claim of Reason: Wittgenstein, Skepticism, Morality, and Tragedy* (Chicago: University of Chicago Press, 1979), 28.
15 Screenplay: Courttia Newland and Steve McQueen.
16 Screenplay: Courttia Newland and Steve McQueen.
17 Paul Gilroy, *There Ain't No Black in the Union Jack: The Cultural Politics of Race and Nation* (Chicago: University of Chicago Press, 1987). Gilroy was a consultant for the series.
18 *Alex Wheatle* is the fourth film in the series. Screenplay: Alastair Siddons and Steve McQueen.
19 Bob Marley and The Wailers, 'Trenchtown Rock', 1971.
20 The Irish Republican Army was created in 1919 to halt British rule in Northern Ireland. It played a prominent part in 'the Troubles', which continued from 1969 for thirty years.
21 Darcus Howe, 'New Cross: The Blaze We Cannot Forget', *The Guardian*, January 17, 2011, www.theguardian.com/commentisfree/2011/jan/17/new-cross-fire-we-cant-forget.
22 See www.alexwheatle.com/.
23 Cavell considers praise and race in 'Fred Astaire Asserts the Right to Praise'. See also my 'Race and Repression in a Dance Routine', *Ethics and Education*, vol. 10, no. 3, 327–42.
24 Stanley Cavell, 'The Interminable Shakespearean Text', in *Philosophy the Day after Tomorrow*, 40.
25 Cavell, 'The Interminable Shakespearean Text', 45.
26 Ralph Waldo Emerson, 'Experience,' *Essays, Second Series*, 1844. In *The Essential Writings of Ralph Waldo Emerson*, ed. Bruce Atkinson, with an introduction by Mary Oliver (New York: Modern Library Classics, 2000).

27 McQueen interviewed by Joy Francis, Words of Colour Productions: www.youtube.com/watch?v=Hjd37Dtyiss.
28 Screenplay by Alastair Siddons and Steve McQueen.
29 It is difficult to resist the association here with images and ideas in Terrence Malick's *The Tree of Life*. Malick's doctoral dissertation was supervised by Cavell.
30 See note 27.
31 Henry David Thoreau, *Walden and Civil Disobedience* (Harmondsworth: Penguin, 2012 [1854]), 64.
32 Thoreau, *Walden and Civil Disobedience*, 142.

PART IV
POPULAR TV AND ITS GENRES

13

The Event of Television: Sitcoms, Superheroes, and *WandaVision*

Stephen Mulhall

Despite its name, the Marvel Cinematic Universe (hereafter 'MCU') has always been involved in television, in its broadcast, cable, and streaming forms. Its centre of gravity during the first three phases of its development has certainly been in the twenty-three movies that collectively constitute 'The Infinity Saga', in which short sequences of films each focusing on individual superheroes (such as Iron Man, Thor, or Captain America) converge as their protagonists come together as the Avengers, and thereafter generate a complex set of self-contained but interrelated adventures involving various subgroups of these characters, eventually culminating in a two-part, six-hour conflict with the Titan Thanos, in which the universe first suffers the loss of half of its population (when Thanos gains control of all the Infinity Stones, whose individual vicissitudes helped interlink the films' storylines), before the remaining Avengers manage to overcome their enemy and recover those lost.

Even during this period, however, the MCU reached repeatedly from cinemas into television. *Agents of S.H.I.E.L.D.*, *Agent Carter*, and *Inhumans* all aired on ABC; *Daredevil*, *Jessica Jones*, *Luke Cage*, and *Iron Fist* streamed on Netflix as individual series before combining as *The Defenders* (a miniature, wholly televisual analogue of the MCU's first phase); and *Cloak & Dagger* appeared on the cable channel Freeform. Moreover, the new, fourth phase of the MCU, conceived after Marvel Studios was integrated into Walt Disney Studios, is even more fully committed to televisual formats. Although this was to some extent an artefact of pandemic-imposed delays in cinematic release dates, the Disney+ streaming service hosted the first element in this phase, *WandaVision*, which was quickly succeeded by *The Falcon and the Winter Soldier* and *Loki*, all before the first film in phase four—*Black Widow*—made it to the big screen; and since then, the appearance of further cinematic and televisual instalments has accelerated in tandem.

One way of understanding the multimedia nature of the MCU is as the inevitable consequence of interlocking economic, technological, and cultural change. When corporate entities have repeatedly subsumed smaller institutions each with a track record in specific media, and the screens in our living rooms, laptops, and phones can with equal facility display content originally created for cinema, broadcast, and streaming, then the way to maximize the commercial value of intellectual property such as that controlled by Marvel Studios is to diversify into as many communicative media as possible, all the while ensuring that the identity of the brand or franchise overwhelms any lingering superficial differences between the media thereby colonized. On this interpretation, the omnipresence of MCU product both indicates and reinforces the increasing irreality of any distinction between different audio-visual media; the MCU's multidimensional cultural imperialism demonstrates the utter irrelevance of inherited assumptions about (and so inherited accounts of) the conceptual and aesthetic distinctiveness of television—in comparison to cinema, and more generally.

But that way of understanding this cultural behemoth is not compulsory. For it might rather be that the MCU has been able to establish and maintain its dominance precisely because those who create its films and shows have a very sophisticated understanding of what differentiates television from cinema (and so what links them), and have utilized their grasp of the distinctive aesthetic possibilities of each medium in shaping the work they do in both. It is this possibility that I will explore here, with the help of *WandaVision*.

In doing so, I will make extensive use of an essay entitled 'The Fact of Television' that Stanley Cavell published in 1982—long before the economic, technological, and cultural developments that have had such an impact on the evolution of television and its place in our lives over the last two or three decades.[1] That fact alone might lead one to suspect its irrelevance to contemporary debates in television studies. If Cavell's range of televisual examples was necessarily restricted to US shows (and UK imports) from the 1970s on his country's main broadcast channels prior to the rise of premium cable services, then how could his attempts to characterize the medium and media of television (together with their material basis) in relation to its distinctive aesthetic possibilities have any bearing on a streaming-dominated medium whose current claims to aesthetic interest have been radically transformed by what commentators have called 'Complex TV' or 'New Television'—showrunner-controlled, long-form narrative works of art such as *The Sopranos*, *The Wire*, and *Breaking Bad*, whose enduring influence on current television is so evident?

And if the object of Cavell's account might be thought to have mutated sufficiently to outflank him, the same could be said of the discursive fields to which his account was intended to contribute. For he focuses on the aesthetics of television by investigating the medium as it has disclosed itself in its distinctive achievements, in a manner familiar from the modernist movements in American painting, sculpture, and literature in Cavell's youth and early adulthood. Philosophical aesthetics in general and television studies in particular, by contrast, are currently well populated with those sceptical of the elitist ideological presuppositions they detect in the very idea of evaluative hierarchies, and with those dismissive of the idea that there is such a thing as the essential nature of the televisual medium (let alone that its distinctive aesthetic possibilities might stand in some internal relation to that nature).[2] In a world where visual images are primarily captured, edited, and otherwise manipulated digitally, and displayed on screens of any size and shape from multiple input formats, it is hardly surprising to observe significant and growing support for the idea that television studies, like film studies, should be subsumed within a much broader field of investigation concerning 'the moving image' or 'the screened image'.

Of course, these sceptics do not lack for opponents, and some of the most interesting recent work in the field has come from them. Ted Nannicelli's *Appreciating the Art of Television* is exemplary in this respect, and I shall return to it.[3] In my view, for philosophers such as Nannicelli, Cavell's essay can and should provide some very congenial support—when it is properly understood. For even if it is wrong to claim that this essay has been largely neglected in television studies,[4] it is at least arguable that its full significance and implications have been missed, and on occasion even by those well versed in other aspects of Cavell's body of work. For example, Martin Shuster's interesting recent book *New Television*[5] gives Cavell a key orienting role; but his way of inheriting the essay on television seems to me to be severely, and peculiarly, limited. Hence, one important aim of my essay is to hold open an alternative way of inheriting Cavell: although I think that that alternative allows us to better understand both the MCU and *WandaVision*, I also believe that it can be far more generally useful.

Cavell on Media, Material, and Modes of Perceiving: Film

'The Fact of Television' is a very dense and demanding essay, so achieving a perspicuous survey of it is challenging, and I will not be able to touch on every interesting aspect. Instead, I will focus on the fact that Cavell there means to characterize television in three interrelated ways: as a medium with a distinctive material basis, exhibiting a distinctive form of aesthetic composition, and inviting a distinctive mode of perception. As we shall see, however, none of these levels or registers of characterization is foundational with respect to the other two—none constitutes an independently established basis from which the other characterizations follow by logical implication; neither are any of the three graspable independently of the other two. Hence, light will dawn, if it dawns at all, over the whole.

Furthermore, Cavell clarifies his claims about television by comparing and contrasting it with the corresponding claims about cinema that he had developed elsewhere. This exponentially increases our exegetical difficulties: at the very least, it means that to get a proper grasp on his conception of television, we need to see it against the background of his more extensive engagement with cinema, which is itself grounded in his general approach to philosophical aesthetics. The misunderstandings inherent in some attempts in television studies to learn from 'The Fact of Television' can often, I believe, be traced to the inaccessibility of these broader contexts, and to the sheer complexity of the material each harbours. So what follows, although complicated enough, is really only a first pass—an attempt to provide at least the indispensable minimum for a more productive engagement with Cavell's essay.

Throughout his career, Cavell takes the concept of a medium to be indispensable in differentiating kinds of artwork, and in understanding specific instances of those kinds; but he sees it as referring not simply to a physical material but to a material-in-certain-characteristic-applications, and hence as having a necessarily dual sense. Sound, for example, is not the medium of music in the absence of the art of composing and playing music. Musical works of art are thus not the result of deploying a medium that is defined by its independently given possibilities; for it is only through the artist's successful production of something we are prepared to call a musical work of art that the *artistic* possibilities of that physical material are discovered, maintained, and explored. We can, of course, identify the independently given physical possibilities of sound qua sound, qua physical phenomenon; but for any such possibility to constitute a way of making art, we must actually deploy it to make art—make something recognizable as a work of art from it.

Philosophers tend to think that possibility is prior to actuality—that something being the case presupposes its being possible; but when our concern is with a medium of art, it is less misleading to say that actuality is prior to possibility—that an aesthetic possibility is only established as such by someone actualizing it. And such aesthetic possibilities of sound, without which it would not count as an artistic medium at all, are themselves media of music—ways in which various sources of sound have been applied to create specific artistic achievements, for example in plainsong, the fugue, the aria, or sonata form. They are the strains of convention through which composers have been able to create, performers to practice, and audiences to acknowledge specific works of art.

In effect, Cavell conceives of an artistic medium as analogous to a language:

> A medium is something through which or by means of which something specific gets done or said in particular ways. It provides, one might say, particular ways to get through to someone, to make sense; in art, they are forms, like forms of speech. To discover ways of making sense is always a matter of the relation of an artist to his art, each discovering the other.[6]

An artistic medium mediates between artist and audience member because it is a medium of communication, a vehicle of meaning; and just like linguistic meaning on a Wittgensteinian conception of it, artistic meaning is constituted by a dialectic between conventions and those employing them. Speakers inherit the norms and conventions of the pre-existing public language they share with other speakers; but that language's continued existence depends upon the collective, and so the individual, willingness of speakers to go on with those conventions. in part by projecting them into new circumstances and contexts, some of which might invite or compel them to revise or otherwise question those conventions, disclosing new possibilities or impossibilities of sense-making in the light of the world's unpredictable yieldings and resistances, and speakers' shifting conceptions of the intelligibility of what other speakers say and do. Speakers at once exploit and extend the meanings of words, and so the medium of communication that they constitute; and without their continued willingness to find sense in the ways individual speakers attempt to make sense to one another, there would be no language, no medium of speech. Linguistic conventions accordingly cannot ground or authorize, in any way that guarantees, the success of these attempts; on the contrary, the continued success of those attempts is what the continued viability of those conventions as ways of making sense consists in.

Four aspects of this analogy are worth noting, in relation to specifically artistic media. First, the primary locus of artistic sense-making is the particular communicative act, the specific artwork: this is where the continued viability of a given artistic convention, or the establishment of a new convention, is exhibited or seen to fail. Hence, second, media are essentially historical phenomena: their constituting conventions can alter over time, sometimes radically, and what was essential to their communicative success at one sociocultural moment might prove to be dispensable at a later one. Third, those at whom that communication is directed are necessarily involved in interpreting or making sense of it (as something that someone might intelligibly have meant to say or do); in short, they must engage in acts of criticism. Works of art are inherently criticizable, and criticism is inherent in any relation to a work of art qua artwork. And fourth, the artistic significance of any work cannot be determined by, and so read off from, the possibilities of its medium: not from its physical possibilities, and not from its aesthetic possibilities either (since each new attempt to exploit them *might* reveal their inability, here and now, to support artistic meaning).

Cavell's approach to film—undertaken in a time when all films utilized analogue photographic technology—bears clear marks of this background:

> You can no more tell what will give significance to the unique and specific aesthetic possibilities of projecting photographic images by thinking about them or seeing some, than you can tell what will give significance to the possibilities of paint by thinking about paint or

> by looking some over. You have to think about painting, and paintings; you have to think about motion pictures ...
>
> The first successful movies—i.e., the first moving pictures accepted as motion pictures—were not applications of a medium that was defined by given possibilities, but *the creation of a medium* by their giving significance to specific possibilities. Only the art itself can discover its possibilities, and the discovery of a new possibility is the discovery of a new medium.[7]

On this approach, however, grasping the significance of specific motion pictures is not only the means through which a particular cinematic medium can and must be discovered; it is also the means through which its material basis is displayed. For if the relevant material is to be grasped *as* the basis of the medium and the media of film, only specific achievements of significance within those media can disclose some property of that material as their ground, as a way of conveying that significance, and so as capable of communicating it (or meaningful modifications of it) more generally.

Accordingly, Cavell defines the material basis of the media of movies not as light, or as photographs, or as sequences of photographs projected on delimited flat surfaces, but as 'a succession of automatic world projections'.[8] That characterization very ostentatiously does *not* characterize the physical means by which movies are made in terms that are graspable prior to and independent of viewing any and all films. It rather condenses or encodes the ways in which successful works in the various media of film have given specific point to those physical means, and so disclosed them as capable of such modes of sense-making, according to Cavell's critical account of his encounters with those films in the seventy pages that precede it. The literariness of its mode of perspicuous presentation is Cavell's way of acknowledging this doubled aesthetic mediation (involving his critical appreciation of specific cinematic artworks), and of indicating the extent to which its full implications might outrun their original promptings (as is generally true of aesthetic significance). Cavell's immediate gloss on his formulation brings this out:

> 'Succession' includes the various degrees of motion in moving pictures: the motion depicted; the current of successive frames in depicting it; the juxtapositions of cutting. 'Automatic' emphasizes the mechanical fact of photography, in particular the absence of the human hand in forming these objects and the absence of its creatures in their screening. 'World' covers the ontological facts of photography and its subjects. 'Projection' points to the phenomenological facts of viewing, and to the continuity of the camera's motion as it ingests the world.[9]

It would take a book fully to unpack the significance of those terms, individually and collectively, and to show how their grammar—although initially shaped by analogue cinematic technology—can fruitfully be projected into digital environments.[10] Here, I simply want to emphasize that the whole formulation counts as 'aphoristic', in the sense Cavell defines when interpreting the role of aphorisms in Wittgenstein's later philosophical writing.[11] It is a mode of exhibiting the clarity achieved by exercises of critical appreciation that simultaneously acknowledges the obscurity from which that clarity comes—reflecting not only the dense idiosyncrasy of the layers of sense his account has laid down, but also his sense that there is something constitutively mysterious about cinema's seductiveness and our responsiveness to it. So when Cavell characterizes the material basis of the medium of television, we need to understand that it too functions aphoristically: its obscure clarity aims to condense the results of critical engagement with what he takes to be successful instances of the medium and media of television, whilst acknowledging our enigmatic fascination with it.

In the case of cinema, the relevant media through which the medium and its material basis were disclosed to Cavell—its distinctive modes of aesthetic achievement—were genres, and genres of two particular kinds. The first kind predominates in *The World Viewed*, and is there labelled 'genre-as-cycle'. Cavell arrives at the claim that cycles of films (such as Westerns, horror movies, Civil War movies) constitute a genre, and so an aesthetic possibility of the cinematic medium, in part because they are an apt home for the presentation and investigation of human types—types such as the Villain, the Fallen Woman, or the Sergeant. Such types incarnate human individualities rather than individuals: the actors who realize them embody a distinctively cinematic acknowledgement of human individuation, which emphasizes the separateness of one type of person from all others, rather than their similarity with others of the same type. The other kind of cinematic genre is the principal concern of Cavell's two other book-length studies of film, *Pursuits of Happiness* and *Contesting Tears*:[12] the first focuses on what he calls 'comedies of remarriage', the second on 'melodramas of the unknown woman', and both are instances of what Cavell names 'genre-as-medium'. For both kinds of genre, to belong to a genre is to be a member of it: but whereas one can roughly just see whether or not a film is a member of a genre-as-cycle such as the Western or the horror movie (in part, by recognizing the types that populate it), membership of a genre-as-medium imposes more demanding conditions.

Each comedy of remarriage, for example, shares something with every other genre member; but that is not a property or set of properties but an inheritance, together with a questioning relation to that inheritance, and so to its fellow inheritors: '[T]he members of a genre share the inheritance of certain conditions, procedures and subjects and goals of composition, and ... in primary art each member of such a genre represents a study of these conditions, something I think of as bearing the responsibility of the inheritance.'[13] That inheritance centrally involves what Cavell calls 'a problematic of marriage established in certain segments of the history of theatre'.[14] One source is Shakespearean romantic comedy, in which a young pair overcome individual and social obstacles to their happiness and achieve resolution in marriage; the other is Ibsen's dramatic concern, exemplified in *A Doll House*, with the struggle for equality of consciousness between a woman and a man, and with the necessity and the possibility of reconceiving marriage so that it can be a site of such mutual acknowledgement. Comedies of remarriage remake these sources by casting a married woman as their heroine, and taking as their goal getting their central, older pair together *again*. Marriage is thus represented as inherently subject to the fact or the threat of divorce, hence as worth preserving or recovering only if both parties prove themselves willing to remarry—as if to be married just *is* to be willing to remarry, every day.

If we call this a myth of marriage, then each member of the remarriage genre embodies a way of making sense of that myth's way of making sense of things (of marriage, but also—in the terms of Cavell's construction of it—of sexuality, society, desire, separateness, finitude, and so on). Each such critical evaluation therefore amounts to a critical evaluation of the interpretations of all its fellow members, a view of the myth that is also a view of all the other views of that myth. Since each such film interprets the unifying myth in its own way, one genre member might in principle differ in any given respect from any other; but it can maintain its claim to membership of the genre by compensating for whatever feature of the myth it lacks—for example, by introducing a new clause to its retelling of the myth which proves to contribute to an illuminating re-description of the genre as a whole.[15] We may also, however, find that a new feature brought to the generic conversation by another film negates some central provision of the unifying myth—that it doesn't allow us to tell the same story differently, but rather decisively changes the story. If so (and whether it *is* so is of course a critical judgement rather than the registration of an observable fact), then the genre-as-medium to which this film belongs is different, and an adjacent genre is thereby identified. It is through this kind of negating operation that the melodramas of the unknown woman are derived from the comedies of remarriage.

These operations of compensation and negation are what justify Cavell in calling such genres instances of 'genre-as-medium'. For although all genres count as media insofar as they constitute a possible mode of aesthetic communication, and some instances of genre-as-cycle might significantly question their generic conventions, instances of cinematic genre-as-medium require that that membership is earned by interrogating, testing, and revising the conventions and resources that constitute it in a particularly fundamental way. In each comedy of remarriage, for example, the central pair converse about the very topics (the nature of marriage, sexuality, desire, and individuality) about which the film they inhabit is in conversation with the other remarriage comedies. And because these films make the question of their generic identity such an explicit preoccupation, they not only instantiate the processes of alteration over time that Cavell sees as characteristic of any communicative medium, but contribute centrally and deliberately to it. For each, membership of their genre in effect requires that they acknowledge, interrogate, and modify the nature of that cinematic medium, and so that of every one of its members.

Thus far, we've seen what Cavell takes to be the material basis of the media of cinema (a succession of automatic world projections), and the distinctive form of its aesthetic work (the genre-member mode of composition). What he regards as its distinctive mode of perception he characterizes as 'viewing'—an apparently innocuous term which is in fact precisely as specific as (because it is grammatically dependent on) the constitutive terms of his characterization of the material exploited to achieve this perceptual mode. On Cavell's account, when we look at a photograph of an object, we see that object (the particular real thing present to the camera), and not some surrogate, representative, proxy or likeness of it (as when we see a painting of an object, or a model of it); and that object forms part of a world that is recorded along with it, whose larger extent is cropped from the photograph by the camera. The implied presence and explicit rejection of that larger world are thus as essential to the experience of a photograph as what it explicitly presents; and this phenomenology carries over to screened projections of motion pictures.

This is one sense attaching to Cavell's claim that the material basis of cinema genres is a succession of automatic *world* projections: the cinema screen screens us from the world projected upon it (that world is present to me, whilst I am not present to it); and it does so automatically (rather than as a matter of convention, which is how our absence from the world of a play is achieved). The cinema screen captures a world that is in every feature indistinguishable from reality; but the price we pay for the world's presentness is the screening of human subjectivity from that world. Reality is made present, at the cost of ensuring our absence, which places us in the position of viewing the world of the film as if from without—a position whose conditions are stringent and on first inspection significantly disabling, but that in fact enable certain distinctive kinds of aesthetic achievement:

> The fact that in a moving picture successive film frames are fit flush into the fixed screen frame results in a phenomenological frame that is indefinitely extendible and contractible ... [It] is the image of perfect attention. Early in its history, the cinema discovered the possibility of *calling* attention to persons and parts of persons and objects [e.g., close-ups]; but it is equally a possibility of the medium not to call attention to them but, rather, to let the world happen, to let its parts call attention to themselves according to their natural weight.[16]

Cavell on Media, Material, and Modes of Perceiving: Television

Now I'm finally in a position to summarize Cavell's understanding of the medium of television: its material basis is a current of simultaneous event reception (rather than a succession of automatic world projections); its distinctive form of aesthetic composition is the serial-episode principle (rather than the genre-member principle), and its distinctive perceptual mode is that of monitoring (rather than viewing).

Before unpacking some implications of these interrelated characterizations, I want to emphasize that they presuppose the same understanding of the concepts of 'medium', 'genre', and 'individual work' that are presupposed in Cavell's work on film, which aligns him with those who continue to believe that the concept of a medium remains a useful, even an indispensable, resource in understanding the distinctive aesthetic possibilities of television. Cavell would thus be very much in sympathy with Ted Nannicelli's critical evaluation of Noël Carroll's general scepticism about the very concept of a medium, and in particular about the suggestion that aesthetic achievement in a given medium should or must exploit its distinctive properties.

Nannicelli rightly identifies some strong and highly questionable assumptions that underpin Carroll's scepticism. The first is that any concept of a medium must be a strongly essentialist one—according to which it possesses a timeless, unchanging essence (like a natural kind); and the second is that the only candidates for such essential characteristics must be the medium's physical properties, characterized independently of any communicative or aesthetic employment of them. This second assumption feeds into a third: that anyone who thinks that grasping the nature of a medium is relevant to understanding the nature and value of artistic work conducted within it must believe that any aesthetically excellent work in that medium should or must use only properties of the medium that are unique to it (that is, the physical properties invoked in the second assumption). This allows Carroll to portray all medium-specificity theorists as imagining that a study of paint or photographs will yield a grasp of the aesthetic possibilities of painting or film, and so dictate how an excellent work of art in either medium must be constructed.

Nannicelli, however, points out that media are cultural rather than natural kinds, and so are essentially historical phenomena: they evolve, in the light of similarly evolving human goals and purposes, and their unity or identity over time is thus more akin to that of a family or a nation (a matter of genealogy and teleology rather than physics). More specifically, a medium should be understood as 'a cluster of relatively coherent, stable practices of making things in a particular vehicular medium'.[17] With suitable adjustments for differences of cultural and philosophical contexts, that provisional definition seems to fit with the basic thrust and the fundamental shape of Cavell's approach. Indeed, much of what Cavell says about the relation between the medium and media of film and television and their material bases is as if designed to buttress Nannicelli's critique of Carroll; and his way of arguing that both a medium and its material bases are disclosable as such only by successful individual works of art offers something like the inverse of the logical and conceptual procedures that Carroll assumes to be essential to the work of medium-specificity theorists.

A further meeting of minds emerges when Nannicelli characterizes the distinguishing characteristics of the medium of television. For he claims in particular that '[t]elevision and film differ in virtue of having quite distinct sets of practices for individuating their works temporally, establishing the temporal duration of those works, and affording viewers temporal access to those works'.[18] Televisual works are temporally subdivided in a variety of ways (format, series, season, episode); they can be indefinitely prolonged without losing organic unity; and these features inform both the creative practices of those working in television and the practices of receiving, interpreting, and evaluating those works (as narratives are shaped around commercial breaks, cliffhangers are created between episodes, or the passing of diegetic time is aligned with the real time that elapses between moments of access to the narrative—all formal features that have outlived the original exigencies of televisual broadcasting in the products of cable and streaming services). Such temporal prolongation brings out the priority of the series or the format over the individual episode, and so underlines a central contrast with the medium of film, which Nannicelli claims prioritizes the individual film over any larger aesthetic forms or types to which it belongs.

The consonance with Cavell's account is striking: for his initial characterization of the distinctive media of televisual art focuses on their deployment of a serial-episode principle. Two immediate consequences he draws from this are, first, that unlike film (whose compositional principle is genre-member, which prioritizes the individual member, or at least does not prioritize the genre as what is memorable, treasurable about the medium of film), television prioritizes the format over its instances (we treasure not an individual episode of *I Love Lucy* but the show or the series); and second, that the relation between narration across episodes and narration within an episode in a television series becomes aesthetically significant.

Cavell's point is not that films don't exhibit a mode of serialization: it is rather that it helps in understanding the difference between the medium of film and that of television to consider further how television series differ as media from film serials (of the kind that dominated Saturday morning shows for cinema-going children of a certain age). For a show like *I Love Lucy*, and sitcoms more generally, the default requirement is that the narrative comes to a classical ending each time; but Cavell notes that *Hill Street Blues* was already questioning that feature of the series format, and notes further that the (then merely projected) sequence of *Star Wars* movies questions the standard movie serial demand *not* to come to a classical ending before the final episode. These are plainly aspects of the cluster of features that Nannicelli christens 'temporal prolongation'.

Once these consonances are clearly seen, of course, they might prompt an exploration of more specific differences between Cavell's and Nannicelli's approaches. A Cavellian might, for example, query Nannicelli's explicit wish to separate the business of appreciating the art of television from aesthetically appreciating it.[19] If this simply means acknowledging that appreciating art involves more than focusing on it as a generator of aesthetic experience (a concept which has certainly been given controversial interpretations in the history of the philosophy of art), then this may be eminently sensible. But it is striking that Nannicelli's listing of the features of televisual narrative that result from the medium's temporal prolongation doesn't explicitly declare that their disclosure as aesthetic possibilities of the medium was the work of artistically successful series (leaving it open to his reader to think that their significance can simply be read off from empirical acquaintance with the structure of their 'vehicular medium').

Whatever might result from such explorations, one can only regret the fact that many of Nannicelli's insights and emphases might not have required such extended restatement and defence if Cavell's essay had been properly attended to thirty-five years earlier. But in some ways, there is more for readers of that essay to regret (or perhaps there is regret of a more piercing sort) in the way Cavell's work has been explicitly taken up by an author well aware of Cavell's extended work on film and his essay on television. For although Martin Shuster builds his account of three series falling under his category of 'New Television' on an ontology of television that he derives explicitly from Cavell's writings, he does so by drawing on Cavell's account of the medium and media of film, entirely ignoring his parallel or complementary account of the medium and media of television.

Shuster's general claim is as follows:

> Roughly with *Twin Peaks*, film and television become intertwined historically and aesthetically in ways that suggest a novel medium, a medium that combines elements—automatisms—of each. For example, the procedural and serial elements of television come to be combined with the aesthetic conventions of film and ... with classic film genres like the gangster and the western ... [T]he elaboration as much as the connections between these media that allow for a new one ... fundamentally rests on the ontology sketched in this chapter.[20]

That ontology is of course centred around (the viewing of projected) worlds, even though Shuster must know that in 'The Fact of Television' Cavell explicitly contrasts television with film by characterizing the material basis of televisual media in terms of (the simultaneous reception of) events. So Shuster must believe that 'new television' belies Cavell's event-centred account of television; but he doesn't say why, here or anywhere in his book. Our only clue comes at the single point at which Cavell's television essay is explicitly cited—in footnote 17 to his book's 'Introduction'—where Shuster remarks that 'Cavell largely finds the [televisual] medium wanting'.[21] Neither the belief nor the remark seem justified.

Shuster's belief that new television somehow outstrips or falsifies Cavell's account is not only unargued; it also seems highly questionable. As we have already seen, Cavell's claim that the compositional principle of television is serial-episode (rather than genre-member) provides a perfectly appropriate lens through which to make sense of the long-form narrative structures of shows such as *The Wire* and *Justified*. It places them in the lineage of shows such as *Hill Street Blues*, which were already reformulating the aesthetic significance of the relation between the narrative arcs of individual episodes, seasons, and series (we might call this aspect of television's temporal prolongation the relation between events and their narrative backgrounds or contexts), and thereby implies that the aesthetic and ontological originality of such series (as opposed to their aesthetic worth) are being overestimated. I cede to no one in my admiration for *The Wire*, but what makes it so treasurable is the excellence of the acting, writing, and overall creative control: its compositional structure certainly modifies prior modes of extended dramatic narrative in television, sometimes significantly, but hardly constitutes a reason to declare the creation of a new hybrid medium.

As for Shuster's belief that Cavell disdains the medium of television: to see what is wrong with this, we need to look more closely at the implications of Cavell's emphasis on the interrelatedness of serialization, events, and monitoring.

What mode of attending is captured by the concept of monitoring? Some of its facets are implicit in a security guard's manner of attending, via his bank of monitors, to the empty corridors leading from points of entry to a building; and Cavell emphasizes (long before its explicit exploitation in contemporary digital broadcasting) how the same mode of access to reality underpins that staple of televisual coverage, the sports event:

> [A] network's cameras are ... placed ahead of time. That their views are transmitted to us one at a time for home consumption is merely an accident of economy; in principle, we could all watch a replica of the bank of monitors the producer sees ... When there is a switch of the camera whose image is fed into our sole receiver, we might think of this not as a switch of comment from one camera or angle to another camera or angle, but as a switch of attention from one monitor to another monitor ... The move from one image to another is motivated not, as on film, by requirements of meaning, but by requirements of opportunity and anticipation—as if the meaning is dictated by the event itself. As in monitoring the heart ... —say, monitoring signs of life—most of what appears is a graph of the normal, or the establishment of some reference or base line, a line, so to speak, of the uneventful, from which events stand out with perfectly anticipatable significance. If classical narrative can be pictured as the progress from the establishing of one stable situation, through an event of difference, to the reestablishing of a stable situation related to the original one, [television's] serial procedure can be thought of as the establishing of a stable condition punctuated

by repeated crises or events that are not developments of the situation requiring a single resolution, but intrusions or emergencies—of humour, or adventure, or talent, or misery—each of which runs a natural course and thereupon rejoins the realm of the uneventful.[22]

The classic televisual formats of talk show and sitcom each relate events to the uneventful in their own ways. The former repeatedly stages the ordinary improvisatory business of taking up, maintaining, and concluding conversations with strangers; and each episode in *I Love Lucy* equally exemplifies the situation of that sitcom, with each generated by introducing an element of difference into it—an event that generates the comedy, reaches its natural end, and returns us (characters, watchers, and creators) to our stable starting point.

This idea of (event-)monitoring projects very easily into the contexts of 'new television'. For these series have predominantly gravitated towards the kinds of dramatic situation for which monitoring seems a likely eventuality within the fictional universe (drug dealers, gangsters, and assorted other forms of criminality arrayed against the forces of law and order); monitoring is in fact the basic premise and governing figure of *The Wire*, as its title declares. Their long-form narratives also allow them to follow *Hill Street Blues* by essaying different modes of balance between narratives within an episode and narratives arcing across both episodes and seasons, thereby interrogating the extent to which the accumulation of foreground events can engender slow but fateful shifts within the original 'situations' to which we are returned (problematizing the distinctness of what Cavell calls classical narrative and serial procedure by disclosing uneventful change). More generally, Cavell's illustrative image of banks of monitors transposes itself with equally remarkable ease into the world of streamed television—where coverage of the Olympics takes the form of dozens of simultaneous feeds of different live events, or where my Netflix home page presents me with an unrolling grid of icons for digital box sets, each of which awaits only a switch of my attention to begin unfolding its sequences of narrative events, and which together imply a multiverse of simultaneously accessible currents of serialization.

None of this strikes me as an account driven by, or inciting, disdain for the medium. First, insofar as Cavell takes media to be media of successful artistic communication, to offer his kind of characterization of our televisual medium and media is to presuppose available instances of aesthetic excellence in television whose achievements have disclosed its distinctive artistic possibilities. Second, Cavell insists that it takes real creative talent to invent the situations of good sitcoms, or to bear up under the burden of hosting talk shows, just as the features of everyday human life that such formats acknowledge—our capacity for improvisation, our hunger for the unrehearsed or unscripted, our ability and desire to respond to that which is new or unexpected—hardly constitute human meannesses or impoverishment. But (third) Cavell's clearest declaration of the human and philosophical significance of the way television can relate events to the uneventful lies in his explicit alignment of it with the way in which the *Annales* historians relate events to the uneventful.[23]

In a short essay published at roughly the same time ('The Ordinary as the Uneventful'),[24] Cavell argues that those historians have a legitimate and illuminating interest in getting beyond the familiar dramas of narrative history to the permanencies, or anyway the longer spans, of common life. To get that uneventful background into focus is not to discount the more episodic or momentary events around which other historical narratives turn. It is rather to invite the question of how the shorter and the longer spans of human forms of life relate to each other, and how both relate to their geographical, climatic, and geological (call it their planetary) contexts; and this rethinking of the historicality of our existence amounts to inviting us to reconceive our conception of human existence as such.

In this sense, the *Annales* project warns us that a prevailing concept of the historical event risks theatricalizing human existence, by attracting our attention to flashing, dramatic occurrences in a way that distracts from uneventful processes of change (historical changes of longer duration, and shifts in their non-human context) that may be at least as fateful. The traditional concept of an event allows our attention to be dictated by the precept and example of what a fairly definite public already attaches a definite importance to; the proffered alternative is to let our attention and our discourse determine our real interests for themselves—so that the human being, thinking historically about itself, should interest itself differently in human existence. And this not only brings the *Annales* project into alignment with that of ordinary language philosophy—which aspires to free us from the dictates of the history of philosophy's definite conceptions of what is of interest to human reason; it also suggests an internal relation between Cavell's conception of philosophy and his conception of the aesthetic possibilities of television. For if televisual formats depend upon relating events to the uneventful, then they can either reinforce our culture's ways of privileging dramatic events and dictating our modes of interest in them, or instead encourage us to attend to their enabling uneventful background, and thereby to reconsider what does or should really interest us about both.

WandaVision

The MCU is patently built on the serialization principle: it derives from a universe of multiple, interacting serial narratives created by what we would now call graphic novels; and like them, its narratives centre around beings in whom the achievement of individual identity is facilitated or frustrated by enhanced powers in ways that amount to an intriguing variation on Cavell's theme of cinematic types and the genres-as-cycles that they inhabit. Unsurprisingly, then, the creators of the MCU quickly appreciated the internal relation between their cinematic compositional principles and those of television, with the *Agents of S.H.I.E.L.D.* series constituting an exemplary instance of the aesthetic possibilities it facilitates.

The first season of that series aired at a point which ensured that its mid-season break would roughly coincide with the release of *Captain America: The Winter Soldier*, in which it is first revealed that the enemy organization HYDRA had extensively infiltrated S.H.I.E.L.D. and was using it to pursue its own authoritarian goals. This is one of the best of the 'phase two' movies, but it inevitably concentrates on events at the top of the organization, and on the planetary scale of destruction embodied in HYDRA's plan to use huge satellite-linked helicarriers to assassinate millions of potential enemies. It thereby risks theatricalizing the existential threat HYDRA poses in the sense abhorred by the *Annales* historians, telling its tale in terms of great men and their world-defining individual struggles. But when *Agents of S.H.I.E.L.D* returned from its break, it began to track the more quotidian consequences of those struggles. A key member of the central team is revealed as a HYDRA agent, and the impact of that individual betrayal on every other team member carefully articulated; and the long, draining, and stressful campaign actually to follow through on Captain America's foiling of the helicarrier plot and eradicate HYDRA at every level of S.H.I.E.L.D.'s organization takes up not only the rest of that first season, but several seasons thereafter. In this sense, the television show brought into view the uneventful background to the film's pivotal events, and showed how the victory won by a small group of superheroes not only radically altered the territory on which ordinary men and women lived their professional and personal lives, but could in fact only be realized as a victory by their willingness to make it real—to rewrite every crucial element of the structures and institutions that had made both the betrayal and its overcoming possible.

Once the first three phases of the MCU's development had been completed, its creators naturally turned to television to help launch phase four; but the way in which *WandaVision*—the first series to be released—went about this (re)creative business broke new reflexive ground. For its first three episodes take the form of a situation comedy, in which Wanda Maximoff (Elizabeth Olsen) and Vision (Paul Bettany)—two romantically linked Avengers involved in the cinematic struggle against Thanos, in which Vision is definitively destroyed—appear as happily married inhabitants of a small town called Westview undergoing the typical trials and tribulations of sitcom life whilst trying to disguise the superpowers that define them. Each of these episodes amounts to a formal and substantial homage to classical US sitcom series from differing historical eras—initially filmed in front of live audiences, and lovingly recreating the set design, camera positions, costumes, and quick-fire dialogue familiar from *The Dick Van Dyke Show* and *I Love Lucy* through *Bewitched* to *The Brady Bunch* and *Malcolm in the Middle*. However, as each episode jumps from one style to the next and from black-and-white to colour, anomalies begin to accumulate, until—with Wanda having just undergone a massively accelerated pregnancy and given birth to twins—she expels a neighbour who begins to talk of events involving her in the MCU, and we discover that Wanda's sitcom is taking place in a real town in the contemporary United States, and has attracted the attention of S.W.O.R.D. (a counterpart of S.H.I.E.L.D. initially focused on extraterrestrial threats but now on nanotechnology and sentient weapons).

We gradually learn that Vision's death—coming after Wanda's parents and brother have met violent ends—has pushed her to the brink of madness: having arrived at the town where Vision had bought a plot of land on which to build a house in which they might grow old together, she is driven to use her powers in unprecedentedly powerful ways to transform the town into a sitcom backdrop and to control the minds and lives of its residents so that they take on the role of its supporting cast and extras. This Herculean effort to deny the reality of her latest trauma (and her own exceptional status) becomes increasingly hard to maintain, and is ultimately abandoned—in part because of the suffering it inflicts on the real inhabitants of Westview, in part because the effort of maintaining it has helped her to understand the full extent of her powers, and so her true identity: she is the Scarlet Witch.

But why does this effort at denial take the form of a potted history of American television's situation comedy format? The preceding serialized narrative of Wanda Maximoff in the MCU provides one dominating reason: her childhood in war-torn Sokovia engendered a consuming love for those programmes, because her father earned a living by selling DVD box sets of such American shows during the conflict, and so their family spent many evenings watching the DVDs he hadn't managed to sell. Episode 8 of *WandaVision* re-presents this part of Wanda's story in more detail than was provided in *Avengers: Age of Ultron*, and in a way that airs a number of complex issues.

On the one hand, those shows allowed the Maximoff family to share an imagined world of love and safety in a time of untrammelled violence; on the other, they did so by presenting a version of reality in which the kinds of events that interrupt this rewarding uneventfulness essentially deny the ways in which reality can actually revise or upend the ordinary—so that we find in the sitcom format's unceasing return to the uneventful a means of denying its true significance. This is why the relevant episode shows how one such evening of viewing is ended when a missile hits their house, killing both parents, and leaving the two children to survive for days in the rubble. They are trapped by the close proximity of another missile, still apparently functional and clearly marked as the product of 'Stark Industries', the conglomerate founded by the father of Tony Stark, otherwise known as Iron Man—the Marvel character with whose series of films the MCU really began.

In this way, *WandaVision* affirms a sense Cavell expresses in his essay, that our enjoyment of television and our anxieties about it alike indicate a displaced fear of what it monitors—'the growing uninhabitability of the world'.[25] But more specifically, the show acknowledges the immensely troubling way in which the United States colonizes the rest of the world both culturally and militarily, with the latter undermining the apparently more benign nature of the former (perhaps even declaring its true function); and it simultaneously acknowledges its own participation in that ongoing domination (as it adds one more witty, self-aware, and artistically sophisticated series to that bulldozing sequence of series, both cinematic and televisual).

A further element of *WandaVision*'s critique of its own form lies in its intensification of a surprisingly common strand of the various sitcoms it mimics: the extent to which female competence manifests itself as access to the occult (most obviously in *Bewitched* and *I Dream of Jeannie*). It's as if the very idea of female autonomy is not sufficiently managed by being restricted to the domestic sphere: even there, its reality can only be acknowledged as a mode of witchhood, hence as involving not only the supernatural but a potentially dark or eldritch side of that realm. Here, *WandaVision* works hard to subvert this denial of female power by showing that Wanda's powers are being distorted in their sitcom format (harming not only herself but the others that she recruits to reinforce her fantasy), that they can be fully realized only by transcending its limits, and that in so doing they can help constitute an unprecedented kind of self-affirmation.

We mustn't forget, however, that these critiques of the US sitcom format are themselves conducted by means of a sitcom, and one which is exceptionally aware not only of what the nature of that format has so far revealed itself to be, but of its internal relation to the medium of television as such. On the former front, *WandaVision*'s incorporation into itself of a condensed history of the sitcom declares its participation in that format's accelerating self-awareness, and its ability to find new aesthetic possibilities for the format in acknowledging and transcending its previous enabling and limiting conditions (the kinds of possibility evident not only in sitcoms such as *Seinfeld*, *The Office*, or *Curb Your Enthusiasm*, but also in the ways that much more classically constructed series have incorporated radically heterogenous elements—as when [UK] shows such as *One Foot in the Grave* or *Not Going Out* undertake to account for a suburban household's acquisition of a flourishing pot plant in the downstairs toilet bowl, or to integrate a classical narrative arc of love, engagement, marriage, and children as the uneventful background to equally surreal episode-length dramas). In this respect, the sitcom is well established within the condition of modernism, in which its relation to the history of its own medium is an undismissable question (neither simply accepted nor flatly dismissed).

As for the Cavellian suggestion that the sitcom format is exemplary of the televisual medium and its aesthetic possibilities: *WandaVision* is as if made to validate and exploit that perception. For S.W.O.R.D. discovers what is really going on in Westview by tuning into the broadcast frequency emerging from it on which Wanda's show is alone accessible, and utilizing ancient television monitors to do so—using the naked eye reveals nothing (even when one knows that something is awry in the real Westview), because the relevant mode of perception is that of monitoring. And the astrophysicist who first discovers this also discovers that the broadcast signal is interwoven with a broader energy field sustaining the sitcom's sequence of events that modulates cosmic microwave background radiation (CMBR)—the lingering traces of the Big Bang. *This* is how *WandaVision* conceives of the medium of distinctively televisual creative power: and it entails that both its and its protagonist's creative work (their chaos magic) is neither a mere illusion nor something created *ex nihilo*. It is made out of reality, but reality rewritten or revised at a molecular level—the level at which repeated transitions between the world of the sitcom and the real world from which it can be monitored engender hitherto-occluded superpowers (as with Monica Rambeau [Teyonah Parris]), rather than reinforcing that occlusion (as Wanda wishes). One might say that CMBR is the epitome of the uneventful background against which the apparently important events of life are monitored—that is, facilitated and anticipated.

So understood, the nature of the medium of television—that is, its ability to disclose the relation between events and the uneventful—is here disclosed as internally related to cinematic events, of the kind that MCU movies both depict and exemplify. *WandaVision* tells us that, just as Cavell foresaw in his essay, the risk of theatricalizing human existence that reaches a kind of apotheosis in superhero narratives can be alleviated by maintaining an openness to specifically televisual modes of advancing those narratives. It even suggests that there is something essential to those modes of transcending the human that is fully responsive to television's distinctive capacity for either reinforcing or redirecting our sense of what is truly important and interesting about the protagonists of such narratives.

In this sense, *WandaVision* was not only a bewitching instance of 'event television': it amounted to a televisual interrogation of the event of television—of its mode of interrupting not only the unfolding history of the MCU but that of cinema in general, and of its capacity to revise our concept of an event, and so our conception of the interweaving of events and the uneventful in human existence.[26]

Postscript

A further step in this cross-media dialogue about media is taken in *Doctor Strange in the Multiverse of Madness* (Sam Raimi, 2022), which unfolds the ominous implications of *WandaVision*'s concluding depiction of Wanda living in an isolated cabin, having relinquished her hold over Westview, but preoccupied by reading the Darkhold (the book of dark sorcery bequeathed her by Agnes [Kathryn Hahn], her primary antagonist). That depiction alerted the audience to the possibility that Wanda's realization of her true identity as the Scarlet Witch, with the untrammelled access it gives her to universe-altering power, might threaten humanity rather than enhancing her willingness to protect us (and thereby disclose the dark side of the American ideal of self-perfecting). The film shows us that the Darkhold has infected Wanda with the belief that her two children, who were central to the fantasy of ordinary life she used Westview to construct and who disappeared when she ceased to impose her traumatized desires upon it, exist in one of the alternate universes that make up the Multiverse—the gradually revealed framework within which phases four and five of the MCU's development play out. Her plan is to use America Chavez (Xochitl Gomez), who can travel between universes at will, to locate the one that includes her children and to possess her counterpart in that universe using a power known as 'dreamwalking'—by which she can inhabit their mother's body and acquire every aspect of her life.

Phase four's notion of the Multiverse offers the MCU a number of advantages. Above all, it is a means of accommodating multiple storylines for the same character, analogous to the graphic novels' capacity to reboot or reset storylines at regular intervals; and as with such graphic retellings, which are often prompted by the desire to see what happens when different creators of narrative and images are let loose on familiar characters and worlds, so the films making up phase four have each used different directors, with individually strong but very heterogeneous stylistic signatures—ranging from Chloé Zhao's awestruck receptivity to planetary shifts of culture, geography, and history (in 2021's *Eternals*) to Sam Raimi's love of the horror of death-in-life (the zombie, the undead). This strategy (we might call it the MCU transforming itself into the MCM) has radically disrupted the tendency established in previous phases to adhere to a single, unifying cinematic vision—seen most clearly in the Russo brothers' expanding sphere of influence in phases two and three, and standing in sharp contrast to that presented by its dour and ponderous DC counterpart. It expresses an aspiration to reflect the burgeoning multiplicity of narrative content into a variousness of cinematic form—an aesthetic multiverse. The resulting lack of predictability in its phase four films has unsurprisingly led to a mixed critical reception, which often seems to manifest a desire to have more of the same (admittedly very satisfying) original recipe, without registering sufficiently clearly the risk of diminishing returns.

But Wanda's transposition from *WandaVision* to Raimi's re-envisioning of Doctor Strange specifically raises the question of the relation between her two incarnations, and thereby the question of what distinguishes an alternate universe from a fantasy. For the Wanda of the television series came to recognize her fantasy for what it was, and to relinquish both it and the cruelty inherent in imposing it on the real lives of the ordinary citizens of Westview; but the Scarlet Witch of the film presents herself as believing that those fantasized children really exist in an alternate universe, and aims cruelly to impose herself on them (and their mother) before ultimately relinquishing that project. In this sense, the Scarlet Witch appears oblivious to her own achievement at the end of *WandaVision*: the fantasy Wanda overcame there as she became the Scarlet Witch has been reconfigured in

Raimi's film as something that is actually happening in an alternate universe, and his Scarlet Witch is introduced to us as once again in its thrall—quite as if she has forgotten her own creation of it, let alone her transcendence of its clutches. There thus seems to be a radical discontinuity between Elizabeth Olsen's televisual and cinematic incarnations of her character—to the point at which one might begin to suspect that the Wanda of *WandaVision* and the Scarlet Witch of *Multiverse of Madness* are two different people.

This cannot be explained by Wanda's transformation into the Scarlet Witch, since that occurred at the end of *WandaVision*; and although *Multiverse of Madness* implies that it is explained by the deleterious effects of her reading the Darkhold (as indicated in the television series' final sequence), that would only explain the Scarlet Witch's acquisition of a delusory belief that her children exist in an alternate universe, whereas the film she inhabits is premised upon, and so unconditionally affirms (to her and to us), the reality of that universe. So how are we to understand this transposition of the basic terms on which *WandaVision* presented Wanda's need for, and her manipulation and emancipation of, Westview?

On one level, this challenge raises the question of whether the very idea of a multiverse is (ultimately indistinguishable from) sheer fantasy—not so much a point at which the imagination expands upon a scientific understanding of reality as a point at which scientific understanding has been infiltrated by a fantasy of what reality could be. The matter is equally pressing on an internal narrative level if we reflect on the capacity for dreamwalking: for if counterparts can possess one another, to present that power as a kind of dreaming, and so as a version of our imaginative powers at their least inhibited, suggests that inhabiting a fantasy of oneself and inhabiting a counterpart of oneself might become as difficult to distinguish from one another as a fantasy from reality (especially given that fantasies are precisely that with which reality can be confused).

But a further range of implications emerges if we recall that there is a third Wanda to be considered: the mother of the children in the film's alternate universe. She too is played by Elizabeth Olsen; and since the Scarlet Witch intends to possess her through dreamwalking, she must be one of her counterparts. But this alternate Wanda appears entirely to lack the capacity for chaos magic; and since she also gives no indication of possessing the precursor powers that were instilled in Wanda Maximoff by HYDRA's experimenting upon her with an Infinity Stone, and that made her eligible to join the Avengers, she doesn't seem to have any better a claim to be a counterpart of the woman who became the Scarlet Witch (in the real world of the film). In short, the Wanda of this alternate universe appears simply to be an ordinary human mother: more precisely—and if we set aside the apparent absence of a counterpart to Vision, whose presence is perhaps implied by the existence of the children—she represents the realization of the fantasy that governed the behaviour of the Wanda of *WandaVision*, and that the Scarlet Witch of the films inherits from her: the fantasy of being ordinary or everyday, and so of setting aside the burdens of being a superhero.

Doctor Strange in the Multiverse of Madness thus projects the fictional content of *WandaVision*'s sitcom as an alternate reality within its fictional multiverse; what was first a sequence of fictional events whose creation, broadcasting, and monitoring amounted to an event in the real world is transposed into a self-contained world that the Scarlet Witch views from without, and proves unable to enter (because she learns that possessing alternate Wanda could not give her the authentic love of the alternate's children, and thereby learns that it is sheer fantasy to think that we might take possession of a life that could have been ours if only we had chosen differently at some time in the past—as if taking ownership of the one and only life we have to lead might be achieved by disowning it in favour of someone else's).

It is the shared content of these fictions that gives substance to the presumption that the Wanda of *WandaVision* and the Scarlet Witch of *Multiverse of Madness* are one and the same person; and it is the difference in their (and our) relation to that content that discloses the extent and the nature of their non-identity. For their shared fantasy is articulated by each in a way that is informed by, and so reflects, the different media (the distinct aesthetic universes) in which they are incarnated. Wanda's fantasy of herself undergoes a monitored sequence of events disrupting and reconstituting an uneventful situation; the Scarlet Witch's fantasy of herself inhabits a world viewed whose integrity depends upon the assured absence of her viewing self. One might accordingly say that Raimi's projection of the Scarlet Witch simultaneously declares his indebtedness to, and his capacity and obligation to transform, his televisual predecessor—to reclaim his protagonist as a cinematic phenomenon who is marked but not determined by her prior transposition into that alternate medium.

Notes

1 Stanley Cavell, 'The Fact of Television', reprinted in *Cavell on Film*, ed. William Rothman (New York: State University of New York Press, 2005).

2 For a particularly interesting and nuanced example of the former kind of scepticism, see Michael Z. Newman and Elana Levine, *Legitimating Television: Media Convergence and Cultural Status* (Abingdon: Routledge, 2021), which interrogates the evaluative hierarchies imposed within the history of television, particularly in discussions of more recent examples of highly valued series such as those counted as 'Complex' or 'New' television. For a massively influential example of the latter kind of scepticism, see Noël Carroll, *Theorizing the Moving Image* (Cambridge: Cambridge University Press, 1996).

3 Ted Nannicelli, *Appreciating the Art of Television: A Philosophical Perspective* (Abingdon: Routledge, 2017).

4   A view argued for by Sérgio Dias Branco in 'Situating Comedy: Inhabitation and Duration in Classical American Sitcoms', in *Television Aesthetics and Style*, ed. Jason Jacobs and Steven Peacock (London: Bloomsbury, 2013).
5   Martin Shuster, *New Television: The Aesthetics and Politics of a Genre* (Chicago: University of Chicago Press, 2017).
6   Stanley Cavell, *The World Viewed: Reflections on the Ontology of Film, Enlarged Edition* (Cambridge, MA: Harvard University Press, 1979), 32.
7   Cavell, *The World Viewed*, 31–32.
8   Ibid., 72.
9   Ibid.
10 William Rothman and Marian Keane, *Reading Cavell's* The World Viewed: *A Philosophical Perspective* (Detroit: Wayne State University Press, 2000) takes on the first task; David Rodowick's book *The Virtual Life of Film* (Cambridge, MA: Harvard University Press, 2007) argues for the continued usefulness of Cavell's characterizations of film's material bases in a digital world.
11 Stanley Cavell, 'The *Investigation's* Everyday Aesthetics of Itself', in *The Cavell Reader*, ed. Stephen Mulhall (Oxford: Blackwell, 1996), 385.
12 Stanley Cavell, *Pursuits of Happiness: The Hollywood Comedy of Remarriage* (Cambridge, MA: Harvard University Press, 1981); *Contesting Tears: The Hollywood Melodrama of the Unknown Woman* (Chicago: University of Chicago Press, 1996).
13 Cavell, *Pursuits of Happiness*, 28.
14 Ibid.
15 Ibid., 29.
16 Cavell, *The World Viewed*, 25.
17 Nannicelli, *Appreciating the Art of Television*, 63.
18 Ibid., 64.
19 Ibid., 6–7.
20 Shuster, *New Television*, 46–47.
21 Ibid., 205.
22 Cavell, 'The Fact of Television', 76–77.
23 Ibid., 78.
24 Stanley Cavell, 'The Ordinary as the Uneventful', in *The Cavell Reader*.
25 Cavell, 'The Fact of Television', 84.
26 I'd like to thank my daughter, Ellie, for her research assistance on this project—both for advice about online information sources, and for her company in the cinema and living room over the last dozen years.

14

Love, Remarriage, and *The Americans*

Sandra Laugier

At a time when the spectres of the Cold War have returned, it is time to take a fresh look at the magnificent series *The Americans* (broadcast on FX for six seasons from 2013 to 2018), created by Joe Weisberg—a former CIA agent—and Graham Yost. One of the best series of this new century, it captured viewers' imaginations, and, despite its tragic dimension, became a source of the most intense pleasure and joy. Touching on geopolitics in a prophetic way, the series has even prompted a Russian adaptation project. *The Americans* manages to combine moral and political relevance with the singular charm of its main characters, a couple of KGB agents, Philip (Matthew Rhys) and Elizabeth (Keri Russell). It proves once again that the strength of a television series lies in its personification of ethical issues, its capacity to foster an attachment to fictional beings who become a real part of our lives and thus of our experience, as much as in the series' unparalleled *narrative* complexity. *The Americans* has been part of viewers' lives in recent years and has left a profound and enduring mark on them: through its moral radicalism, the power of its characters, no matter what side they are on, its meticulous representation of the sometimes tedious work of espionage, and the political analysis it produces. Finally, and this is quite rare in television series, it illustrates in an exemplary way the genre of remarriage, which Stanley Cavell made a matrix of Hollywood cinema, and its capacity for moral and political education through forms of overcoming scepticism.

The Americans is part of the corpus of contemporary 'security' series that have proliferated after September 11, even though it is set in Reagan's America. In recent years, there has also been a noticeable multiplication of works paying homage to the 1980s: the wonderful films *A Most Violent Year* (J.C. Chandor, 2014), *Foxcatcher* (Bennett Miller, 2014), *Dallas Buyers Club* (Jean-Marc Vallée, 2013), *Argo* (Ben Affleck, 2012), *Call Me by Your Name*

(Luca Guadagnino, 2017), and *The Traitor* (Marco Bellocchio, 2019)—not to forget, in lighter genres, *Guardians of the Galaxy* (James Gunn, 2014) and *Wonder Woman 1984* (Patty Jenkins, 2020). For television series, the focus is perhaps even more striking: the 1980s appear as foundational for the twenty-first century, returning viewers to a world before the fall of the Wall, before the Iraq war, and of course before September 11. How can we not notice the number of recent series that are set in the Reagan years? Besides the mythical *The Americans*, there is *Halt and Catch Fire* (AMC, 2014–17), *Show Me a Hero* (HBO, 2015), *Stranger Things* (Netflix, 2016–), *GLOW* (Netflix, 2017–19), *The Deuce* (HBO, 2017–19), *Dark* (Netflix, 2017–20), *Chernobyl* (HBO, 2019), *Cobra Kai* (Netflix, 2018–), *When They See Us* (Netflix, 2019), *Pose* (FX, 2018), *Deutschland 83, 86, 89* (AMC, 2015–20), *The Queen's Gambit* (Netflix, 2020); *Physical* (Apple, 2021–), *This Is Us* (NBC, 2016–22) for much of its story, and *The Crown* (Netflix, 2016–), which for its fourth season narrates the Thatcher years and the arrival of Diana, as well as the French series *OVNI(s)* (Canal+, 2021 and 2022).

Ordinary Spies

The Americans is brilliant in recalling and reanimating the dualism of the bipolar world of the early twenty-first century—a time when the threat of terrorism replaced the Cold War in representation and politics, and the imagined end of communism heralded the cultural victory of the capitalist world. It is true that Russia has long been present in the security genre, as signalled by the moment in *House of Cards* (Netflix, 2014–18) when President Underwood (Kevin Spacey) confronts his terrifying Russian counterpart Petrov, and then the latter's troubled exchanges with Claire Underwood; and of course, by the last two Russian seasons of the series *Le bureau des légendes* (Canal+, 2015–20), which also very clearly herald Russia's hardening.

The Americans is part of a growing genre of spy series centred on the KGB, with shows like *Spies of Warsaw* (BBC, 2018), *Allegiance* (NBC, 2015), *Vigil* (BBC, 2021), etc. But the originality of the series lies in the fact that it opens at the beginning of the Reagan years, a time at the end of the Détente, of anti-communist tensions, and of the resurgence of McCarthyism under Reagan's influence; in an America that still calls itself the 'free world' for those few years that precede the disintegration of the East, which is (almost) never shown in the series. Philip and Elizabeth Jennings, two KGB agents who have been undercover in the United States for fifteen years, live in a suburban neighbourhood of Washington, DC, with their two children, presenting to the outside world the image of the perfect American family … while secretly conducting intelligence missions, infiltrations, assassinations, and kidnappings. Philip and Elizabeth pose as husband and wife. After pretending for years, and even having two children together, Paige and Henry, everything changes when they begin to develop genuine feelings for each other and to question, in different ways, their double life and the cause that has carried them so far. The ironic title 'The Americans' refers to them, these Americans, while also evoking the world into which their mission has plunged them. But the series has a strong point of distinction. The characters, despite their occasional doubts (especially Philip, who likes the capitalist way of life, while Elizabeth remains staunchly beholden to Russian values), are committed and sincere communists, ready to do anything to defend their cause, especially Elizabeth. The series demonstrates the moral power of serial writing in the way that it resolutely puts the viewer on their side, eliciting in the American public an attachment to characters who are 1) spies, 2) communists, 3) atheists, 4) killers, 5) deceivers of their children and friends, and—worst of all—6) occasional adulterers (but only when on missions).

Of course, turn-of-the-century series have accustomed us to enjoying characters who are morally dubious (Tony Soprano[1]), neurotic and unreliable (*Six Feet Under* [HBO, 2001–05], *The Wire* [HBO, 2002–08]), difficult and fragile (*Mad Men* [AMC, 2007–15]), or downright evil (*House of Cards* was until *Succession* [HBO, 2017–] the best example, but *Game of Thrones* [HBO, 2011–19] has diversified the field). But *The Americans* shifts the paradigm yet again, and elicits something else entirely: a strange moral adherence, like a nostalgia for the good—which is expressed in criminal acts.

Without doubt, the plot point that gives the series its tension and its romantic texture is the development that marks the first episodes: Philip and Elizabeth, who have until now coldly played the role of the perfect couple as 'professionals', after years of living together and having two children, fall in love with each other during a disturbing mission. The rest of the series simply deals with this transformation, which they never recover from, and which complicates their lives, their sexuality, their mission, their work, and their relationship with their children. Beware: we are entering the territory of *remarriage*, a fundamental structure of Hollywood cinema analysed by Stanley Cavell (1981)—very present in cinema beyond the initial genre of remarriage, but exploited only in a few rare series, such as *Dream On* (HBO, 1990–96), *How I Met Your Mother* (CBS, 2005–14), *The Affair* (Showtime, 2014–19), etc. In the remarriage genre, a couple separates, or loses itself (in this case, Philip and Elizabeth were living a life of 'quiet desperation', as Thoreau would say, on the emotional level), and later on achieves a reconciliation through conversation and fuller recognition of the other.

The remarriage comedies present, according to Cavell, the couple as an image of the political union. As in George Cukor's *The Philadelphia Story* (1940), which features a remarriage at the site of the American Declaration of Independence, the question of the private relationship becomes a way of posing the political question: that of the human connection to society, of the possibility of a genuine conversation, and of a communal public life. This is the question of the 'State of the Union' (the title of another film illustrating the genre, which refers to the annual address of the US President to the nation). Elizabeth and Philip propose, in an original way, the serial reworking of the theme of remarriage and, in so doing, carry the perfectionist demand for a state that is able to ensure a minimum of happiness for its citizens. Hence the ongoing debate between the two of them, despite their status as spies, about where happiness (for all) can be found. Elizabeth and Philip are, to American society, ordinary people, and it is this ordinariness, however constrained and complicated by their actions, that gives them a special moral quality. And, unlike Frank and Claire Underwood in *House of Cards*, our characters in *The Americans* carry the moral requirement altruistically, without much personal, material, symbolic benefit to themselves—and in this respect, paradoxically remind us that the pursuit of happiness requires forgotten or invisible forms of political idealism.

The nostalgia for the 1980s also offers many reasons to get attached to the series. For it has some extraordinary assets: the lead actors, Keri Russell and Matthew Rhys, carried by an erotic tension that extends, as we know, into the actors' private lives; the children, who unlike the children in most TV series, are intelligent and endearing; the clothes and, of course, Philip and Elizabeth's wigs and accessories. Ah, the wigs! The glasses! The technological apparatus, both sophisticated and low-tech. Although the videography is melancholic and even at times morose, the details of the period are always perfectly achieved—that is, without turning the series into a nostalgia fest. The series is indeed centred on the art of disguise, taken literally, as symbolizing deception, the 'private' as secret, but also constantly revealed—the truth of external expressiveness.

The series' creator, Joe Weisberg, defined it as essentially a story about marriage: 'International relationships are just an allegory for human relationships. Sometimes when you're struggling in your marriage or with your child, you feel like it's a matter of life and death. For Philip and Elizabeth, it often is.' Joel Fields, the other producer, described the series as working on different levels of reality: 'The most interesting thing I observed during my time in the CIA was the family life of officers who served overseas with children and spouses. The reality is that, for the most part, these are people who are living their lives, of which work is a part.'[2] It is this relationship to the 'life that the heroes live' that gives the series its realistic dimension—and thus presents a context that appears authentic. In *The Americans*, everything is in the details, and the fact of choosing Russian actors, or those who speak Russian perfectly, to play the Russian characters we see most, whether they are in the *Rezidentura*[3] or in Russia, is another element of realism in the series. Nina, Oleg, and Arkady Ivanovich are all engaging characters, not just props, and they are essential to the series. The attention to detail can be heard even in the music, which always makes sense in relation to the plot and the era: the pilot alone includes Fleetwood Mac's 'Tusk', Quarterflash's 'Harden My Heart', and Phil Collins' 'In the Air Tonight', which sets the tone for the series, as do songs by Yazz, Tears for Fears, U2, Soft Cell, Dire Straits, Kenny Rogers, Elton John, and Peter Gabriel; finally, after Stan and his friends break up, there is 'Brothers In Arms' by Dire Straits. One episode of the fourth season will forever change the way you hear Soft Cell's 'Tainted Love'.

Scepticism and the Knowledge of Others

Elizabeth and Philip get to know each other in the first few episodes but will remain unknown to *us*, especially in terms of the erotic, intimate dimension of their relationship. *The Americans* is a series that deals with the question of scepticism, like the melodramas of the last century that Cavell analyses in *Contesting Tears*,[4] but through the themes of espionage, betrayal, and concealment, and therefore in a way that is always emotional and often challenging. The melancholic story of the unfortunate Martha, an FBI employee whom Philip marries in order to use her in his mission, is emblematic of such trials; her fate is particularly distressing. But Martha is only one of the many love stories that *The Americans* presents, which are always tragic or at best melancholy in action and outcome. There's the teenage girl, Kimberly, one of the first major roles for Julia Garner (who was also featured in *Ozark* [Netflix, 2017–22] in a prominent role) whom Philip seduces; there's the unfortunate recovering alcoholic whom Elizabeth befriends in the hopes of tricking her; there's Young-Hee, the one friend Elizabeth ever manages to make and whom she obviously betrays; there's even their daughter, Paige, a young, idealistic believer ... recruited by her own mother to become a spy. As in the remarriage comedies, the intimate bonds are also a symbolization of the public bonds: the fate of Elizabeth and Philip's marriage is as threatened as that of the Soviet Union (which *we know* will collapse soon, shortly after the series' storyline ends—this is our secret). *The Americans* is a dark series in which every episode ends in heartbreak or disappointment, and that ultimately ends, as we might imagine for the Soviet Union, in tragedy—even if the two heroes survive. In these respects, the show has a depth and maturity that is exceptional among television series.

One of the charms of this series is precisely that it is really and specifically *for adults*—neither for teenagers nor for 'young adults'—an audience segment that has become rarer today (*Mad Men* and *The Affair* are the last powerful representatives addressed to such audiences). This maturity is what makes *The Americans* a series that is both essential and still marginal, effectively unknown despite its quality. It is surprising because, on the surface, the show seems like it could be watched by anyone: after all, it features two attractive actors as married spies with a secret life. Played differently, it could be a comedy (like *True Lies* [James Cameron, 1994] or *Mr. and Mrs. Smith* [Doug Liman, 2005]). By day they pretend to be boring travel agents. By night they disguise themselves, have sex with other people, take part in elaborate espionage operations, and, more often than not, kill. Dark—and so, then, perhaps dark comedy. In fact, the series remains dramatic. There are some memorably harrowing scenes, laborious murders, an excruciating sequence of home-made dentistry and another one where a corpse is stowed away and folded into a suitcase, all of which dismiss thoughts of comedy. That is to say, there's no fun or distance or ado about any of this. Similarly, when Philip is forced by work to seduce a beautiful and intense fifteen-year-old girl (Kimberly), there is nothing exciting or amusing about it and there is never any semblance of justification or positivity. Kimberly is vulnerable, desperate for attention, and she both irritates and affects Philip, who tries to distance himself from her and is unsure how to cope—despite all the training he received in the USSR. He is visited by flashbacks in which we see how he and Elizabeth were trained to have sex with strangers in a way that appears to the viewer to be particularly violent towards them, and certainly not sexy, not fun—and not funny. Philip discusses these memories with Elizabeth, and refers to his relationship to Kimberly in terms of *simulating*—not just orgasm but intimacy and love. This conversation is adult, sceptical, and quite radical, posing profound questions about relationships, the truth of contact with others, the possibility of faking feelings or even one's very humanity. Thus, while Philip speaks with a teenager, such scenes are not fitting for teenage sensibilities.

By evoking this couple of spies—Philip and Elizabeth—who discover each other and yet remain strangers to each other until the end, *The Americans* thus raises the question of how contact with others is central to the reality of experience. In his beautiful essay 'Experience', the American philosopher Ralph Waldo Emerson discusses the difficulty of being close (*next to*) the world in relation to the experience of bereavement (in his case, the death of his son, Waldo, two years earlier) and generalizes it to experience as such, taken as a whole under the sign of bereavement and loss—that is, of the *impossibility* of making contact with others: 'Was it Boscovich who found out that bodies never come in contact? Well, souls never touch their objects. An innavigable sea washes with silent waves between us and the things we aim at and converse with.'[5]

The discovery of Emerson's transcendentalism, taken up by Cavell, is that the object of 'enquiry' is the human subject and its strangeness to self and others.[6] Experience cannot teach us anything, not because it is insufficient in itself, as the traditional philosophy of knowledge says—but because we do not *have* it. This is the experience of scepticism. It does not *touch* us. Hence the upheaval of the first episode of *The Americans* in which there is a discovery of the capacity to be touched, the first escape from scepticism, which also involves the recognition of a violent past. The upheaval of the rest of the series is the difficulty of dealing with this new sensitivity to the other (Philip and Elizabeth, respectively) and to the other characters. Emerson again: 'I take this evanescence and lubricity of all objects, which lets them slip through our fingers then when we clutch hardest, to be the most unhandsome part of our condition.'[7] Scepticism is not only a formulation of the impossibility of knowing the world, but an expression of our refusal to recognize (*acknowledge*) others, to make ourselves sensitive and open to them.

Cavell's reading of scepticism amounts to asking: do we really want to know (ourselves)? For it is not *only* a question of being able to know, but of *wanting to know*; and when the desire to know is mixed with and abandoned to the denial of knowledge, the refusal to know, it takes the form of scepticism. It is the avoidance of reality and of the other that proves to be crushing. How do we get around this inevitability, which in Shakespeare's work is often fatal? By the opposite of avoidance—namely, *recognition*. Cavell's idea, both obvious and unprecedented, is to start again with comedy, as a reversal and conversion of tragedy, against a background of similar data. What in tragedy is avoidance of the intolerable idea of human separation becomes, in comedy, a happy acceptance of this inescapable state. Scepticism cannot be overcome by new *knowledge*. The only response to scepticism is *acknowledgement*, whether of the world or of others.

Cavell discovers this acceptance in cinema in the genre of what he calls 'remarriage comedy'. In *Pursuits of Happiness*,[8] he links the Shakespearean legacy to comedy, showing that a whole group of films released in Hollywood in the 1930s and 1940s can be read as a response to scepticism: included in the list are *It Happened One Night* (Frank Capra, 1934), *The Awful Truth* (Leo McCarey, 1937), and *The Philadelphia Story* (George Cukor, 1940). In these films, the main aim of the plot is not (as in the classic or romantic comedy) to unite the central couple, but to *reunite* them after a separation. It is this pattern of loss and reunion that structures these films, and that carries the emotional weight of great shows like *The Americans*, *The Leftovers* (HBO, 2014–17), and *The Affair*. In these films and series, overcoming scepticism—the wall that separates me from the other—means re-establishing a lost relationship with the world. These films and series show that our condition is one of separation, represented in this context by divorce (or the *threat* of divorce), and that overcoming it requires both more and less than knowledge: an ordinary conversation. This conversation figures a set of 'trades', as Cavell put it, that are not merely linguistic. Philip and Elizabeth find the source of their first remarriage in the sudden erotic tension ('In the Air Tonight' …) generated by a dangerous mission.

The scepticism that builds a wall between people and the world, and between humans themselves, is constantly represented in remarriage comedies: by the blanket held up by Peter Warne (Clark Gable) in the motel room of *It Happened One Night*, or by the swinging door in the final scene of *The Awful Truth*: both films end with the collapse of the wall. In *The Affair*, it is the divorce brought about by 'the affair'; in *The Leftovers*, it is the loss of the world due to the disappearance of a small part of its inhabitants; in *The Americans*, it is a life of prevalent deception.

The philosophical strength of the comedy of remarriage lies in the fact that it does not deny the separation of beings, nor does it seek to overcome it, for example in a fusional romantic relationship: instead, reconciliation is the acceptance of the state of separation and difference, through the establishment of a new problematic, that of *equality*. Accepting the *reality* of the other means accepting to be their equal, both the same and different—to be open to ordinary conversation. This is why the refutation of scepticism is achieved through feminism, and in *The Americans*, it is not a coincidence that the female character is the strongest.

In Cavell's *Contesting Tears*, where he deals with cases of melodrama, scepticism is represented as the impossibility of conversation, the presence of loneliness, and the attendant loss of speech and reality (there are such moments, to be sure, which seem irredeemable in *The Leftovers* and *The Americans*). It is as if the cinematographic could in every sense of the word *domesticate* scepticism, make people recognize the reality and inevitability of separation, and convert it into a desired repetition of the everyday.

Remarriage comedies comically portray the essential feature of scepticism— the misunderstanding and loss of others—and show the ability of the heroes and heroines of these films to overcome this state. The instrument of this reunion is that which is threatened or denied in scepticism, namely language, conversation, of which the remarriage comedies offer, in the joy of the early days of talking movies, remarkable examples. Conversation remains the guiding thread in the relationship of the couples in the remarriage series, who, after a momentary estrangement, never stop talking to each other. Cavell showed how scepticism was the theoretical, or intellectual, translation of a human anxiety that is both fundamental but also ordinary—that of contact with the world and with others. This idea will find its place and resolution on the cinema screen, and sometimes on television, not by the projection of the world but by the serialization and recognition of characters in time, Cavell says in *The Claim of Reason*: 'At the origin of scepticism, there is the attempt to transform the human condition, the condition of humanity, into an intellectual difficulty, into an enigma. (To interpret "a metaphysical finitude as an intellectual lack").'[9] *The Americans*, by introducing deception into the everyday, into the intimate, and into the sexual, continues the cinematic formulation of scepticism, which had first found its expression in the comedy of remarriage. What is *pretending*? What are the criteria for a successful feint? J.L. Austin posed these very concrete questions in his essay 'Pretending' (in *Philosophical Papers*[10]) and placed it at the heart of his theory of knowledge.

These questions are also constantly posed in *The Americans*, and in the fourth season they take on a specific, sexual meaning—summarizing the whole issue of the relationship with the other. At the very end of the episode where Philip has a revealing conversation with Kimmy, Elizabeth asks him 'Are you faking it with me?'—and Philip mentions the difficulty of 'faking it' in his job, 'on duty' ('Salang Pass', [s3:e5]). To simulate here is not only to simulate enjoyment, climax, but also attachment, sharing, affect, life together. 'Sometimes', he admits. But he hugs her and adds, 'Not now.' This seemingly discreet moment is crucial, highlighting the power of the feeling that unites the two protagonists, their mutual and parrhesiastic sincerity, and the essence of their marriage. But this type of scene, of which several examples could be cited in *The Americans*, also reveals the epistemological and moral radicality of the series and the renewed capacity of the espionage genre to ask the question of the connection between humans, and the strategic place that the erotic relationship finds in it (I am thinking here of great espionage films such as *Notorious* [Alfred Hitchcock, 1946], or those of Éric Rochant, *Les patriotes* [1994] and *Moebius* [2013], which are echoed by the series *The Bureau*).

To arrive at a certain style of intimate conversation is to invent forms of expression, says Cavell; it is to accept something of human finitude. This question constantly surfaces in *The Americans*. 'It is equally to acknowledge that your expressions in fact express you, that they are yours, that you are in them … to acknowledge your body, and the body of your expressions, to be yours, you on earth, all there will ever be of you.'[11] It means accepting one's condition, which is to be expressive—hence to be mortal. This is how conversation, both ordinary and cinematic, is defined: as acceptance of the language condition—our form of life in language—and of exposure to others. The television series has become the privileged place for such exposure, and the television actor, like the film actor, has this mysterious capacity, by bearing expression, to constitute the experience of the spectator.

To let oneself be known by the other is to lose control, to make oneself vulnerable—as Kimberly (Julia Garner) or Martha (Alison Wright) are with Philip; as Stan (Noah Emmerich), the FBI agent, is with Nina (Annet Mahendru) and others like Sandra (Susan Misner) and Renee (Laurie Holden); as Nina, a Soviet diplomat and double agent, is with Oleg (Costa Ronin), an employee of the Russian embassy; as Oleg is with Stan, as they become friends, inventing the only bromance in the series. And Elizabeth? Not with anyone. Her separation from others, her alienation, is unique and central to the emotional force of the series; 1980s feminism weighs on our understanding of her character.

The Americans is thus a series about the difficulty of being (or appearing as) an ordinary human. The series is focused on the ordinary human, woman and man, and not, like so many contemporary series of this century, on 'difficult men' and on exemplary and narcissistic anti-heroes whose inner conflicts are supposed to interest us (*Mad Men*, *Breaking Bad*, or even *The Bureau*). For *The Americans* also broke new ground by presenting an unlovable, radical, and violent female character, far from any stereotype. As Keri Russell said, it is exciting and rare for the female character to be 'the tough one', Philip being more vulnerable and accessible.

Completely dedicated to her homeland and the cause, and thoroughly anti-American, Elizabeth is certainly one of the most ruthless and passionate characters on television, although we have seen scarier villains. Russell eschews the sweet Felicity and gives us Elizabeth, a violent woman who does not trust anyone and does not mind killing, while Philip, as the seasons progress, cannot stand being a weapon for the KGB, or using one.[12] Russell noted this reversal in an interview: 'It was interesting that Philip was the most emotional and engaging character in the story.'[13] Russell's performance in *The Americans* is probably the most impressive of the ten outstanding ones in the show. Elizabeth does a lot of unacceptable things throughout the series, yet remains a powerful and endearing figure; this character is a milestone in serial feminism.

Let's not forget another taboo broken by the series, which is adultery, a crime that is normally even more unforgivable in TV series than murder: both Elizabeth and Philip must necessarily sleep with other people, or even become romantically involved, as part of their missions. In some cases they *marry* other people. The fact that we can easily forgive and understand them is an indication of the power of the series to represent *duty* and *work*—words that constantly come up in the Jennings's conversations.

These are ordinary relationships, symbolized by neighbourly relationships (*next*, i.e., both beside and apart: like Stan who is beside the Jennings). There is a sense of care built up over the series' six seasons—the mutual care of the heroes and the care that we painfully feel for them, as evidenced by the very real anguish that seizes us when they are in danger. It is this investment that inscribes the series in the daily routine of the spectators and in their ordinary lives that reflect those of our heroes, at least in their diurnal habits. In the end, we become attached to this ordinary side of Philip and Elizabeth, in order to better appreciate and recognize the dark, unknown, *uncanny* part of them—but also, in order to better grasp what it is that constitutes an 'ordinary life', an American life, of which Philip and his children dream, against their beliefs (unlike Elizabeth, as we shall see).

Human Security

The Americans exemplifies what can be called a third wave of ambitious series—after the great HBO works of the turn of the century such as *The Sopranos*, *Six Feet Under*, and *The Wire*. The early 2010s were indeed an extraordinary time for television. Firstly, there were the groundbreaking works such as *Breaking Bad* (AMC, 2008–13) and *Game of Thrones*, but also *Banshee* (Cinemax, 2013–15), *The Walking Dead* (AMC, 2010–22), *Hannibal* (NBC, 2013–15), and *Fargo* (FX, 2014–20) that followed the HBO classics. Then, streaming services like Netflix launched their own creations, which have since become classics in their own way: *Stranger Things*, *Narcos* (Netflix, 2015–), *House of Cards*, *Ozark*, etc. And there has been an important development of the security genre, of which *Homeland* is representative, but which also includes *The Americans*.

Joe Weisberg, creator of *The Americans*, is a former CIA officer. In 2007, after leaving the CIA, he published *An Ordinary Spy*, a novel about a spy who completes the final stages of his training in Virginia and is transferred overseas. After reading Weisberg's novel, Graham Yost, the executive producer at FX, discovered that Weisberg had also written a pilot for a possible spy series. Weisberg was fascinated by the stories he had heard of agents serving overseas as spies, while raising their families. Hence the idea of focusing on a whole family of spies, rather than just one person. Weisberg says that the CIA inadvertently gave him the idea for a spy series:

> While I was taking a lie detector test to get into the CIA, they asked me, 'Are you joining the CIA to get experience in the intelligence community so you can write about it later?' That had never occurred to me. I was joining the CIA ... because I wanted to be a *spy*. But the second they asked that question I thought, 'Now I'm going to fail the test'.[14]

In fact, Weisberg's work in the CIA not only inspired some of the storylines in the series, but more importantly, gave the show its technical and realistic polish by incorporating tactics and methods learned in his training, such as dead drops and communication protocols.

The number of films and series revealing the 'backstage' of democratic regimes facing the terrorist threat has grown significantly since 2001 (in addition to *Homeland* [Showtime, 2011–20] and *The Bureau* [Canal+, 2015–20], there are *The Looming Tower* [Hulu, 2018], *Fauda* [Yes Oh, 2014–], *False Flag* [Channel 2, 2015–], *Kalifat* [Netflix, 2020], *The Girl from Oslo* [Netflix, 2021], and *Tehran* [Apple TV+, 2020–22], to name a few). These works provide strong common cultural referents, which populate ordinary discussions and political debates. Security series pose the question of the relationship between reality and fiction in a new way: even fictionalized and dramatized, reality always catches up with their characters—even if, for *The Americans*, it is ten years later, and curiously, at the moment when it is finally recognized as one of the greatest series.

With *24* and then *Homeland* and *The Americans*, it is not 'reality' that influences fiction, but rather 'reality' *and* 'fiction' that co-determine each other. The reflexive capacity of these works gives them a role in a collective democratic conversation and allows everyone to familiarize themselves with the issues, here historical, of democracy and geopolitics.[15] The security series, which includes *The Americans*, but also *The Bureau* and *Homeland*, offers a dive into very specific professional worlds, those of espionage or intelligence, and the form of life associated with them. They modify the collective *experience* by revealing secret universes unknown to the public, but also by presenting the point of view of the 'enemy'. They are matrices of intelligibility, demonstrating that the series can not only represent but also *analyse* international conflicts, as well as national policies. September 11 was thus the moment of an upheaval in narrative practices, which led to a change in the moral, political, and geopolitical ambition of the series. This genre of security series became an opportunity to shake the historical American domination of series, by multiplying the political points of view and demanding more and more from the viewer. *The Americans'* gamble was only possible in this context: to take the point of view from the East.

Through their aesthetic format (long-term, weekly, and seasonal regularity, often viewed in a domestic setting), the attachment to the characters they cultivate, the democratization and diversification of their viewing methods, these twenty-first-century series allow, for many subjects, a specific form of education and the constitution of an *audience*. They allow us to consider the powers of fiction in the analysis and perception of espionage or terrorist violence, in the transmission and sharing of meanings and values. This leads to taking into account their degree of *reflexivity*, while reconsidering the question of 'realism'—no longer defined as verisimilitude or stylistic 'likeness', but as impact and action on the 'real', including the show's audiences.

The 2001 attacks have also disrupted the way in which films and television series are being made. Like the rapprochement initiated during the First and Second World Wars, September 11, 2001 precipitated the renewed proximity between security actors and creators of all kinds in the fields of consulting and writing. The CIA–Hollywood collaboration, already formalized in the mid-1990s with the creation of a Liaison Office on the model of existing cooperation between the FBI, the Pentagon, and Hollywood, has entered a new chapter with such productions as *24*, *Alias*, *Homeland*, *The Americans*, and in cinema, *Argo*, *Zero Dark Thirty* (Kathryn Bigelow, 2012), etc. The number of works benefiting from a more or less important involvement of security actors have multiplied. However, series have been able to escape becoming the pure expression of American domination, and *The Americans* is a remarkable proof of the possible complexity of approaches, and of a blurring of the status of representation: neither completely fictional nor completely documentary, these in-between fictions have thus accompanied—or even anticipated—real events. This is the case with *Homeland*, whose fifth season in 2015 featured Daesh cells preparing an attack on European soil; and today with Volodymyr Zelensky's series, *Servant of the People* (Слуга народу, Kvartal 95, 2015–19) which showed him as an ordinary citizen who is suddenly elected president of the Republic, and which in a few years paved the way for him to become the very real president of Ukraine, a soon-to-be warring nation of which he is the leader and *showrunner*.

In the world of television series, September 11 became a catalyst for the advent of the security genre. Like the espionage genre, security series function as a perpetual preparation for war,[16] and a glorification of the *clandestine* or *illegal*. This includes *The Americans*, even though the time and the characters of the series are out of sync with the post-September 11 world, and allows them to return to the political and moral stakes of the Cold War. The power and intelligence of the series lies in its ability not only to forge the viewers' attachment to characters that represent America's enemy, but also for its six seasons to keep reminding us that neither September 11 nor the fall of the Berlin Wall put an end to the Cold War.

The Americans, which is based on the story of an authentic program of KGB sleeper agents infiltrated in the United States, the 'Illegals', leaves nothing to chance, like its heroes on a mission: building up plotlines in the first season that are only resolved five seasons later, and demanding a great deal from the viewers—showing respect for them.

The Americans is a paradox. While it is an American series, its heroes are the emblematic enemy of the United States. Moreover, the series has managed to make American viewers fall in love with Russian spies because it has achieved moral complexity, a space where black and white do not exist, and neither do the good nor the bad guys. It is in this respect that the series cultivates moral education. Moral ambivalence is the genius of *The Americans* and its formative power. The series is *perfectionist* not only because of this moral demand, but also because it requires a certain attention, the ability to open up to a particular universe: where the colours are far from bright, the setting is often dark and the night dense, the scenes can drag on and on, the fights are confusing and laborious, the murders are painful and tinged with a dull horror, and the relationships are deceptive and disappointing.

With or Without You

Philip and Elizabeth are simultaneously spouses and lovers, spies and partners in the field, colleagues at the travel agency that serves as their cover, both Americans and Russians—they represent several kinds of lives within them. They are so fascinating because of their profession, but also because of their ambivalence and differences. For their cover, they had to erase everything about their Russian origins and leave it all behind. Yet in a life of lies they manage to be quite sincere and open in their feelings for each other, which does not come naturally, but is indeed a perfectionist work, progressing on the screen through the seasons. It is this perfectionism that is signalled by their remarriages (plural, as remarriage occurs several times in *The Americans*) and that allows the series to end, teaching us to let our heroes go.

The end of a great show is always a difficult parting, especially when its characters are as strong as these. *The Americans*, which appeared in the midst of the heyday of television series and was erased in favour of other, more addictive shows, never made a fitting impact in the ratings or the critical reviews, but it did create a deep attachment among its ardent fans, and it is now coming back to the fore. The meticulously plotted and written ending of the series is particularly exemplary; and it is remarkable that the attachment to the series has crystallized precisely around this final season. The excellent Noah Emmerich (the neighbour and FBI agent, Stan) shows the full extent of his talent here, where his role becomes essential. The children, Paige and Henry, are characters in their own right who also become more prominent. The realism of the series is also in seeing the children grow up, and Elizabeth and Philip transform and harden physically as well as morally (especially her). Oleg is one of the most difficult to abandon to his sad fate—and we later find Costa Ronin, just as crucial, in the last season of

Homeland. The last season of *The Americans* achieves a particularly realistic way of depicting the murders carried out on missions by Elizabeth and Philip—more and more laborious, interminable, and horrible, as if to indicate the weariness of the protagonists, often physically registered in their bodies. Finally, the last season demonstrates its ability to *transform* viewers by taking them completely by surprise, making them love these *Americans*, even as they are also spies and KGB assassins—shaking and crying for them when they are finally burned.

The Americans' audience is those who became so attached to its characters and its procedures that they impatiently awaited the return of the seasons and, during the period of two to three months, each weekly episode—an old-fashioned way of watching that has nothing to do with the binge-watching instituted by Netflix. The series was consumed in the real temporality of its six years, with the acceleration of the last one, becoming part of the viewers' routine and daily lives that reflect those of our heroes. One wonders how in the current context new viewers will devour all six seasons of the show.

The final season of *The Americans* brings the Hollywood structure of remarriage full circle, implemented at least three times in Elizabeth and Philip's story: at the very beginning, when after years of pretending to live together, including the making of children, they fall in love with each other; at the time of their 'real' clandestine Orthodox marriage, which will eventually lead to them being discovered by the FBI; and at the very end, when they have to figure out a new life together, 'back home' (but: *there is no place like home*). This final reunion, a tragic version of the comedy of remarriage, is the result of a final subversion, the *abandonment of the children*, that goes in both directions. Elizabeth and Philip abandon their son to a life they know is better, and are abandoned by their daughter on a station platform, in one of the most moving and surprising scenes in the series. Here, we understand that the 'Americans' arc, in fact, Paige and Henry. It is at this point, and in the key scene before it, the eleven terrible minutes of exchange in a car park between Stan and Philip, that the show constitutes our ability as viewers to separate ourselves from the characters, and from the work itself. After years of intimacy with our heroes, we identify for the first time with Stan, who suddenly *lets go* of Elizabeth and Philip, as if to teach us to let go of them too, and to carry on without them, who will now also be without us, but who will remain within us ... all to the tune of U2's 1987 song 'With or Without You'.

Sometimes a show itself teaches us to detach ourselves from the characters: this is the case in *Mad Men*, which in its last season gradually weakened our link to Don Draper, or radically at the end of *Six Feet Under*, where the succession of deaths of all the characters cut the thread, asserting and visualizing the metaphysical purpose of mortality. In *The Americans*, it is the children who abandon their parents, and teach us to let them go too. The episode is entitled 'Start', like a new beginning, but difficult and uncertain, and without us, with new terms that parties must agree to if they are to grow and move on. By suddenly excluding us from the fate of the Americans, the series displays its scepticism in its final moments.

The scene in which Stan confronts his friends in the car park is one of the most poignant in the series and the culmination of the slow process of building a friendship. Noah Emmerich delivers his best scene, revealing the damage that lies can do: 'You made a joke of my life', he says in despair. Philip responds with equal sadness: 'You've been my only friend in my whole fucking life. All these years, it was my life, the joke, not yours.' Scenes like these create real, bitter, flesh-and-blood characters that become deeply embedded in our experiences. They also draw narrative possibilities for the 'future' of these characters who are abandoned by the heroes, and whom we must therefore leave, too. 'You have to take care of Henry', Paige said as they left the garage. 'He loves you, Stan', Philip said, his eyes finally tearing up. 'Tell him the truth.' Philip leaves Henry in Stan's keeping, entrusting him to the audience.

The Jennings then travel by train, each on their own passport. There is a checkpoint. They pass through. The relief is intense … as is the brutal shock of suddenly seeing Paige on the platform, staying behind at the last moment. Each in turn, and separately, the parents discover that their daughter is definitely gone, that she has abandoned them as they abandoned their son. They do not share this experience and do not see her both at the same time. This scene, which evokes radical scepticism, stays in one's memory because here too, for the last time, our heroes must remain impassive, even if their features tremble—expressing both dissimulation and horror. This masterful scene ends with the pain of others, and also a form of comfort: Stan arrives at Henry's public school to tell him the truth, seamlessly embracing the role of parental figure—which he, in fact, has always played.

One of the saddest, most *uncanny* moments in *The Americans* is Elizabeth's dream, which is shown just after Paige's traumatic abandonment, on the way to Russia. Elizabeth is in bed with Gregory, her old lover, who died five years before. In the dream she is young again. 'I don't want a child anyway', Elizabeth tells Gregory. She senses that something is wrong. Her room is filled with art—paintings and prints that cover the wall, as if her room were a gallery. On the bedside table, there is a picture in a frame: it is her children, Paige and Henry, but younger. Their faces are sad. When the camera pulls back, it reveals a gigantic painting with a face of a mysterious woman, hidden by a veil of sadness. It is the painting she received from Erica, the dying artist who marked her. This *uncanny/unheimlich* atmosphere is present in all of the last images of the series: Stan stares at his wife Renee in the dark, wondering if their relationship is also a sham, since Philip has (not without calculation) instilled doubt just as they were leaving ('I don't know how to tell you this, but Renee might be one of us'). He contemplates the Jennings's house, the ghost of his friendship with Philip. Scepticism and anxiety set in through the aesthetic of this scene—that of the *uncanny*. Notably, this final season of *The Americans* is contemporaneous with the third season of David Lynch's *Twin Peaks* (*Twin Peaks: The Return*, 2017); the conclusion of *The Americans* is in a sense equally strange and frightening. Some critics have imagined that the series' conclusion and the couple's return to Moscow plays out against the background of the end of the USSR and a possible reunion with their children in a less divided world. But the tragic tone of the ending is irredeemable. No return or reunion is possible, no more so than in Lynch—the family is definitively separated.

These sceptical series feed on our past, showing it to be irretrievably past and yet the source of our present insecurity—how the present-day return of the Cold War confirms the profound realism of *The Americans*. It is like *Back to the Future*, where we go to the past—but cannot change anything about the present. It is not a matter of aesthetic charm à la *Mad Men*. What is shown to us on the small screen is then, as Cavell noted of the cinema screen, a world from which we are excluded; we are like Carrie Mathison in front of her screen, observing Brody's intimacy in *Homeland*. 'A screen is a barrier. It screens me from the world it holds—that is, makes me invisible. And it screens that world from me.'[17] The world *projected and viewed* in the cinema does not exist (any more) and I cannot be part of it. Victor Perkins noted that 'we are powerless in relation to the image because it presents actions already performed and recorded; it gives us no influence and allows no possibility of intervention'.[18] These series, set in the 1980s, take up the question of the ontology of cinema and present us with a nostalgic but relentless unfolding of action and history, in the way that the 1980s scenes of *This Is Us* lead irrevocably to the death of the father, which we must wait for with a mixture of anxiety, curiosity, and inevitability.

In these respects, these series of our time that take us back to the Reagan years have become, like cinema, 'a moving image of scepticism'.[19] They do not just make us appreciate life as it used to be, but also broaden our range of experience through fiction. If they take care of us, it is not by putting us back into the world, but by *separating* us from it, by shielding us from it, showing us a reality in which we are absent and powerless—through which we can still dream about and regret, like something out of a myth. Certainly, these series often aim to make us *revise* our vision of the past (*When They See Us* on Netflix, which revisited the terrible story of the Central Park Five, is one of the most beautiful examples) and, if possible, to repair or atone for mistakes. They break with an implicit historicism and the illusion of a global and shared progress of humanity. They succeed in demonstrating the influence of the 1980s—the rise of global capitalism—on the present catastrophes. But above all, they show us a vanished world, which we can no longer see as a step towards a better future. Now *The Americans*, a sceptical tragedy of remarriage, a spy novel, and a treatise on (im)morality, also carries a power of premonition for the present moment, where we feel as if we have dreamed the fall of the Berlin Wall and find ourselves back at the beginning, prepared again, ready. Start.

Notes

1. Tony Soprano is the main protagonist of the TV show *The Sopranos* (HBO, 1999–2007).
2. June Thomas, 'A Conversation with *The Americans* Showrunners Joe Weisberg and Joel Fields', *Slate*, 31 January 2013.
3. *Rezidentura*: Soviet clandestine cell based in foreign territory.
4. Stanley Cavell, *Contesting Tears: The Hollywood Melodrama of the Unknown Woman* (Chicago: University of Chicago Press, 1997), 272.
5. Ralph Waldo Emerson, 'Experience', *Essays: Second Series*, in *Essays and Lectures*, ed. Joel Porte (New York: The Library of America, 1983), 473.
6. Stanley Cavell, *A Pitch of Philosophy* (Cambridge, MA: Harvard University Press, 1984), 217.
7. Emerson, 'Experience', 473.
8. Stanley Cavell, *Pursuits of Happiness: The Hollywood Comedy of Remarriage* (Cambridge, MA: Harvard University Press, 1981).
9. Stanley Cavell, *The Claim of Reason: Wittgenstein, Skepticism, Morality and Tragedy* (New York: Oxford University Press, 1979).
10. J.L. Austin, *Philosophical Papers*, ed. J.O. Urmson and G.J. Warnock (Oxford: Clarendon Press, 1979).
11. Cavell, *The Claim of Reason*, 551.
12. Felicity's breakthrough part was in *Felicity* (J.J. Abrams, Matt Reeves, 1998-2002, WB).
13. Maureen Ryan, 'Keri Russell and Matthew Rhys Break Down the "Devastating" Finale of *The Americans*,' *New York Times*, March 30, 2018.
14. Joe Weisberg, interview By Laura M. Holson, *New York Times*, March 29, 2013.
15. See Sandra Laugier, *Series under Threat*, Open Philosophy 5 (1), 155–67 (2021), *En confinement, du care en séries* (Paris: AOC, 2021), *Nos vies en séries* (Paris: Flammarion, 2019) and *TV-Philosophy. How TV Series Change our Thinking* (Exeter: University of Exeter Press, 2023).
16. Luc Boltanski, *Énigmes et complots* (Paris: Gallimard, 2012).
17. Stanley Cavell, *The World Viewed: Reflections on the Ontology of Film* (Cambridge, MA: Harvard University Press, 1971; expanded edition 1979), 24.
18. Victor F. Perkins, *Film as Film: Understanding and Judging Movies* (New York: De Capo Press, 1993 [1972]), 71.
19. Ibid.

15

True Detective: Existential Scepticism and Television Crime Drama
Robert Sinnerbrink

The three seasons of *True Detective* (HBO, Nic Pizzolatto 2014–19), especially season 1 (2014), were celebrated for their historical realism, moral complexity, and addressing of social themes. But they are also exemplary televisual explorations of the varieties of scepticism that morally engaged crime dramas are well placed to examine. Drawing on Stanley Cavell's philosophical engagement with epistemic and moral scepticism in relation to cinema, I extend this approach to the television crime drama, taking *True Detective* as my philosophical case study. Pizzolatto's existentially slanted series explores not only epistemic and moral scepticism but also what we might call existential scepticism—a thoroughgoing questioning of the contemporary bases of social existence extending to institutions of law and order, the family, religious belief, morality, love, and the possibility of transcendence.

Introduction: Scepticism and Television Crime Drama

Long-form television series are often praised for their capacity to world-build, to create dynamic, complex, and intersecting character arcs, and to provide more substantial time and narrative space for emotional engagement with characters than regular-length movies. Something similar could be said, I suggest, of the capacity for long-form television series—especially the television crime drama—to stage and explore the problematics of *scepticism* in all its varieties. Television crime drama is particularly suited to examining and exploring *epistemic and moral scepticism*: the limits of our capacities to know what happened or discern the truth, coupled with critical reflection on the limits of our moral-psychological accounts of evil, understanding violence, the possibility of justice, and dealing with trauma. To this we can add *existential scepticism*, a more pervasive sceptical attitude towards the meaning, value, or possibilities of human existence that can also encompass epistemic and moral scepticism. These themes are all central to one of the most celebrated television crime dramas of recent years, Nic Pizzolatto's *True Detective* series (season 1: 2014; season 2: 2015; season 3: 2019). Season 1 focuses on what I shall call *existential* scepticism, which explores the intertwining of metaphysical speculation and moral scepticism, pessimistic philosophy and the problem of nihilism, traversing scepticism as a means of accepting our finitude and dealing with the limits of knowledge, action, and meaning. Season 2 strips away any metaphysical background, or postsecular/spiritualist elements, presenting a thoroughly secular critique of social institutions from the perspective of *moral* and *socio-cultural* scepticism: what we could describe as a televisual critique of the decay of contemporary American culture and society. The scepticism here is pervasive, with little sense of how traversing this sceptical terrain—here closely aligned with an interrogation of masculinity and patriarchy—might enable a practical or social transcending of it. Season 3 focuses on the moral, social, as well as philosophical implications of *epistemic* scepticism, especially resulting from the limits of memory and pressures of time in the aftermath of traumatic experiences (not only in the form of violent crime but also other forms of loss). The other two forms of scepticism (existential and socio-cultural) are also addressed but the third season emphasizes the inevitable finitude of knowledge and morality, given the vicissitudes of time, memory, ageing, and consciousness. These intersecting strands of scepticism—existential, epistemic, moral, and socio-cultural—are woven together without offering a definitive resolution but also without succumbing to a pessimistic nihilism or loss of belief in the everyday. In this way, I suggest, the three seasons of *True Detective* thus substantiate Cavell's claim that cinema, or in this case cinematic television, can both stage and overcome, present and critique, the varieties of sceptical experience shaping contemporary sensibilities.

How does television figure in relation to the problem of scepticism that, for Cavell, gives cinema its philosophical import? Can television offer ways of responding to scepticism, or is it characterized by its avoidance of this very problem? How does the ontology of television differ from that of film, and how might television therefore offer a different response to the problem of scepticism? To explore these questions, I turn to Cavell's reflections on television and explore how these might help us read and understand the *True Detective* series.

Television as 'a Current of Simultaneous Event Reception'

Cavell's 1982 essay 'The Fact of Television' provides a fascinating interpretation of television as a medium, but also offers striking responses to these questions concerning scepticism.[1] His reflections are driven by a simple question: given the dominance of television as a popular medium, why has it been neglected by philosophers and film theorists? What does this 'refusal of interest' or 'fear of television' signal in a cultural sense?[2] More specifically, what relationship does television have to the problem of scepticism, which for Cavell is definitive of cinema's philosophical significance?

Assuming that television has 'come of age' as a medium of art—a point beyond question in the 2020s, the 'golden age of television'—Cavell develops an enquiry into the medium of television in order to arrive at a deeper understanding of our apparent (philosophical or intellectual) aversion to that medium. Cavell notes immediately the difference between individual films that are taken to reveal (or acknowledge) the nature of the medium, and the case of television, wherein it is 'the program, the format' that reveals it.[3] In contrast with Cavell's observation regarding standard television formats, we can note that those televisual works typically taken as exemplars of the art of television—long-form series such as *The Wire*, *The Sopranos*, or *Breaking Bad*, for example—are usually treated in a manner akin to cinematic works, and are described as sharing an aesthetic kinship with cinema.[4] This would also hold true, I suggest, for *True Detective*, which again serves as an exemplary case of 'cinematic television' that nonetheless also embodies and exploits key features of the medium of television and the format of the television serial.

What to make of the 'format' of television from an aesthetic perspective? Television, according to Cavell, works according to the *serial-episode* principle, in contrast to the genre-member principle familiar from cinema (taking genre here in Cavell's sense of the 'genre-as-medium').[5] In the genre-as-medium concept, there are internal features shared by members of the genre, and also divergences that involve correlated 'compensations' introduced by new members of the genre in order to accommodate these variations.[6] Externally, one genre 'negates' an adjacent genre when there is a shared feature that negates another feature of the adjacent genre. Genres can refine themselves in relation to each other, and even form a system of genres through these relations of negation—a feature that indicates their philosophical significance.[7] Interestingly, the three seasons of *True Detective* can also be understood via Cavell's concept of 'genre-as-medium' thanks to the divergences and compensations that distinguish and relate each season to the others, which taken together we could describe as existential or metaphysical detective fiction.[8] This 'cinematic' dimension of *True Detective*, however, coexists with its televisual 'serial-episode' dimensions, the serialization and repetition of consistent elements across episodes that adds variation within a coherent whole. It is this combination of cinematic genre-as-medium and televisual serialization features which makes the long-form 'cinematic' televisual series so distinctive.

Cavell identifies the serial-episode format as television's distinctive mode of composition, which describes the manner in which television reveals or acknowledges its medium.[9] The contrast here is with his account of cinema as a medium, which he famously defined as '*a succession of automatic world projections*'.[10] In *The World Viewed*, Cavell remarked on the ontological difference between live television and film, with the former being closer to the scenario of a 'prosthetic' image with a direct causal link to its referent—an image presented simultaneously with what is happening before the camera.[11] The more interesting point Cavell makes is that what is presented as happening 'live' on television is not (an event in) the world but rather 'an event standing out from the world': the televisual image does not reveal events so much as *monitor* or 'cover (as with a gun)', a mode of perception oriented 'to keep something on view'.[12] Television 'creates' an event that exists adjacent to, or simultaneously with, events in the world, but renders them as *televisual* events that are essentially an expression of our visual *monitoring* of everyday reality (as opposed to viewing a portion of a cinematic world, the 'world viewed' as definitive of cinematic experience).

On this basis, Cavell ventures a definition of the material character of television as '*a current of simultaneous event reception*'—a direct conceptual contrast, term for term, with the definition of cinema as '*a succession of automatic world projections*'.[13] With television the focus is on *simultaneity* rather than succession: a focus on *the present*—the live moment, the now, with what is current, but also connoting the electrical circuits of telecommunication networks (or, to update his account, on-demand digital streaming platforms). Broadcasting need not be essential to television since the essential unit is the individual (television or digital) monitor, an observation that has proven prescient with the decline of broadcast television and the rise of on-demand digital streaming of content. The monitor is what allows televisual engagement to be defined by *monitoring* (rather than viewing): a mode of perception that tracks or receives what is current, of simultaneous events that are monitored or scanned (in an associative manner) rather than viewed (as a projected world). Successful television formats (sitcoms, game shows, sports and cultural coverage, talk shows, news, and entertainment) are those that reveal or acknowledge the conditions of perceptual monitoring, and do so via a 'serial-episode mode of composition'.[14] Again, long-form television serials, with their hybrid forms of cinematic/televisual narration, challenge this distinction between the two mediums, showing the complex manner of their interaction.

Cavell notes the ubiquity of 'talk', with its repetitiveness and its improvisatory aspects, including the interview, which again will play a central role in the police procedural/crime investigation dimensions of *True Detective*. As we shall see, the latter features extensive sequences of 'talking heads' (detectives Marty Hart [Woody Harrelson] and Rust Cohle [Matthew McConaughey]) addressing CID investigating detectives' interview questions about the unorthodox investigation in which the two partner-detectives were involved, in the wake of a murder case they worked together during the 1990s. The police procedural also spans what Cavell describes as the two poles of the *event*—that which breaks with the everyday, and the uneventful, that which comprises the everyday[15]—yet also examines the inevitably sceptical situation of uncertainty and inaccessibility concerning the truth of events in the past or how the effects of traumatic events continue to shatter the present and shape the future.

The monitoring of events occurring simultaneously in the present (television) is contrasted with the viewing of a succession of events generating changing narrative situations across time (cinema). For Cavell, the serial procedure in television is a way of monitoring the play of the eventful and the uneventful, a procedure for establishing 'a stable condition punctuated by repeated crises or events that are not developments of a situation requiring a single resolution, but intrusions or emergencies ... each of which runs a natural course and thereupon rejoins the realm of the uneventful'.[16] This pattern of both sequential narrative developments—spread across multiple timelines—and the contingent appearance of 'intrusions and emergencies' set against the enduring background of the uneventful or ordinary offers a fitting and productive framework for understanding the long-form television serial. Once again, it is striking how the long-form series spans both dimensions of cinematic viewing and televisual monitoring, both dimensions of changing narrative situations and the episodic monitoring of events—eventful and uneventful—while articulating these episodes across multiple time frames and across the narrative development of related characters across multiple seasons.

As Cavell observes, popular television's emphasis on the present is countered by 'the extraordinary spans of narrative time commanded by serialization',[17] which can last for years thanks to the structuring of the serial according to successive seasons. This compression and elongation of time are central to soap operas and long-form serials, whose organizing events, however disruptive, are in the end explorations, as Cavell remarks, 'of the interminable everyday, passages and abysses of the routine'.[18] These events in their serialized repetition command an order of time 'incommensurate with film time', enabling both a plurality of temporally extended forms of narrative development and a plurality of distinctive character arcs, which help explain the powerful forms of character-directed emotional engagement such serials can elicit. Although the programming of episodes that traditionally were broadcast weekly, in a ritualized chronological sequence, has given way to on-demand streaming with its capacity for individual choice and variation, the periodic release of seasons, along with the sheer amount of time required to watch their episodes, means that there remains a sense of the ordering of time, a rhythm of narrative serialization. The latter becomes thematic in *True Detective*'s quotidian reflections and metaphysical speculations on time and meaning. Indeed, as Cavell remarks, the extended time span of seasons in serials stands in stark contrast with the transient character of individual episodes; the aesthetics of serial-episode construction suggest a philosophical parallel between conceiving of time as repetition (recalling Nietzsche's eternal recurrence) and time as transience (recalling Heidegger on finite temporality).[19] These philosophical dimensions of the two modes of time, as we shall see, are thematized in *True Detective*, with Rust Cohle explicitly referencing Nietzsche's conception of eternal recurrence in the first series, and all three seasons emphasizing the existential finitude of mortality, meaning, memory, and consciousness.

What of the (intellectual) fear or anxiety Cavell claims television evokes? What does this avoidance or aversion to television—as the medium of the uneventful and/or the everyday—tell us about cultural-historical anxieties or philosophical concerns in the post-war period? Here Cavell points to the coincidence between the rise of television after World War II, which historically and politically means 'after the discovery of concentration camps and of the atomic bomb', and related social and cultural shifts in post-war sensibilities including 'the decline of our cities and the increasing fear of walking out at night, producing the present world of shut-ins'.[20] This coupling of the post-war recognition of a threat to human existence on the planet and a pervasive historical-cultural sense of anomie and groundlessness are indicative of a broader (sceptical) malaise.[21] What the fear or aversion towards television suggests, for Cavell, is a fear of 'deworlding' (already identified by Heidegger in the 1950s[22])—an uncoupling of the bond between us and the world, between us and the earth, a fear that the world no longer offers a meaningful or secure home for human beings: 'the fear that what [television] monitors is the growing uninhabitability of the world, the irreversible pollution of the earth, a fear displaced from the world onto its monitor (as we convert the fear of what we see, and wish to see, into a fear of being seen)'.[23]

Cavell describes here what other philosophers (like Heidegger and Arendt) have described as a withdrawal or ungrounding of our shared social, historical, and existential familiarity with the world (the 'uninhabitability of the world'), coupled with a fear of the human-driven threat of nature's demise or the loss of the natural dimension of the world, both of which are displaced by an anxiety about the self in relation to an 'alienated' represented world reduced to a panoply of images.[24] As Cavell notes, Heidegger regarded the threat to our sense of world—and threat to our 'essence' as human beings—as bound up with the transformation of the world into the 'world-image' [*Weltbild*], one of the symptoms of the 'forgetting of Being' defining the nihilism of technological modernity. What Cavell finds thought-provoking is this dissonance between the indifference towards television and its ubiquity as a medium monitoring the everyday, as though what television monitors were somehow anxiety-inducing or threatening—the anxiety attending the threatened loss of the everyday world itself. Television monitors the everyday, yet our aversion to it suggests an anxiety concerning the everyday and the threat that this poses to our very existence in a habitable or meaningful world. The 'fear' or aversion to television suggests a repression of anxieties about the viability of our familiar sense of the world, the meaningfulness and validity of our everyday being-in-the-world. It suggests 'a reference line of normality or banality so insistent as to suggest that *what* is shut out, that suspicion whose entry we would at all costs guard against, must be as monstrous as, let me say, the death of the normal, of the familiar as such'.[25]

These reflections on the existential significance of television resonate with other remarks that Cavell makes concerning the existential significance of film in relation to our sense of a world and of nature surviving our own demise. Conviction in prevailing historical and ideological narratives of progress, and the role these played in popular film, began to wane in the aftermath of World War II, withering in the Cold War period. Cavell starkly articulates the post-WWII/Cold War mood of historical and cultural scepticism, a mood arising 'in the knowledge, and refusal of knowledge, that while we had rescued our European allies, we could not preserve them; … that the stain of atomic blood will not wash and that its fallout is nauseating us beyond medicine, aging us rapidly'.[26] These beliefs, for Cavell, were replaced by forms of scepticism towards possibilities of individual and social freedom, and progressive democratic transformation, that have since become questionable. Much like Deleuze,[27] Cavell identifies a post-war form of scepticism or nihilism that is registered, articulated, and worked through in varieties of popular film, and more recently, I would add, in television serials such as *True Detective*.

Indeed, television, in what I am calling an existentialist sense, intimates the sense of crisis afflicting us in relation to world and earth (nature), both of which we recognize are in crisis, while also repressing this intuition—it 'makes intuitive the failure of nature's survival of me'.[28] The anxiety towards television's power of evoking the familiar points to the waning of our belief in its redemptive possibilities: it points to the pervasive scepticism concerning the meaningfulness of the world, an attitude suppressed through distraction or denial—in short, a background pessimism or nihilism towards the everyday. As Cavell remarks, if television 'probed for intelligible connections and for beauty among its events',[29] it might offer more critical insight into our sceptical cultural-historical condition. I suggest that *True Detective* offers the kind of televisual existential (philosophical and ethical) response to scepticism and nihilism that Cavell calls for in 'The Fact of Television'.

True Detectives

True Detective is one of the most successful medium- to long-form anthology television serials of the last decade. The first season (2014) attracted rave reviews, impressive audience numbers, and a dedicated online fan base, whose arcane speculations on the inner meaning of various elements of each episode became an internet phenomenon and important paratext. As Sheehan and Alice point out, *True Detective* had the distinction of generating 'a compendium of literary and philosophical texts—in short, a reading list'; knowledge of such esoteric references, unusual for a television series, was taken to enhance viewers' understanding and appreciation of the series.[30] Many commentators have noted the same, exploring and analysing the allusions and influences including '[f]ictional and nonfictional works pertaining to the Southern Gothic, "weird fiction", and existentialist and antinatalist philosophies' dealing with pessimism and nihilism (Schopenhauer, Nietzsche, Ligotti, Zapffe, and Cioran).[31] Focusing principally on the ruminations and reflections of Detective Rustin ('Rust') Cohle, many critics highlighted the philosophically 'pessimist' and antinatalist elements of Cohle's worldview.[32] Cohle's pessimism was contrasted in the series with his partner Martin ('Marty') Hart's more pragmatic, conventional affirmation of the value of religion, family, and social institutions (such as the police and the law), and his firm but brittle belief in the moral necessity of their struggle against crime and violence. I would suggest that these important philosophical dimensions of the series—deepened and extended in seasons 2 and 3—are concerned more with varieties of *scepticism* (existential, social, and psychological). By focusing on season 1, the most popular and critically acclaimed of the three, critics have foregrounded the role of pessimist philosophies and existential nihilism; but they paid less attention to how this existential scepticism is broadened in the other two seasons to encompass societal institutions, family and gender relations, politics and government (season 2), along with the possibility of knowledge, reliability of memory, finitude of consciousness, unstable character of identity and subjectivity, and ambiguity of narrative (season 3). Although I can only sketch these themes here, and shall focus too on season 1—indeed, each series would be deserving of its own detailed interpretation and extensive analysis—I wish to examine how *True Detective* thematizes and explores *existential scepticism* in ways that Cavell's philosophical account of scepticism in cinema—here extended to television—might help us better understand.

The much-imitated opening credits of *True Detective* set the mood for the metaphysical crime drama to follow. Set to 'Far From Any Road', a brooding 'alt-folk' ballad by The Handsome Family, the credits feature haunting stylized images of industrial landscapes, urban decay, Southern revivalist churches, and desolate swamps superimposed over the faces and bodies of the various protagonists and minor characters coupled with disturbing anticipatory tableaux from the episodes to come. The bodies and places coalesce, embedded in a dark and disturbing world in which untold crimes unfold. The Southern Gothic mood is deftly established, mingled with a noirish industrial squalor and dark hints at conspiratorial plots and shadowy fringe-dweller figures.

An opening prologue follows, showing the dark silhouette of a man carrying what looks like a body in a field towards a tree at dawn, setting fire to a collection of twigs, and starting a blaze in the bluish-lit field shown in long shot. This obscure sequence is followed by an abrupt shift to police drama, with a close shot of a camera lens, followed by the video recording of an interview with Detective Martin ('Marty') Hart, in the present (2012) by two members of the Louisiana State Police CID. Hart's testimony is interpolated with video footage of an interview with Hart's partner, Detective Rustin ('Rust') Cohle, also responding to questions concerning a murder case he and Hart investigated, and apparently solved, back in 1995. As Sheehan and Alice note, this 'meta-investigation' of the case provides a framing narrative for both the crime and the investigation of it, which has been reopened for critical consideration. The interviewing CID detectives Maynard Gilbough (Michael Potts) and Thomas Papania (Tory Kittles) are impassive and evasive, revealing little to either the detectives or the viewer as to their reasons for interviewing Hart and asking questions about Cohle. The murder case in question is a disturbing ritualized killing, with a young woman's body found kneeling and bound before a large tree, as though in prayer, crowned with thorns and deer antlers, displaying a spiral tattoo-like marking on her back, and surrounded by mysterious doll-like stick figures suspended from the tree above her.

Cohle is introduced as a brooding, meticulous investigator, attentive to details and bringing sophisticated psychological and philosophical knowledge to such cases (his nickname, Hart tells the interviewer detectives, was 'the Taxman' because of the large ledger notebook he used at crime scenes). Cohle's past is obscure (the records from his Texas days were redacted) and Hart tells of seeing Cohle's empty and bleak apartment—without furniture, a mattress on the floor, a solitary cross on the wall—which 'kinda made me feel for the guy'. Hart, by contrast, is earthy and practical, affable but ill-tempered, a self-described 'regular dude', a family man and churchgoer, as opposed to Cole's solitary misanthropy. At the same time, he has a capacity for insight (although not always towards himself) and for shrewd appraisals of Cohle's character. He reminds Cohle of the difficulty of distinguishing between evidence that confirms a hypothesis or narrative, and evidence that makes sense because one takes the narrative for fact, which means one risks self-deception: 'you attach an assumption to a piece of evidence, you start to bend the narrative to support it. Prejudice yourself.' Hart's observation can be taken as a moment of critical self-reflection that encapsulates the philosophical problem—the threat of scepticism—driving the entire series.

He invites Cohle over for dinner—while they are still at the murder scene—something that Cohle says he 'had a problem with' since that day happened to be his daughter's birthday. As he tells Cohle's wife Maggie (Michelle Monaghan) later that evening, his two-year-old daughter was tragically killed in an accident and the grief of her loss destroyed Cohle's marriage. Cohle turns up on Hart's doorstep drunk and dishevelled, tatty bunch of flowers in hand, frightening Hart's two young daughters. The death of Cohle's daughter, and its traumatic effects on him and his capacity for relationships, reverberate throughout the series: this tragic event provides essential context for interpreting Cohle's striking professions of pessimist and antinatalist philosophical views—a point frequently overlooked by commentators, who tend to take Cohle as a philosophical porte-parole for the entire series.[33] As Cohle remarks later (using an image lifted from Ligotti's *The Conspiracy Against the Human Race*[34]), his philosophical pessimism appears to be linked to his daughter's death: 'Think about the hubris it must take to yank a soul out of non-existence into this ... meat. A force of life into this thresher. My daughter spared me the sin of being a father.'[35] The combination of his dead daughter's birthday coinciding with the discovery of the shockingly posed corpse of Dora Lange sets the scene for Cohle's obsessive dedication to investigating and solving this case.

The dual structure of the series—the framing investigation of the investigators and the latter's investigation of the ritualized murder—sets up the sceptical problematic in an acute and powerful manner: the nature of the crime, the way it was investigated, even the identity of all the perpetrators, remain enigmatic, despite apparent resolutions, right until the end of the first series (and even then many questions are left unanswered, much to the chagrin of many viewers and critics).[36] Why Dora Lange—the young woman whose grisly murder sparks the story—died and what other forces or unknown agents were ultimately responsible for her death remain obscure. Why Cohle is of particular interest to the CID interviewers, and what his ultimate motivations were, also remain enigmatic, even as they provide both the dramatic and philosophical backbone of the series. Indeed, the ultimate unknowability of the crime—not only the true perpetrators but the ultimate meaning of it—remain out of reach. The revelation at the end of episode 1 of season 1, where the interviewing detectives show Cohle the photograph of a recent murder that bears the hallmarks of the Dora Lange ritualized killing, suggests that Cohle and Hart captured and killed the wrong man, or that others involved in her killing remain at large. Either way, the sceptical problem of the unknowability of the crime, its perpetrators, and its ultimate meaning is starkly underlined. Cohle's 'true detective' status is marked by his obsessive dedication to solving the crime even as he recognizes that it may be impossible to do so. Nothing ever gets resolved, the next crime or victim appears, perpetrators keep the upper hand; these sceptical laments are uttered throughout the series and serve as a framing perspective for *True Detective* as a whole.

Cohle's intellectual and philosophical bent as a detective is coupled with his intuitive, even mystical side. He describes to the interviewing detectives the 'visions' or hallucinations he sometimes experienced while on the job (which he explains as neural flashbacks, chemical damage from his time as a deep undercover drug dealer, although it remains unclear whether this is what he really believes or just a more acceptable account he offers to Hart), visions that he usually knew were not real yet that often guided his detective work.[37] This clash between exoteric and esoteric knowledge is part of what makes Cohle such a fascinating detective figure, and undercuts that claim that he simply embodies a pessimistic antinatalist perspective rejected by Hart and the community.[38] As he remarks at the end of episode 2, when he and Hart find a striking clue—a painted mural of a half-naked female figure sporting deer antlers—in an abandoned burned-out church building, most of the time he thought his visions were irrational, but other times 'I thought I was mainlining the secret truth of the universe'. This experience will recur in the first season's climactic encounter with the 'Yellow King', the serial killer Cohle and Hart have been tracking, where Cohle has a metaphysical epiphany just before encountering (and being stabbed by) the killer.[39]

In this respect, he clearly embodies a figure who straddles the divide between a naturalistic, psychological perspective (his assiduous study of the psychopathology of serial killers and interest in anthropological dimensions of religious cultic practice) and a supernaturalistic, metaphysical perspective on the horrific events being investigated (revealed by his hallucinatory visions and investigative intuitions). He remains divided between a naturalistic rationalist account of criminal violence and a more metaphysical view of the reality of evil—a contradictory figure combining 'the Taxman' and mystic seer in one. Cohle's own sceptical uncertainty about his intellect, his knowledge, and his intuition and visions reflects his general attitude of combining rational detective work ('observation and deduction,' as he remarks) with intuitive belief and speculative insight, his sense that there are reasons behind why people act the way they do but that there is also a hidden order or dimension to our experience that we cannot fathom or reveal.

Some of his more pessimistic philosophical pronouncements are made during an 'old-time' church revivalist meeting. He and Hart have gone there to question a preacher concerning the 'Friends of Christ' Church where two detectives found a painted 'occult' female figure, a vital clue since it strongly resembles the posed corpse of Dora Lange. His Nietzschean scepticism towards religion—that it provides merely a comforting metaphysical 'fairy tale' for the ignorant and the weak—is contrasted with Hart's more pragmatic, communitarian defence of religion as creating a spirit of community and shared orientation towards the common good. Cohle replies that a common good resting on illusions is no good at all. Hart insists that, without shared moral or religious beliefs, people would be free of moral constraints and have licence to do anything, to which Cohle responds that they would do exactly what they do now, 'just out in the open'. Interestingly, Hart expresses greater scepticism towards the capacity of human beings to live rationally in the absence of religion: what we would have in a fully atheistic world, he claims, is a 'freak show of murder and debauchery', whereas Cohle insists that, if the only thing keeping an individual from being decent is the expectation of 'divine reward', then that person is corrupt or to blame, not society, and such individuals should be exposed for their moral weakness.

Cohle's scepticism towards morality and the meaning of existence—his combined Nietzschean and Schopenhauerian nihilism—becomes clear in his critical rejection of religion. There is something disturbing, he remarks, about people gathering in groups, reassuring themselves via religious myths 'that violate every known law in the universe', just so that life can be made meaningful and bearable. Later he repeats the claim, adding a more sceptical angle concerning religion as a technique of domination: that human beings evolved religion to control, dominate, and exploit one another. Cohle explains to Hart that preaching is a kind of transference, the 'transference of fear and self-loathing to an authoritarian vessel', and that religion is simply existential catharsis: 'He [the preacher] absorbs their dread with his narrative. Because of this, he's effective in proportion to the amount of certainty he can project.' Religious belief, for Cohle, echoing William S. Burroughs and Richard Dawkins, is a 'language virus' designed to manipulate and corrupt the community.[40] It rests on a fantasy of metaphysical optimism concerning the way of the world, what Nietzsche called the 'Socratic Optimism' underpinning both Christianity and modern science.[41] Rust Cohle calls it the 'ontological fallacy of expecting a light at the end of the tunnel': 'that's what the preacher sells, same as the shrink ... The preacher, he encourages your capacity for illusion, then he tells you it's a virtue.' Cohle's combination of Schopenhauerian pessimism, Nietzschean nihilism, and naturalistic critique of religious-based morality could not be more starkly expressed.

Hart offers a pragmatist retort, using plain language rather than 'ten-dollar words'. For someone who sees no point in existence, he remarks, Cohle 'sure seems to fret about it a lot', and even sounds (existentially) 'panicked'. Like Nietzsche's nihilist, Cohle 'frets' about the meaning of existence, professing that it ultimately has none but, like most people, he cannot evade the quest for meaning that defines human experience, most likely due to 'his programming', as he remarks—his social conditioning and innate psychological needs. For his part, Hart defends the role of traditional social institutions and sources of meaning (family, religion, community, and the law), yet his behaviour and conduct contradict these earnest professions of faith (his philandering, marriage break-up, breakdown of relations with his daughter, cynical ripostes to his wife Maggie's conservative father, violent outbursts, and so on). Although Hart calls out Cohle's ambivalent attitudes towards religion, existence, and purpose, his own professions of faith and belief in ordinary social institutions seem as 'panicked' as Cohle's, although his hypocritical ambivalence takes the form of conventional endorsement coupled with moral indifference and practical neglect.

The two detectives' relationship starts to deteriorate as they get no closer to solving the case, whose leads and implications begin to sprawl confusingly and dramatically. Hart finds Cohle increasingly arrogant, obsessive, and erratic, as Cohle's account of the case begins to incorporate conspiratorial elements implicating not only a shadowy ring of powerful paedophiles but police, church, and government figures, who facilitate the kidnapping, abuse, and killing of vulnerable young girls and women from the fringes of the Bayou region. Cohle, for his part, sees Hart as an unimaginative hack and conventional moral hypocrite who is too wedded to institutionalized police culture to see the real core of the crime and too distracted by his own bad-faith desires to be a 'true detective'. Their deteriorating relationship not only reflects their conflicting existential attitudes towards crime and justice but the idea that penetrating to the heart of any one case demands a commitment, discipline, and self-sacrifice that few police are willing or able to make—a willingness to sacrifice oneself for the truth.

Cohle and Hart come to blows, after Maggie seduces Cohle to take revenge on her cheating husband. After a brutal fist fight at the Police Headquarters car park, their relationship is terminated, until Cohle, who quits the police force in disgust, contacts Hart years later with new evidence concerning the case of Dora Lange. It becomes clear that the murders have continued, and that they may not have convicted the right killer. The two detectives, both 'true' though often at variance with each other, continue to work together incognito, finding meaning and purpose in a case that now has sprawled in ways that point to a sinister web of conspiracy, child abuse, kidnapping, murder, and political corruption. Indeed, Cohle now has evidence implicating politicians and church leaders, suggesting a collusion with the police that has allowed these crimes to continue. Indeed, the CID investigation of Cohle, which appears to be an attempt to pin the murders on him, adds weight to what Hart had hitherto regarded as Cohle's paranoid conspiracy theories. As evidence, Cohle shows Hart shocking video footage—stolen from a safe in Reverend Billy Lee Tuttle's (Jay O. Sanders) sprawling mansion—of one of the young girls (Marie Fontenot) whose disappearance they have been investigating being sexually abused in a ritualized manner before being killed. Hart is devastated and disgusted, with no choice now but to help Cohle solve the case to honour the memory of the young victim. Having pieced together clues and information over several years, it is not Cohle but Hart's intuitive detective work that finally cracks the case: his recollection of a green-painted house he photographed years ago while questioning neighbours, together with the sketched image of an individual, with scars, their suspect, who turns out to be a house painter connected to the Tuttle family, a figure once described by a child witness as a green-eared 'spaghetti monster'.

Both detectives question their suspect—'lawnmower man' Errol Childress (Glenn Fleshler), former house painter and school groundsman—in a squalid and decaying Southern Gothic mansion. Before they arrive, we see the disturbing Childress, the 'Yellow King' in his 'kingdom' of Carcosa, keeping his father chained to a bed, having perverse incestuous relations with his mentally impaired half-sister, and displaying unsettling acting skills by imitating James Mason (as Cold War spy villain Phillip Vandamm from *North by Northwest*). Cohle arrives and sights Childress standing still in the overgrown 'garden': he shouts at him to 'get on his knees' but Childress stands his ground, says 'no!', then flees into a labyrinthine enclosure of tree-tangled tunnels. As Cohle gives chase, attempting to confront and slay the killer, calling Hart for backup, Cohle has a metaphysical vision—of 'form and void', to quote the episode title, a swirling vortex illuminated against the dark—just before his final confrontation with the killer (Childress stabs and nearly kills Cohle, who manages to retrieve Hart's dropped gun and shoots Childress in the head before he can kill Hart). Recovering later in hospital, Cohle narrates, in tears, an epiphany he experienced before being attacked by Childress. He 'shouldn't be here' (be alive) since he had a vision, or rather a felt sense, as his 'definitions' dissolved into nothingness, as he 'let go' of consciousness and awaited death, of a deeper dark, a deeper intuited sense of love as binding him to his dead daughter, a sense of being bound through this love to the dark 'substance' of the cosmos. His grief upon waking was to find that he was still alive instead of merged with his daughter in the void. Hart helps Cohle 'escape' the confines of the hospital, and as they walk, they discuss the meaning of what they experienced, against a black night sky. Cohle describes it as 'the oldest story in the world', that of light versus dark, good versus evil; Hart observes that the dark seems to have 'claimed most of the territory'. Cohle agrees but later corrects Hart's observation that the dark has become all-encompassing. Despite the vision of darkness devouring goodness, it seems to him that 'the light may be winning', a moment of insight marking a possible transcending of existential scepticism.

Many viewers were disappointed by this apparently optimistic ending, which reverses, or ameliorates, the pessimism that had characterized Cohle, and for many the entire series, throughout season 1.[42] For pessimist critics, this ending could be taken as a gesture of containment and reconciliation, returning the protagonists to social reality as reconciled and affirming of the status quo.[43] Joseph Packer and Ethan Stoneman, for example, cite Norwegian deep ecologist and pessimist philosopher Peter Wessel Zapffe's claim that there are deeply entrenched anti-pessimist strategies in human beings typically used to undermine and neutralize pessimist beliefs and rhetoric (distraction, isolation, anchoring, and sublimation).[44] Indeed, such 'optimist biases' would, at first glance, also seem to vitiate *True Detective*, especially with its 'optimistic' finale: 'one could find no more fitting instance of Zapffe's idea of anchoring than the arc of *True Detective*'.[45] They go on to claim, however, that a deeper analysis of the show reveals an abiding commitment to pessimism, despite season 1's apparently reconciliatory conclusion. Indeed, the typical containment strategies and neutralizing rhetoric evident in such artistic works require an 'esoteric' approach to effectively convey pessimist views. For these reasons, Packer and Stoneman argue that *True Detective* is a complex doubled text, one that invites an esoteric 'pessimist' reading as opposed to its' apparently 'optimistic' surface meaning. Following Leo Strauss's controversial claim that certain (modern and ancient) philosophers had to 'disguise' their true but subversive doctrines under the cloak of conventional doxa in order to avoid religious or political censure, leaving sufficient clues in the text to alert more philosophical readers, they argue that attentive or careful viewers of the show—noting blatant errors, contradictions, cryptic clues, and suggestive symbols—can discern the true, hidden, or esoteric meaning of *True Detective* as an affirmation of philosophical pessimism that had to be disguised or concealed using the conventional trappings of the police procedural and crime drama. As they remark, 'what those who endeavor to dig past the show's iridium hues discover is not a convoluted narrative about the light overcoming the dark—or even a grisly murder story—but a complete and utter blackness of the kind associated with the weird, cosmic pessimism of Thomas Ligotti and H.P. Lovecraft'.[46]

What is the evidence for this esoteric pessimist interpretation? Rust Cohle's pessimism, as they note, is explicitly marked and obvious to any viewer—not only in Cohle's pessimistic philosophical pronouncements but in his manner, movement, and expressions.[47] He even offers Hart a frank self-description of his philosophical pessimism, drawing on concepts, themes, and phrases associated with Schopenhauer, Zapffe, and Ligotti:

> I consider myself a realist, but in philosophical terms I'm what's called a pessimist ... I think human consciousness was a tragic misstep in evolution. We became too self-aware. Nature created an aspect of nature separate from itself. We are creatures that should not exist by natural law ... We are things that labour under the illusion of having a self. This accretion of sensory experience and feeling, programmed with total assurance that we are each somebody, when in fact everybody's nobody ... I think the honourable thing for our species to do is to deny our programming. Stop reproducing. Walk hand in hand into extinction. One last midnight, brothers and sisters opting out of a raw deal.[48]

As many critics have observed, Cohle's speech borrows from the writings of antinatalist pessimists such as Ligotti (such that Pizzolatto was even accused of plagiarism).[49] Indeed, his repeated 'pessimist' refrains have been taken as expressing *True Detective*'s philosophical stance, which is why the end of season 1 was criticized as inauthentic or implausible. Packer and Stoneman offer five reasons why one should be sceptical concerning the 'optimistic' ending and offer instead an 'esoteric' reading of the series as disguising its pessimistic 'anti-message'. The first reason is the authoritative intellectual, ethical, and professional stature granted Cohle as a character (as a highly intelligent, morally authentic, and exceptional detective), which makes him the porte-parole for *True Detective* as a whole.[50] The second is Cohle's 'all-consuming attentiveness', considering every detail in context, despite realizing that the more he knows, the less he knows, the more the darkness grows; this suggests that we should not abandon his perspective simply because of his apparent 'conversion' at the end.[51] The third is Cohle's explicit commitment to philosophical pessimism, which remains undiminished despite his 'weakness' at the end, an example of what Ligotti calls the 'conspiracy against the human race' (our propensity to embrace optimistic beliefs in order to perpetuate life that is only a source of suffering and pain).[52] The fourth is the fact that Cohle, despite his attention to detail and esoteric knowledge, does not think to follow up on the 'Yellow King' reference. This is either a sign of his incompetence (which is unlikely) or else an indication that Chambers' influential example of 'weird fiction' does not exist in the universe of *True Detective*. It suggests, rather, that *True Detective* belongs within the fictional world of 'weird fiction'—that it is yet another tale within the 'Yellow King' universe—with its overarching pessimistic worldview.[53] The fifth is that Cohle's Nietzschean critique of religion remains intact, with little evidence that he has abandoned this view in favour of a mystical intuition of love or union with nothingness. Viewed 'esoterically', his earlier words foreshadow the illusoriness of the show's 'religious' conclusion, and thus undermine the image of Christ-like resurrection he appears to undergo at the end of the final episode.[54]

Although Packer and Stoneman make a strong case for considering a pessimistic 'esoteric' reading of the series, I would query their evidence supporting the claim that Cohle's epiphany should be taken as masking or disguising *True Detective*'s underlying commitment to a pessimistic philosophical worldview. Firstly one might interrogate the assumption that Cohle is the sole authoritative 'philosophical' voice of the show whose intellect, character, and actions mark him as (morally and philosophically) 'superior' to Hart's more conventional take on morality and meaning. Cohle himself offers many qualifying, ironic, and self-critical remarks—about his unstable state of mind, drug history, failed relationships, familial trauma, and depressive states—that ought to make us cautious about simply accepting his many 'pessimistic' pronouncements as revealing the 'truth' of the series. His quasi-mystical near-death experience is presented not as a drug-induced hallucination, but as a moment of metaphysical intuition and existential insight, a profoundly transformative experience, in confronting death, of being able to sense both the darkness (death) and light (love) expressive of cosmic nothingness. Rather than read the latter as an inauthentic cover-up of his more authentic pessimism, we could read his former pessimism as, at least in part, a nihilistic symptom of his inability to accept mortality, death, and love as intrinsic to human finitude.

We should also recall Hart's cautionary criticism, in the first episode, to resist the temptation to 'bend the narrative' to fit one's hypotheses, lest one end up prejudicing oneself (or engaging in self-deception). Hart's own self-deceptions do not detract from the truth of his statement, which I take as essential to understanding the *True Detective* fictional universe. Indeed, Cohle's pessimism appears to be as much a defensive means of coping with the traumatic loss of his daughter as an existential expression of his authentic worldview. Her death is the event that defines his character and the reason given for the breakdown of his marriage, his alienation from his colleagues, and his self-destructive behaviour as a long-term undercover narcotics agent. His motivation—and the basis for his authentic commitment as a 'true detective'—stems from a combination of pain at the traumatic loss of his daughter, a desire to numb himself through all-consuming dedication to the impossible task of resolving the worst of crimes, and a strong sense of seeking justice for those forgotten, excluded, or deemed dispensable by 'the system'. His overtly pessimistic pronouncements—which would undermine the validity of his dedication to detective work and desire to seek justice for the victims of violent crime—should be read as a means of dealing with the pain of existence, of traumatic suffering, and a way of reconciling himself with unbearable loss. Nihilistic pessimistic philosophies too can serve as a means of 'preserving life', as Nietzsche noted of Schopenhauer, and as Cohle appears to acknowledge thanks to his metaphysical epiphany.

It is Cohle's existential encounter with death, mortality, and evil—the 'moment of vision' in which his existence is reduced to 'nothingness'—that enables him to come to terms with his existential scepticism and reconcile himself with the pain of human, all-too human, reality. This kind of insight need not mean the abandonment of his sceptical beliefs but is rather a traversing of nihilism (as Nietzsche put it) or 'coming to terms' with (existential) scepticism that acknowledges our finitude, the limits to human knowing, yet one that retains a sense of the possibility of transcendence despite our finite existential condition. Indeed, Cohle only denies the idea that 'there is only darkness' and suggests that the struggle against evil is not entirely in vain—a not unreasonable view—while acknowledging that they only caught one perpetrator, so that the greater evil represented by the shadowy network of other perpetrators remains beyond reach. The series' more general acknowledgement of finitude, loss, and limits appears to remain intact. Although the 'Yellow King' is killed, much concerning the case—the sprawling network of abuses, perpetrators, crimes, and conspirators—remains unresolved, which is the lesson of *True Detective* overall: an exploration of the insurmountable character of scepticism coupled with the need to come to terms with the inevitable limits we confront as finite beings. As Cohle remarks: 'Nothing is ever fulfilled. Nothing is ever over.' In this sense, we should qualify Cohle's final statement: he agrees with Hart that darkness seems to prevail, but notes that this is not the right way to view things—it is not that there is only darkness but that small victories in the struggle between good and evil are still meaningful and worthwhile. His experience of a felt sense of love coupled with the nothingness of existence prompts him to say, 'the light is winning', despite the pervasive darkness. Scepticism, whether epistemic, moral, or existential, remains part of our condition, an irreducible feature of our being-in-the-world; this is not an argument for pessimism but rather a challenge to come to terms with scepticism in ways that enable us to live ethically in 'the long bright dark'.

Notes

1   Stanley Cavell, 'The Fact of Television', *Daedalus*, vol. 11, no. 4 (1982), 75–96.
2   Cavell, 'The Fact of Television', 75–76.
3   Ibid., 77–78.
4   See, for example, Sarah Cardwell, 'Television Aesthetics', *Critical Studies in Television: The International Journal of Television Studies*, vol. 1, no. 1 (2006), 72–80.
5   Cavell, 'The Fact of Television', 79.
6   Ibid., 80.

7   Ibid., 80–81.
8   See Paul Sheehan and Lauren Alice, 'Labyrinths of Uncertainty: *True Detective* and the Metaphysics of Investigation', *Clues: A Journal of Detection*, vol. 35, no. 2 (Fall 2017), 28–39.
9   Cavell, 'The Fact of Television', 85.
10 Stanley Cavell, *The World Viewed: Reflections on the Ontology of Film*, Enlarged Edition (Cambridge, MA: Harvard University Press, 1979), 72–73.
11 Cavell, *The World Viewed*, 26.
12 Ibid., 26, quoted in Cavell, 'The Fact of Television', 85.
13 Cavell, 'The Fact of Television', 85.
14 Ibid., 86.
15 Ibid., 89.
16 Ibid.
17 Ibid., 92.
18 Ibid.
19 See Friedrich Nietzsche, *The Gay Science*, trans. Walter Kaufman (New York: Vintage Books, 1974), Book IV, #341; and Martin Heidegger, *Being and Time*, trans. John Macquarrie and Edward Robinson (Oxford: Basil Blackwell, 1979), Part IV, #67 ff.
20 Cavell, 'The Fact of Television', 95.
21 We should note that Cavell is referring specifically to the post-war social and cultural context in the United States.
22 See Martin Heidegger, 'The Age of the World Picture', *Off the Beaten Track*, trans. and ed. Julian Young and Kenneth Haynes (Cambridge: Cambridge University Press, 2002), 57–85.
23 Cavell, 'The Fact of Television', 95.
24 See Martin Heidegger, 'The Age of the World Picture'; and Hannah Arendt, *The Human Condition*, second edition (Chicago: University of Chicago Press, 1998 [1958]), 248–57.
25 Cavell, 'The Fact of Television', 95.
26 Ibid., 62–63.
27 See Gilles Deleuze, *Cinema 2: The Time-Image*, trans. Hugh Tomlinson and Robert Galatea (Minneapolis: University of Minnesota Press, 1989), 171–172.
28 Cavell, 'The Fact of Television', 95.
29 Ibid., 96.
30 'Sheehan and Alice', 'Labyrinths of Uncertainty', 28.
31 Sheehan and Alice, 'Labyrinths of Uncertainty', 28. See also Joseph Packer and Ethan Stoneman, '"I'm Bad at Parties": The Philosophical Pessimism of *True Detective*', in *A Feeling of Wrongness: Pessimistic Rhetoric on the Fringes of Popular Culture* (Pennsylvania: Penn State University Press, 2018).
32 See Jonathan Elmore, 'More than Simple Plagiarism: Ligotti, Pizzolatto, and *True Detective*'s Terrestrial Horror', *Dialogue: The Interdisciplinary Journal of Popular Culture and Pedagogy*, vol. 4, no. 1 (2017), http://journaldialogue.org/issues/v4-issue-1/more-than-simple-plagiarism-ligotti-pizzolatto-and-true-detectives-terrestrial-horror/; Mathijs Peters, '"A Giant Gutter in Outer Space": On the Schopenhauerian Themes of HBO's Hit Series *True Detective*', *Film International*, 15 December 2014,

http://filmint.nu/a-giant-gutter-in-outer-space-on-the-schopenhauerian-themes-of-hbos-hit-series-true-detective/

33   See, for example, Packer and Stoneman, "'I'm Bad at Parties'". Cohle's self-identification as a pessimist antinatalist is made early in episode 1 of season 1, in the first police car ride scene between him and Hart: 'I consider myself a realist, but in philosophical terms I'm what's called a pessimist.'

34   Thomas Ligotti, *The Conspiracy Against the Human Race: A Contrivance of Horror* (New York: Hippocampus Press, 2010).

35   In discussing Norwegian deep ecologist philosopher Peter Wessel Zapffe, Ligotti remarks: 'Zapffe's thought … has the value of advancing a new answer to an old question: "Why should generations unborn be spared entry into the human thresher?"' Ligotti, *The Conspiracy Against the Human Race*, 74.

36   See Packer and Stoneman, "'I'm Bad at Parties'", especially the notes to chapter 2, 181–84.

37   The fact that we see some of Cohle's hallucinatory sequences—while driving and when about to confront the 'Yellow King' killer in the labyrinthine maze near his derelict property—suggest that these episodes remain ambiguous between 'naturalistic' and 'supernaturalistic' perspectives on the world.

38   See Packer and Stoneman, "'I'm Bad at Parties'" for a reading of *True Detective* as a Straussian 'esoteric' text that masks its deeper pessimistic meaning. I take issue with this reading below.

39   The 'Yellow King', along with his city of 'Carcosa', are references to Robert W. Chambers' *The King in Yellow*, a highly influential collection of 'weird fiction' short stories published in 1895 that was admired by H.P. Lovecraft. In these stories, there is a fictional play, *The King in Yellow*, which causes anyone who reads or sees it to fall into despair and madness. See Packer and Stoneman, "'I'm Bad at Parties'", 73–74; Michael M. Hughes, 'The One Literary Reference You Must Know to Appreciate *True Detective*', *io9 Gizmodo*, 14 February 2014, https://gizmodo.com/the-one-literary-reference-you-must-know-to-appreciate-1523076497

40   See William S Burroughs, *The Adding Machine: Selected Essays* (New York: Arcade Publishing, 1986), 47; and Richard Dawkins, 'Viruses of the Mind' (1991) in *Dennett and his Critics: Demystifying Mind*, ed. Bo Dahlbom (Oxford: Blackwell, 1993), 13–27.

41   Friedrich Nietzsche, *The Birth of Tragedy*, trans. Walter Kaufman (New York: Random House, 1967), #18.

42   See Packer and Stoneman, "'I'm Bad at Parties'", 62 and the notes at 182 for a discussion of viewers' and critics' negative reactions to the final episode of season 1.

43   Ibid., 62ff.

44   Ibid., 60. Zapffe argues that pessimist beliefs encounter resistance because they conflict with deep-seated 'biases' in favour of life, meaning, and purpose. When confronted with pessimistic theories, people tend to deploy anti-pessimistic strategies as a means of 'inoculating' themselves against their 'anti-message' of pure negation.

45   Ibid.

46   Ibid., 50.

47   Ibid.

48 In the script for *True Detective*, Cohle advises Hart to start with Schopenhauer if he wishes to understand philosophical pessimism. The idea of consciousness as a superfluous, 'unnatural' product of evolution that now hinders us comes from Zapffe. The call for human extinction as ethically desirable is associated with antinatalist thinkers such as Ligotti and David Benatar.
49 See Elmore, 'More than Simple Plagiarism'.
50 Packer and Stoneman, "'I'm Bad at Parties'", 68–70.
51 Ibid., 70–71.
52 Ibid., 71–73.
53 Ibid., 73–75.
54 Ibid., 75–76.

Index

A

Adam's Rib 103, 153
Adorno, Theodor 57, 63n15, 66n46, 122–23, 128–29, 222, 224, 233nn1–2
Aeneid, The 237
Affair, The 21, 290, 294
After Finitude 132
Agee, James 7
Agent Carter 265
Agents of S.H.I.E.L.D. 265, 280
Alias 299
Alice, Lauren 311
Alighieri, Dante 122
Al-Jamil, Tahani 136
Allegiance 289
Allende, Salvador 195
Allen, Robert C. 203, 218n96
All in the Family 93
Amelia Lopes O'Neill 206
Americans, The 16, 37, 53, 288–304
Anagonye, Chidi 137
Anderson, Amanda 131
Anderson, P.T. 4
Apollo astronauts 91
Appreciating the Art of Television 267
Argo 288, 299
Aristocrat and the Peasant, The 106
Armstrong, Jesse 68–70, 77–79
Arnold, Matthew 137
Arriagada, Jorge 206
Art Television 154

Aude, Françoise 206
Audience, The 88
Austin, J.L. 137, 256, 295
Authoritarian Personality, The 123
Avengers: Age of Ultron 281
Awful Truth, The 43, 103, 211, 294

B

Balasco, Byron 50
Balfour, Jodi 86
Bandirali, Luca 10
Band Wagon, The 256
Banshee 297
Baron Noir 21
Barton Fink 175
Benjamin, Walter 130, 191
Bergman, Ingmar 13
Berlant, Lauren 113–14, 115
Bewitched 93, 280
Big Bang Theory, The 140
Big Little Lies 11
Black Atlantic 241
Black Cat, The 195
Black Jacobins, The 255
Black Panther 12
Black Widow 265
Bleak Liberalism 131
Blixen, Karen 204
Blood Simple 175
Bloom, Allan 6
Boardwalk Empire 37
Bonham Carter, Helena 92

Bordwell, David 195
Brady Bunch, The 280
Breaking Bad 44, 52, 60, 164, 266, 297, 307
Breton, André 110
Brideshead Revisited 12–13
Bringing Up Baby 103, 139
British Royal Family 85–96
Bronfen, Elisabeth 23
Budd, Mike 200, 217n70
Buffy the Vampire Slayer 11, 158–60, 162
Bureau, The 298
Burroughs, William S. 108, 316
Busby, Margaret 259n2

C

Cabaret 122
Cain, James M. 175, 185
Caldwell, John Thornton 86–87
Call Me by Your Name 288
Capra, Frank 155
Carroll, Noël 203, 274
Carter, Joelle 40
Cash, Johnny 42
Cavell, Benjamin vii–viii, 37, 44
Cavell, Stanley
    Cities of Words 19, 35–36, 47, 101, 103, 110, 112, 116, 118n39, 136, 141, 152–53, 158, 166
    Claim of Reason, The 47, 118n44, 134, 295
    Conditions Handsome and Unhandsome 136
    Contesting Tears 11, 271, 292, 295
    'Fact of Television, The' 4, 17, 24n7, 31–37, 90, 97n24, 156, 165, 192, 202, 218n91, 266–68, 306–7, 311
    Little Did I Know 47–48
    Must We Mean What We Say? 34–35
    Philosophy the Day after Tomorrow 240, 255
    Pursuits of Happiness 11, 17–18, 32–36, 43, 54, 90, 103, 168n22, 220n122, 271, 294
    Senses of Walden, The 3
    World Viewed, The 3, 7, 15, 31–35, 37, 40, 90, 155, 193, 196–97, 271, 308
Cerisuelo, Marc 174–76, 185–86, 188n7, 189n38
Césaire, Aimé 241, 260n11
Chandler, Raymond 175
Charles III, King of the United Kingdom 89
Chernobyl 289
Chigurh, Anton 175
Churchill, Winston 88
Cities of Words 19, 35–36, 47, 101, 103, 110, 112, 116, 118n39, 136, 141, 152–53, 158, 166
Citizen Kane 44, 90
Claim of Reason, The 47, 118n44, 134, 295
Clayton, Alex 10
Clémot, Hugo 23
Cloak & Dagger 265
Cobra Kai 289
Coen, Joel 174
Cohle, Rust 310, 313
Collette, Toni 11
Comer, Jodie 11
Common Cause, The 130
complex TV 9–10, 84, 118n38, 146, 148, 151n35, 154–59, 165, 223–25, 227, 266
Complex TV: The Poetics of Contemporary Television Storytelling 10
Concept TV 10
Conditions Handsome and Unhandsome 136
Contesting Tears 11, 271, 292, 295
Corcuff, Philippe 163, 169n44
Cornfield, Michael 230, 234n28
Cornillon, Claire 146, 150n33

INDEX

Cortínez, Ariel 207
Cosby Show, The 93
Cox, Brian 68, 80–81, 83
Craig, Steve 200
Crowder, Boyd 43–44
Crown, The 23, 85–96, 289
Cruel Optimism 113
Csikszentmihalyi, Mihaly 2, 24n6
Cukor, George 290
Curb Your Enthusiasm 13, 27n45, 282

D
Dallas 32
Dallas Buyers Club 288
Daredevil 265
Dark 289
David, Larry 2
Davies, Byron 10, 23
Dawkins, Richard 316
Deadwind 94
Deadwood 31, 35, 38
de Beauvoir, Simone 180
Debru, Claire 175–76, 185–86, 188n7, 189n38
Defenders, The 265
Deleuze, Gilles 311, 322n27
Delinquent Spectatorship 199
Democracy and Education 230
Descartes, René 112, 136, 178
Deuce, The 289
Deutschland 83, 86, 89 289
Devereaux, Michelle 23
de Vries, Hent 23
Dewey, John 16, 20, 230
Dexter 164, 175
Dialectic of Enlightenment 129
Dick Van Dyke Show, The 280
Divina Comedia 122
Doctor Strange in the Multiverse of Madness 283, 286
Doing Philosophy at the Movies 176
Doll House, A 272
Dorcé, André 218n92
Double Indemnity 175
Dragnet 37

Dream On 290
Dunnes, Irene 11
Dynasty 32

E
Eco, Umberto 224, 234n13
Edward VIII, King of the United Kingdom 89
Eisenhower, Dwight D. 89
Eliot, George 137
Eliot, T.S. 68
Elizabeth II, Queen of the United Kingdom, 85–98
Emersonian perfectionism 21, 35–36, 44–46, 107, 143
Emerson, Ralph Waldo 20–22, 35–36, 38, 40, 42, 44–48, 102, 104, 107, 111, 136–37, 141, 143, 147, 149n3, 152–53, 159, 179–81, 186, 190n51, 256, 293
Emily in Paris 15, 94
Emily of New Moon 110
Engell, Lorenz 10, 26n41
Eternal Sunshine of the Spotless Mind 146

F
'Fact of Television, The' 4–5, 8–9, 17, 31–37, 90, 97n24, 154–55, 165, 192, 199–202, 211, 217n79, 218n91, 266–68, 276, 306–7, 311
Falcon and the Winter Soldier, The 265
False Flag 298
Fantasy Island 200
Fargo 173–90, 297
Fauda 298
Fey, Tina 14
Fiedler, Leslie 2
50 First Dates 146
Fitzgerald, Ella 8, 247
Foot, Philippa 136
Foucault, Michel 137, 149n7
Foxcatcher 288

Foy, Claire 89
Frears, Stephen 86, 88
Freud, Sigmund 47–48, 57, 65n39, 152, 218n93
Friends 140
Fromm, Erich 57, 65n39

G

Game of Thrones 290, 297
Gandhi, Leela 130, 134n3
García, Alberto N. 10, 26n42
Garner, Julia 292
Gaslight 103, 153
Genette, Gérard 203, 211, 218n95, 219n117
George VI, King of the United Kingdom 91
Gerrits, Jeroen 10, 62n1, 167n9
Giddens, Anthony 229, 234n23
Gilmore, Richard A. 174, 178–79, 180–81, 186
Gilroy, Paul 241, 260n17
Girard, René 189n37
Girl from Oslo, The 298
Girls 21
Glenn, John 91
Glissant, Édouard 241
GLOW 289
Godard, Jean-Luc 5
Goddard, Michael 205, 215nn34–35, 220n126
Godfather 127
Goggins, Walton 40
Going, Joanna 50
Golden Boat, The 198–99
Golden Compass, The 204
Good Place, The 23, 118n41, 135–51
Goodman, Paul 2
Graham, Billy 86
Grant, Cary 43, 107, 139
Grant, Susannah 11
Greenaway, Peter 199
Grillo, Frank 50
Groundhog Day 146
Guardians of the Galaxy 289

H

Habermas, Jürgen 123
Halt and Catch Fire 289
Hamlet 69
Hammett, Dashiell 175
Handmaid's Tale, The 11, 15, 164
Hannibal 175, 297
Harlan County, USA 44
Harper, William Jackson 138
Harris, Jared 86
Has, Wojciech 204
Hatchuel, Sarah 146, 147, 148, 150n33
Haven, C.K. Dexter 107
Hawks, Howard 139
Hawley, Noah 175, 184
Hazard, Patrick 7
Heat 13
Heidegger, Martin 131, 134n4, 310
Hepburn, Katharine 11, 107, 139
Her Boy Friday 106, 109, 113
Hill Street Blues 31, 36–37, 156, 158, 275, 277–78
His Girl Friday 43
Hitchcock, Alfred 4
Hitchcock: The Murderous Gaze 38
Holland, Jack 227, 233n4
Homeland 23, 222–35, 297, 298–99, 303
Horkheimer, Max 57, 123
House of Cards 164, 169n47, 289, 291, 297
Howe, Darcus 237, 238, 241, 242, 254, 260n21
How I Met Your Mother 140, 290
Hudelet, Ariane 147, 151n35
Hunger 254

I

Ibsen, Henrik 137, 153, 195
I Love Lucy 1, 32, 91, 275, 278, 280
I May Destroy You 21
Immediate Experience, The 17
im/moral perfectionism 152–70
Inferno 122

Inhumans 265
Iron Fist 265
It Happened One Night 36, 153, 155, 294

J
Jacobs, Jason 31, 37
Jaffe, Oscar 43
James, C.L.R. 255
James, Henry 137
Jenkins, Tricia 223, 228
Jessica Jones 265
Jokes: Philosophical Thoughts on Joking Matters 189n41
Jonas, Nick 50
Juliet 22
Justified 23, 31–48, 52, 277

K
Kalifat 298
Kant, Immanuel 136–37, 149n2, 152–53, 177–79, 184, 186
Kellman, Gerri 71
Kidman, Nicole 11
Killing Eve 11
King Lear 68–84
King, Regina 11
Kingdom 50–66
Kings and Queens of Africa for Children 258
Klossowski, Pierre 194
Kopple, Barbara 44
Kumar, Deepa 228
Kundnani, Arun 228

L
Lady Eve, The 194
L.A. Law 37
Lanier, Douglas 67
LaRocca, David 23, 85–96
Laugier, Sandra 16, 163, 223, 232, 243, 289–303
Lauria, Matt 50
L.A. Takedown 13
Lear, Norman 5

Leave It to Beaver 87
Leftovers, The 294–95
Leonard, Elmore 38, 39, 44
Levi, Hagai 13
Levinas, Emmanuel 122
Ligotti, Thomas 312, 313, 319, 323n35
Litoral 23, 191–221
Little Did I Know 47–48
Little White Dove 198
Locke, Alain 259
Locke, John 153
Loki 265
Looming Tower, The 298
López, Ana M. 202, 218n92
Lord of the Rings, The 204
Lord, Tracy 107
Lost 15, 21, 146
Lovecraft Country 12
Lovecraft, H.P. 12, 319
Lovers Rock 244–45, 257
Lukács, György 54
Luke Cage 265
Lundegaard, Jerry 176
Lynch, David 4, 212, 303
Lyotard, Jean-François 115, 120n84
L Word, The 11

M
Macé, Éric 225, 226
Mad Men 15, 52, 301, 303
Mafiosa 21
Malcolm in the Middle 280
Malle, Louis 5
Maltese Falcon, The 39
Mangrove 236, 239–40, 244
Mann, Michael 13, 87
Maria Isabel 198
Marley, Bob 259
Marnie 44
Mars, Veronica 165
Martín-Barbero, Jesús 202
Martin, Brett 123
Marx, Karl 121
Mathison, Carrie 224

Matrix, The 8
Maurice, Thibaut de Saint 23
Maximoff, Wanda 285
McGowan, Todd 212
McLuhan, Marshall 2
McQueen, Steve 12, 23, 236, 243
Meadows, Charlie 175
Medea 22
Meillassoux, Quentin 132
Mendoza, Jason 136
metatelevision 85–96
Miami Vice 87
Milch, David 31
Mildred Pierce 175
Mill, John Stuart 153
Milos, Stavros 178, 189n30
Mindhunter 175
Minima Moralia 122
Minnelli, Liza 122
Minnelli, Vincente 256
Minow, Newton N. 2
Mittell, Jason 10, 137, 146, 147, 156–57, 158, 164, 165, 223, 224
Moebius 296
Monash, Paul 38
Morgan, Peter 86, 88, 91, 94
Moss, Elisabeth 11
Most Violent Year, A 288
Mr. and Mrs. Smith 292
Mulhall, Stephen 23, 85, 137
Muller, Karl 71
Multiverse of Madness 285
Must We Kill the Thing We Love? 44
Must We Mean What We Say? 34–35
My Dinner with Andre 5
Mysteries of Lisbon 199

N

Naked 22
Nannicelli, Ted 10, 267, 274
Narcos 21, 297
Narration in Light 87
Nation, The 7
Newcomb, Horace 6–7
New Girl 140

New Television 10, 23, 154, 267
Nietzsche and the Vicious Circle 194
Nietzsche, Friedrich 191, 194, 316
Nilsson, Harry 106
No Country for Old Men 175, 184
Not Going Out 282
Notorious 296
Now, Voyager 103
Numéro Deux 5
Nussbaum, Emily 138, 227, 233
NYPD Blue 31

O

O Brother, Where Art Thou? 175, 182
O'Connor, Flannery 44
Odyssey, The 182
Office, The 282
Oh Brothers! 175
Oh, Sandra 11
Olsen, Elizabeth 285
Olsson, Jan 10
Olyphant, Timothy 40
One Foot in the Grave 282
Ordinary Spy, An 297
Oswalt, Bill 180–81, 184
Ozark 23, 121–34, 297

P

Packer, Joseph 318, 320, 323n38
Paisley, Brad 43
Palmer, Laura 165
Palm Springs 146
Peacock, Steven 37
Pears, Louise 227
Perez, Gilberto 87
perfectionism, im/moral 152–70
Perkins, V.F. 87, 303
Peyton Place 32, 38
Philadelphia Story, The 36, 43, 21, 107, 153, 290, 294
Phillips, Tom 199
Philosophical Investigations 240
Philosophy the Day after Tomorrow 240, 255
Physical 289

Pippin, Robert B. viii, 23, 97n11
Pizzolatto, Nic 306
Plato 189n39
Poehler, Amy 14
Poetics 195
Poetics of Cinema 192–94, 199–200
Pomerance, Murray 86–87
Poniewozik, James 95
Porter, Dennis 201
Postman Always Rings Twice, The 175
Postman, Neil 2, 24n8
Prince Charles 91
Princess Diana 88
Princess Margaret 91–93
Profumo Affair 260n3
Protestant Ethic and the Spirit of Capitalism, The 125
Pursuits of Happiness 11, 17–18, 32–36, 43, 54, 90, 103, 168n22, 220n122, 271, 294

Q
Queen's Gambit, The 289
Queen, The 86, 88, 97n15

R
Raising Arizona 175, 180, 182
Red, White and Blue 248, 257
Rhys, Matthew 291
Rochant, Éric 296
Rodríguez-Remedi, Alejandra 204, 215n27, 218n100
Rohmer, Éric 112
Rothman, William 10, 23, 287n10
Rowley, Christina 223
Roy, Logan 68
Ruiz, Raúl 23, 191–213, 214n11, 215n27, nn32–35, 216nn47–48, 217n65, 218n83
Russell, Keri 291, 296
Russian Doll 23, 101–20

S
Sanchez, Kiele 50
Saraband 13

Sarmiento, Valeria 206
Scanlon, T.M. 136, 145, 149n2
Scenes from a Marriage 13
scepticism 104, 108, 116, 136, 229, 288, 292–97, 305–24
Scott, A.O. 4, 25n13
Scott, Darrell 43
Scrubs 140
Searcy, Nick 40
Seinfeld 93, 282
Seinfeld and Philosophy 22
Seldes, Gilbert 7
Senses of Walden, The 3
Serial Shakespeare 68, 77
Serious Man, A 180
Servant of the People 299
Seven Seconds 11
Sevier, C. Scott 143
Sex and the City 11, 21
Sex Education 94
Shaw, G.B. 137, 152, 195
Shayon, Robert Lewis 7
Sheehan, Paul 311, 322n8
Shellstrop, Eleanor 135, 148
Show about the Show, The 94
Show Me a Hero 289
Shuster, Martin 10, 23, 133, 223, 232, 267, 276, 277
Silence of the Lambs 175
Simpsons and Philosophy, The 22
Sinnerbrink, Robert 23
Six Feet Under 53, 297, 301
Sloterdijk, Peter 128
Small Axe 12, 23, 236–61
Smith, Matt 89
Snoats, Gale 175
soap operas 3, 32, 35, 37–38, 154–57, 192, 198–205, 210–11, 309
Sopranos, The 21–22, 37, 52, 158–62, 266, 297, 307
Soprano, Tony 161, 164, 166, 304n1
Spielberg, Steven 13
Spies of Warsaw 289
Spigel, Lynn 10
Standish, Paul 12

Stanwyck, Barbara 11
Star Wars 13, 275
Station Eleven 15
Steimberg, Oscar 201, 217n82
Steinman, Clay 200
Stella Dallas 103, 153
St. Elsewhere 37
Stevenson, Robert Louis 197
Stewart, Garrett viii, 4, 85
Stewart, James 21, 109
St John Passion 258
Stoehr, Kevin L. 163–64, 169n42
Stone, Alison 117n36, 119n59, 265, 285
Stoneman, Ethan 318, 320, 323n36, 324n50
Stranger Things 289, 297
Strauss, Leo 318, 323n38
Streeter, Thomas 3, 24n11
Succession 23, 67–84, 122, 126, 290
Suicide Club 197
Switch Image, The 10

T
Tehran 298
Teillier, Jorge 194
telenovelas 201–4
Television Aesthetics and Style 10, 26n41
Television after TV 10, 26n38
Tele-Visions 26n36
television philosophy, Stanley Cavell and 1–24
Television Studies after TV 10, 26n39
Television: The Critical View 7
Terrone, Enrico 10
Thinking Outside the Box 10, 26n37
This Is Us 289, 303
Thompson, Emma 133
Thompson, Kristin 156, 158, 217n70
Thoreau, Henry David 3, 111, 152, 181, 259, 290
Three Crowns of the Sailor 204–6
Toles, George 87
Top of the Lake 11
Traitor, The 289
Travolta, John 133
Treasure Island 199
True Blood 53
True Detective 23, 305–24, 324n48
Tube Has Spoken, The 10
Tucker, Jonathan 50
TV Dante, A 199
TV: The Most Popular Art 7
Twentieth Century 43
24 299
Twin Peaks 303

U
Ulmer, Edgar 195
Ulysses 182, 187
Unbelievable 11
Uncanny Cinema 87
Uprising, The 255

V
Verfremdungseffekt 96
Vermeule, Blakey 7, 164
Vernon, Frank 68, 71
Vigil 289
Voice of Chile, The 208
Voir 97n15
Vulvokov, Nadia 101

W
Wald, Christina 68, 84n4
Walking Dead, The 297
WandaVision 23, 85, 265–87
Wandering Soap Opera, The 198
War of the Worlds 21
Warne, Peter 294
Warner, Deborah 68
Warshow, Robert 7, 17, 19, 22
Watchmen 11–12
Wayco Roystar 69
Weber, Max 65n34, 125
Weeds 52
Weiner, Norbert 2
Weisberg, Joe 288, 291, 297–98
Weldes, Jutta 223

Welles, Orson 204
West Wing, The 21
Wever, Merritt 11
What We Owe to Each Other 136, 145
Wheatle, Alex 260n18
Wheatley, Catherine 23, 26n35, 104
Whedon, Joss 11
When They See Us 289
Why Theory? 10
Williams, Raymond 2, 244
Wilson, George M. 86–87
Winter's Tale, A 112
Wire, The 22, 266, 277–78, 290, 297, 307
Witch, Scarlet 285
Witherspoon, Reese 11
Wittgenstein, Ludwig 10, 20, 63n13, 102, 118n44, 193, 197, 240, 269, 271
Wizard of Oz, The 17
Wonder Woman 1984 289
Woodley, Shailene 11

World in Action 238
World Viewed, The 3, 7, 15, 31–35, 37, 40, 90, 155, 193, 196–97, 271, 308

X

X-Files, The 158

Y

Yost, Dave 97n22
Yost, Graham 288

Z

Zahedi, Caveh 94
Zapffe, Peter Wessel 318–19, 323n44
Zaveri, Alan 106
Zea, Natalie 40
Zelensky, Volodymyr 299
Zero Dark Thirty 299
Zickgraf, Ryan 132, 134n7
Žižek, Slavoj 212, 220n123
Zunshine, Lisa 7, 25n27

CPSIA information can be obtained
at www.ICGtesting.com
Printed in the USA
JSHW020006100723
44339JS00001B/3

9 781804 130186